Inventing the Needy

Inventing the Needy
Gender and the Politics of Welfare in Hungary

LYNNE HANEY

University of California Press

BERKELEY   LOS ANGELES   LONDON

This book is a print-on-demand volume. It is manufactured
using toner in place of ink. Type and images may be less sharp
than the same material seen in traditionally printed University
of California Press editions.

University of California Press
Berkeley and Los Angeles, California

University of California Press, Ltd.
London, England

© 2002 by the Regents of the University of California

Library of Congress Cataloging-in-Publication Data

Haney, Lynne A. (Lynne Allison), 1967–
    Inventing the needy : gender and the politics of welfare in Hungary /
Lynne A. Haney.
        p.   cm.
    Includes bibliographical references and index.
    ISBN 978-0-520-23102-3 (alk. paper)
    1. Public welfare—Hungary—History.   2. Hungary—Social
conditions—1945–1989.   3. Hungary—Social conditions—1989–.
4. Women—Hungary—Social conditions.   5. Hungary—Social
policy.   I. Title.
HV260.5.H36   2002
362.5'09493—dc21   2001027816

Manufactured in the United States of America

For my mother, Janice Peritz,

my grandmother, Catherine Yurko,

and my great-grandmother, Hannah Palmer

Contents

Tables

Acknowledgments

Not only is this book about welfare, but it is also the product of an enormous amount of welfare. Since I began conducting research in Hungary in 1987, I have invented many needs for this project and for myself. Luckily, I have also been the recipient of multiple forms of social assistance: institutional, intellectual, material, and familial forms of welfare sustained me as I researched and wrote this book.

Most broadly, this book would not have been possible without the institutional support of the University of California. From start to finish, the book was a product of this outstanding institution. In the 1980s, many sociologists at the University of California at San Diego engaged my sociological imagination and deepened my understanding of East/Central Europe. In particular, I thank Martha Lampland, Charles Nathanson, Gershon Shafir, and Jeff Weintraub. During most of the 1990s, I was fortunate to be part of the Sociology Department at the University of California at Berkeley. At Berkeley, I received all the intellectual support that a graduate student needs and deserves. I am especially grateful to members of my dissertation committee, Michael Burawoy, Nancy Chodorow, Jerome Karabel, and Mary Ryan—all of whom, in their own ways, left an imprint on my sociological development and on the ideas advanced in this book. I am particularly indebted to Michael Burawoy, who served as my mentor and most benevolent "need interpreter" for nearly a decade. Michael provides a model as a theorist, an ethnographer, and a teacher that I will always strive to emulate. While at Berkeley, I formed many friendships that continue to sustain me. Among others, I thank Shana Cohen, Sharon Cooley, Laura Lovett, Ágnes Mihalik, Lisa Pollard, Elizabeth Rudd, Suava Salameh, Elsa Tranter, and my fellow Global Ethnographers. Finally, I am grateful to the University of California Press, especially to Naomi Schneider for her unflagging support of this book and to Pamela Fischer for her excellent editing of it.

Other institutions provided invaluable social assistance for this project. My colleagues, students, and friends at New York University have nurtured and supported me through the arduous task of research and writing. I am especially grateful to those who took the time to read and comment on portions of this book, including Danielle Bessett, Dalton Conley, Ailsa Craig, Jo Dixon, Kathleen Gerson, Linda Gordon, Kate Gualtieri, Liena Gurevich, Barbara Heyns, Ruth Horowitz, Robert Jackson, Jair Kessler, Jayati Lal, Gita Reddy, Olga Sezneva, and Mary Taylor. Beyond the borders of particular departments and universities lies the broader institution of academia, which is comprised of many scholars who have encouraged me and embraced my work. For providing feedback on the ideas expressed in this book, I thank Julia Adams, Lisa Brush, Nanette Funk, David Kirp, Gail Kligman, Sonya Michel, Ruth Milkman, Ann Orloff, Mark Pittaway, Balázs Szelényi, Iván Szelényi, Katherine Verdery, Miklós Vörös, Peggy Watson, and Marely Weiss.

Not only are Hungarian institutions the object of this study, but they also provided the support needed to complete it. In the late 1980s, the then Karl Marx University of Economic Sciences opened its doors to U.S. students like me. Working behind those doors were exceptional scholars such as István Rév and Júlia Szalai, both of whom helped to instill in me an interest in and a passion for their country. As I conducted the research for this book, the Institute of Sociology of the Hungarian Academy of Science offered an ideal home base. Thanks to László Bruszt, Vera Gáthy, and Ferenc Miszlivetz for facilitating my connection to their institution. Many sociologists from the ELTE Institute for Social Policy and Social Work shared their time and ideas with me. I am especially grateful to Mária Adamik, Zsuzsa Ferge, Gábor Hegyesi, and Léna Szilvási for teaching me so much about the Hungarian welfare system. Clearly, one of my biggest Hungarian debts goes to those working in the welfare institutions I invaded on a daily basis. Although I cannot mention them by name, they know how much I appreciated their help and valued their friendship. For their tireless support as I struggled to gain access to these welfare institutions, I thank Karolina Bor, Rita Falvai, Judit Karczag, Zsuzsa Matusek, and Ágnes Réti.

Research of this scope and magnitude could not have been conducted without an enormous amount of material welfare. For language study, I was supported by a two-year Foreign Language and Area Studies Fellowship and a summer grant from the American Council of Learned Societies. The data collection was funded by the International Research and Exchanges Board and the Joint Committee on Eastern Europe of the American Council of Learned Societies and the Social Science Research Council. While I wrote the dissertation on which this book is based, I received financial assistance in the form of a Chancellors' Dissertation Fellowship and a Phi Beta Kappa Dissertation Award. Finally, a Postdoctoral Fellowship from the American Council of Learned Societies and a Faculty Fellowship from the Remarque Institute at New York University gave me the time and the space to turn the manuscript into this book.

All this institutional, material, and intellectual support was a necessary but insufficient precondition for the completion of this book. Without a considerable amount of familial welfare, the book would have never come to fruition. My female lineage, to which I dedicate the book, passed on an incredible legacy of strength, determination, and humor. Among other things, my mother taught me what it means to be a scholar, a feminist, and a mensch. I thank my father for instilling in me a strong sense of social justice and a view of social science that encompassed this broader politics. My sisters, Jessica Peritz and Erin Haney, continually reminded me of what's important in life and kept my priorities in check. Finally, my deepest gratitude goes to my *élettárs*, András. For a decade, he joined me in crossing the U.S./Hungarian divide, both literally and figuratively. I thank him for tolerating my many absences, for securing my overall well-being, and for making it all worthwhile.

Introduction
Conceptualizing the Welfare State

In 1954, a young Hungarian woman initiated a case in a Budapest welfare office. As her case developed, it exemplified key shifts in the structure of Hungarian welfare. When Mária Kovács, then seventeen years old, discovered she was pregnant, her family had just moved to Budapest from the countryside. Space was limited, money was tight, and Mária's parents saw only one solution for their daughter: to get married and move out. Yet Mária knew this was not an option; since their sexual encounter, the father of the baby had not spoken to her. Frightened, Mária went to a local state office, the Gyámhatóság. One of the four caseworkers in the office was assigned to her case. She began by tracking down the father of Mária's baby. Within a week, she had the reluctant father in her office. After a lecture on socialist responsibility and threats of a paternity test, she "convinced" him to pay 20 percent of his wages to Mária in child support. She then arranged through the Ministry of Labor to have his wages attached until the child turned eighteen. Next, the caseworker turned to finding Mária employment. Mária's lack of education and slight physical disabilities made this a difficult task. Yet, within a month, Mária had secured work as an assistant at a local market.

After these material issues were resolved, the caseworker mobilized Mária's extended family to come to her aid. She wrote letters to all membersof this network, informing them of Mária's situation and asking for assistance. The caseworker followed the letters with visits to Mária's relatives living in the area—grandparents, cousins, aunts, and uncles. On these home visits, she assessed each relative's ability and willingness to help Mária. It was not clear whether Mária knew or approved of this process; she was not consulted at any point. Mária was therefore surprised when, just before her daughter, Judit, was born, her caseworker informed her of an arrangement she had worked out with an elderly uncle. In exchange for household help, Mária would receive a room in his flat and childcare for Judit. Mária agreed to the arrangement, and her case closed soon thereafter.

Seventeen years later, in 1972, the Kovács case reopened when Judit became pregnant. On her mother's advice, Judit went to the Gyámhatóság for help in determining the father's identity. By then, the welfare office had doubled in size, and Judit was met by an intake officer who assessed her needs. The officer informed Judit that it was against regulations to administer paternity tests to more than one man. Instead, she advised Judit to take three years of maternity leave. Judit followed the suggestion and took leave from her job as a cleaning woman to stay home with her daughter, Kati. Two years later, a district nurse was sent to evaluate Kati's overall "well-being." The nurse found Judit and Kati living with Mária in a one-room, dilapidated flat. Worried that Kati was not being cared for properly, the nurse referred the case back to the Gyámhatóság and recommended that Judit receive public assistance.

This time around, a caseworker was assigned to Judit's case. She met with Judit in the office and allocated temporary assistance to support the baby. A home visitor was then sent out to assess Judit's eligibility for regular support. On this visit, she quizzed Judit about her cooking abilities and interrogated her as to why her flat was not furnished or cleaned appropriately. Unsatisfied with Judit's answers, the visitor referred her to a family expert. After a series of psychological exams, the expert diagnosed Judit as "overly identified" with her mother and claimed that Judit therefore was an ineffective mother. She warned that if the cycle were not broken, Kati would reproduce Mária's and Judit's dangerous paths. Within weeks, Kati was placed in an institution for neglected children. Throughout the 1970s, Judit appealed for Kati's release. Each appeal prompted a new home visit, another domesticity test, and lectures about how to improve her mothering. State officials pleaded with Judit to undergo child-rearing counseling. At first Judit resisted their pleas. But in the early 1980s she acquiesced. Judit and Mária repainted their flat and purchased new furniture. They went to counseling together. By Judit's own admission, she began to feel less "ambivalent" about her role as a mother. State psychologists agreed and rewarded her with weekend home visits with Kati.

In 1986, Judit initiated a final appeal to have Kati returned permanently. She had addressed all of her "needs" as a mother and believed she was entitled to care for Kati. Yet when the home visitor arrived to assess her appeal, she was armed with a new set of surveillance tools. Using a ruler, she measured the size of Judit and Mária's flat and deemed it too small to house three women. Using means tests, she found that the women lived well below the subsistence level. And, using income formulas, she determined that the women's combined income was insufficient to support three people. The appeal was then rejected, and these women were deemed "materially" needy and unable to provide for Kati. All subsequent appeals were rejected on the basis of these women's poverty and material deprivation. In 1989 a caseworker defined them as "pathologically unruly" and "chronically deprived," thus ending any hope they had to have Kati released to their care.

The Kovács case provides a dramatic example of the reconfigurations of Hungarian welfare from the earliest years of state socialism to the present. Over this thirty-five-year period, Mária's and Judit's needs were constructed in three different ways. Mária's needs were conceptualized in societal terms by a welfare system that sought to reconstitute her institutional relations. Mária was acknowledged as having multiple needs that required various kinds of assistance. As a "shunned woman," she was thought to be in need of assistance tracking down a "deadbeat dad." As a potential worker, she was thought to be in need of employment. As a mother, Mária was thought to be in need of childcare and stable housing. And, as a member of a kinship network, she was thought to be in need of familial support. All these needs coexisted and were weighted equally. Two decades later, Judit's status as a mother was elevated to primary importance. Her needs were "maternalized" by a welfare apparatus that sought to reconstitute her role as a mother. No one conducted a paternity test for Judit; no one helped her find better work; and no one attempted to mobilize her extended kin. Instead, her dealings with the welfare apparatus revolved around her identity as a mother. Then, in contemporary Hungary, these women's needs were "materialized" by a welfare system aimed at the bureaucratic regulation of poverty. Their needs were collapsed into one, material need; their neediness was defined in strictly monetary terms. In short, over this period, the Kovács women's needs were first socialized, then maternalized, and finally materialized.

The Kovács case also highlights how these shifting conceptions of need were embodied in both social policies and institutional practices. At the time of Mária's pregnancy, few social policies were aimed at women in her situation. Instead, the state provisions of the era coalesced around wage labor. Mária's access to social support was based on her position in the labor force. Only through work could she receive subsidized material goods and services. In fact, Mária used these work provisions to move into her own flat in 1956. When Judit came of age, a different set of policies was in effect. By the 1970s, a subsystem of welfare had emerged that decoupled welfare from work status. Judit's access to support was based on her role as a mother. The three years of paid maternity leave and the family allowance she received were available to all mothers; the income support she obtained was allocated to mothers who demonstrated domestic competence. If Kati follows her mother's path, she will probably confront a version of the second set of policies that Judit encountered. In contemporary Hungary, Kati's income rather than her work history or maternal status will structure her choices. Income tests will determine whether she can take maternity leave and for how long. They will also decide whether she can receive a family allowance. And the median income in her neighborhood will affect her eligibility for public aid. Thus, these three generations of women will have had their lives shaped by three distinct regimes of social policy.

Finally, the Kovács case offers a glimpse into the workings of welfare institutions. At this level, their story reveals differences in the practices of Hungarian welfare—changes in the size of the welfare apparatus and the structure of welfare institutions. In Mária's time, only one welfare agency existed, and just one caseworker handled her case from start to finish. Without financial assistance to distribute, the caseworker turned to existing social institutions and networks. She tracked down the child's father and mobilized Mária's extended family. This type of help contrasts with the approach Judit encountered two decades later. Numerous state actors were involved in Judit's case, from caseworkers to home visitors to family experts. They all had their own tools to assess Judit's problems. Using domesticity tests, caseworkers evaluated Judit's housekeeping and deemed her incompetent. Drawing on psychological tests, family experts saw Judit's unresolved issues with her mother as the source of her ineffective mothering. Together, these evaluations led to Kati's institutionalization. In subsequent years, when Judit appealed to have Kati returned to her, she confronted yet another set of welfare practices. Armed with poverty tests, welfare workers documented the size of her flat, her income, and her material resources. In the end, Judit was defined as too "deprived" to care for her daughter. Hence, over the course of these women's lives, the Hungarian welfare system became increasingly specialized, segmented, and punitive.

FROM STATE IDEOLOGY TO STATE
WELFARE REGIMES

These transformations in the state policies and institutional practices of the Hungarian welfare system, from 1948 to 1996, provide the frame for this book. By examining "transformations" in the plural, my analysis presents an alternative to the historical periodization advanced by many area specialists. Political sociologists of Eastern Europe, or "transitologists" as they often call themselves, tend to adhere to a bifurcated model that breaks the region's history into the clearly demarcated periods of "state socialism" and "welfare capitalism." Guided by this static periodization, transitologists oppose the re/distributive systems operative before and after 1989, using what David Stark and László Bruszt term "the method of mirrored opposition."[1] Because these systems are thought to be so qualitatively different, scholars avoid systematic comparisons of them.[2] Instead, the presumably rigid state-socialist model is juxtaposed to the dynamic quality of welfare capitalism—an approach that has led to the homogenization of state socialism and to the censoring of the past.

Although much of East European historiography rests on this opposition, some scholars have begun to advance more nuanced accounts of social change in the region, particularly those social scientists who eschew grand narratives of systemic transition in favor of analyses of distinct social processes or relations. Realizing that yawning gaps existed between state ideology and reality, many of these scholars have documented the ongoing transformation of state intervention in the productive arena. For instance, scholars of Hungary tend to agree that three, as opposed to two, productive regimes have prevailed since the inception of state socialism. According to them, the first regime arose in the immediate postwar era and was characterized by "bureaucratic state coordination" and "centralized redistributive intervention."[3] This was a time of the state's usurpation of society, when the "dictatorship" presided over "need."[4] The post-1968 period then ushered in a second regime, that of "reform socialism," which was based on the state's partial withdrawal from the productive realm. With the rise of the second economy came a diversification of economic practices; as the market took over many redistributive and disciplinary functions, bureaucratic coordination gave way to a partial commodification, and the state's paternalism became more "mature."[5] This period was followed by the third, post-1989, era of further diversification, privatization, and "marketization." Here scholars' analytical focus shifted from the singular to the plural—from socialism to capitalisms, from the ruling elite to bourgeoisies.[6] Thus, instead of falling back on simple dualisms, these area specialists developed historical accounts of the diminishing level of state control and of the diversification of state/productive relations.

Other scholars of Eastern Europe have begun to use a similar approach to analyze changes in state intervention in the reproductive arena. Like analysts of the productive sphere, these scholars found that the evolution of state regulation did not fall into simple, dichotomous periods. In fact, they discovered that reproductive intervention could also be classified according to three, rather than two, distinctive regimes. Instead of viewing these regimes as leading to a progressive reduction in state control, these scholars have highlighted the fluctuations in state regulation—moments of heightened intervention and of retreat.[7] Through an analysis of state policies and propaganda, they have traced the socialist state's first reproductive regime to the immediate postwar period, when abortion was banned and access to contraceptives was highly curtailed. In the reproductive arena, "bureaucratic state coordination" bred a coercive body politics, whereby women's bodies were centrally monitored and their reproductive desires were trumped by the needs of the party/state.[8] As in the productive arena, the second, post-1968, reproductive regime was marked by a lessening of state control and, in some cases, by relative state withdrawal. In this sphere, a new cohort of demographers and reproductive experts took over some of the state's disciplinary functions; they regulated reproduction with an arsenal of scientific techniques and procedures. Then, in the third, post-1989, period, state surveillance was stepped up again, through new abortion legislation, contraceptive policy, and pronatalist demagoguery. Here, too, scholars have emphasized the diversity of the current regime, consisting as it does of a plurality of new levels of state regulation and intervention.

To a large extent, my analysis of Hungarian welfare is rooted in this tradition of critical East European studies. Following these area specialists, I also resist grand narratives of systemic transition, preferring instead to study the dynamics of change within a particular social arena. And, like critical area specialists, I also reject the method of mirrored opposition and the dichotomy between "state socialism" and "capitalism" it implies; instead I explicate ongoing social processes that transcend taken-for-granted periods or "systems." By challenging these rigid approaches, area specialists not only will construct a more accurate historical sociology of the past but will develop a fuller understanding of the region's present and future. Clearly, 1989 did not wipe the slate clean in Eastern Europe.[9] Historical legacies continue to constrain and enable state development, both within and among the countries of the region.[10] Such legacies also condition the expectations different social groups have of the state and how they react to its metamorphosis.[11] Only by disrupting rigid historical dichotomies and models will area specialists unearth the complex reconfigurations of state involvement in social life.

At the same time as I share the historiographic approach of critical area specialists, my analysis seeks to broaden prevailing understandings of state regulation itself. Overall, the dominant trend in East European studies has been to chart changes in the level of state involvement in social life. Both transitologists and critical area specialists have been centrally concerned with how state intervention waxed and waned over time. Their work has thus centered on the twists and turns of elite formation and rule—whether those elites are party/state officials, economic planners, intellectuals, politicians, or policymakers.[12] This scholarly preoccupation is somewhat understandable: because the Communist state's ruling elite frequently portrayed itself as completely in control, social scientists have, not surprisingly, evaluated it in similar terms.[13] Although this focus on the degree of state control has fostered important insights, it has deflected attention from an analysis of changes in the kind of state engagement in social life. This book embarks on this analysis by looking at shifts in the nature of state regulation, modes of welfare entitlement, and conceptions of need over a fifty-year period. In doing so, it broadens the historical focus to expose what Michael Burawoy has called the "subterranean alternatives" of socialism and postsocialism—that is, the meanings the subjects of state regulation attached to that regulation and the ways they maneuvered to protect themselves from it.[14]

This shift to the study of the state "from below" not only involves a historical refocusing but also requires a conceptual retooling. Most generally, it calls for an alternative model of the state itself. Throughout this book, I approach the state as a layered entity, comprised of multiple and even conflicting apparatuses. At one level, I conceptualize the state as layered with redistributive and interpretive apparatuses.[15] States not only create provisions to redistribute benefits but also articulate historically specific conceptions of need. By constructing "architectures of need," states define who is in need and how to satisfy those needs. Moreover, state processes of redistribution and interpretation stand in complex relation to one another. As states embark on given redistributive paths, they give rise to particular interpretations of need and images of the needy. These interpretations and images then shape what is feasible at the redistributive level. By conceptualizing the state as both a redistributor and a need interpreter, I extend the analysis of Hungarian welfare beyond the mere level of state involvement to probe the shifting nature of state engagement in social life.

In this conceptualization of the state, I highlight another form of layering: states also comprise layers of social policies and institutional practices. State processes of redistribution and interpretation operate on multiple terrains. One such arena is the political propaganda produced by state actors at the national level.[16] Yet this ideological work must be translated into concrete social provisions. By defining eligibility criteria, policies determine which social groups to target and which needs to fulfill. And these policies must then be implemented and grounded in the lives of real people; they must be integrated into real institutions. This requirement makes the practices of welfare institutions another key state arena to investigate. Compared with those engaged in policymaking, a wider range of state actors engages in this on-the-ground work, from professionals to caseworkers to social workers. Together, these state actors set the immediate conditions of redistribution and the meanings associated with it. Instead of giving analytical priority to one of these layers or assuming that one can be subsumed by the other, I approach the state as a loosely coupled system.[17] This book takes the state as a composite of subsystems that can be in sync or at odds with one another and thus opens up the space for a study of state politics that is not reducible to the politics of elites.

In order to capture these two forms of state layering, I deploy the concept of a "welfare regime." Coined by Gøsta Esping-Andersen and elaborated by others, this concept usually refers to the links welfare systems build among the state, the family, and the market.[18] In this book, I reconceptualize the term to emphasize the different subsystems that constitute the state itself. On the one hand, I conceive of welfare regimes as encompassing distinct policy apparatuses—collections of redistributive programs that shape the structure of social life and give rise to social conceptions of need. Here I posit that welfare regimes vary according to the site of their redistributive mechanisms, the mode of benefit allocation, and the nature of claims-making. On the other hand, I view welfare regimes as embodying networks of welfare agencies—local bodies that shape clients' lives and interpret their needs in direct and immediate ways. Here I argue that welfare regimes differ in the kind of workers employed in institutions, their work organization, and their understanding of clients' problems. In my conceptualization, welfare regimes are historically specific combinations of state policies and institutional practices that together set the terms of state redistribution and interpretation.

Using this conceptual framework, I propose a three-tiered periodization of Hungarian welfare regimes. Unlike transitologists' accounts, this periodization is not a dichotomous one; it bears a closer resemblance to the three-tiered regime models proposed by critical area specialists. Yet unlike these other regime models, which trace the rise of the third regime to 1989, my periodization holds that all three welfare regimes took root prior to 1989. Based on archival, interview, and participant-observation research, this book explicates the contours of the welfare society of 1948–1968, the maternalist welfare state of 1968–1985, and the liberal welfare state of 1985–1996. Overall, these regimes encoded different architectures of need. They were based on divergent understandings of who was in need and how their needs should be met: the welfare society targeted social institutions, the maternalist welfare state targeted social groups, and the liberal welfare state targeted impoverished individuals. Different architects designed these regimes. While the welfare society was the product of economic planners and unions, the maternalist and liberal regimes were built from the blueprints of ascendant groups of professionals. Table 1 summarizes the constellation of state apparatuses in each regime and the architects who constructed them.

My periodization of Hungarian welfare regimes begins in the earliest years of state socialism, 1948–1968, an era of social, economic, and political transformation. Instead of viewing this period as a time simply of bureaucratic collectivism, I argue that it was also marked by a new approach to welfare. The goal of the period was to create a welfare society in which the well-being of Hungarians was secured in existing social institutions. Material needs were to be met through efficient economic organization, while "caring" welfare work was to be done in the family. State policies were deployed to remake these institutions. This period saw the introduction of societal policies designed to reshape economic and social life. Many of these policies were embedded in the state's centralized wage structure, employment guarantees, and price subsidies. Others were connected to enterprises. These policies included benefits-in-cash, such as family allowances and pensions, and benefits-in-kind, such as socialized healthcare, childcare, and eating facilities. This distribution of benefits placed economic planners and unions at the core of this regime. To the extent that societal policies were discretionary, they were connected to work position and performance. Hence, this regime's policy apparatus consisted of plan and work-based provisions aimed at restructuring social life to secure the population's welfare.

At the level of welfare agencies, the welfare society designated one state body, the Gyámhatóság, to regulate existing social institutions.[19] There was no segmentation within Gyámhatóság offices; one caseworker handled the entirety of a case, from start to finish. Without any welfare funds to distribute, welfare workers focused on social integration: they hooked clients into work, nuclear family, and extended-family structures. Married women, who were already embedded in these institutions, were helped to negotiate their different social roles and demands. Single mothers, who were more marginalized, were helped to enhance their institutional integration and support networks. The spheres of work and family were the targets of these

Table 1. *Overview of Hungarian Welfare Regimes*

	Regime Type		
	Welfare society (1948–1968)	*Maternalist welfare state (1968–1985)*	*Liberal welfare state (1985–1996)*
Architecture of need	Social institutions	Social groups	Social classes
Architects of need	Economic planners, unions	Economic reformers, demographers, psychologists	International agencies, sociologists, economists
Policy Apparatus	*Societal policy*	*Maternalist policy*	*Social policy*
Site of re/distribution	Central plan, enterprise	National government, local government	Local state bodies
Mode of re/distribution	Universal, work-related	Universal, domesticity tests, psychological exams	Means tests, income tests
Eligibility criteria (entitlement claim)	Labor-force participation, work position	Labor-force participation, motherhood, maternal competence	Material need
Institutional Apparatus	*Singular structure: Gyámhatóság*	*Bifurcated structure: Gyámhatóság, Nevelési Tanácsadó*	*Tripartite structure: Gyámhatóság, Nevelési Tanácsadó, Család Segítő*
Type of welfare workers	Caseworkers	Caseworkers, family experts	Caseworkers, social workers
Work organization			
Division of labor within agencies	Low	Medium	High
Division of labor among agencies	—	Amateur vs. expert	State vs. nonstate

institutional practices. The conception of need underlying this regime was therefore quite structural in nature, rooted in the smooth functioning of social institutions and networks.

By the late 1960s, this societal-welfare model gave way to a more differentiated welfare regime. From 1968 to 1985, a maternalist subsystem of welfare formed out of the welfare society. Rather than conceptualizing this period as one of state withdrawal, I argue that it was a moment of state redeployment—a time when a targeted arm of social policy arose to decouple work from welfare and to shift re/distribution from the enterprise to the national government. The overall architecture of need then changed, and women's needs as mothers were separated from those of other social groups. New labor policies forbid women from doing work that could impair their reproductive abilities; a new childcare grant gave women three years of subsidized mothering for every one year of wage labor; and new child-rearing funds assisted mothers financially. Embedded in these provisions were new eligibility criteria and modes of distribution. Motherhood became a key entitlement claim, while domesticity tests became a common way to allocate support. Hence, a policy apparatus that was once oriented toward entire social institutions narrowed to target Hungarian mothers.

As the social-policy apparatus became more differentiated, welfare institutions became increasingly specialized. As a result, welfare workers began to assess how well their clients fit the "good-mother mold"—a narrow set of domesticity standards that determined how clients were dealt with and what kind of aid they received. Caseworkers no longer attempted to integrate clients into existing institutions. Instead, they used the new policies under their control to shape how women mothered. Moreover, in 1968 a network of Child Guidance Centers was established. Staffed by a new cadre of family experts who considered it their job to "rationalize" the Hungarian family, these centers saw mothers as the source of and the solution to a wide range of familial problems. They drew in large numbers of mothers for child-rearing counseling. In doing so, they further shifted the state's focus from the family as a whole to mothers. Welfare agencies solidified and strengthened the new maternalist arm of the welfare regime.

Finally, in the mid-1980s, the Hungarian welfare regime was reconfigured yet again. As its universal and maternalist arms collapsed into one discretionary apparatus, it began to resemble a liberal welfare regime. The social conception of need was then etched out on the terrain of social class, as the poor became the targets of the welfare system. In the late 1980s, local and global actors launched an assault on universal policies: they withdrew employment guarantees, they dismantled price subsidies, and they means-tested child-rearing assistance. In the mid-1990s, they took on the remaining maternalist policies, subjecting the maternity-leave and family-allowance systems to income formulas. Once means testing became the central method of redistribution, Hungarians could no longer stake claims to social support on the basis of their contributions as workers or mothers. Material deprivation was now the only recognized eligibility criterion. Moreover, as welfare funding was decentralized, local governments became the main site of redistribution. This system bred variation among locales and led to further class differences in welfare allocation.

A similar materialization of need characterized the institutional welfare structure of the period. Welfare work became even more specialized and segmented. Local Gyámhatóság offices now operated as public-assistance centers; casework was transformed into piecework. As poverty tests replaced domesticity tests, caseworkers reduced all clients' problems to material issues and focused on the bureaucratic regulation of poverty. These changes gave rise to new discourses about clients' pathologies and individual defects. A similar dynamic was at work in the Family Support Services, the most recent addition to the welfare system. Created in 1986 to alleviate the problems of impoverished families, these institutions were run like traditional poor-relief centers. The new cadre of social workers saw their job in strictly material terms: they set out to teach clients to economize and change lifestyle "defects" as a way of curtailing poverty. Once organized around the "needs" of social institutions and then of mothers, the welfare system was now aimed at the "needy" classes.

As I trace these state inventions of the needy, my goal is not to analyze each and every policy established over this period. Rather, my objective is to chart general reconfigurations in the social conception of need in different layers of the Hungarian welfare system. Hence, throughout this book, I adhere to a fairly broad definition of welfare—a definition that does not oppose redistribution and interpretation, needs and rights, or policies and practices.[20] I conceptualize welfare as a state project that encompasses all these dimensions. Welfare states set social boundaries; they determine which groups fall inside the redistributive sphere; and they structure who gets which resources and on what terms. With this broad definition of welfare, I attempt to bridge common divides among structural, poststructural, and cultural analyses of welfare.[21] This conception of welfare was also somewhat of an empirical necessity; had I defined welfare narrowly, as state interventions into the market or as income-maintenance programs to assist the poor, I would not have been able to capture the dynamics of both socialist welfare and welfare capitalism. The broader definition of state boundary work allowed me to draw into view the shifting contours of welfare inclusion and exclusion in all three regimes—and how these regimes evolved from the regulation of social institutions, then of social groups, and finally of individuals.

FROM SEX-SEGREGATED TO GENDERED WELFARE STATES

These Hungarian welfare regimes encompassed more than distinct modes of state regulation. In redrawing the boundaries of welfare, they had concrete effects on gender relations. Through their regulatory work, these regimes ascribed meaning to the social categories of gender: they defined the "appropriate" attributes and responsibilities of women and men. As the policies and practices of the welfare society reconstituted the spheres of work and family, they defined what it meant to be a "good" parent, spouse, worker, and family member. As the maternalist state fixated on reproduction, it demarcated who was responsible for child rearing and what "good" mothering entailed. And as the liberal welfare state targeted the materially needy, it narrowed the definition of "care work" and accentuated the financial roles of parents and spouses. In short, these three welfare regimes were premised on different gender regimes; their conceptions of "neediness" were based on distinct gender constructs.

While East Europeanists have had little to say about how states construct need or how these constructs are gendered, feminist scholars have produced a rich literature on this topic. After years of debating whether welfare states are gendered, Western feminists have taken up the more complicated task of illuminating how the state treats men and women differently.[22] Yet they still disagree about how to view the state and how to analyze its gendered underpinnings. Some feminist scholars view the state as a regime of provisions with different redistributive outcomes for women and men. Others approach the state as a site of national-level political struggle fraught with battles over gender meanings. Still others take the state as a site of local-level implementation with practical effects on women's lives. This theoretical division of labor has produced detailed explications of how state spheres shape gender relations. Yet this division comes with a key limitation: it has bred partial accounts of state gendering processes and blinded feminists to the multiplicity of state arenas within which gender relations are played out.

Because feminist regime analysis operates at a high level of abstraction, it appears to provide the most general account of state constructions of gender. Influenced by the work of Esping-Andersen, these feminist scholars have developed typologies of state-policy regimes.[23] Some feminists adjust Esping-Andersen's "three worlds of welfare capitalism" to account for gender.[24] Others replace his typology with their own models, which emphasize gender as the main axis of state variation.[25] What unites this feminist work is a specific approach to the welfare state—a view of the state as a constellation of national-level policies that redistributes benefits. These scholars take policy structures as evidence of eligibility claims and trace their material consequences for women. In this way, regime analysts have uncovered who gets what in different policy structures. And while this redistributive focus illuminates the material relations of gender, it obscures other relations. Because regime analysts often take policy constellations as given, they tend to ignore the historical processes through which welfare regimes are built. From the standpoint of redistributive outputs, it is difficult to explicate the discursive and political battles underlying state re/formation. By centering on the state as "need satisfier," regime analyses obscure the state's role as "need interpreter."[26]

By contrast, feminist historiographers of the state place this interpretive work at the center of their analyses. Instead of asking how states vary, they investigate why states develop in divergent ways. They have constructed new origins stories to reveal how female reformers, influenced by maternalism and professionalism, participated in the building of Western welfare states.[27] They have also dissected the scripts adhered to by male political actors, recasting battles between labor and capital and movements of militarism to expose their gender agendas.[28] By conceiving of the state as a site of political struggle, feminist historians address the key limitation of regime analyses: they illuminate how real institutional actors construct states; they portray state building as a complex process, fraught with ideological conflict. But because of their focus on national polities, most feminist historiographies fall short of providing a full explication of state interpretive processes. They tend to accept reformers' intentions at face value and rarely follow their scripts back to locales to see how they were translated into practice. These analyses thus avoid the tricky terrain of policy effects. Their focus on the interpretive obscures the practical—that is, how state policies dis/arm women in their concrete, everyday struggles.

Working from a more local perspective, some feminist scholars have begun to address the practical implications of welfare states. Although their analyses are limited in scope and underdeveloped theoretically, they share a focus on welfare practices and implementation. These scholars examine how a variety of state actors, from social workers to juvenile-court officials to caseworkers, shape the nature of benefit allocation.[29] Their work exposes the gender norms encoded in state practices and illuminates how institutions translate women's needs into administrative cases or therapeutic cases or both.[30] Moreover, these scholars frequently probe clients' relationships with the state itself, investigating how female clients appropriate or transform state constructions to protect themselves.[31] Local welfare analyses are thus strongest where regime analyses and historiographies are weakest: they are attuned to on-the-ground institutional arrangements and the power dynamics between caseworkers and clients. And they address the complicated issue of gender effects by explicating the imprint that state practices leave on gender relations in everyday life. Yet these local-level analyses are also weakest where the other two feminist approaches are strongest: because their studies are rarely framed around comparable categories, their work often appears case-specific. Without an explication of the redistributive and political contexts surrounding institutional practices, these analysts find it difficult to theorize from their local-level studies.[32]

In effect, these feminist approaches to the welfare state offer different insights into state gendering processes. While feminists who view the state as a policy regime are well positioned to illuminate who the state targets and its redistributive effects, they are less able to analyze gender as an interactive, negotiated process. While studies of national-level political struggle reveal how welfare politics are infused with gender meanings, they frequently miss the concrete manifestations of these constructions. And while accounts of welfare implementation expose the dynamics of caseworker/client interactions, they are ill-equipped to situate these local interactions in broader contexts.

This study of Hungarian welfare bridges these conceptual divides to build a more encompassing analytical framework. Just as my theorization of the layered state fosters a more historically grounded narrative of state development, it also offers new insights into how states shape gender relations. This theorization extends beyond a particular state arena to trace the development of multiple state apparatuses. It links the redistributive and the discursive—illuminating the interpretive underpinnings of specific redistributive patterns as well as the redistributive consequences of particular discursive constructs. And it connects policy and practice by locating state constructions in both national policy formulation and local implementation.

As feminist regime analysts have shown, welfare systems shape gender relations through sex-segregated spheres of redistribution. To some extent, my account draws on these insights to unearth broad shifts in the conduits of welfare. Over this fifty-year period, the Hungarian welfare system became increasingly segregated by sex. The welfare society brought both men and women into its sphere of influence. To the extent that it redistributed resources differently, it better equipped women. This regime not only encompassed policies to incorporate women into the labor force but also included a network of institutions that intervened into family life on women's behalf. In late state socialism, the state's focus shifted to women. Left to be regulated by the market and the second economy, men fell outside key arenas of the welfare system. New distinctions then surfaced among women; the welfare apparatus separated "good" from "bad" mothers and surveyed them accordingly. Finally, in the most recent period, new groups of women moved outside the state's sphere. Now defined as the terrain of the poor, the welfare apparatus targets the materially needy. Hence, there was a progressive narrowing of those treated by the welfare system: its targets shifted from women and men, to women, to the impoverished. My analysis echoes this narrowing: different social groups move in and out of the narrative just as they moved in and out of the welfare apparatus itself.

Although this book does reveal changes in the targets of the welfare apparatus, its central narrative is not about the welfare system's treatment of women and men. Underlying this story of sex segregation is a deeper story about shifting interpretations of gender. To capture these shifts, it is necessary to move beyond an account of who was regulated by the state to probe changes in how this regulation operated. In Hungary, these levels were intertwined: as these welfare regimes narrowed their client base, they engaged in a series of interpretive acts to redefine "neediness." Through this boundary work, the welfare apparatus recognized a different array of gender identities. Since the inception of state socialism, there was a progressive reduction in the number of identities recognized by the welfare apparatus. Of these regimes, the welfare society worked with the most diverse group of identities. Its policies and practices sought to constitute "appropriate" worker, spousal, and parental attributes. By defining neediness in such broad terms, the state cast its regulatory net wide enough to include men and women. In late socialism, this repertoire of recognized identities narrowed. Instead of acknowledging clients as multiply situated, this regime responded to clients as mothers and workers, with preference given to the maternal. In doing so, the state redefined neediness in maternal terms that largely excluded men. Finally, the current welfare regime operates with the narrowest repertoire of identities. Working with the seemingly gender-neutral distinction of rich or poor, this regime reduces its female and male clients to the materially needy.

In addition to this quantitative shift in the number of recognized identities, these welfare regimes drew out qualitatively different identities in clients. In the welfare society, women and men were viewed according to their social contributions as workers and family members. This acknowledgment of women's contributory roles underlaid efforts to integrate women's work and family lives. And this recognition of men's important roles as spouses and fathers propelled state actors to intervene into domestic relations. This emphasis changed with the rise of the maternalist welfare state. In this regime, men's contributions as family members were deemphasized, while women's roles as mothers were highlighted. Even with this shift, women's identifications were still positive, connected as they were to their valued work as child-rearers. With the rise of the liberal welfare state, this recognition of women's contributory roles has been lost. No longer based on women's positive identities as workers or mothers, entitlement is conferred in negative terms; it is based on what women lack financially or materially. Hence, my conception of state gender regimes will illuminate how structural and redistributive changes in the welfare apparatus were coupled with quantitative and qualitative shifts in state-recognized gender identities.

With this broad conception of state gender regimes, I also advance an alternative way to assess the implications of state constructions for clients. To unearth these effects, I follow other feminist scholars and turn to the local. Yet unlike these feminists I keep my local-level analysis situated in a larger regime framework as I dissect the dialectics of domination and resistance in each welfare regime. As welfare states distribute benefits and construct need at the national level, they organize the space within which clients maneuver at the local level. This concept of "client maneuverability" is preferable to traditional notions of agency or autonomy for several reasons. These traditional concepts are too often understood in either/or terms—states give agency or they deny it; states increase autonomy or they undermine it. Maneuverability allows for the possibility that states can both constrain and enable those targeted.[33] States shape client maneuverability by demarcating the rhetorical possibilities for claims-making and defining how participatory the prevailing needs talk is. They also affect maneuverability by extending concrete tools to clients to defend their interests. Through their redistributive and interpretive work, welfare states determine the amount of space available for clients to maneuver discursively, practically, and institutionally.

While other scholars of Eastern Europe have also analyzed the implications of state development for gender relations, too often their work is infused with liberal ideals about the state's role in social life. In their accounts, the state intrudes while women resist; the state strikes at private relations while women struggle to escape its iron fist.[34] This approach misses the complex ways that women and men can use state policies and institutions to protect themselves. Over this period, Hungarian clients did not passively acquiesce to state domination. Nor did they engage in continual acts of resistance. Instead, clients actively participated in the state's interpretive work—sometimes accepting, and other times rejecting, state understandings of their needs. But they always strategized to gain discursive and practical resources, even when the regimes they lived under progressively narrowed their room to maneuver.

In early socialism, clients maneuvered to negotiate their many social responsibilities. Their strategies were thus integrative in nature: they utilized state resources to become embedded in work and family structures. As the maternalist welfare state narrowed its focus to women's child rearing, female clients' maneuvering became more constrained. Their strategies then took on an expansive quality: they struggled to draw into view the larger context in which they mothered and to reengage state actors in their domestic relations. With the emergence of the liberal welfare state, clients' space to maneuver was reduced further. This reduction then gave rise to excavational strategies as clients strategized to resurrect their significance as mothers and to demand state assistance for their child rearing. In this way, links were forged between the form of state dominance and the type of client strategizing; as welfare regimes demarcated the terms of inclusion and exclusion, they provoked particular responses as clients maneuvered to protect their own well-being.

CONSTRUCTING THE ANALYSIS

My historical account of Hungarian welfare is based on research I carried out in Budapest from 1993 to 1995. Although my examination of the policy apparatus relies on national-level data, my investigation of welfare practices is rooted in two Budapest districts. By grounding the institutional analysis in Budapest, I clearly privileged urban populations. While I could not entirely control for this urban bias, I did employ research strategies to grapple with it. Before choosing the districts, I collected demographic data on the size, income distribution, and ethnic composition of Budapest's twenty-two districts. From these data, I located two districts of similar size, but with varied populations. In order to protect the identities of my subjects, I am unable to reveal the precise districts; anonymity was the main constraint that those in charge of these institutions placed on my research. Thus, throughout this book, I use the pseudonyms "szegénytelep" and "ipartelep" to identify these locales.[35]

When I began my research in 1993, the population of each district hovered around 100,000; szegénytelep had 93,741 residents, and ipartelep had 110,042. This population size was similar to that of other locales within and outside Budapest.[36] Although these districts were similar in size, the characteristics of their inhabitants differed. Szegénytelep has historically been an impoverished area. In 1993, 16 percent of its residents were unemployed, higher than the national rate of 13 percent.[37] It was one of the most ethnically diverse areas in Budapest; roughly 7 percent of the inhabitants defined themselves as Roma, or "gypsy."[38] By contrast, ipartelep has historically been one of Budapest's most industrialized areas, with a large manufacturing sector. It had working-class, middle-class, and bourgeois pockets. This economic diversity was coupled with relative ethnic homogeneity— roughly 3 percent of its residents identified themselves as Roma in 1993.[39] The differences between these districts allowed me to examine welfare development in locales with different populations. And these districts' demographic parallels to larger Hungarian trends enabled me to ensure that my findings were as generalizable as possible.

Given my substantive focus on welfare policies and practices, it was not sufficient to analyze only welfare expenditures and redistributive patterns. Instead, I collected four types of data. First, I carried out an archival study of 1,203 case files produced from 1952 to 1995 by three key welfare institutions—Child Protective Services (Gyámhatóságok), Child Guidance Centers (Nevelési Tanácsadók), and Family Support Services (Család Segitő Szolgálatok). My case sample was selected randomly, according to the year the cases were initiated. I sampled approximately one hundred cases from each institution in each decade under examination. Since these institutions classified cases by family name, I did not choose my sample on the basis of the sex of the client. Instead, when analyzing these cases, I studied which family members were targeted, how they were regulated, and whether and how they strategized to change the nature of this regulation. Second, for the contemporary period, I supplemented this archival work with eighteen months of ethnographic research in local welfare offices. I had access to all parts of these institutions: I attended staff meetings, observed caseworker/client interactions, and accompanied welfare workers on home visits. Table 2 provides an overview of the different types of cases I reviewed through my archival and ethnographic research.

Third, I conducted thirty-one interviews with Hungarians affiliated with the welfare apparatus from 1952 to 1995. My respondents included case-

Table 2. Overview of Case-File Sample by Topic and Period (by percentage
of caseload)

Type of Case	Welfare Society (1948–1968)	Maternalist Welfare State (1968–1985)	Liberal Welfare State (1985–1996)
I. Work-Related	47%	32%	21%
A. Needed work	60	17	84
B. Needed better work	23	77	14
C. Needed better work relations	17	6	2
II. Family-Related	69	81	13
A. Spousal problem	27	19	31
B. Parental problem	41	76	69
C. Extended-family problem	32	5	—
III. Poverty-Related	6	18	78
A. Inappropriate housing	91	27	44
B. Insufficient wages	9	14	30
C. Material endangerment	—	59	26

NOTE: These case categories are not inclusive; some cases were classified in more than one way. For more on my approach to this case-file analysis, see the Methodological Appendix.

workers, psychologists, government officials, and policymakers. These interviews provided me with a fuller understanding of the evolution of welfare work, as well as of shifts in the policy sphere. Because some respondents had worked outside Budapest, they provided a check against the urban bias of my other empirical materials. Fourth, to gain a more complete perspective on policy development, I collected a wide range of primary and secondary source materials on social programs and laws produced at the enterprise and the national level. At the enterprise level, I examined records from a group of five factories in the Csepel region of Budapest to ascertain the precise nature of enterprise re/distribution and its effects on workers' everyday lives. At the national level, I analyzed a plethora of documents to determine the broader trajectory of state redistribution and interpretation of need as well as the existence of potential rural/urban cleavages in the allocation of social benefits.

Using all these data, I construct a comparative analysis of the development of Hungarian welfare from the inception of state socialism to the present. In this book the historical analysis is broken into three parts, which correspond to the three Hungarian welfare regimes. Each part includes two chapters—one devoted to the state architecture of need as embedded in policies and practices, and one devoted to client maneuverability and the gender strategies provoked by the regime. Part One traces the contours of the welfare society of 1948–1968. In Chapter One, I examine how this regime socialized need in an attempt to remake the basic institutions of social life. Drawing on national-level policy data and documents from a complex of factories in the Csepel region of Budapest, I explicate how central-plan and enterprise-related benefits linked entitlement to recipients' institutional positions. In addition, I draw on 407 case files from two Gyámhatóság offices to describe how welfare workers restructured clients' institutional relations. In Chapter Two, I use the case files to evaluate client maneuverability in the welfare society. I illuminate how the prevailing conception of need bred client strategies of integration by exploring how married women and single mothers appropriated state resources to transform the form and the content of their institutional relations. In doing so, I argue that both groups of clients found ways to enhance their institutional and social integration.

Part Two moves to the late socialist period and explicates the dynamics of the maternalist welfare state of 1968–1985. Chapter Three analyzes how social conceptions of the "needy" were reinvented in maternal terms. Based on policy data and interviews with government officials, I examine how the welfare system regulated the quantity and quality of motherhood. I also analyze 586 case files from the two welfare institutions of the period, the Gyámhatóságok and Child Guidance Centers, to reveal how welfare work became increasingly specialized. Through these cases, I trace the rise of the "good-mother mold" and the evaluative distinctions welfare workers made between the domestically competent and incompetent. In Chapter Four, I interpret these cases from the perspective of female clients. I argue that clients' room to maneuver in this regime varied according to which side of the good/bad–mother divide they fell on. While "good" mothers were able to expand the prevailing needs talk to speak of their needs as spouses and as women, "bad" mothers were more constrained in their strategizing. This chapter traces the emergence of punitive welfare practices and their implications for female clients' maneuvering.

Part Three analyzes the liberal welfare state of 1985–1996 to reveal how the "needy" were reinvented yet again, this time in material terms. Chapter Five describes how neoliberal discourses of poverty regulation transformed the national and the local policy apparatuses: universal and maternalist welfare provisions were dismantled and were replaced with means-tested poor relief. Through a study of 210 case files and ethnographic research, I examine how the materialization of need transformed casework into piecework and widened the social distance between welfare workers and clients. I also document how these welfare shifts reduced clients' identities to the materially needy and thus bred new mythologies about the pathologies of the Hungarian "welfare cheat." In Chapter Six, I draw on this case-file and ethnographic material to illuminate how the materialization of need further reduced clients' room to maneuver. The chapter also examines how this regime prompted client strategies of excavation as female clients reasserted their contributory identities as child-rearers and their sense of maternal entitlement. The concluding chapter draws out a series of broader lessons from this case study, lessons that can inform Western welfare state theory and politics. Finally, in the Appendix, I provide a detailed methodological discussion of the archival, interview, and ethnographic data used in this book.

Part 1

THE WELFARE SOCIETY, 1948–1968

1. Socializing Need

The Restructuring of Social and Economic Institutions

The post-World War II period was one of the most difficult eras in modern Hungarian history. With much of the country's basic industry and infrastructure demolished in the war, the population faced extreme material hardship. Half of Hungary's national assets had been destroyed; over one third of its railways and nearly all its bridges were unusable; and one fourth of its housing stock was severely damaged.[1] After the country's forced "inclusion" in the Soviet bloc, the Hungarian government was enormously constrained in how it could approach postwar reconstruction. This was a period of state-engineered transformation clearly dictated by the Soviet model. By the early 1950s, industry, mining, and banking were nationalized, and agriculture was collectivized.[2] Amidst these profound changes, there was little room for open dissent or contestation. As the brutal history of political purges and forced collectivization reveals, repression awaited those who overtly challenged the political and economic order under construction in the period.[3]

Although this was certainly an era of high Stalinism, it was also a time when a new welfare model was introduced. Unlike the West European states of the era, Hungary did not create a system of targeted social provisions and family policies. The economic realities and political commitments of the period prohibited Hungary from following this path. Faced with the daunting task of rebuilding the basic infrastructure and industry demolished in the war, the government simply did not have the resources to build an extensive welfare system. There were also ideological impediments to the creation of such a system. Within the new socialist order, there was to be no need for social policies associated with the West. Poor-relief programs were considered a relic of the bourgeois past; social policies targeted at specific economic classes were deemed divisive and even reactionary. To demonstrate its antipathy to this welfare model, the government dissolved the Ministry of National Welfare in 1952 and replaced it with the Ministry of Health.

Yet this metamorphosis at the ministry level did not mark an end to all welfare provision. Over the first two decades of state socialism, the party/state set out to establish a welfare society in which the well-being of the population was to be secured in existing social institutions. At the national level, a series of societal policies were introduced to reshape the institutions of economic and social life. Many of these policies were built into the economic plan, embedded in its wage structure, full-employment provisions, and price subsidies. Others were linked to specific enterprises. These included benefits-in-kind such as socialized healthcare, housing, childcare, and eating facilities, as well as benefits-in-cash such as family and marital allowances. These policies were connected by their focus on social institutions as the site of the allocation of state resources.

The societal-welfare model also included a network of local agencies, the Gyámhatóság. These institutions operated out of district councils throughout the country. Staffed by a small group of caseworkers, these agencies intervened into everyday life to ensure clients' welfare by integrating them into work and family institutions. For those not already tied to such structures, caseworkers did some "networking": they secured employment, tracked down deadbeat dads, and mobilized extended families. For those already embedded in such structures, caseworkers regulated these institutions to make sure they operated properly. Like societal policies, these agencies focused on their clientele's institutional context and connections.

This chapter explores the inner workings of the early socialist welfare regime. Through an examination of its re/distributive and interpretive practices, I reveal how the architecture of need in the period was constructed around existing social institutions. In this regime, there was a close fit between these state terrains; together, they transmitted consistent messages about the nature of social entitlement. State re/distributive policies and practices did not link entitlement to the needs of individuals or social groups. Instead, they interpreted the institutions of economic and social life as "in need." Societal policies reshaped work and family institutions, while welfare agencies linked clients to these structures. At both levels, assistance claims were based on clients' collective roles and responsibilities. In this era, the relationship between the state and its clients was mediated by the existing institutions of work and family.

This analysis of the early welfare regime departs from the existing historiography of the period in two primary ways. First, most of the scholarship on early state socialism denies the existence of a welfare apparatus. It takes the party/state's ideological appeals at face value to argue that the regime's inability to recognize poverty forced it to abolish all welfare policy. As a result, this scholarship tends to reduce the regime's policy apparatus to the economic organization of state socialism.[4] Although much of the regime's welfare apparatus was rooted in its economic structure, a complex system of policies and agencies did operate with the explicit goal of securing the population's well-being. As Hungarian sociologist Zsuzsa Ferge characterized it, the regime was "societal" in nature and invested in altering the "profile of society."[5] According to Ferge, the provisions of early socialism were not simply palliative measures designed to ameliorate poverty. They had far loftier goals: they sought to restructure nothing less than "basic human and social relations."[6]

To a large extent, my analysis draws on Ferge's insights into this regime's societal underpinnings. Yet it also complicates her account. In Ferge's analysis, the "state" appears as disembodied and separated from actual policies, while "society" is analyzed in vague terms, disconnected from actual social institutions. Instead of falling back on abstract characterizations, I work with a more specified unit of analysis. While I also look to the economy to understand the societal-welfare regime, I explicate the precise state terrains and institutions through which this regime operated. Most important, I differentiate between state policies and practices, revealing how these state levels reshaped social life in distinctive, albeit complementary, ways. At the national level, I draw on policy data to show how economic planners created societal provisions in line with the demands of industrial reorganization. At the enterprise level, I examine documents from a group of factories in the Csepel region of Budapest to reveal the ways trade unions participated in the interpretation of workers' needs. At the level of welfare agencies, I analyze 407 case files to show how caseworkers transmitted these messages to families. In doing so, I explicate the precise social institutions remolded in the period. State actors did indeed attempt to change the profile of society, but they did so by targeting three main institutions—the workplace, the nuclear family, and the extended family. In short, I provide a grounded analysis of the social actors, spaces, and principles underlying the early socialist welfare regime.

Second, this analysis expands the confines of the existing historiography by unearthing the gender regime of the welfare society. While little scholarly work has been done on this welfare system, there is even less work on its gendered nature. Most feminist scholars dismiss this era as "Stalinist" and begin their work in the late socialist period.[7] The few gender analyses of this early period examine the state's gender regime through the lens of the party—its political discourse or iconography.[8] While insightful, these analyses give rise to overly abstract conceptions of the state that are disconnected from its actual policies and practices. They rarely address the gendered implications of centralized planning or of enterprise assistance schemes. And they do not even acknowledge the existence of state agencies or caseworkers in the period. These gaps have led feminists to view "Stalinist emancipation" as focused primarily on women's position in the labor force and to argue that because the regime never rethought gender oppression in the home, it failed to undermine the source of gender subordination.[9]

Here, too, my narrative shifts the unit of analysis by moving from the level of political ideology to the level of state policy and practice. In doing so, I advance a somewhat different argument about the gender regime of the Hungarian welfare society. While this state was undoubtedly concerned with women's roles as wage laborers, work was only one institution that underwent reconstruction. The state also sought to remake familial institutions, in both their nuclear and extended forms. One of the main goals of this welfare regime was to connect these institutions and to locate women in different social spheres. The policies and practices of the period recognized women's many roles and identities; they acknowledged women as workers, spouses, mothers, and family members. The early socialist state worked with an expansive understanding of women's social positions—an understanding that stemmed largely from its socialized conception of need.

REMAKING THE INSTITUTIONS OF SOCIAL LIFE: THE SOCIETAL POLICY REGIME

Soon after its ascendance to power in 1948, the Hungarian Workers' Party (MDP, Magyar Dolgozók Pártja) embarked on wide-sweeping legal reforms to alter the most fundamental of social relations—those between citizen and government, worker and employer, husband and wife, and parent and child.[10] Like those enacted in other East European countries, Hungary's reforms ended decades of patriarchal family law that codified female dependence on men.[11] They constituted a new family form that served as the basis for the era's policy regime. Rhetorically, the 1949 Hungarian constitution guaranteed women equal rights, equal working conditions, increased legal protection, and new maternity and child protection institutions. The constitution also pledged a formal commitment to marriage and the family, promising to "defend" this institution.[12]

While these promises sounded appealing as discursive constructs, the

1952 Family Law was the government's first attempt to translate this legal theory into concrete provisions. First, the law set new guidelines for marriage by delineating those who could enter this institution. The law required that all Hungarians submit marital applications to state councils and gain the approval of local judges; minors who wanted to marry had to convince council caseworkers that they were knowledgeable about what marriage entailed.[13] Second, the 1952 law set new rules for how couples could exit this institution. In essence, it introduced a version of "no-fault divorce," which allowed either partner to initiate divorce proceedings. In these proceedings, applicants had to demonstrate that their marriage had "decayed" (*megrom-lott*). Applicants then underwent a waiting period to ensure that their marriage was "beyond repair" and they had not made a "rash" decision to dissolve it.

Third, the 1952 law also set new property relations for couples. It gave women joint ownership rights to property obtained during marriage. These rights were particularly significant in the sphere of housing since over 65 percent of Hungarian flats remained in private hands through the 1960s.[14] In divorce cases, women had the right to reside in commonly held flats. When children were involved, the parent with custody (usually the mother) was guaranteed access to the family flat. And when the father was the formal owner of the flat, the mother had the right to reside in his flat until a state flat became available.[15] As the law phrased it, these provisions were designed to "protect" women from material loss and to make marriage a more "egalitarian" institution for both partners.[16]

Fourth, the 1952 law set new guidelines for familial structure and responsibility. It effectively outlawed single parenthood by requiring children to have two officially recognized guardians. If it was unclear who a child's father was, local caseworkers conducted paternity tests. Once paternity was established, fathers were "encouraged" to marry their children's mothers.[17] If they refused, they were forced to "acknowledge" their offspring and to support them "materially" and "morally."[18] In addition, the law fixed new paternal responsibilities by establishing an extensive system of child-support payment and enforcement. Fathers were required to pay roughly 20 percent of their wages to support their children.[19] These funds were taken directly from fathers' wages and transferred to mothers via the Ministry of Labor. The law also held workplaces responsible for such transfers. Enterprises were required to supply caseworkers with accurate data on fathers' wages and to help transfer them to mothers. If they did not, they were held legally accountable and subjected to fines.[20]

Taken together, these provisions painted a legal portrait of the new

Hungarian family. They created an image of what the family should look like—how Hungarians should join this institution, what their responsibilities were within it, and how they could leave it.[21] This portrait was not simply an ideological image. Once constituted, it served as the basis on which a complex of state policies formed. Few of them were family policies in the classical sense of the term; they were not provisions to supplement the incomes of certain families.[22] These policies were linked to workforce participation rather than charity. They tended to be available to most classes of Hungarians. And they took the institutions of work and family as the social bodies in need. Rather than constituting a distinct policy apparatus, these provisions were diffused throughout different economic and social terrains, including centralized planning and the organization of enterprises.

Economic Planning as Social Planning

One reason social scientists have not theorized the welfare regime of early state socialism is because many of its key re/distributive mechanisms were rooted in economic planning.[23] Since centralized planning has been the domain of economists preoccupied with economic efficiency, few analysts have viewed planning as a form of welfare re/distribution. For instance, János Kornai's work, influential for both economists and sociologists, analyzes economic planning from the standpoint of production and productivity.[24] Kornai characterizes the state-socialist economy as dominated by centralized bureaucratic coordination. Through its re/distributive intervention in the operation of firms, this centralized coordination produced soft budget constraints.[25] Firms were prompted to usurp investment resources, and as a result state-socialist economies were "resource constrained" and plagued by chronic shortages.[26] In Kornai's analysis, centralized planning was important for its deleterious effects on economic production, productivity, and efficiency. While insightful, Kornai's analysis obscures how central planning was a primary form of welfare re/distribution in the first two decades of socialism. Planning certainly structured the relationship between the centralized state and individual firms. Yet the plan was also the mechanism through which the government engaged in broader social engineering and reshaped general social relations.[27]

Working with a broader notion of the plan, sociologist Iván Szelényi extends Kornai's analysis to the sphere of social inequality.[28] Szelényi criticizes Kornai for focusing only on planning's damaging effects on efficiency; he then analyzes its effects on class structure. Through survey data on housing, Szelényi found that subsidized housing actually benefited the elite. He discovered that subsidized flats were allocated to high-income groups, while low-income groups were forced to build their own housing without subsidies.[29] This finding led him to conclude that "more redistribution and more government money spent on public housing were advantageous to the rich; less money for public housing but improved mortgage conditions were beneficial for the poor."[30] Eventually, these findings prompted Szelényi to view centralized planning as the primary source of inequality under state socialism and to call for the introduction of the market and formal welfare re/distribution to counter such inequality.[31]

Szelényi's analysis of centralized state coordination was path breaking. By examining planning as a distinct form of re/distribution, it marked an important departure from overly economistic analyses. Szelényi's work evaluated the effects of planning not only on economic efficiency but also on class relations. Of course, while housing policy may have exacerbated existing social inequalities, socialist re/distribution encompassed more than the allocation of state flats. It also included full-employment provisions, wage policies, and price subsidies—all of which Szelényi takes for granted in his work but refrains from analyzing as such. Moreover, while Szelényi offers an extraordinary account of the re/distributive consequences for class relations, centralized coordination reshaped other social relations. Through these centralized provisions, the national state participated in both need interpretation and need satisfaction. These policies can then be analyzed as welfare provisions in the broadest sense of the term—as attempts to define the population's needs and to formulate the best mechanisms for meeting them.

More specifically, at the heart of the Hungarian societal policy regime were its full-employment provisions. As early as 1947, the Hungarian constitution proclaimed that it was the right of all Hungarians to work. As Ferge put it, "All those who were of working age should avail themselves of the right to work. The state guarantees the opportunity to work and the stability of employment."[32] Work was thus constituted as a basic social need; it was both a right and an obligation in the period. Beginning in 1950, all ablebodied men not gainfully employed were deemed "publicly dangerous work avoiders" and were subjected to fines and imprisonment.[33] The same year "unemployment" (*munkánelküliség*) was officially abolished; the word was replaced by more neutral terms such as "labor surpluses" and "labor redundancies."[34] Unemployment compensation was introduced in 1954, but its benefits were so minuscule that few Hungarians used it. By 1957, the provision covered only those who were physically or mentally unable to work.[35] As a popular slogan of the period put it, the regime gave workers the daily gift of "eight hours of work, eight hours of rest, and eight hours of entertainment."[36]

Yet full employment was as much a gift for the regime as it was a gift from the regime. The postwar model of reconstruction was based on rapid industrialization. Increased labor-force participation was a key component of this program. Full-employment policies served to mobilize the population into state manufacturing and thus were connected to the regime's general policy of speedy industrialization. The government's first five-year plan called for a massive increase in industrial employment—from 1949 to 1954 half a million workers were to be drawn into industry.[37] Of these new positions, 50 percent were to be skilled, 25 percent semiskilled, and 25 percent unskilled. The majority of these positions were also to be in heavy industry. Similarly, the regime sought to centralize the workforce in large factories and enterprises. Overall, many of these goals came to fruition: by 1953, four hundred thousand new industrial workers had entered the labor force; by 1954, industrial employment had increased by nearly 50 percent; and, by 1955, 70.3 percent of the labor force were employed in enterprises with at least five hundred workers.[38]

This centralized push toward full employment had important implications for women. The regime's need for an expanded labor force placed different, and often contradictory, demands on women. Because the demand for labor largely outpaced its supply, women's reproductive labor became of central concern. According to even the most conservative estimates, 5 percent of the Hungarian population had been killed in the war.[39] The difficult economic conditions of the period exacerbated the situation and led to falling birthrates. This decline provoked consternation in the party leadership. In 1949, they reacted by instituting a series of reproductive policies that restricted the availability of abortion and subjected the medical profession to heightened surveillance.[40] Then, in 1953, the government completely banned abortion, even when the mother's health was in jeopardy. The resulting "Ratkó regime," named after the female Minister of Health, criminalized abortion and curtailed access to birth control; women were thus forced to subordinate their reproductive desires to the state's economic needs. Although the Ratkó laws did increase birthrates, the effect was only temporary: these laws were repealed in 1956, after which time the Hungarian birthrate plummeted to record lows.[41]

The government looked to women not only as reproducers of the future labor force but also as an untapped source of productive labor. In its 1949 five-year plan, the government projected that women would constitute 38 percent of the industrial labor force. Yet their numbers lagged far behind this projection; in 1950, only 24 percent of industrial laborers were women.[42] In 1951, the government passed a decree that ordered an increase in women's

Table 3. Female Employment Rate, 1949–1970

Year	Percentage of Women in Labor Force	Percentage of Labor Force Female
1949	35	29
1955	45	33
1960	53	36
1965	60	40
1970	65	42

SOURCES: KSH, *Time Series of Historical Statistics, 1867–1992*, p. 37, and Iván Pető and Sándor Szakács, *A Hazai Gazdaság Négy Évtizedének Története, 1945–1985*, pp. 675, 677, 712.

employment rates.[43] Two years later, the National Planning Office instituted quotas for industrial retraining programs—women were to constitute 30 to 50 percent of newly trained workers and apprentices. As a result, women's participation in the paid labor force soared. While 20 percent of women were employed outside the home in 1941, this number rose to 45 percent in 1955, and 60 percent in 1965.[44] Table 3 has these data. In reality, these numbers were probably much higher since many women who were formally defined as "housewives" actually worked long hours on the land.[45] The increase in female employment becomes clear when employment rates are examined by region. In 1955, close to 70 percent of Budapest women were employed outside the home, while 43 percent of women in small cities and 20 percent of women in villages were employed. By 1960, these percentages had risen to 75 percent for Budapest women, 48 percent for women in small cities, and 25 percent for women in the countryside.[46]

With time, women also became increasingly integrated into different economic sectors. Before retraining quotas were introduced in 1950, women constituted 19 percent of construction apprentices, 16.7 percent of mining apprentices, and 11 percent of metallurgy apprentices.[47] After 1950, their representation in these fields changed. As Table 4 reveals, women's employment in agriculture declined, while their presence in industry increased dramatically.

In order to facilitate women's entrance into the paid labor force and new industrial sectors, the government engaged in a great deal of ideological work. It attempted to redefine the meaning of wage labor in women's lives. The political propaganda of the period equated work with female emancipa-

Table 4. Percentage of Labor Force Female by Economic Sector, 1949–1970

Year	Economic Sector				
	Agriculture	*Industry*	*Commerce*	*Transportation*	*Construction*
1949	55	15	39	8	5
1960	38	35	50	17	11
1965	37	39	59	21	14
1970	38	43	62	23	14

SOURCES: KSH, *Time Series of Historical Statistics, 1867–1992*, pp. 44, 67, and Iván Pető and Sándor Szakács, *A Hazai Gazdaság Négy Évtizedének Története, 1945–1985*, p. 675.

tion. Through a selective reconstruction of the past, the regime linked women's historical oppression to their exclusion from the paid labor force.[48] By bringing women into the labor force, the regime presented itself as undercutting female subordination.[49] In addition, wage labor was said to be a central avenue for female self-realization. Political ideology and iconography emphasized how the collective and women's work groups mitigated against the isolation of "domestic drudgery."[50] Wage labor was also presented as a way for women to contribute to the building of socialism. Through these ideological practices, the regime attempted to constitute work as a social and personal "need" for women.[51]

In addition to this ideological pull, the massive entrance of women into the labor force was the result of an economic push caused by the wage policies of the period, which constituted the second component of the early socialist welfare regime. Analyzing the centralized wage structure of the period is quite a complex task, as it fulfilled many functions for the regime—functions that were historically variable even within the first two decades of state socialism. In the decade following the war, the wage system was a tool for securing the large labor force necessary for reconstruction. Economic planners abolished the family wage, setting wages so low that few families could exist on just one wage. This depression in wages then increased the supply of cheap labor needed for rapid industrialization. The wage structure was also used to alter the class structure. In 1931, 57 percent of Hungarian incomes fell into the first quintile, and 38 percent into the second and third quintiles. By 1962, these percentages had been reversed— with 35 percent located in the top quintile and 59 percent in the second and third.[52]

Income data on specific occupational groups also reveal that the regime

Table 5. Average Monthly Income by Economic Sector and Type of Worker, 1950–1965 (in forints)

	1950	1955	1960	1965
Economic Sector				
Industrial	736	1,209	1,609	1,756
Agriculture	414	922	1,357	1,511
Construction	618	1,193	1,611	1,794
Commerce/trade	597	973	1,401	1,567
Transportation	631	1,112	1,503	1,749
Type of Worker				
Manual	587	1,164	N/A	1,771
Technical	1,166	1,884	N/A	2,182
Administrative	824	1,205	N/A	1,691
Manager	N/A	2,649	N/A	5,537

SOURCES: Iván Pető and Sándor Szakács, A Hazai Gazdaság Négy Évtizedének Története, 1945–1985, pp. 685–686, 688, 691, and KSH, A Nők Helyzéte a Munkahelyen és a Családban, pp. 13–14.

tried to close the income gap separating those working in different economic sectors and in manual and nonmanual positions.[53] For instance, in 1950 manual laborers' wages were 50 percent of those of technical workers; by 1965, this percentage had increased to 81. Table 5 has income data for different economic sectors and work positions.[54]

The centralized wage system was also one of the main mechanisms the regime used to secure a basic subsistence level and to ensure that minimum wage levels did not fall too far below the average. In this period, minimum wage levels tended to be calculated in household terms; the wage system was itself premised on a two-wage-earner family. Government statisticians expended an enormous amount of energy pinpointing the different factors that impinged on family income. They conducted elaborate studies of children's effects on family income by calculating precisely how much each child reduced the real family income and where small, medium, and large families were located in the class structure. They carried out complicated studies of spousal occupational and income patterns, tracing marital patterns within and across income groups to determine whether families were clustered in an income bracket because both spouses were in similar occupations. They also examined the effects of "housewives" on family income by testing whether this was a "luxury" of families whose primary wage earner was well paid.[55] All these data then informed policy decisions about how to structure the wage system to ensure the well-being of different types of families.[56]

It is quite difficult to evaluate whether this wage structure actually secured a decent standard of living for families in the period. Since there was no official "poverty line," it is hard to translate these data into meaningful statements about the population's material well-being.[57] However, the existing data do reveal that per capita income and wages increased steadily after 1955. Real income rose by roughly 61 percent while wages rose by over 63 percent from 1955 to 1965.[58]

Another reason why it is difficult to assess material well-being through income data is that these data do not account for the third component of the regime's plan-related benefit scheme—centralized price subsidies. Like the socialist wage structure, price subsidies served many purposes for the government. First, they were a way to secure a minimum standard of living. Second, price subsidies were a tool to alter consumption patterns. By subsidizing certain goods, economic planners steered consumption in specific directions.[59] Third, selective subsidization was a way to make consumption consistent with the regime's production priorities and to bring the supply and demand of certain goods in line. Finally, price subsidies were family-based. Subsidy levels were often set according to calculations of what different families could afford.[60] In some areas, the amount of the subsidy even varied by household size and family structure.[61]

The system of subsidies can be broken down into two main categories: subsidized goods and socialized services. Of the two, there are fewer debates about the egalitarian effects of subsidized goods, particularly subsidies for basic necessities. Until the early 1950s, the Hungarian economy was plagued by hyperinflation, which led to chronic price increases and food shortages.[62] In 1951, the government attempted to stabilize the situation by leveling off food prices and introducing a massive price reform. While prices for basic foodstuffs shot up in 1952, they stabilized in the following decade. From 1952 to 1962, basic food prices increased at an average of 3–6 percent per year.[63]

This stabilization was achieved largely through subsidies on basic foodstuffs.[64] Four general "tiers" of subsidies existed in the period.[65] At the top were subsidies for bread and sugar. These goods were subsidized so heavily that they became affordable for most social classes. Over half the calories consumed by Hungarians in this period were derived from bread alone. The second tier included subsidies for dairy products and eggs. They were subsidized less heavily, yet their consumption rates were 10–20 percent higher than prewar levels.[66] The third tier of subsidies included meat and poultry. Subsidized at lower levels, their consumption rates were roughly the same as prewar levels. Finally, the fourth tier consisted of "negatively subsidized" goods such as alcohol, tobacco, and coffee. Hence, consumption of these "luxury" items decreased by 30–50 percent.[67]

As with the wage structure, it is difficult to assess whether these subsidies helped secure a basic standard of living for the population. Yet family expenditures for basic necessities did seem to stabilize after 1953. While the massive price reforms of the early 1950s had a destabilizing effect on prices, the proportion of family budgets devoted to food and clothing remained fairly steady afterward.[68] In 1953, 37 percent of the average family budget went to food; this percentage increased to 47 in 1960. A similar pattern characterized clothing: in 1953, families devoted 12 percent of their budgets to clothing, while in 1960 they allocated 15 percent.[69] Moreover, consumption rates indicate that Hungarians were consuming more during this period. From 1950 to 1965, food consumption increased by 44 percent; after 1955, there was a fivefold increase in the purchase of consumer durables such as televisions, refrigerators, telephones, and household appliances.[70]

In addition to subsidizing specific goods, the state also subsidized numerous services. The most important of these were childcare and housing. The state-socialist childcare system was quite complex and consisted of local-government and enterprise-based facilities. The state-run sector encompassed a network of nurseries (*csecsemőotthonok*) and kindergartens (*óvodák*). Both facilities were heavily subsidized in the post-1953 period, although to different degrees. From 1953 to 1965, there was a huge expansion of the nursery system: the number of state-run nurseries increased by close to 500 percent.[71] The system of kindergartens did not expand quite as rapidly. Few new kindergartens were built prior to the early 1950s, despite the "baby boom" of the Ratkó regime. From 1950 to 1960, the number of kindergartens increased by only 40 percent. The demand for kindergartens clearly outpaced supply. In 1955, 28 percent of Hungarian children were in kindergartens; by 1960 this percentage had increased to 34. And, by 1965, still only 50 percent of those who wanted to place their children in kindergartens were able to do so.[72]

Placement in subsidized childcare was based on several criteria. Applicants for council (local-government) childcare were ranked according to four main criteria: the mother's employment status, household structure, the number of children already in childcare, and the existence of extended family networks. In this way, workforce participation was combined with familial need to determine who received council childcare.[73] The availability of enterprise childcare was also considered when assigning children to spaces in state-run centers. Women employed in enterprises with on-site childcare facilities often were instructed to apply first to their workplaces. For some women, this created a problem since it left them responsible for getting children to and from childcare. Many women preferred to use state-run facilities in their neighborhoods, which enabled them to mobilize other family members to transport children to childcare.[74]

Similar eligibility criteria determined the allocation of subsidized housing. The socialist housing structure was also quite complex, in both ownership form and allocation mechanisms. Three forms of residential property prevailed in the period. Owner-occupied flats were those inherited or built by individual occupants. Cooperative flats were those built with the support of government loans. In 1950, 86 percent of all flats fell into one of these types; by 1960, the number had dropped to 74 percent.[75] Council flats were residences owned by the government and leased to occupants at a subsidized rate.[76] In 1950, 14 percent of all flats were council flats; by 1960 the number had increased to 26 percent.[77]

All three forms of housing were subsidized by the central government, albeit in different ways and to different degrees. Hungarians who owned their flats had access to twenty-five-year government loans to offset maintenance and construction costs. Those who wanted to build cooperative flats had to pay a 10 percent deposit to the government.[78] They were then eligible for a thirty-five-year loan at a low interest rate.[79] They also received a 20 percent subsidy to cover maintenance and construction costs. Moreover, beginning in the early 1950s, occupants of cooperative flats were given an additional 10 percent subsidy for each child they had (or contracted to have) in their first three years of residence.[80] Council flats operated according to a three-tiered subsidy system—in which 75, 25, or 6 percent of all maintenance costs were covered by state grants.[81]

Because council flats were the most heavily subsidized and did not require an initial capital investment, they were the most sought after. As with childcare, the allocation of council flats was based on a combination of labor-force participation, personal/political connections, and familial need. Prior to 1971, applicants for council flats had to submit formal recommendation letters from their employers. In these letters, employers assessed the applicant's "value" to the enterprise and overall "social importance." This requirement opened up the system to class inequalities since workers' enterprise positions determined their "value," as well as their ability to influence the placement process. According to some estimates, as many as 80 percent of the applicants for council flats were managers or professionals.[82] Yet occupational privilege did not determine the whole process. Once an application reached the local council, it was ranked according to a point system in which familial need was central. Applicants received points based on number of children and family structure. Ultimately, their final ranking helped to determine whether they received a council flat, its size, and the subsidy level. This point system may have undercut the influence of personal or political connections: although 80 percent of housing applications may have been submitted by managers and professionals, it is estimated that 60 percent of council flats were allocated to these groups.[83]

Taken together, these plan-related benefits constituted a large part of the societal policy regime of the period.[84] In constructing these policies, economic planners not only attempted to satisfy the population's needs but also interpreted them. Full-employment policies positioned work as a basic need for men and women alike; the wage structure made work a practical need for families; and the system of price subsidies defined what families needed to survive materially. These interpretations were linked to the larger demands of industrialization and production. Thus, national-level policies also fulfilled the economic needs of the regime. In doing so, they often satisfied the needs of different social groups in contrasting ways—class position and family structure clearly affected the allocation of centralized services. A similar dynamic characterized the distribution of enterprise-based benefits in the period.

Welfare at Work

In addition to benefits distributed through central economic planning, many societal policies were based in individual enterprises. Through their workplaces, Hungarians had access to benefits-in-kind and benefits-in-cash. This access was particularly prevalent in the post-1956 period because of an overall decentralization of welfare allocation. In large part, this move to bolster the role of enterprises was a response to the 1956 Hungarian revolution. The industrial working class played a critical role in this uprising; it created workers' councils in factories as one of its first revolutionary acts.[85] For the postrevolutionary János Kádár regime, gaining the loyalty of the industrial working class was quite a pressing issue. The subsequent "Kádár compromise" sought to secure this loyalty by increasing living standards and building "refrigerator socialism."[86] Following the revolution, state wages increased—in 1956 they rose by 11 percent and in 1957 by 18 percent.[87] Another goal of the Kádár government was to link workers more closely to their workplaces. This objective was achieved through the movement of welfare re/distribution to enterprises. In this way the regime personalized "state benevolence" and showed its commitment to workers directly at the workplace.[88]

Yet bolstering the role of enterprises in the allocation of welfare benefits did not mean that workers became central to policy implementation. Rather, it gave a select group of trade-union officials increased control over the administration of social benefits. Trade unions had become central players in this system in 1950, when they were incorporated formally into centralized planning at the national level. In the early 1950s, the Central Committee of Hungarian Trade Unions formed two subsidiary committees to steer policy formation. The National Social Security Council, comprised of trade-union representatives from different economic branches, was responsible for social-policy formulation and innovation, while the Central Committee on Social Insurance, comprised of union bureaucrats, had authority over policy administration. Yet both these bodies focused their work upward, in an attempt to shape the direction of centralized economic planning.

In the mid-1950s, this trade-union network began to extend downward, to the local government and enterprise levels. Officials from local councils (*tanácsok*) were given more decision-making power and administrative control within their locales. At the same time, trade-union presence in factories became stronger. In workplaces with over one hundred employees, "pay-out" centers distributed benefits to workers directly. New union subcommittees were established in these enterprises to guide and control welfare allocation within firms.[89] Their tasks varied: they regulated working conditions; they developed social facilities in factories; they introduced programs to improve the situation of specific groups of workers; and they allocated social aid to families with special needs. In a sense, these tasks constituted "social work for the workers."[90]

Although local trade unions gained increased influence over welfare distribution, central regulation of the structure of enterprise-based benefits remained. Beginning in the mid-1950s, firms were required to submit yearly "social plans" to the Central Committee of Hungarian Trade Unions and the Ministry of Labor. This requirement was designed to lessen the variation among enterprises in the benefits available to workers. In these plans, enterprises outlined the mechanisms used to improve working conditions and employees' "everyday lives." They reported on six areas: their measures to assist female and manual workers; their wage structure for different workers; their professional training for employees; their working conditions; their health programs; and their general welfare program, including provisions for employee meals, transportation, childcare, and housing.[91] Firms were also required to demonstrate that their welfare programs took into account employees' social and family conditions as well as the quality of their work.[92] In this way, familial need and work performance were to guide enterprise re/distribution.

In practice, these principles applied differently to various types of enterprise assistance. From an analysis of primary and secondary documents from five Csepel enterprises, I discovered that workplace provisions fell into two categories: benefits provided at work and benefits received through work.[93] These provisions were distributed according to distinct principles. Most benefits-in-kind allocated at work were available to all workers irrespective of their enterprise position or familial need. For instance, many enterprises operated canteens where workers could purchase inexpensive meals while on the job. Csepel factories also had sales in which employees could obtain goods at discounted prices. Until the late 1940s, most of these goods were basic necessities, such as milk, bread, eggs, and vegetables.[94] In the mid-1950s, Csepel enterprises began to provide workers with access to "luxury" items such as meat and coffee, as well as household appliances like refrigerators and vacuum cleaners.[95] To make these goods available to a wide range of workers, enterprises allowed them to purchase items on "credit" and to make monthly payments from their wages.[96] Enterprises also gave their workers cultural subsidies, such as discounted theater, opera, and cinema tickets.[97] In the summer, many enterprises organized weekend trips to Lake Balaton.[98] These trips were highly subsidized and were provided to workers on a first-come, first-serve basis. Finally, enterprises with over four thousand workers operated special polyclinics to give workers medical advice, medicine, baby food, and milk for nursing mothers.[99]

Other benefits-in-kind seemed to be allocated in a less egalitarian fashion. For example, there appears to have been two tiers of workers' vacations—those available to all workers and those contingent on one's enterprise position and connections. Employees with access to the best vacation homes and resorts were located at the upper echelons of enterprises.[100] Similar inequities were at work in the allocation of childcare; because "high-status" workers often mobilized their professional connections in the enterprise to secure placement for their children, fewer spaces were left for less well-positioned workers.[101]

At the same time, other enterprise benefits-in-kind were distributed primarily on the basis of family structure and need. The allocation of enterprise housing appears to be have been influenced more by familial need than by bureaucratic privilege. Much of the housing allocated through enterprises took the form of rooms in barrack-style workers' hostels.[102]

While such collective arrangements did not offer the kind of living conditions preferred by those at the upper echelons of enterprises, they were desirable for other groups of workers, particularly in the mid-1950s, when large-scale urbanization brought masses of workers to industrial cities that did not have adequate housing infrastructures. Family need largely determined workers' ability to secure enterprise housing. For instance, a study of six Hungarian enterprises from 1952 to 1965 indicated that family structure was the key factor determining who received enterprise housing.[103] Workers with children were given top priority, followed by married couples, and then individual men.[104] Among men, those with families outside the cities where they worked were given top priority since they were thought to need subsidized housing in order to be able to fulfill their family obligations.[105] Male workers from the countryside who had no family networks within commuting distance of their workplaces also had priority. Hence, those benefits that were not sought after by "prestigious" workers were allocated according to workers' family structures and needs.

Workers who secured placement in enterprise housing then had access to a series of additional services and benefits-in-kind. Hostel records from five Csepel factories indicated that enterprise housing was organized to meet workers' diverse needs. Hostel residents received cultural subsidies unavailable to other groups of workers. On a weekly basis, they had access to films, dance recitals, and concerts at highly discounted prices.[106] Hostels also offered numerous evening classes and programs: reading groups organized by the hostel library; cooking classes run by the hostel canteen; dance classes organized by the hostel sports club; and writing classes offered by the hostel newspaper.[107] In addition, hostels regularly organized family outings and activities, including weekend arts and sports programs for children, after-school activities for teenagers, and collective cooking arrangements for women.[108] On Sundays, they often organized "collective childcare schedules" in which parents worked an hour at the hostel day-care center and then could leave their children there for the rest of the day.[109] Finally, hostel residents ran discussion and support groups that dealt with topics as diverse as how to handle marital problems, rebellious children, and aging parents.[110]

In addition to these benefits-in-kind, enterprises provided benefits-in-cash to their employees. These benefits tended to be allocated according to workers' familial needs. In fact, many enterprises created "family cashiers" (családi pénztárok) to distribute cash benefits. Because most of these benefits were centrally conceptualized, there was less room for discretion or bureaucratic influence at the point of allocation. Four main types of benefits-in-cash were distributed by enterprises. First, the most extensive benefits-in-cash were family allowances, monthly payments distributed to families to offset the costs of child rearing. When introduced in the 1930s, family allowances targeted state workers and civil servants. In 1948, the Hungarian government extended eligibility to industrial workers with three or more children; in 1959 the program was expanded to include agricultural workers with three children, industrial workers with two children, and single parents with one child. Allowances were provided to families with one child if the child were disabled or ill. As a result, the proportion of families entitled to the allowance increased by nearly 35 percent from the late 1950s to the early 1960s.[111] The amount of the allowance varied by the number of children in the family. Since large families were thought to have "special" needs, they were given more money. Yet, overall, family allowances constituted approximately 20 percent of the average wage.[112]

Beginning in the mid-1950s, family allowances were distributed at the enterprise level. In the first two decades of state socialism, family allowances were attached automatically to the fathers' wages. Exceptions were made only for single mothers who refused to reveal the identities of their children's fathers. In all other cases, family allowances were given to male "heads of household," even when children no longer resided with their fathers. The family-allowance system therefore assumed a particular domestic structure—the nuclear family, headed by a man.

Second, maternity-leave provisions were administered at the enterprise level. Until the mid-1960s, women who were employed for at least 270 days prior to childbirth were given twelve weeks of fully paid leave; women who had worked for 180 days prior to birth were provided twelve weeks of leave at 50 percent of their previous salary.[113] A woman in either group was eligible for an additional month of support if the birth had been "irregular." Once back at work, new mothers were given two hours of paid "nursing time" per day until their infants were six months old and, after that, an hour per day until they reached nine months. Enterprises were also required to provide mothers with baby food and nursing milk. These provisions were distributed through trade-union offices in enterprises: union officials calculated mothers' work histories, wage levels, and benefit levels. Fathers were not entitled to these benefits unless they were single parents.

Third, enterprises granted short-term leave for families. In this period, the "housework holiday" was introduced to give families time to take care of their "special responsibilities."[114] Women with two children were given one day off per month without pay, while women with three or more children received two days off. Hungarian families also were the beneficiaries of a system of paid leave. For each child, families received two additional days of paid leave per year. Workers with small children had access to additional sick leave.[115] The assumption underlying all these policies was that families with young children had special needs and required more time and resources to fulfill them.

Finally, enterprise unions had special funds that they distributed to workers on a per-case basis. Most unions provided marital allowances to newly married workers. To obtain these funds, married couples had to apply to the family cashier and demonstrate they needed additional funds to pay for their weddings or to set up house. Similar familial criteria were used to allocate "emergency aid." These funds were set aside for families with temporary material problems. Unlike other enterprise-based assistance, emergency aid was accompanied by home visits. On visits, union officials assessed the applicant's level of familial need. In my sample of Csepel factories, I found that 62 percent of these funds went to the families of workers who had been injured in work accidents; 27 percent went to workers who cared for sick children, parents, or spouses.[116] The remaining 11 percent went to female workers who had been left by their husbands. As a union official wrote in 1958 when he approved aid to one such woman: "Her husband left her between one day and the next. She does not know where he disappeared. As part of our collective, we cannot leave her and her family in this condition. This is an emergency situation we must resolve."[117]

Like plan-related benefits, enterprise provisions were not just re/distributive in nature. They also articulated a specific conception of need. Here the architects of need were trade-union officials. They carried out the interpretive and allocative work involved in welfare re/distribution; they determined what kind of housing, cultural, and financial assistance workers needed. In many ways, their conception of need was more grounded in workers' everyday lives than was the conception of need embodied in the central plan. It was also guided by principles of familism. Although workers' positions affected their access to some fringe benefits, most enterprise provisions were based on familial need. This centrality of the family and the household was even more salient in the practices of welfare agencies in the period.

INSTITUTIONAL FAMILISM AND GYÁMHATÓSÁG WELFARE PRACTICES

While the scholarly literature on the societal policies of early socialism is limited, almost no work has been done on this regime's institutional welfare practices. Both Hungarian and Western social scientists have tended to interpret the abolition of the Ministry of Welfare in 1952 as signifying an end to all direct welfare assistance. Yet the Ministry of Welfare's reincarnation as the Ministry of Health did not mark an end to welfare work. After the Ministry of Welfare was dissolved, the government created a network of child protection agencies, the Gyámhatóságok. These institutions operated out of local state offices in every district of the country; they were located in the heart of the party/state apparatus. They therefore ended up playing a critical role in mediating between national-level policies and Hungarian families. They provided the link between the regime's conception of need and everyday life by translating its discursive constructions to clients in direct and immediate ways.

The Gyámhatóság was formed out of the prewar orphanage system, the *árvaszék*. During World War II, the *árvaszék* evolved into an important force at the local level. These offices grappled with the problems of those who had lost family members in the war, mainly by placing abandoned children in state institutions or adoptive families. Thus, these offices were not "welfare institutions" in any sense of the term. Although they occasionally conducted charity work, their responsibilities were confined to organizational issues relating to orphans.

Instead of scaling back these institutions in the postwar period, the government transformed them into more general welfare agencies. These institutions not only retained their control over adoption and institutionalization but took on new, more traditional welfare responsibilities. Staffed by two to three caseworkers, most of whom were women with limited education, postwar Gyámhatóság offices had responsibilities that fell into two categories. First, they were responsible for maintaining the large bureaucracy surrounding the family. All families had contact with Gyámhatóság caseworkers in this capacity since these offices were required to register each child born in their districts. Caseworkers also made recommendations in child-custody cases, set visitation rights, enforced child-support arrangements, and resolved housing problems. Second, caseworkers oversaw the general upbringing of the children in their districts. In this capacity, the Gyámhatóság acted both as a parental assistance center that advised parents on how to organize family life and as a coercive body with the legal authority to institutionalize "endangered" children. There was no segmentation among welfare agencies in this period. The Gyámhatóság carried out all "welfare" work; it combined the legal assistance, social work, and child protection that are usually located in separate institutions in Western welfare states.

Moreover, there was little segmentation within Gyámhatóság offices.

Although these agencies dealt with a variety of cases, they did not divide their work by task.[118] The same caseworker conducted bureaucratic and child protection work. Caseworkers handled the entirety of a case—from registering newborns to tracking down deadbeat dads to making recommendations in child-custody disputes to institutionalizing children who lived in dangerous environments. They stayed with their cases from start to finish. Importantly, Gyámhatóság caseworkers had few financial resources at their disposal, so they could not allocate funds to clients. Instead they used existing social institutions to resolve clients' problems. They regulated these institutions to ensure that they cared for their members; they smoothed over conflicts that surfaced in the workplace or home; and they advised clients on how to remain integrated in these networks.

These two components of Gyámhatóság work—its lack of segmentation and the paucity of its financial resources—had profound implications for the conception of need articulated in their welfare practices. The absence of a rigid division of labor within these offices enabled caseworkers to see clients' different social positions. Welfare workers were accorded a sense of clients' numerous social roles and the ways they intersected in everyday life. In this period, clients were recognized as having a series of collective identities; they were acknowledged as workers, parents, spouses, and family members. Moreover, given the limited resources at caseworkers' disposal, they tended to conceptualize need in social terms, as connected to clients' levels of institutional integration. While the societal policies of the period sought to reconstitute the institutions of economic and social life, welfare offices tried to reshape Hungarians' relationship to these institutions by incorporating clients into three key institutions—the workplace, the nuclear family, and the extended family.

Casework as Employment Work

In contrast with the professionalism exhibited by caseworkers in later decades, early Hungarian caseworkers saw their work as socially transformative. In conferences, staff meetings, and interactions with clients, caseworkers often spoke about the "new era" they operated in—a period characterized by new social roles and relations.[119] Caseworkers connected these social changes to their own work, positioning themselves as direct links between broad structural change and Hungarians' everyday lives. As the head of one Gyámhatóság office put it in his 1953 institutional summary, "This is a revolutionary period and our work is revolutionary. Across occupational groups, regions, and generations, lives are changing and we are here to guide and control these changes."[120]

While these shifts were indeed occurring across social terrains, for women they were particularly pronounced in the sphere of wage labor. For the first time in Hungarian history, men and women were expected to participate in the labor force. Caseworkers seemed aware of the profound effects of this new position for women and their families. Thus, they set out to do the practical work involved in incorporating women into the paid labor force. In the process, caseworkers transmitted important messages about women's needs as wage laborers.

The centrality of clients' positions as workers surfaced in their initial contact with Gyámhatóság caseworkers. The first questions caseworkers asked clients in all kinds of situations inevitably revolved around their work lives. Divorced parents with custody or visitation disputes were interrogated about their work histories. Minors who sought permission to marry were required to submit documentation of their employment status. Parents who wanted to change their children's legal guardianship had to prove the new guardian had stable employment. Couples who wanted to adopt children had to demonstrate that they were gainfully employed. And parents who sought help resolving domestic conflicts were met with a litany of questions about their work lives. Caseworkers then used this employment information to assess what clients needed above and beyond their specific requests. These "needy" clients fell into three categories: those who needed to find work; those who needed to resolve problems at work; and those whose families needed to become supportive of their work lives.

In the decade following the war, caseworkers devoted a considerable amount of time to clients in the first category—28 percent of the cases I reviewed from the period involved unemployed clients, the overwhelming majority of whom were women. Unemployed women were greeted with questions about why they were not working. Motherhood was not an acceptable excuse. Caseworkers often lectured these women about the relationship between wage labor and familial well-being. For example, in 1952 a female client was scolded by her caseworker for ending her employment in order to care for her rebellious son. As the caseworker recounted after a meeting, "I informed Mrs. Kárpány that the time was over when she had to stay at home to secure the family. Her family will be better if she works and feels herself strong."[121] Or as another caseworker wrote about one of her clients, a housewife whose son refused to attend school, "Her son sees her as unproductive. If he saw her as productive, he would be more productive in school himself."[122] Caseworkers often spoke of these unemployed women in pejorative terms, deeming them "irresponsible" and even "unprepared" for child rearing.

Caseworkers did more than lecture clients about wage labor. They also spent time advising clients about work possibilities. Gyámhatóság offices often seemed like employment centers, with caseworkers documenting the intricacies of clients' experience and skills. They then used this information to instruct clients how to secure employment, particularly those with few formal skills. For the difficult cases, caseworkers contacted local enterprises to ask whether they needed additional workers and to recommend their clients. When a caseworker learned that a woman who came to the Gyámhatóság in 1953 with a bureaucratic problem had only a fourth-grade education, the caseworker agreed to assist her and eventually helped the woman find a job in a local textile factory. The caseworker then followed up to ensure that she kept her job.[123]

For clients who had stable employment, caseworkers often intervened to resolve work-related problems. Caseworkers regularly helped women reschedule their work hours so they could meet their family demands. For instance, in 1960 a recently divorced woman came to the Gyámhatóság for advice on how to control her teenage sons' unruly behavior. She worked the night shift, and thus the boys were free to "roam the streets of the city into the night." The woman's appeals to her supervisor to change her shift were denied, until her caseworker "requested" that he help the woman. She was then transferred to a job in the same enterprise with only daytime hours.[124] Caseworkers also advised clients about how to get along with supervisors and co-workers. In a 1963 case a woman had such terrible relations with her co-workers that her family suffered the consequences. While on a home visit to the workers' hostel where the woman lived with her husband and five-year-old daughter, the caseworker discovered that the young girl had no friends in the day-care center. After inquiring about this situation, she learned that the mother's colleagues so despised her that they forbid their children to play with the girl. The caseworker then asked the head of the center to pay special attention to the girl so she would not suffer from her mother's bad work relations. She also initiated meetings with the mother to instruct her on how to become part of the "collective."[125]

Other caseworkers took active roles in their clients' work lives. Occasionally, they visited clients at work to get a first-hand look.[126] When they saw something that disturbed them, they did not hesitate to intervene. In 1962 a woman was referred to the Gyámhatóság by the manager of her housing complex (házmester). In a letter to the Gyámhatóság he expressed his concern that the woman was always "nervous" and drank to "calm herself down." After an office meeting in which the caseworker was unable to detect the source of the woman's stress, she paid a visit to her workplace.

There she found the woman working in a brigade that was "too advanced" for her skill level. The woman worked at a far slower pace and appeared embarrassed as a result. So the caseworker took it upon herself to suggest that the woman be transferred to another brigade that made her feel less "nervous."[127]

In other instances, caseworkers attempted to make clients' family lives more compatible with their work lives. This kind of assistance was more time consuming since it frequently involved reshaping family members' attitudes toward female employment. These work/family conflicts surfaced most often between spouses, with husbands exhibiting frustration with their wives for not "caring" for them properly. All sorts of men voiced such complaints in this period, using them as arguments to bolster their divorce appeals or to extend their visitation rights. Men also blamed their wives' work lives for general marital tensions and child-rearing difficulties. Caseworkers meticulously documented their complaints and took it upon themselves to change men's attitudes. They lectured men about how they should be more accommodating. A good example is the 1955 "beef-stew case." It began when a man wrote a letter to the Gyámhatóság to complain that his wife had stopped caring for him once she began to work. To support his accusations, he made repeated references to how she no longer cooked his favorite food, Hungarian beef stew. The caseworker then scolded him for his selfish preoccupation with beef stew, explaining that the "needs of the collective" outweighed his "need for beef stew."[128]

In some cases, caseworkers did more than lecture these men: they took the radical step of demanding that men contribute to domestic upkeep. Usually, these demands were framed in terms of the man helping the woman with *her* domestic duties.[129] This was the stance that one caseworker took in a 1958 case in which the husband complained incessantly about how dirty their flat had become since his wife started doing "social work" on Saturdays. The caseworker retorted, "Well, Mr. Sebők, what do *you* do on Saturdays? What stops you from doing the cleaning?" She then threatened to find him some "social work" of his own if he refused to help his wife.[130] In 1961 a man claimed that the household "fell apart" every year in the fall. His wife worked in a fruit-canning factory and worked long hours in the fall to turn fruit into preserves. In response, the caseworker reminded the man that since his work in an iron factory was not seasonal, he could pick up the slack for his wife. She even provided him with a list of cleaning tasks that had to be done in the fall.[131]

In all of these ways, Gyámhatóság caseworkers constituted work as a central part of clients' lives; they evaluated clients' "needs" through the prism of wage labor. This preoccupation with work was not simply ideological. While caseworkers did echo the prevailing discourse of wage labor, their interest in clients' work lives was also materially motivated. In this period, Hungarians received basic necessities through their workplaces. Caseworkers' assessments of clients were colored by this material reality. When they encountered unemployed clients, caseworkers became concerned for their future well-being. Since caseworkers did not have resources to support clients, they had to connect them to institutions that could. As one caseworker who worked in the Gyámhatóság in the 1960s revealed to me in an interview, "The best way to put it is that I was practical. Of course I bowed to the communists. Everyone did. But I did my job. I protected the families of my district."[132] In this era, such protection meant hooking clients into work institutions and regulating their work relations.

A "Father" for Every Child

Caseworkers' focus on clients' work lives did not deflect them from familial experiences. One of the most distinctive features of welfare work in the period was the belief that clients' needs as workers did not negate their needs as family members. State actors viewed these spheres as complementary: wage labor was important for clients' material well-being, while the family was both materially and emotionally essential. Yet families were left largely on their own to decide how to fulfill such "caring" functions. Caseworkers attempted to locate clients in nuclear family structures; they worked hard to impose this family form on their clients. Once clients were embedded in this familial structure, state caseworkers rarely sought to alter the nature of their familial relations. Unlike the sphere of work, where state actors readily intervened to reshape clients' relations, caseworkers were reluctant to become involved in familial dynamics. Their concern was with the form of their clients' families not the content of their familial relations.

The preoccupation with the nuclear family permeated all aspects of casework, but it surfaced most clearly in the amount of time caseworkers devoted to establishing legal paternity.[133] Such investigations were particularly important in the early 1950s because of the 1952 Family Law's requirement that children have two legally recognized guardians. This requirement presented practical nightmares for the Gyámhatóság, forcing caseworkers to spend an inordinate amount of time on paternity cases. In doing so, they transmitted messages about men's contributory roles as family members—messages about how mothers needed the support of fathers, wives needed the help of husbands, and children needed to be raised by two parents.

These messages did not always fall on sympathetic ears. Caseworkers encountered many women who claimed not to know the identity or whereabouts of their children's fathers. These women gave caseworkers long lists of men, proclaiming that any of them could have been the father. Without genetic tests, caseworkers had to interview these men and their acquaintances to establish paternity; this work could take years. Other women changed their stories about the fathers' identity, providing caseworkers with new names when the earlier ones did not materialize. Still others insisted that the fathers had disappeared abroad and could not be located. But caseworkers were relentless: they followed up every lead, all the while instructing women that they needed paternal support and their children needed two parents.

One of the best examples of client recalcitrance and caseworker persistence occurred in a paternity case that ran for over seven years. When the Gyámhatóság first contacted Mrs. János in 1953, her husband was in prison. She informed her caseworker that her husband was not the father of her son: the father was a former lover who had since moved to Slovakia to marry another woman. She hoped this information would end the case; it did not. After a year of translated letters, the Hungarian consulate found the man, who denied that he was the boy's father and claimed that Mrs. János was pregnant when they met. So the caseworker initiated an international paternity investigation involving interviews and medical exams in several languages. Another year elapsed before she discovered that he was not the boy's father. The caseworker then conducted a paternity test on Mrs. János's husband—an investigation that was equally complicated given the man's imprisonment. It took another year for the caseworker to learn that he was not the father either. She then confronted Mrs. János, who revealed that the "real" father was an old friend who had since moved to another part of Hungary. It took two more years to discover that he, too, was not the father. Frustrated, the caseworker decided to list Mrs. János's then ex-husband as the legal father. But just before the documents were drawn up, Mrs. János came to the Gyámhatóság with the "real" father at her side—a young soldier she had recently married. Before she changed her mind, the caseworker drew up the papers and signed them. The case closed in 1960.[134]

While some women demonstrated such foot dragging, Hungarian men tended to exhibit all-out resistance to paternity testing. Their resistance infuriated caseworkers: they interpreted it as proof of these men's disregard for the "Hungarian family." Caseworkers approached these cases as if they were on a mission. They showed overt disgust at the stories these men told. For instance, in 1956 one man tried to get out of a paternity suit by arguing that he was in the army when his girlfriend became pregnant. As the caseworker angrily responded, "Excuse me Mr. Bálint. We all know that army men have sex. This story does not help your case."[135] In 1954, a man claimed that he could not be the father of a young girl because, as he put it, "She was born in April and I stopped having sexual relations with her mother in October. It is impossible." The caseworker then suggested that he return to primary school and learn basic math skills.[136]

Of all the excuses that men used to escape paternal obligations, those that angered caseworkers most were claims that the children's mothers were "promiscuous." These accusations enraged caseworkers; men who made them were subjected to extensive investigations of their sexual lives. A man informed a caseworker in 1955 that "everybody knows Mária Jenő has many lovers. It will take years [to find the father]." In response, the caseworker conducted interviews with his acquaintances, most of whom corroborated that he was the father. Within a month, she had legally designated him as the father. As the case closed, she snidely noted that he would be dealing with the case for a long time in the form of eighteen years of child-support payments.[137]

This focus on paternity seemed to indicate that state caseworkers placed an emphasis on biological familial ties. As time went on, this was not the case. Through the late 1950s, caseworkers faced a slew of paternity cases; by the early 1960s the Gyámhatóság was inundated with cases involving legal-guardianship changes. Roughly 30 percent of the cases I reviewed from 1958 to 1965 involved such changes.[138] In most cases, mothers wanted to transfer paternal rights to their new spouses or "life partners" (*élettársak*). To secure Gyámhatóság approval for these changes, clients had to demonstrate two things. First, they had to show that the new father was employed. Second, they had to prove that they were in a "stable family relationship." Caseworkers used one phrase repeatedly in assessing these cases: the couple had to have an "orderly, peaceful family life" (*rendes, békés, családi élet*). Home visits were not required to determine whether they did; office proclamations of these men's commitment to women and their children usually sufficed even for the "repeat transfers" by clients who continually switched their children's legal fathers. For instance, from 1960 to 1962, one woman changed the identity of her son's father four times. Each time the new father-to-be came to the office to proclaim his commitment to the woman and her son. As the fourth father stated in 1962, "I have lived with Ildikó for six months. I want to give her son my name because I love him." This was enough to convince the caseworker.[139] For caseworkers, what mattered most was the family form, not the nature of family relations.

Of course, decisions to cede paternal rights were not determined by mothers and caseworkers alone—legal fathers had to agree to give up their paternal rights. These men rarely posed an obstacle. Yet in approximately 15 percent of the cases I reviewed, fathers resisted the transfers. Most frequently, caseworkers persuaded these men to change their minds. Their modes of argumentation were quite indicative. Caseworkers began by mobilizing legal arguments to convince fathers of the importance of codifying existing family relations into law. They often cited the 1952 Family Law's emphasis on "legally consistent" familial relations. If this argument did not work, caseworkers drew on the needs of children, explaining how "disturbing" it was for children not to share their mothers' names or how "confusing" it was when the men they lived with had no formal authority over them. If neither argument was persuasive, caseworkers questioned fathers' commitments to their children. They gathered information on the times fathers canceled meetings with their children or missed child-support payments. For example, in 1962, a father who refused to cede his paternal rights to his ex-wife's new husband was accused of being selfish: "My records show that you did not pay support for the first year of your daughter's life. Were you thinking of her then?" His only option was to get a lawyer to fight the transfer; eventually, he turned over his paternal rights.[140]

Caseworkers pressured biological fathers to cede paternal rights only if mothers had lined up new nuclear families. When mothers had not, caseworkers took the opposite approach: they worked to keep biological fathers responsible for their offspring. In effect, they used their control over child custody and visitation to re-create the semblance of a nuclear family. The Gyámhatóság set visitation in divorce cases, and caseworkers took this work quite seriously, meticulously documenting parents' work schedules to arrive at visitation arrangements. The resulting agreements seemed like complicated treaties designed to bring peace to two warring factions. They outlined the exact days fathers could see their children; they specified precisely when fathers were to pick up and return their children; and they stated the penalties for tardiness. Fathers who were more than fifteen minutes late for two visits lost one meeting with their children. Those who were "chronically tardy" had their visitation cut in half until they became reliable. Some of these men seemed genuinely distraught over these restrictions and questioned the need for complicated arrangements. Those who raised such questions received speeches about the importance of maintaining consistent familial connections.

After these visitation agreements were drawn up, caseworkers policed both parents to make sure they adhered to them. In part, they had to convince mothers that fathers should continue to play important roles in their children's upbringing. Mothers who tried to limit the amount of time fathers spent with their children were subjected to lectures about how two parents should be involved in child rearing. For instance, in 1959 the mother of a young boy was reprimanded for denying her husband access to his son. The caseworker explained that her ex-husband's presence not only gave her support but also provided her son with a male role model.[141] Far more common were fathers who failed to maintain regular contact with their children. This behavior enraged caseworkers: they saw such men as shirking domestic responsibilities and showing disrespect for the family itself. So they lectured these men about paternal responsibility. Missing one visit or being late to as few as two visits was enough to get a father pulled into the Gyámhatóság for a lecture. "Do you know what your son feels in those fifteen minutes when he waits for you?" a caseworker asked a father in 1961. "You are a role model for him. What kind of example do you give him?"[142] For the "chronically irresponsible," caseworkers resorted to threats, promising to dissolve visitation rights or report the fathers to their workplaces if they failed to improve their behavior. In effect, caseworkers forced clients to maintain nuclear family ties, even when these familial structures had formally broken down.

State caseworkers used their control over child support to achieve similar ends. Just as they manipulated visitation to secure familial contact, they used child support to establish clear financial responsibilities among family members. In this capacity, caseworkers engaged in direct action. They had the institutional means to be proactive: caseworkers were vested with the legal authority to enforce child-support arrangements. For divorced couples, such enforcement was fairly straightforward. Caseworkers simply attached the father's wages until his offspring turned eighteen. The centralization of the economy facilitated this solution; caseworkers could locate fathers' workplaces with few difficulties. Thus, caseworkers usually completed this work in a few weeks. They also adjusted child-support payments to compensate those women whose ex-husbands refused to turn over their family allowances. Recall that family allowances were given to male heads of households. In some divorce cases, these allowances never found their way back to the mothers and children, so caseworkers developed their own transfer route: they increased the men's child-support payments by the amount of the family allowance.

Even more creative were the strategies caseworkers used to secure child support from men who had left Hungary. This was a particularly acute problem in the post-1956 period, when many Hungarian men emigrated abroad, leaving their wives and children behind in Hungary. Caseworkers struggled relentlessly to track down these men; they contacted foreign embassies and Hungarian consulates to locate them. Through these international bodies, they pressured fathers to support their offspring. In one amazing 1958 case, a caseworker spent months tracking down a deadbeat dad who had immigrated to France. Once she located him, she sent him a photo of his two sons. On the back of the picture, she wrote: "It costs a great deal to raise children in Hungary, too. Do not forget your Hungarian responsibility." A few weeks later, the boys' mother received an undisclosed amount of money to cover her child-rearing costs.[143]

In this way, caseworkers' regulatory practices largely targeted men. They sought to discipline men; they defined spousal and parental roles in ways that centrally placed men's domestic contributions; and they policed men's familial obligations with determination. Yet their police work rarely impinged on the nature of familial relations: caseworkers never questioned why so many men shirked their domestic duties or why some women seemed loath to keep these men in their lives. Caseworkers saw the nuclear family as in "need" of a redefinition of responsibility, but they did not problematize clients' relationships to the nuclear family itself. They assumed that this family form was in clients' best interest and struggled to position it as a central part of their lives.

All Their Kin

Caseworkers' focus on the nuclear family did not exclude other family ties. As they connected women to work institutions and men to nuclear families, caseworkers also sought to locate their clients in extended family networks. Their vision of ideal domestic arrangements had the nuclear family situated in a larger orbit of extended families. Caseworkers viewed extended families as complementary to nuclear families—as networks that could support the nuclear family. They also used extended families to resolve issues typically addressed through the workplace. When these other institutions broke down, caseworkers had extended kin come to the rescue. Approximately 32 percent of the case files in my sample from the period involved extended families. In carrying out this work, caseworkers transmitted messages about the interconnectedness of the institutions of work, the nuclear family, and the extended family and of how the extended family could become a safety net for those who had fallen out of the workplace and the nuclear family.

This institutional interconnectedness was encoded in the initial questionnaires administered to Gyámhatóság clients. Until the mid-1960s, these questionnaires were quite short and were designed to elicit general information about clients' social locations and resources. Questions fell into four categories. First, there were questions about clients' work lives. Second, there were inquiries about clients' nuclear families and their children's legal guardians. Third, there was a series of questions on their health history. The fourth area of inquiry revolved around clients' extended-family networks. Here caseworkers determined whether clients had relatives living in the area. They also obtained information about these relatives—their ages, occupations, living arrangements, and relationship to the client. Together, this information guided caseworkers' assessments of clients' needs. In many cases, caseworkers drew on extended families as temporary and permanent solutions to their clients' problems at work and home.

As temporary solutions, caseworkers used extended families to address material issues unmet by clients' workplaces. Although families had priority in obtaining enterprise benefits, they often had to endure long waiting periods. In these cases, caseworkers helped clients locate relatives who were willing to assist them, particularly clients with housing problems. The 1957 Jancsó case is a good example of this kind of casework. This family of four had recently migrated to Budapest and were living with Mrs. Jancsó's cousin. Accommodations were already cramped, but when the cousin became pregnant, they had to move out. Although Mrs. Jancsó had applied for housing through her workplace, she was told that it could take years for space to become available. Convinced that she would have to turn her children over to state care, Mrs. Jancsó begged for assistance. Unable to secure council housing for her, the caseworker sent letters to other relatives in the area, requesting their help on behalf of the "local government council." Eventually, the caseworker "convinced" one of Mrs. Jancsó's aunts to give them a room in her flat. The caseworker even wrote up a formal agreement to assure the aunt that the situation was only temporary.[144]

Caseworkers carried out similar kinds of work for clients in need of childcare. Here they focused on clients' elderly relatives. They sent letters to determine whether relatives were retired and on pensions. If so, caseworkers tried to convince them to use their retirements "productively." In 1962, after a caseworker learned that a client with childcare problems had an elderly aunt who was a retired nursery school teacher, she convinced the elderly woman to continue her work raising the "next generation."[145] For those who had no relatives in the area, caseworkers often helped relocate relatives to Budapest. For example, after a mother of three was left by her husband in 1953, the caseworker encouraged her to send for her mother, who lived in a distant village. When the mother encountered difficulties migrating, the caseworker advised her how to secure the necessary approvals and make the move as smooth as possible.[146]

In addition to filling voids left by clients' workplaces, caseworkers also used extended families to pick up the slack for nuclear families. They frequently mobilized extended families to come to the aid of female clients unable to fulfill their caretaking responsibilities. When these women became ill, caseworkers turned to their mothers, sisters, and aunts for domestic help. This tendency to turn to female relatives was indicative of larger cultural assumptions about child rearing: despite the social and ideological changes of the period, child rearing was still perceived as a female domain not to be fully entrusted to men. In one 1957 case, a mother of three was hospitalized with pneumonia. Although she lived with her husband, the caseworker "convinced" her mother to care for her grandchildren.[147] In a 1961 case, when the mother of two boys suffered a nervous breakdown and was institutionalized, the state caseworker sent letters to all her relatives. Rather than leave the children with their father, she relocated them to their aunt's house. As she wrote in her notes on the case, "Although she [the aunt] lives in a humid, dark flat that is not entirely healthy, it is important that they [the children] stay in the family."[148]

Caseworkers also utilized extended families as permanent solutions to their clients' problems. This was the primary way caseworkers addressed the needs of single mothers, in part because single mothers' problems seemed less temporary than those of married women. Single mothers were more likely to work in unskilled jobs in enterprises without housing or childcare. As a result, caseworkers looked to these women's family networks to solve their material problems. To secure clients housing, caseworkers inquired about the size and comfort level of relatives' flats. They carried out similar work for single mothers in need of childcare. Here caseworkers located relatives who could transport children to school or care for them after school. Usually, these were long-term arrangements, designed to fulfill single mothers' ongoing material needs.

Occasionally, caseworkers had relatives take permanent responsibility for the children of single mothers with especially acute problems, such as alcoholism or mental illness. Rather than institutionalizing their children, caseworkers placed them with extended families. Quite often, they moved the children to distant towns or villages. In some situations, caseworkers arranged for mothers to send relatives money each month until they could take their children back. In other cases, they pressured mothers to turn over guardianship to their relatives. Caseworkers took this route with clients who had serious physical disabilities. As one caseworker put it in 1953 as she tried to convince a disabled mother to transfer legal guardianship of her son to her mother, "This will let you remain in contact with him. So when you get better, he will know you as his mother."[149]

Finally, caseworkers also drew on extended-family networks to take over paternal responsibilities. Although caseworkers could force biological fathers to support their children financially, they could not demand that they play active roles in their children's lives. This lack of paternal involvement was of great concern to caseworkers; they worried about the long-term effects of children's lack of male role models. So they looked for male relatives to serve as father figures. The presence of a man was one of the main criteria used to decide where to place homeless single mothers. For example, in 1965 a young mother moved out of her ex-husband's flat because of his alcohol abuse. Her caseworker helped her locate two relatives willing to assist her: one was an elderly aunt who resided in a large flat in an elite area of Budapest, while the other was a sister who lived with her husband in a small flat in downtown Budapest. The caseworker encouraged her to take her sister's offer because her husband could serve as a father figure for her son. As the caseworker wrote in her case notes, "The flat is smaller but the boy cannot be denied the role model he needs given his father's terrible example and irresponsible behavior."[150]

PERSONAL WELL-BEING THROUGH INSTITUTIONAL WELL-BEING

The welfare society of the first two decades of state socialism was a complex system designed to secure the population's well-being. The state/society relations in this regime were encoded in two distinct realms—national societal policies and local welfare practices. These state spheres worked in complementary ways: societal policies restructured the institutions of economic and social life, while welfare agencies intervened into Hungarians' lives to connect them to these institutions. While both state realms attempted to alter the general "profile of society," they did so by targeting specific institutions and remolding them according to particular models.

As this regime's policies and practices targeted the sphere of work, they ascribed new meanings to wage labor. In this period, the workplace became the main arena within which material needs were to be met. At the national level, full-employment provisions and wage policies constituted wage labor as a social right and an obligation. Through labor-force participation, workers gained access to socialized goods and services. At the enterprise level, the workplace became responsible for providing basic necessities to the population. Work-related benefits connected employees to valuable resources, such as housing, childcare, and vacations. And, at the level of welfare agencies, caseworkers connected work institutions and clients, particularly women: by linking them to employment and improving their work relations, caseworkers defined wage labor as a social responsibility for women as well as men. Together, the policies and practices of this regime remade work institutions and infused them with social significance.

Like the sphere of wage labor, the nuclear family underwent a transformation in this period. Often overlooked in the existing historiography, the changes made to the family were as encompassing as those made to the workplace. The centralized wage structure and full-employment provisions gave rise to a new family form. By creating a material reality in which few families could exist on only one income, the state made the two-wage-earner family the norm. Enterprise provisions also helped to encourage this family form; they made it difficult for workers to exist outside the nuclear family. Workers disconnected from such family structures were at a disadvantage in the allocation of subsidized goods and services. And caseworkers were even more explicit in their policing of the family. Through their regulatory practices, caseworkers made it extremely hard for clients to remain outside the nuclear family. They also set new expectations for those in nuclear families, particularly men: by forcing husbands and fathers to fulfill their domestic obligations, caseworkers redefined familial responsibility to highlight men's contributory roles. In this period, the family took on a new form, with more clearly demarcated obligations for parents and spouses.

While this welfare regime endowed the workplace and the nuclear family with new responsibilities, it also carved out an important role for extended kin. In doing so, the regime formalized previously informal familial links. Welfare agencies of the period mobilized extended families as temporary solutions to their relatives' problems at work and at home. Extended kin also served as long-term alternatives for those who had fallen out of these other institutions. Neither role was "new" to the period; traditionally, extended kin provided critical support for Hungarians.[151] In effect, the regime drew on this tradition. By keeping nuclear families within a larger orbit of extended kin, the regime solidified a familial tradition and regulated the links among these familial bodies.

Through these policies and practices, the welfare regime of the period articulated a distinct conception of need that had interpretive and re/distributive manifestations. At the interpretive level, this regime worked with broad, collective categories. It did not individualize needs; nor did it connect them to the problems of certain social strata. Instead, it transmitted a socialized conception of need based on the notion that the collective welfare could be secured through strong, smooth-functioning institutions.

This broad interpretation of need then had practical implications for the relationship between the state and its clients. It determined whom the state targeted and what kind of assistance claims clients could advance. Because this regime recognized clients as members of collectivities, it cast its regulatory net wide enough to encompass both women and men and to acknowledge the many social locations they occupied. Claims to state assistance were to be couched in such collective terms—on claimants' roles as workers, spouses, parents, and extended kin. Hungarians were not offered handouts to ameliorate material deprivation; they were not given counseling to ferret out the source of their individual problems. Rather, societal policies provided access to socialized goods and services, while state caseworkers provided institutional links. In the welfare society, social institutions and collectivities, as opposed to individuals or groups, were interpreted as those entities most in need.

Of course, these policies and practices did more than interpret need. They were also designed to satisfy need and re/distribute benefits. At this level, the welfare society was open to considerable scrutiny. Given its financial constraints, the state allocated quite meager benefits, which often included only basic necessities. Moreover, when it came to resource allocation, the regime's collective focus became blurred. Its re/distributive practices were riddled with inequities; it frequently allocated goods and services to particular social groups and economic classes, thus exacerbating existing social cleavages. And when it came to distributing political resources, this regime had an abysmal record. In the welfare society, the population lacked the most basic political, civil, and social rights. As a collective, Hungarians were unable to participate in the social politics of the era. At the national level, they could not demand formal involvement in the satisfaction or the interpretation of their needs; there were no formal mechanisms to exert pressure on policymakers or economic planners. At the enterprise level, trade unions wielded almost exclusive control over the allocation of work-related benefits. Within welfare agencies, caseworkers often worked in rigid ways and failed to provide clients the formal channels to alter their course of action.

Thus, there were clear tensions between the interpretive and the re/-distributive dimensions of the welfare society. Although this regime operated with a broad interpretation of need that stressed the social collective, it re/distributed political and material resources in ways that privileged certain social strata. These patterns raise a series of questions about how

Hungarians negotiated the tensions inherent in this regime. Did they find this regime overwhelmingly repressive and confining? Or were they able to utilize the regime to secure their own well-being and to articulate their interests? As I explore in the next chapter, the welfare society did end up providing many Hungarians with the practical and discursive space to maneuver in everyday life.

2. Strategies of Integration
Collectivism and Individualism

The welfare society of early socialism encompassed a unique arrangement of state policies and practices. Its architecture of need was built around existing social institutions: national-level policies and local-level practices were designed to build stronger institutions and to integrate Hungarians into them. This was how the welfare society appeared when viewed from "above," from the standpoint of its architects and designers. Yet this picture obscures what the welfare society looked like from "below," from the perspective of those it targeted. Such a picture is far more difficult to paint. While the regime left behind a plethora of records conducive to social-scientific analysis, clients produced few retrievable artifacts. As a group, they were restricted from participating formally in the era's social politics; thus, they did not create the kinds of documents that social scientists are accustomed to studying. So while it is always difficult to reconstruct a view of a welfare system from the perspective of its clientele, this task is particularly complicated with respect to early socialist Hungary.

In constructing this view from below, the historiography on state socialism is of limited help. Not only is there a paucity of historical work on the period, but the few existing analyses examine this era from the top down. They begin from the perspective of state ideology and then hypothesize what this ideology must have meant to those it targeted. This approach has given rise to two general conclusions about the early socialist state. The first is the commonly held notion that this regime was overly intrusive and invasive. This characterization permeates the work of feminists and non-feminists alike; both argue that the early socialist state maintained a strong hold on the public and private realms, on the labor market and the family.[1] Having set out to radically restructure society, the state is thought to have extended its reach to all social realms, leaving no social space untouched:

through its monopoly of power, the state is said to have redefined what it meant to be a good citizen, worker, parent, and spouse.[2] And it did so without much input from below, with the "dictatorship" taking precedence over "needs."[3] The state's totalizing impulses are even said to have intruded on women's sense of self by dictating how they should dress, carry themselves, and relate to their sexuality.[4] While most analysts of Hungary do distinguish between pre- and post-1956 and argue that the Kádár era was marked by the state's partial withdrawal from the private realm, their main concern is still with the high level of state intervention and control in the period.

This argument about the state's intrusiveness is often coupled with a second general conclusion about the early socialist state: that it was conservative, even traditional, in character.[5] Scholars of Eastern Europe frequently indict the Communist state for failing to live up to its revolutionary promises. Juxtaposing ideology and reality, these scholars have debunked official proclamations of the "workers' state" and have revealed the mechanisms through which bureaucratic control was exerted over the working class.[6] Rather than undermining class oppression, the regime is said to have substituted one set of exploitative relations for another. Similar arguments have been advanced about the gender ideology of the period. Despite its rhetoric of emancipation, feminist scholars maintain that the regime failed to challenge the division of labor within the home.[7] As a result, patriarchal authority simply shifted from individual men to men as a collective embodied in the state.[8] Through analyses of ideological ploys and metaphors, feminists chart the rise of a particular form of state power: one in which the state positioned itself as a benevolent, protective father and positioned women as passive, infantile beneficiaries of state kindness.[9] Thus, instead of abolishing patriarchal power, the early socialist state is said to have ushered in a transition from private patriarchy to public patriarchy.[10]

While all these arguments raise important questions about the limitations of the early socialist state, they are based almost exclusively on the ideologies emanating from state structures. This preoccupation with ideology has left scholars unprepared to explicate the politics of implementation or the ways citizens related to the state in their everyday lives. For instance, in her study of labor control, sociologist Martha Lampland found a critical disjunction between ideology and implementation in the period.[11] While the regime trumpeted collective sentiments in its media and propaganda, its everyday techniques of rule targeted individuals; through the piece-rate system, wage policies, and labor surveillance, collectivism gave way to the individuation of workers.[12] It is precisely these kinds of complications that get obscured through purely ideological accounts of the socialist state.

In this chapter, I embark on a historical excavation of how the regime's societal policies were implemented and how they shaped everyday life. Moving beyond the level of ideology, I analyze a collection of Csepel enterprise records and 407 Gyámhatóság case files for what they reveal about Hungarians' interpretations of and responses to the welfare society. Through citizens' words and actions as recorded in these historical documents, I advance a view of this regime from "below." In doing so, I argue that this regime ended up providing Hungarians with more resources than is usually posited. Almost paradoxically, the regime's collective focus gave individuals the ability to protect themselves by allowing them to maneuver among institutions to defend their interests. And the regime's desire to control social institutions inadvertently empowered those connected to these institutions by enabling them to harness the state's concern with public and private relations to secure their own well-being

More specifically, at the interpretive level, the welfare society established an expansive discursive terrain on which needs claims could be advanced. Its focus on collective categories enabled citizens to couch their appeals for state assistance in several idioms. Needs claims could be framed by one's position as a worker, parent, spouse, or extended-family member. In fact, women utilized all these positions when arguing for state aid. They also made connections among their institutional positions to stake claims to different state resources; they used their roles as parents to argue for special benefits at work, and they drew on their roles as workers to secure assistance with their family lives. Because these needs claims were based on institutional roles rather than individual deprivation, they were not laden with blame or contempt. Thus, at the interpretive level, this welfare regime provided citizens a broad repertoire of discursive resources with which to claim state assistance.

The resources available in this regime were not only discursive; Hungarians could also extract practical resources for use in their everyday struggles. Although the welfare society was riddled with re/distributive inequities, its expansive reach opened up possibilities for those connected to it. By politicizing social institutions, the regime infused new social spaces with power. In the process, it unintentionally provided powerful weapons for citizens to appropriate in their daily struggles. Given the political centrality of wage labor, women could strategize to improve their positions in the paid labor force; they utilized caseworkers to gain full-time employment, acquire new skills, and improve their working conditions. Given the political importance of the workplace, female workers could then maneuver to secure other material resources, such as housing, childcare, and household goods. And given the regime's emphasis on the nuclear family, women could extract tools to alter their domestic arrangements: by siding with women in domestic battles, caseworkers became valuable weapons for disciplining men and regulating familial responsibility. Caseworkers were also a resource for those who sought to reintegrate themselves into their extended-family networks. Hence, by subjecting work and family institutions to public scrutiny, the regime enabled many Hungarians to resolve the material and practical problems confronting them.

Although the welfare society offered an array of such possibilities, Hungarians' ability to utilize them depended largely on their institutional locations. Because the regime conceptualized need in institutional terms, citizens' practical and discursive maneuverability was closely linked to their social position. This chapter examines how two groups of women—married women with children and single mothers—fared in this welfare regime.[13] Their institutional positions differed: married women with children were connected to existing institutions, while single mothers were more isolated. These positions then shaped their needs, interests, and strategic possibilities. Overall, married women with children strategized to integrate the spheres of work and family, while single mothers maneuvered to become incorporated into these institutions. As they maneuvered, both groups advanced a critique of how social institutions operated in the period. Through their strategizing, they prompted state actors to move beyond a limited preoccupation with institutional form and to become involved in the content of their institutional relations.

MARRIED MOTHERS AT WORK

The economic and social transformations underway during the first two decades of socialism had profound effects on gender relations. In the workplace, women and men were employed together, occasionally even side by side. In the domestic realm, the full-time homemaker/caretaker became the exception. By 1959, 79 percent of all women living in Budapest were employed outside the home; 73 percent of those with children were in the paid labor force.[14] By the mid-1960s, these numbers increased to 84 percent and 78 percent, respectively.[15] Thus, a majority of women were expected to be workers as well as mothers and wives. While this situation accorded many women new opportunities, it also presented them with new dilemmas. Faced with a series of social and familial demands, women had a multiplicity of needs related to their public and private lives.

In this period, most Hungarians confronted severe economic and material difficulties.[16] The rise of the two-wage-earner family was in many ways a response to these difficult material circumstances. Yet the two wages that went into family income were rarely equal. This period was marked by gender-segregated labor markets and work patterns. In 1959, over 40 percent of employed women worked only part-time. Many did not do so by choice: a 1959 survey found that 70 percent of part-time workers wanted full-time employment. Of those women who landed full-time employment, only 12 percent worked in skilled positions and 25 percent in semi-skilled jobs. This labor-market segregation was reflected in the wages of men and women. On average, women's wages were 60 percent of men's.[17] This wage differential remained steady throughout the socialist period. Thus, in their new public roles, women had a series of needs as workers—needs connected to their access to paid employment, occupational segregation, and wage disparities.

Moreover, women also experienced conflicts negotiating their roles as workers and as caretakers. While it is questionable whether men enjoyed the regime's gift of "eight hours of work, eight hours of rest, and eight hours of entertainment," it is unimaginable that working women divided up their days in such a humane way. This breakdown failed to account for the time women devoted to domestic upkeep, work that was particularly time-consuming given the difficult economic conditions. Women had to deal with chronic food shortages, run from store to store for basic foodstuffs, stand in long lines to purchase necessities, and cook and clean without basic household appliances.[18] Time-budget studies conducted in the period revealed that most women divided up their days in a far less leisurely way than was portrayed in the regime's slogans. On average, women spent nine hours working, seven hours sleeping, seven hours caretaking, and an hour relaxing. Of the seven hours devoted to caretaking, two were spent cooking, two cleaning, two shopping, and one caring for children. These studies also found that 61 percent of women reported that they were entirely responsible for domestic upkeep; less than 10 percent claimed to receive help from their husbands.[19]

Yet women's familial needs were not reducible to the unequal division of labor within their homes. The nature of the family was itself under reconstruction in the period. Women and men were struggling over their expectations of each other. Although these subjective changes were difficult to survey or quantify, they came across clearly in Gyámhatóság case files. In these historical records, one can hear women and men at war. Their battles often surfaced in divorce and custody cases. Yet they also emanated from the agencies' child protection cases. When interacting with caseworkers, women proclaimed their domestic dissatisfaction. They complained about their husbands' lack of commitment to their families. They accused men of being aloof and careless fathers. They faulted men for not contributing financially to the family. And they berated men for being selfish and inattentive spouses. As the boundaries of work and family were under renegotiation, married women with children had a series of needs related to their roles as wives and caretakers.

In addition, many married women with children confronted threats to their physical well-being. Although domestic violence and alcoholism were rarely acknowledged publicly, many women experienced such abuse in this era. Because of the official silence on these issues, it is difficult to gauge how pervasive they were. Yet alcohol-consumption rates reveal part of the story: from 1950 to 1965, per capita alcohol consumption increased by 100 percent.[20] The number of alcohol-related deaths close to doubled during the same period.[21] Moreover, one of the only studies to be done on this issue examined the life histories, personality traits, work patterns, and family lives of two hundred male alcoholics. The researchers discovered that 72 percent of these men lived with their wives. Of these, 85 percent reported "severe marital problems" related to their alcohol use, and 30 percent admitted to being "aggressive" with their wives.[22]

Hence, in this period, married women with children faced a series of issues related to their public roles, private relationships, and the dis/connections between them. Yet this group of women was best situated to take advantage of the resources available in the welfare society. Precisely because they occupied so many social locations, they could draw on different identities to stake claims to state assistance; they could maneuver among institutions to secure practical and discursive resources. In the process, they waged a profound battle against the organization of work and family in the period.

Improving Material and Work Lives

Just as the welfare society constructed need in collective terms, most Hungarian women emphasized their institutional locations when they presented their problems. As they interacted with state actors in their workplace or local Gyámhatóság offices, married women with children focused on their institutional needs and contributions. Rather than separating their public and private needs, they presented them as interconnected. By taking the regime on its own terms, married women with children extracted discursive and practical resources to secure their material well-being.

At the discursive level, women couched their appeals for state aid in several idioms: they spoke of their needs as workers, mothers, wives, and family members. At the workplace, their assistance claims were rarely based only on their responsibilities as workers. Rather, they were framed around their work and familial needs. Enterprise records from the period reveal that married women with children often used their positions as workers and family members to stake claims to additional socialized goods and services. For instance, through the mid-1950s, many state enterprises held weekly sales in which employees could purchase material goods at discounted prices. Married women with children frequently demanded special access to these sales. Some argued that they were entitled to first dibs on these goods; others thought they should be able to purchase more of these items. Both groups justified their appeals for special treatment on the basis of their needs as workers, mothers, and wives. As a female textile worker argued in 1951, "I have two boys and a husband who consume more food. It is only fair that I be allowed more than my childless colleagues."[23] In one factory, a small group of female workers pressured the enterprise to introduce new regulations that allowed married women with children to purchase twice as much at sales because they had "more mouths to feed" and "more dirt to clean."[24]

As these enterprise sales became less frequent in the late 1950s, female workers with families demanded special working hours and time off. Above and beyond the "housework holiday" given to all working mothers, female workers argued for more time off to allow them to fulfill their social responsibilities. In 1958, a small group of female workers from a Csepel metal factory proposed that they be given more flexibility to set work hours; they justified their appeals by arguing that they had more responsibilities than other workers did. In 1954, one female worker even argued that her family roles be added in when determining her "worth" to the enterprise; she pointed out that her social obligations entitled her to special benefits.[25]

These appeals were not simply discursive victories: female workers made them in order to gain concrete material resources. In addition to obtaining more items at enterprise sales, married women with children gained access to material goods unavailable to other groups of workers. For instance, enterprises often received shipments of coveted household appliances like refrigerators and vacuum cleaners. Since the demand for these items exceeded their supply, enterprises held contests to determine who would receive them. These contests required workers to submit applications to prove they needed a particular item. In reviewing the contests from a Csepel factory in 1950–1955, I discovered that 85 percent of the successful applicants were married women with children who combined good work records with familial need. "My two sons never lend a hand with the housework," a female worker wrote in 1954. "I am so tired after my long days at the enterprise. A vacuum cleaner would greatly improve my life and work abilities."[26]

Female workers also strategized to gain access to the vacations organized by enterprises. Here, too, demand exceeded supply, so enterprises were forced to hold contests to allocate these vacations. And here, too, married women with children mobilized their contributions as workers and family members to bolster their appeals. Many argued that they were subjected to more pressure and were thus entitled to vacation time. Their strategizing seemed to pay off: proportionately, female workers secured more vacation places than did other groups of workers.[27]

Women who lived in enterprise housing were even more successful in carving out material resources based on their roles as workers and family members. In fact, placement in enterprise housing was itself contingent on one's ability to demonstrate familial need. Once secured, enterprise housing put female workers in a position to stake claims to further material resources. Although most workers' hostels were financed through enterprise and centralized state budgets, factory committees operated them. Many female workers used their connections to these committees to facilitate their work lives. In one Csepel factory, female workers organized the hostel to suit their needs: they structured the childcare center to coincide with their work schedules; they planned collective meals on the weekends; and they held "family days" during which their husbands and children could come to the factory to see how they worked.[28] These women also ran clubs and support groups to help them juggle the demands of work and family. In 1958 a union official justified these expenditures by arguing that in order to become "good workers" employees had to have "orderly family lives."[29]

In addition, married women with children used their contributions as workers and family members to squeeze income support out of their workplaces. Many enterprises set aside "emergency" funds to distribute to workers on a per case basis.[30] These funds tended to go to female workers who could demonstrate familial need. For instance, in 1950 a female worker wrote to her factory committee to explain that her husband was extremely ill and in need of constant care. Her request for two months of paid leave was approved because of her "strong work history" and "family problem."[31] Four years later another female worker appealed to the same committee to ask for a stipend to care for her two newly adopted children. Deeming her a "diligent" worker, they awarded her support to secure a "stable life" for her children.[32] In a 1957 case a woman requested supplemental wages to care for her family while her husband was out of work. This request prompted a home visit by a union official. When the official found the woman's husband bedridden and "legitimately incapacitated," he awarded her support for the duration of her husband's illness.[33]

Female clients connected to Gyámhatóság offices used similar strategies. Since these agencies were responsible for protecting the family, one would assume that clients with children couched their needs claims in a familial idiom. This was not entirely the case. Rather, they frequently linked their public and private problems, skillfully maneuvering within the existing discursive terrain to argue for state support. By establishing a discursive connection between their public and private responsibilities, women were able to utilize caseworkers to resolve work-related problems. Clients with bureaucratic problems framed their requests around their work lives to resolve their problems: those who sought new apartments argued that they wanted to live closer to their workplace; those who sought guardianship changes justified them through appeals to the new fathers' work histories. Other women were able to secure better employment from caseworkers. Married women with children who worked part-time frequently had caseworkers help them find full-time work. In one 1953 case, a mother of two came to her local Gyámhatóság office to change the legal guardianship of her son. To justify the appeal, she mentioned that she was unable to make ends meet without full-time employment. The caseworker then helped her strategize to increase her work hours.[34] In one 1952 case, a cleaning woman came to the Gyámhatóság, ostensibly to turn her children over to state care. Crying, she told the caseworker that she could not support the children because of her small salary. The caseworker then went into job-placement mode, and, after a few meetings, the woman had found employment as a porter in a government ministry—a position that paid more than her previous job had.[35]

Other clients appropriated caseworkers to undercut occupational segregation. Women working in unskilled jobs frequently relied on caseworkers to help them locate better positions. Women also had caseworkers conduct similar job searches for their children. For instance, in 1955 a female client told a caseworker that she felt guilty because her son was an unskilled worker just like her. After their discussion, the boy secured a position in a local factory where he could "learn a skill."[36] In another 1957 case, a client mentioned to her caseworker that her son dreamed of becoming a table maker. By early 1958, the boy was an apprentice to a local table producer. According to his mother, this job gave him the "opportunity to do work he finds meaningful."[37]

Finally, female clients used caseworkers to locate work that was more compatible with their family lives. These women tended to work at quite inconvenient times—on weekends, early in the morning, or late at night. They regularly complained that their schedules forced them to leave their children alone or with unreliable spouses. Such complaints, if voiced frequently enough, could push caseworkers into job-placement mode. Perhaps the best example was a 1962 case of a female client who had a nighttime job as a cleaning woman. She was referred to the Gyámhatóság by a neighbor who became concerned when he saw her six-year-old son sleeping in the courtyard of their building. In her meeting with the caseworker, the client revealed that her husband regularly kicked the family out of the house in his drunken tirades. The caseworker then helped her find work in a post office sorting mail. As the caseworker wrote in her notes, the day job enabled the client to protect her son from her husband's "crazy behavior."[38]

Hence, through their workplaces and local Gyámhatóság offices, married women with children uncovered a series of practical resources. They secured these resources by emphasizing their institutional positions and framing needs claims around their social contributions.[39] In this regard, married women with children remained within the prevailing discursive boundaries. They never challenged state officials' preoccupation with wage labor. Nor did they question caseworkers' institutional practices. Instead, they made the most of these practices to improve their work and material lives. Yet this group of clients was able to expand another aspect of this regime's conception of need: they forced state actors to become engaged in the content of their familial relations.

From Familial Form to Familial Content

Although the Gyámhatóság was designed to protect and regulate the family, state caseworkers were quite reluctant to become embroiled in clients' domestic problems. Caseworkers' biggest concern was with clients' family form; from their perspective, Hungarian families simply needed clearly defined obligations. By demarcating family responsibilities and codifying them into law, caseworkers believed they were securing familial well-being. For them, family protection was essentially a bureaucratic or juridical issue to be resolved through strict legal guidelines, paternity tests, guardianship arrangements, and financial obligations. This preoccupation with the legal form and bureaucratic underpinnings of the family created discursive boundaries around welfare work. Just as material problems went unacknowledged in official discourse, domestic turmoil remained outside welfare workers' conception of need.

In their interactions with caseworkers, married women with children disrupted these discursive boundaries. More than any other group of clients, these women were well situated to carry out such disruptions. They were embedded in the kind of familial structures that caseworkers idealized: they resided in nuclear families, with legally codified relations and obligations. Despite their family form, these women voiced domestic concerns and experienced domestic turmoil. Female clients often spoke about their aloof, unresponsive husbands. They complained about men's irresponsible child-rearing practices. And they exposed violent partners who drank heavily and beat them regularly. In effect, they raised issues that extended beyond the form of their families and impinged on the content of their familial relations—problems that could not be resolved through simple bureaucratic regulation. By raising such issues, these clients stretched the boundaries of what constituted social well-being.

To ensure that state caseworkers recognized their appeals, married women with children couched them in familiar idioms. They drew on the existing discursive terrain as they expanded it in two main ways. First, married women with children linked their appeals for familial support to their social contributions as workers. This was one of the most striking features of these early case files—clients rarely framed their domestic pleas in strictly familial terms. Rather, they claimed that they deserved help because they were wives, mothers, *and* workers. Some clients drew on these social roles to convince caseworkers of their worthiness. "I am a diligent, hard-working seamstress who suffers pain at the hands of my husband," wrote one woman in 1954. "I ask for nothing more than an end to this pain."[40] Clients seeking help with divorce disputes often framed their appeals in work terms. They claimed that their difficult familial relations caused them to become ineffective workers.[41] Others claimed that work demands had made their spouses ineffective partners. Many women who sought help with child support connected their requests to their limited work options. Unable to secure well-paid or full-time work, they needed financial assistance from their children's fathers.[42] Still other clients used their roles as workers to legitimize requests for more on-going familial intervention. Preoccupied with domestic distress, they argued that they had become inattentive workers. By citing domestic turmoil as the source of work difficulties, these women "deprivatized" the family; by making a link between production and reproduction, they turned marital conflicts into social problems of collective concern.[43]

Second, married women with children presented their husbands' problems in social terms. In their written and verbal appeals to the Gyámhatóság, they complained about their husbands' irresponsible behavior at home and at work. These clients held their spouses to dual standards, simultaneously faulting them for failing to fulfill their public and private responsibilities. "My husband is dangerously aggressive," wrote one client in 1953. "He is a lazy, unruly worker. He walks around the flat screaming; he cannot pay attention at work; and he wanders around the city when he should be at home or in his workplace."[44] In her portrayal, this woman conflated her husband's domestic and work deficiencies. Or, as another woman wrote about her husband in 1955, "His colleagues say that his work suffers since we live separately. I ask for help on their behalf too. Without it, everyone suffers."[45]

Such discursive connections were a means to an end: by drawing out the collective consequences of their husbands' problems, these women sought to reconfigure their familial relations. And many of them reached their goal. Married women with children mobilized state resources to force men to become better fathers by convincing caseworkers to regulate the quantity and quality of time their husbands spent with their children. In effect, they expanded the Gyámhatóság's definition of fathering. They pushed caseworkers to recognize that fathering not only was a legal or financial obligation but also implied devoting time and energy to children. The Gyámhatóság was literally inundated with complaints about fathers' limited contact with their children. Female clients told stories of men who never spent time with their children and who came home too exhausted to interact with them. "He does not understand what guardianship means," wrote one woman in 1957. "He believes it is just signing a paper. It is more. Comrade, please help teach him this."[46]

Female clients were also concerned about the quality of their husbands' child-rearing practices. They complained that their husbands did not know how to "entertain" children; they faulted men for not exhibiting enough affection for their children; and they accused their husbands of being "brutal" with their children. While some clients simply wanted caseworkers to lecture their husbands about proper child rearing, others went further. They used the Gyámhatóság as a threat, as a way to force men to alter their behavior. For instance, a number of clients threatened to switch their children's legal guardians if their husbands did not change. Caseworkers' willingness to turn guardianship over to male relatives or acquaintances bolstered their threats; it provided women with ammunition in their battles to make their husbands better fathers. A few women even used the Gyámhatóság's ability to claim legal paternity, warning men that the *tanács* (local councils) could always become the legal father.[47]

Married women with children also mobilized the Gyámhatóság to make their spouses better husbands. Approximately 23 percent of the cases I reviewed involved male alcohol abuse. Most women who raised this issue cited it as the source of their marital problems, arguing that alcohol caused their husbands to be particularly uncaring and brutal. Given that alcohol treatment centers were almost nonexistent, many women turned to the Gyámhatóság. They had caseworkers serve as "objective" third parties to convince their husbands that their behavior was destructive. "He does not listen to me when I tell him that his behavior violates the collective good," wrote one woman in 1955.[48] Or, as another woman wrote in 1960, "He stays out late to play music and drink. The neighbors complain and I complain. He sells my belongings for alcohol. If he is not punished, he will continue and I cannot go on."[49] In response, state actors often lectured men about the evils of alcohol, explaining that "overindulging" was against the "new social ethos" and undermined "peaceful family life."[50] When such instruction proved ineffective, caseworkers became more interventionist. They threatened men who refused to turn their salaries over to their families. They created budgets for female clients, which delineated how much their husbands should contribute to household expenditures. They even paid visits to clients' homes to ensure that men met these financial obligations.

Married women with children also sought help curbing their husbands' violent behavior. Although domestic violence was rarely discussed explicitly in case files, female clients used code words to signal such abuse, calling their husbands "brutal" (*brutális*), "rough" (*goromba*), or "aggressive" (*agresszív*). Caseworkers were equally indirect when dealing with such appeals. They rarely called these men into the office to lecture them about their abusive behavior. Sometimes caseworkers raised this issue when lecturing men about their alcoholism, as the two problems tended to coexist. But they rarely confronted domestic violence explicitly. When female clients pushed the issue, caseworkers usually referred them to community networks—to neighbors, co-workers, in-laws, or parents. For instance, in 1952 a caseworker told a client to have a neighbor "keep an eye out" for her safety.[51] In 1958 another caseworker had a client ask her mother to stop by her flat after the pubs closed to check on her well-being.[52]

For the most part, these female clients seemed to be interested in improving their domestic lives or in altering male behavior. Yet when their husbands refused to change, some used caseworkers to become less dependent on men. While few of these women could divorce their husbands for material reasons, they did struggle to undercut male control. Frequently, they legally disentangled themselves from their husbands, some by transferring their children's guardianship to men they found more trustworthy or responsible—even when they were still formally married to their children's fathers. The women could then use caseworkers to help solidify these domestic arrangements. This was particularly true of women who continued to reside in the same flats as their (ex)husbands, but insisted on "living separately" from them (*külön-külön élnek*). These women had caseworkers set new household rules and domestic boundaries. In one 1956 case, a mother of two had her caseworker literally divide the rooms in the family flat between herself and her husband.[53] In a 1965 case, a mother of three had her caseworker draw up an agreement to specify exactly how much money her husband had to contribute each month to support the family.[54]

In cases where women and their children lived in particularly dangerous situations, caseworkers could be convinced to go a bit further. While many women used the Gyámhatóság to secure better divorce or child-custody agreements, some clients appropriated caseworkers to leave their marriages altogether. These women felt especially trapped and dependent; they tended to be married to extremely aggressive men. One woman came to an office in 1958 because her husband was "selling" their three daughters to older men for alcohol.[55] In instances like this, caseworkers were activated to help women leave their husbands: they intervened with "higher" authorities to locate housing for these women; they worked to find these women stable or better-paid employment; and they searched familial networks to provide these women social support.

The Dávid case exemplifies this kind of intervention.[56] On Mrs. Dávid's first visit to the Gyámhatóság in 1959, she explained that her husband had a series of problems: he was an alcoholic who treated his family "brutally" and never contributed to the household budget. Initially, Mrs. Dávid simply asked her caseworker to talk to her husband. After these discussions failed to materialize, Mrs. Dávid decided to live "separately" from her husband by moving herself and her two children into one room in their flat. This move exacerbated the conflict. Her husband's drunken tirades became more frequent and violent. One afternoon, Mrs. Dávid came to the office with her son, whose face was covered with bruises. She threatened to institutionalize the boy unless something was done. Such clear evidence of the man's "decay" prompted her caseworker to act. Deeming this an emergency case, she secured for Mrs. Dávid temporary housing; she helped her file divorce proceedings; she attached Mr. Dávid's wages and transferred child-support payments to Mrs. Dávid; and she advised Mrs. Dávid to use her colleagues to protect herself should she be confronted by her husband. When the Dávid case closed in 1961, Mrs. Dávid was divorced and living with her two children in a new flat.

SINGLE MOTHERS: MANLESS WOMEN AND
UNDERPAID WORKERS

Single motherhood was a relatively rare social position in early state socialist Hungary. The structure of the welfare society was not particularly conducive to it. The 1952 Family Law essentially outlawed single motherhood
by requiring that all children have two legally recognized parents. The economic organization of early socialism also presented obstacles for those who
raised their children alone. The centralized wage structure and enterprise-
based provisions were premised on a two-wage-earner family. The familism
of local Gyámhatóság offices also made single parenting hard to sustain. By
lecturing women about the importance of the nuclear family and tracking
down children's fathers, caseworkers sought to impose nuclear-family models on their clientele. As a result, single motherhood tended to be a transitional position that women occupied before marriage and after divorce. In
1949, 12.9 percent of households were headed by women; by 1960 it had
increased to 13.4 percent.[57] Just under one third of these households consisted of recently divorced women who remarried soon thereafter. Hence,
roughly 10 percent of Hungarian households were headed by women on a
regular, long-term basis.[58]

In this period, single mothers faced a unique set of problems. While married women with children were in need of help balancing their institutional
positions, sole mothers' needs were connected to their lack of institutional
integration. First, they tended to be located on the margins of the paid labor
force. Although most single mothers worked outside the home, they usually
occupied peripheral positions in the labor force. Because they tended to
be young, with limited skills, most single mothers had extremely low
incomes—often well below the subsistence level. These women rarely
worked in enterprises with extensive benefit systems, so they often encountered trouble finding stable housing. For the same reason, they also had difficulties securing convenient childcare; they had to spend large amounts of
time transporting their children to and from facilities located in remote
parts of Budapest.

Second, the plight of single mothers was exacerbated by their isolation
from familial networks. Although the financial problems associated with
"manlessness" were alleviated somewhat by the elaborate system of child-
support enforcement, these women received little help with their caretaking
responsibilities. Paternal involvement in child rearing was rare. Moreover,
single mothers were more likely than married mothers to be disconnected
from their extended families. Many were new migrants to Budapest whose

families resided in other parts of Hungary; others had been banished from their families because of their out-of-wedlock pregnancies. Single mothers therefore had a series of needs related to their lack of integration into both the labor force and familial networks.

Given the depth of their material, social, and familial problems, many single mothers turned to local Gyámhatóság offices for assistance. In the two districts of my research, roughly 20 percent of clients were single mothers who headed their households on a regular basis. In their interactions with single mothers, caseworkers exhibited concern about the voids in their family lives. They frequently lectured sole mothers about the superiority of the nuclear family and tried to impose this familial model on them. It was not a smooth fit. To a large extent, the realities of these women's lives forced caseworkers to recognize the limits of their familial ideals. On the one hand, many sole mothers questioned the viability of this family form. For them, the nuclear-family model was simply not an option. Many claimed to be "shunned women," abandoned by irresponsible men. Others were divorced from men who had disappeared from their lives. Still others claimed to have spent only a few nights with their children's fathers.[59] All the Gyámhatóságs' proselytizing could not change this reality: for these women, the two-wage-earner, nuclear family was just not viable.

On the other hand, some single mothers questioned the desirability of the nuclear family. These women wanted to remain manless. While such clients constituted a minority of single mothers, they were the most vociferous. They fought caseworkers' attempts to (re)unite them with their children's fathers. Many rejected these reunions by arguing that men were more trouble than they were worth. Others passively resisted by claiming not to know the names or the whereabouts of their children's fathers. Hence, although their plight was quite difficult, some single mothers opted to remain outside the nuclear family and, in doing so, pushed the limits of the Gyámhatóság's familism.

Yet single mothers were not opposed to institutional reintegration. On the contrary, sole mothers frequently used the regime's institutional focus to secure their own well-being. By staking claims to assistance on the basis of their institutional isolation, single mothers obtained the material and social support necessary to raise their children alone. They used caseworkers to (re)integrate them into the existing institutions of work and the extended family. And they appropriated state institutions to fill the voids left by absent spouses or extended kin. In the process, single mothers maneuvered to carve out an existence for themselves and their children outside the nuclear family.

Needy Workers, Fallen Family Members

When married women with children staked claims to state assistance, they emphasized their social roles as workers, mothers, wives, and family members. The arguments advanced by sole mothers were of a different sort; they could not base their claims on their needs as wives or, in many cases, as family members. Nevertheless, they were not without discursive resources. Sole mothers drew on other identities, the most common of which were the "shunned woman" and the "banished family member." Many claimed to have special needs because of their manlessness and exclusion from extended families. Yet they added a positive inflection to these appeals for support: instead of focusing on what was lacking in their lives, single mothers articulated a desire to be (re)integrated into social institutions in new, more encompassing ways.

Since most single mothers occupied marginal positions in the labor force, they frequently appropriated state caseworkers to change their work positions. Young single mothers were often uneducated, with few employable skills; older single mothers were usually newly divorced or widowed, with little work experience. While the rigidity of the early state-socialist labor market restricted the occupational mobility of many social groups, single mothers were particularly immobile. They faced a unique set of constraints when they tried to increase their mobility. Because they supported their families alone, few single mothers could afford to return to school or to spend time in retraining programs. Such programs also tended to be beyond their reach: they operated out of enterprises that employed few single mothers and were designed to upgrade the skill levels of their workers. Placement in these programs almost always required bureaucratic connections. Single mothers' problems were exacerbated further by the fact that they were sole caretakers and thus unable to attend night school or evening programs.

In this period, many single mothers mobilized caseworkers to overcome these barriers. First, they had caseworkers help them locate existing retraining programs, which were rarely "advertised" publicly. Programs organized by government ministries usually recruited through existing workplaces; those run by unions tended to be limited to their own membership; and those established by enterprises typically drew from their own workforce. Since most single mothers were outside these networks, they used caseworkers to learn about such possibilities. Second, these women appropriated caseworkers to exert bureaucratic influence on placement decisions. For instance, in 1955 a caseworker helped a single mother gain permission to attend a training program run through the Ministry of Light Industry. Although the woman had no experience in this industrial sector, the caseworker wrote a letter stating that she was a "diligent" (*szorgalmas*) woman with great work potential.[60] In 1956, another single mother gained entrance to a special workshop on technical drawing organized by the workers' hostel of a local enterprise. Even though she was not employed in this enterprise, her caseworker's connections enabled her to secure a place in the workshop.[61]

Caseworkers also proved to be assets for single mothers who wanted to improve their existing working conditions. Many single mothers complained that they needed additional social benefits and services to make ends meet. Since these resources were distributed through the workplace, their only real option was to transfer to enterprises with comprehensive benefit schemes. Changing jobs was a bureaucratic nightmare in early socialist Hungary. Prior to the 1968 New Economic Mechanisms, workers were wedded to their workplaces and could gain permission to change them only under special circumstances.[62] Caseworkers came in handy here. While they helped all female clients navigate the maze of bureaucratic regulations, caseworkers approached this task with special urgency for single mothers. They were more likely to serve as references for these women, verifying that they were "orderly" (*rendes*) or "reliable" (*megbízható*). And they more readily used their own contacts to help single mothers gain access to these enterprises. In 1955, a caseworker referred a young, pregnant client in need of housing to an enterprise with a workers' hostel.[63] In 1957, a caseworker connected a young single mother to one of her relatives who worked in a food store; after a short time working as an apprentice in the store, the client gained a paid position.[64]

Single mothers also used caseworkers to negotiate with their workplaces. Some of them mobilized caseworkers to gain full-time work, soliciting letters from the Gyámhatóság that outlined their "special needs" as single mothers. Others appropriated caseworkers to secure "emergency" funds from enterprise unions. These funds tended to go to workers with large families and severe economic problems. When single mothers applied for them, they often attached letters from caseworkers to strengthen their cases—letters that described how, despite the small size of their families, these mothers faced unusual difficulties as heads of "single-wage-earner families."[65] Moreover, while unions usually sent their own home visitors to evaluate workers' eligibility for these funds, a letter from the Gyámhatóság could preempt such visits. For instance, a single mother who received monthly enterprise funds in 1957 avoided all contact with union home visitors. Her caseworker's proclamations about her diligence and severe material needs were enough to secure her regular assistance without union investigations.[66]

In the two districts of my research, I uncovered three cases in which caseworkers actually advised single mothers to secure extra work in the informal economy.[67] Of course, they did not call this "black-market work"; instead, they referred to it as work "on the side." All three of these single mothers suffered from severe economic problems and had been unable to squeeze additional resources from their workplaces. The first was a 1961 case of a mother of three who had fallen into poverty after her husband left her. Even with monthly child support, her wages as a cleaning woman were insufficient to support her family. After numerous attempts to increase her work hours and wages, her caseworker suggested that she do some "night work on the side" to keep her family afloat. The two other cases surfaced in 1963 in the same Gyámhatóság office. Both single mothers had recently migrated to Budapest from the countryside and worked as unskilled laborers (*segédmunkások*). Neither of them earned enough to support their families alone. So their caseworkers suggested that they take sick leave from their jobs and return to their villages to take up some "seasonal" or "extra" work on the land. Obviously, such cases were exceptional. But they do underscore just how far some caseworkers went to secure single mothers' material well-being.

Caseworkers also served as valuable resources for those single mothers who had fallen out of their extended families. Approximately 70 percent of the single mothers in my case sample revealed serious familial conflicts resulting from their out-of-wedlock pregnancies or manlessness. Caseworkers helped them become (re)integrated into these networks. Such reintegration was quite consistent with caseworkers' familial ideals, according to which nuclear families existed in a larger orbit of extended families. Overall, there were two stages to this repair work: familial acceptance, followed by familial integration.

Although single mothers may not have been stigmatized by the state bureaucracy of the period, they did encounter negative views of their behavior within their communities. Many sole mothers described how their families faulted them for their out-of-wedlock births; others claimed to have become the "black sheep" of the family after their children were born. Caseworkers were useful in overcoming this stigmatization. They often advised single mothers how to reconnect with their families. Their suggestions were strikingly similar: in an overwhelming majority of cases, caseworkers instructed single mothers to highlight their identities as "shunned women." Many single mothers already represented themselves in these terms—as women abandoned by irresponsible men. Caseworkers encouraged them to draw on this identification; together, single mothers and caseworkers thus developed a discourse of male abandonment. Playing the victim served many purposes. Most important, it absolved single mothers of blame. They were not rejecting the nuclear family per se; they had just been denied access to it. This construction also made single mothers socially acceptable. It allowed them to appear more sympathetic and needy, as manless, familyless women who needed to be rescued. So although the victim construct left single mothers without much agency, it was a way to regain respectability in the community and to prepare for familial reintegration.

The redemptive quality of this construct may explain why so many single mothers seemed to find it so appealing. It also explains why many of them had caseworkers help them transmit this construction to their families. For instance, in 1958 a single mother asked her caseworker to convince her family that her divorce was not her fault. Because she had initiated the divorce, her family held her responsible, ignoring the fact that her ex-husband had essentially abandoned her. The caseworker helped to collect evidence of her husband's irresponsible behavior and to convince her family that she had "suffered the most."[68] Similarly, in a 1962 case a young, pregnant, and unmarried woman came to the Gyámhatóság after being banished from her family. She explained that her parents believed she was a "whore" despite the fact that the father of the baby had reneged on his promise to marry her. The caseworker advised her to redirect their rage at the man who "deserted her" after "having his way" with her.[69]

Once constituted as "shunned women," single mothers were in the position to ask for concrete, practical assistance from their extended families. This material support took numerous forms. Housing was one of the most pressing issues facing single mothers. Since sole mothers had limited access to enterprise and council housing, they often used their extended kin as long-term solutions to their housing problems. Caseworkers frequently helped them convince their relatives to provide such assistance. They searched single mothers' extended families for relatives with extra space in their flats; they wrote letters to relatives to request assistance; and they paid visits to these clients' relatives to assess their ability to help. As one caseworker put it in 1959, "When a family member is in trouble, it is the family's legal responsibility to help her. The *tanács* does not like those who shirk their domestic duties and does not treat them kindly."[70]

Caseworkers also encouraged single mothers to draw on their extended families to release themselves from some of the burdens involved in raising children alone. Single mothers in need of childcare were advised to have family members watch their children before or after school. For sole mothers in need of basic material goods, caseworkers suggested family loans or borrowing arrangements. Usually, these agreements involved some sort of exchange, with single mothers providing domestic help in exchange for goods and services. For instance, in 1960 a caseworker convinced a recently divorced mother to have her mother pick up her children from school and watch them until she returned from work; she then prepared the evening meal for her mother and children.[71] In a 1962 case a caseworker connected a single mother to her distant cousin. Both women had twins, so the caseworker suggested that they exchange children's clothing, furniture, and bedding.[72] Through such strategizing, single mothers found ways to become (re)integrated into their familial institutions and to protect their well-being outside the nuclear family.

The State as Pseudo-Family

While most single mothers mobilized caseworkers to facilitate their integration into extended family networks, some single mothers used the Gyámhatóság as a replacement for the institution. These women positioned the Gyámhatóság as a familial body; they interacted with caseworkers like family members. Caseworkers responded to them in similar terms, engaging in these women's lives in quite intimate ways. Although these familial connections may have subjected single mothers to new forms of control, they also enabled clients to extract special kinds of state support.

In this period, the most common way that single mothers positioned the state in familial terms was by treating it as a father figure. They spoke of how they needed to be "protected"; they claimed to be in need of help "defending" their respectability; and they deployed familial metaphors that constituted the state as a guardian. Take this letter written by a single mother to the Gyámhatóság in 1967: "I am alone . . . . My parents are dead. When I came to Budapest, I was lost, searching for the protection I yearn for. My son needs this too; he is our child of the national democracy. I do what is best for the social good, on my own. Dear Comrade, we rely on you to raise us in health and security. Please help."[73]

As this letter indicates, single mothers' appeals to paternal authority usually included requests for practical assistance, quite often with ex-husbands or lovers. They wanted someone to protect their honor from men who took advantage of them. They wanted someone to defend their respectability against men who had abused them. And they wanted someone to force these men to take responsibility for their actions. For instance, female clients often used caseworkers to punish ex-husbands through visitation rights. To scold "ineffective" fathers, women had caseworkers restrict access to their children, arguing that they needed institutional recourse to force men to change. As one woman pleaded in 1954, "He must learn. He comes and goes as he pleases, with no concern for the little one. Please, Comrade, teach him about the devastating effects of this."[74] These women were quite likely to position the Gyámhatóság as a father figure in order to track down deadbeat dads. "If my father were here, he would find him [her ex-lover], beat him up, and force him to pay," proclaimed a single mother in 1962. "Since he passed away, I alone must fight this terrible man."[75]

Overall, such paternal appeals seemed to work: while caseworkers helped all their female clients with child-support enforcement, with manless, familyless clients they approached this aspect of their work as if they were on a crusade.[76] Caseworkers chased these men from workplace to workplace, reminding them that they could not shirk their domestic responsibilities. They charted men's movements from county to county, from city to city, all the while letting them know that someone was "watching over them." And they tracked down these men across national borders, writing letters and deploying Hungarian foreign-service officials to remind men of their "Hungarian responsibilities."[77] These caseworkers' discourse was infused with paternalism. As the (male) head of one of a Gyámhatóság office wrote in 1955, "Child-support enforcement is our most important work. We do it for helpless, defenseless, and powerless mothers without the means to defend themselves. This is our real protection work—financial, yes, but also moral, ethical and political."[78]

In addition to positioning the Gyámhatóság as a father figure ready to take on deadbeat dads, single mothers drew on the Gyámhatóság's paternal authority in their negotiations with other institutions. When they were unable to obtain housing, childcare, or family allowances from other state agencies, single mothers portrayed themselves as powerless vis-à-vis the male authorities controlling these resources. They believed they needed the help of a paternal figure in their negotiations, and they asked caseworkers for such assistance. Never mind that most caseworkers were women; these clients were appealing to the paternal power of the Gyámhatóság, of the *tanács*. They asked caseworkers to have enterprise unions place them in workers' hostels. They requested that caseworkers go to battle with local government officials to move them up on the waiting lists for council housing and childcare. They begged caseworkers to negotiate with ministry officials to help them obtain family allowances. They even had caseworkers exert influence over judges. For instance, a 1958 letter written by a single mother beautifully illustrated this construction of the Gyámhatóság as father figure and the client as dutiful daughter: "I write with sorrow and pain. I am a young woman, alone with two children. Their father was an older man, a married man. I am not proud of this seven-year connection, and I learned from my mistakes. Now he has died, and I have no access to material support. Judges and lawyers scorn me. They refuse their help. I am vulnerable and I turn to you [formal] because you help the poor and vulnerable."[79]

Single mothers also placed the Gyámhatóság in a familial position by treating it as a spouse. These women asked for the kind of advice from caseworkers that they would ordinarily have asked their husbands for. Some came to the Gyámhatóság with simple child-rearing dilemmas, asking caseworkers what to feed their children, how to dress them, or where to take them on the weekends. Others sought assistance with more complicated child-rearing problems, such as how to deal with children with learning disabilities or severe behavioral problems. All these mothers prefaced their queries with statements about their lack of parental support and assistance. "When Jozsi acted like this before, my husband dealt with him," proclaimed a single mother in 1954. "Now that he is gone, I must turn to others for this help."[80]

Moreover, single mothers used caseworkers as spouses who could help them allocate their family's resources. Widows often asked caseworkers to create monthly budgets for them.[81] In part, this spousal connection was built into widows' relationship with the Gyámhatóság. On the death of their husbands, widows were required to report to caseworkers and provide information about the financial resources at their disposal. Caseworkers were then responsible for distributing monthly allotments of their husbands' pensions. If they needed more than the given allotment, widows had to appeal to their caseworkers for additional money. In the process, these women regularly positioned state caseworkers as husbands-in-residence. "My husband promised me a refrigerator before he died," one woman proclaimed in 1961. "It is fair that I have this now. We must take it from the budget immediately."[82] As this quote reveals, widows usually used "we" when making their appeals, as if to indicate that they and the state were jointly responsible for their families' well-being and security.

Single mothers who had never been married also positioned caseworkers as spousal figures in order to obtain financial resources. Although the Gyámhatóság did not have any formal funds to distribute, caseworkers could apply for emergency support from the local government. Caseworkers were extremely reluctant to request these funds; altogether, I uncovered only six clients who received aid in these two decades. All were single mothers. And all had formed special, almost spousal, connections with their caseworkers: one of them sent her caseworker pictures from her son's name-day celebration;[83] another had her children send postcards from camp to her caseworker.[84] Like widows, these single mothers spoke to caseworkers about "their children." They framed their appeals for financial assistance in similar terms: their children needed new beds; their children needed new winter clothes; and their children needed to go to summer camp. By drawing state actors into their parenting, these single mothers extracted additional resources to support themselves and their children.

The final way that single mothers placed the Gyámhatóság in a familial position was by using these offices as replacements for their extended families. They regularly turned to these agencies to care for their children. Single mothers who needed the time and the space to resolve their problems worked out short-term "contracts" with caseworkers, putting their children into state care for a few weeks to several years. They then used this time to find employment, to secure stable housing, and to locate childcare. In 1952, a single mother of two asked the Gyámhatóság to care for her children while she searched for work. Within a year, she had found a job as a nurse, and her children were returned.[85] In 1954, a recent divorcée used the Gyámhatóság in a similar way; unable to live in the same flat as her violent ex-husband, she had her son institutionalized until she found a room in a workers' hostel.[86] These kinds of arrangements were especially common in the years following 1956, when many men emigrated and left their wives to care for their children alone. These women were often forced to turn their children over to state care while they put their lives back together.

These contracts were risky for single mothers. They entered into them without any formal guarantee that their children would be returned. The absence of formal political rights or appeals mechanisms made such contracts even riskier. It is possible that single mothers deployed a familial discourse to increase the likelihood that their children would be returned. By positioning the Gyámhatóság as an extended family and framing institutionalization as a form of collective care, they turned these contracts into agreements between family members. If this was their strategy, it seemed to work. In contrast to the situation in late state socialism, when caseworkers often denied mothers access to their children, this Gyámhatóság rarely restricted mothers' access. When these mothers asked for their children back, "uncle state" (*állam bácsi*) usually conceded, with few questions asked.

GENDERED STRATEGIES AND THE WELFARE SOCIETY

The welfare society looks quite different when seen from the perspective of female clients rather than through the lens of state ideology. From this standpoint, it is difficult to sustain commonly held notions of this regime's overly intrusive and conservative character. For women embedded in state enterprises and agencies, this regime was not categorically intrusive or conservative. Rather, it encompassed resources and limitations. In fact, many of the resources provided by this regime were outgrowths of its expansive reach. By subjecting social institutions and relations to scrutiny, it demarcated a broad terrain on which clients could appeal for state assistance. The regime's interpretive underpinnings accorded women rhetorical possibilities for claims-making and institutional tools to defend their interests. Women utilized this space to its fullest extent, drawing on their social contributions to demand state support and maneuvering among existing institutions to protect their well-being.

Yet this strategizing did not take only one form. Women were situated differently in the welfare society, and their different positions shaped their needs and the strategies available to them. Married women with children were well positioned to take advantage of this regime. Because they were situated in multiple social institutions, they could couch their appeals for state support in several idioms, simultaneously speaking of their needs as workers, mothers, wives, and family members. They also linked these institutional positions by drawing on their contributions as family members to gain resources at work and by highlighting their needs as workers to alter their family relations. In effect, married women with children used the regime's collectivism to their advantage; they connected their public and private roles to make their lives more manageable. In the process, many of them stretched the boundaries of the regime's conception of need. As they negotiated with state agencies and enterprises, they implicitly questioned the notion that the form of their families or their employment status was enough to protect their welfare. They sought to change the content of their institutional relations: they struggled to find stable, fulfilling employment and attentive, nonabusive spouses. Through their strategizing, married women with children used the state to alter the content of their institutional relations at work and at home.

Single mothers, however, were less integrated into the institutions of the welfare society. They occupied marginal positions in the paid labor force and were rarely embedded in nuclear families. Yet sole mothers also linked their public and private roles to make their lives more manageable. Here, too, women took the state on its own terms. Some single mothers drew on the state's promise of collective integration to improve their positions in the labor force and to gain acceptance in their extended families. Others utilized the state's familism to push state officials to act like responsible parents or spouses. Instead of becoming passive in the face of state paternalism, these women formed collusive relationships with state actors: as members of a common family, they had the state scold their ex-lovers, care for their children, and protect their material welfare. Almost ironically, mothers utilized state familism to secure an existence for themselves outside of heterosexual marriage and the nuclear family.

At the same time as they strategized, both groups of female clients encountered the limitations of the welfare society. While this regime's interpretation of need was broad, it could also be confining. To secure resources from this regime, female clients had to make gestures to the paternal authority of the state. They had to remain within the existing discursive boundaries; they could not overtly challenge the state's collectivism or familism. Perhaps even more limiting was the pervasive tension between the regime's interpretive expansiveness and its re/distributive narrowness. It cannot be forgotten that these women strategized to secure quite basic goods and services. Nor can it be ignored that such strategizing would not have been necessary if the regime's resources were legally recognized rights. In this period, citizens had a right to positions in the labor force and in legally codified families. They did not have a right to fulfilling work or to supportive family environments. And they did not have the right to demand formally that their institutional relations be made more gratifying or satisfying.

In this way, yet another tension underlaid the welfare society. Despite this regime's collective focus, it ended up breeding quite individualized survival strategies. The primary way clients could alter the nature of their institutional relations was through informal bargaining. Individual clients negotiated with caseworkers; individual workers negotiated with workplaces and union representatives. Although they negotiated in patterned and consistent ways, they rarely did so collectively. Married women with children never came together to demand better working conditions, higher wages, domestic-violence counseling, or alcohol treatment centers. As a group, sole mothers never demanded special labor policies, retraining programs, or family counseling. Instead, these women struggled on their own, maneuvering individually to protect their interests and well-being.

Hence, the lack of rights to the resources of this regime undercut the formation of a collective identity among women with similar needs. This absence then left women unprepared to fight for these resources when they began to evaporate in the last two decades of state socialism. Beginning in the mid-1960s, the welfare society underwent major reform. Rather than transforming the existing resources into collective rights or guarantees, these reforms chipped away at women's discursive and practical maneuverability. They narrowed the interpretive basis of state policies and practices. They reconfigured the boundaries of welfare to release men from state scrutiny. And they reconstituted women's institutional positions by emphasizing their roles as mothers and subjecting them to new forms of regulation. As I explore in the next two chapters, this reconceptualization of need had profound implications for women's ability to protect themselves in everyday life.

Part 2

THE MATERNALIST WELFARE STATE, 1968–1985

The Dynamics of Change: Hungarian Professionals Reform
the Welfare Society

Over the first two decades of state socialism, the Hungarian welfare society
underwent few reforms. Throughout the period, targeted social provisions
associated with a "welfare state" were deemed unnecessary; state policies
and practices were guided by the notion that the well-being of the population could be secured through well-connected institutions. In the mid-1960s,
these assumptions about what the population needed and how to meet those
needs began to change. At this historical juncture, the needs of specific social
groups began to be emphasized. Within the welfare society, access to social
support had been informally based on bureaucratic privilege and social class.
By the late 1960s, assistance was formally linked to specific attributes, the
most important of which was motherhood. In this period, state actors began
to argue that mothers had special needs and the welfare apparatus should be
reoriented to address them. They disconnected the maternal from the familial by proposing new provisions and institutions aimed exclusively at mothers. As a result, women were put under the purview of a maternalist welfare
apparatus that constituted them primarily as child-rearers and caretakers.

This focus on the maternal arose from the work of three groups of professionals—demographers, economists, and psychologists—all of whom
framed the nation's "needs" as antithetical to a societal-welfare model. A
new cohort of Hungarian demographers launched the first attack on the
welfare society. Motivated by demographic data collected in the first two
decades of socialism, they became invested in the quantity control of motherhood. Through the mid-1950s, the Hungarian birthrate remained relatively stable, primarily because of the coercive measures of the Ratkó

regime, which included laws that outlawed abortion and curtailed access to birth control. Thus, until the mid-1950s, the birthrate remained at just the reproduction level. After abortion was relegalized in 1956, the birthrate plummeted to record lows.[1] By the early 1960s, the Hungarian birthrate was one of the lowest in the world. Drawing on these data, demographers warned of an impending disaster and proposed population policies to reverse these trends.[2]

These demographic changes were not unique to Hungary. They also characterized other East European societies experiencing the combined effects of industrialization, urbanization, and high rates of female employment. Throughout the region, demographers projected the long-term implications of the declining birthrate.[3] From Romania to the German Democratic Republic to Poland to Hungary, they used these data to question the viability of the existing policy regimes. Demographers frequently linked these trends to their regimes' overemphasis on production; they claimed that production had taken precedence over reproduction, which led to demographic crisis. They also blamed the Stalinist "ideology of emancipation" for discouraging women from reproducing. Preoccupied with their roles as workers, East European women were said to have abandoned their responsibilities as reproducers.[4]

Plagued by demographic fears, most governments in the region instituted a series of pronatalist policies. On the coercive side, the late 1960s and early 1970s were marked by increasingly restrictive abortion laws. These restrictions were most severe in neighboring Romania: after a brief liberalization period following Stalin's death, a regime of "Romanian-style family values" emerged in 1966.[5] This regime included measures that denied women access to abortion and birth control; it also encompassed public institutions created to regulate reproduction and to disseminate a pronatalist ideology. Although the Hungarian pronatalist regime was not as extreme, it did enact a relatively restrictive abortion law in 1973. Backed by a media campaign that attacked women for being "overly individualistic," the law restricted abortion to targeted groups—those who were unmarried, those with two or more children, those over thirty-five years old, those with severe housing problems, and those with serious health concerns. The law also set up medical lay committees to assess appeals from other groups of women. Although women found ways to bypass these restrictive measures, the law subjected them to humiliating investigations into their reproductive lives.[6]

On the less coercive side, most East European countries responded to their demographic crises by introducing new maternity and family policies.

In Romania, restrictive abortion laws were accompanied by income-tested child allowances, birth bonuses for women with four or more children, mother medals, and two to three months of paid maternity leave.[7] In 1970, the Czechoslovak state established its own package of maternity benefits, which included monthly allowances for families with two or more children, a fixed-rate maternity allowance, birth subsidies, and twenty-eight months of paid maternity leave.[8] Even the Soviet state, which had lagged behind its neighbors in its system of social support, established maternity benefits in 1973; it gave lump-sum birth payments to mothers with three or more children, monthly family allowances to those with four or more children, and sixteen weeks of paid maternity leave to all mothers.[9] The following year, the Soviet state introduced its first income-tested social program—a cash allowance given to impoverished mothers to purchase food for their children.

Although Hungary also followed a pronatalist path, its policies differed from those of other East European countries in two respects. First, instead of focusing on large families, Hungarian demographers proposed policies based on incentives for all mothers.[10] Their goal was to "encourage" all women to reproduce by securing social conditions conducive to raising children. Second, while other East European demographers focused primarily on childbearing, through birth grants and subsidies, Hungarian policymakers centered on child rearing. They proposed a support system that included universal family allowances, a three-year paid maternity leave, and birth payments. Thus, Hungarian policies were broader in scope: they encompassed benefits that supported both the birth and the rearing of children.

In part, Hungary's pronatalist path resulted from the convergence of demographic shifts with economic changes that were largely unique to Hungary. While demographers were contemplating the implications of the declining birthrate, economists were in the process of designing a series of reforms to restructure the economy. By the mid-1960s, postwar reconstruction and industrialization were complete. Until this time, the regime's policy of full employment had been consistent with its larger economic imperatives. The primary way the regime had secured full employment was through job creation—from 1950 to 1965 industrial employment increased by 5–6 percent annually; by the mid-1960s, the growth rate slowed to 1 percent.[11] The regime's ability to secure full employment was waning, and the need for female labor was lessening. The children of the postwar baby boom had also come of working age and had to be incorporated into the labor force. By the mid-1960s, the government had even begun to speak of labor "surpluses" and "redundancies."

The government also began to give economists more room to formulate measures to address these economic issues. After Stalin's death and the 1956 revolution, economists utilized splits in the party/state to gain the political and professional space necessary to exert influence over the direction of the economy. Economists also began to form international networks; they gained access to journals such as *Business Week* and the *Wall Street Journal* and engaged in academic exchanges with their counterparts in U.S. universities.[12] Through these exchanges, Hungarian economists gained exposure to new economic ideas, such as econometrics and linear programming. These ideas soon permeated their thinking, leading them to view the economy as a "mechanism" to be tinkered with like an engine. They conceptualized the market in similar terms—as a mechanism that could be incorporated into central planning to enhance economic efficiency.

This professionalization process culminated in the mid-1960s with the introduction of the New Economic Mechanisms (NEM). In 1964, the government established an advisory committee to draw up proposals for reforming the existing "economic mechanism." The committee's proposals were authorized in 1966; the NEM reforms were implemented in 1968.[13] The main goal of the NEM was to integrate markets into central planning. Profits became a measure of an enterprise's economic success; production became more closely tied to supply and demand. The NEM also gave individual enterprises more control over production: enterprises were held accountable for economic efficiency and accorded more autonomy in their hiring, firing, and decision making. The objective was to force enterprises to rid themselves of internal labor reserves and thus improve efficiency.[14] The formula was a risky one. Among other dangers, it heightened fears of labor surpluses and unemployment—concerns that were particularly acute for the regime since much of its legitimacy still rested on its ability to secure full employment and a decent standard of living for the population.[15]

Hence, by the late 1960s economic reformers and policymakers faced the complicated task of siphoning off workers from the labor force without provoking mass unemployment. Here their "needs" coincided with those of demographers. Social policies that focused on women's reproductive responsibilities were one way to secure economic downsizing and to increase the birthrate. By emphasizing women's roles as mothers, these provisions encouraged women to exit the labor force, albeit temporarily. In effect, paying women to devote themselves to full-time child rearing served the interests of both economists and demographers.

Clearly, these demographic and economic problems presented real dilemmas for the socialist state. The regime could have resolved these problems in a variety of ways. It did so by redefining the meaning of motherhood and maternal responsibility. And this decision to accentuate the maternal emanated largely from a third group of professionals, Hungarian psychologists. After a ten-year hiatus, the psychology department reopened at the University of Budapest in 1957. The first cohort of psychologists focused on the sphere of production and industrial relations, conducting elaborate studies of worker fatigue, work accidents, and the "neuroses" of assembly-line workers.[16] By the early 1960s, many of them had turned their attention to the reproductive sphere, and they developed a branch of "educational" or "child-rearing" psychology (*nevelési pszichológia*). In 1962, they established the Institute of Child Psychology and the National Child-Rearing and Children's Clinic, which diagnosed childhood disorders and conducted family therapy. Their objective was to produce a new generation of effective workers by reshaping child-rearing patterns. Here their preoccupation with the maternal surfaced most explicitly.

Throughout the 1960s, child-rearing psychologists conducted countless empirical studies on child development. Their studies were published in two influential journals, *Pszichológiai Tanulmányok* (Studies in Psychology) and *Magyar Pszichológiai Szemle* (Hungarian Review of Psychology). Although they were cloaked in scientific discourse, many of these articles had a radical tone; psychologists wrote as if they were uncovering new social phenomena and analyzing them in unique ways. As a prominent child psychologist trained in the 1950s explained in an interview, "It was an exciting period. We were doing research that had been forbidden. We were talking about individuals and discussing psychological issues that no one had examined before."[17] In other words, their work was guided by an individual model of action that diverged from earlier models of the institutional basis of identity. Just as economists viewed the economy as a mechanism to be adjusted, psychologists conceptualized the psyche as a mechanism to be tinkered with. Their research centered on how to adjust children's psychological mechanisms, such as their emotional learning, school performance, identity formation, and social adaptation.[18] They also studied the psychological underpinnings of "deviant" behavior, including the activities of youth gangs, juvenile delinquency, and family violence.[19]

Mothers loomed large in psychologists' studies of children's psychological mechanisms. Psychologists found that infants developed faster and more consistently when they had "close contact" with their mothers.[20] They discovered that children were emotionally stable if their mothers cared for them "rationally."[21] They determined that children performed better academically if their mothers remained at home and involved in their schooling.[22] They revealed that teenagers were more socially adaptable if they had good mothering.[23] Mothers were also used to explain abnormal child development and delinquent behavior. For example, two psychologists explained the gang involvement of two brothers in this way: "Their mother belongs nowhere, socially and culturally. She lives as an outcast, and her children grew up with this. This leads them to delinquency."[24] An influential study of the period, a 1966 investigation of parents' effects on personality development, exemplified this approach. Studying hundreds of children at play, it found that most of them mimicked their mothers or acted like maternal figures. This finding led the psychologist to conclude that children see and act in the world through their mothers and that state experts should thus begin to direct their work at mothers.[25]

Such conclusions about the centrality of the mother were quite typical of this research. When psychologists offered prescriptions for healthy child development, their recommendations were strikingly similar: mothers needed to devote more time and energy to child rearing. Well aware of the economic impediments to full-time child rearing, the psychologists frequently called for new policies to allow women to focus on their children, especially during the first three years of children's lives, when, psychologists believed, the main oedipal issues are resolved and negotiated. As a psychologist stated in 1965, "The most pressing issue for us is to establish the predominance of domestic care of children, from birth to the beginning of school."[26] Other psychologists proposed training for new family "experts" who would rationalize child rearing and secure the quality control of motherhood.[27] They imagined that these experts would work out of a network of guidance centers that intervened in family life and taught effective caretaking skills.[28]

Psychologists' recommendations did not remain confined to their academic journals. Each year, they seeped out of these circles to reach a broader audience. In their annual conferences, psychologists informed government officials and state practitioners of their findings and prescriptions. In 1965, when the Hungarian Psychological Association held a national conference devoted to child psychology, psychologists' recommendations flooded out of their small institutes and into the hands of party/state officials. The meeting consisted of over thirty-seven lectures in which psychologists inundated the audience with their ideas about healthy child development. In attendance were high-ranking party/state officials and policymakers. One message resounded throughout the conference: mothers needed the time and the resources to take child rearing seriously, and the state had to facilitate their carrying out this responsibility. As the head of the Hungarian Psychological Association put it in his opening address:

> The correct relationship between mother and child is one of the most important factors of the family that, on account of emancipation and the participation of women in productive work, is loosened more and more in every respect. This involves the diminished importance of the role played by the family, a danger appearing in the laxity of sexual morals of youth, their deviance, and their irresponsible behavior. This problem has to be resolved by the development of rational, socialist, moral care-taking, in harmony with the establishment of conducive economic con-ditions.[29]

His statement encompassed all three of the professional forces that converged in the 1960s to push for the reform of the welfare society. Demographers were preoccupied with the quantity control of motherhood, psychologists with the quality control of motherhood, and economists with economic efficiency. Together, their appeals paved the way for the emergence of a maternalist welfare apparatus out of the welfare society.

3. Maternalizing Need
*Specialization and the
Quality Control of Motherhood*

Throughout the 1960s, Hungarian professionals launched an attack on the welfare society. By the end of the decade, their appeals had been translated into state policies and practices. The historical convergence was striking. In early 1968, the New Economic Mechanisms (NEM) were introduced to incorporate market mechanisms into centralized planning. Later that year, a child-care grant (Gyermekgondozási Segély/GYES) was established to provide mothers with three years of paid maternity leave. By the end of the year, the institutional welfare apparatus had expanded with the advent of Child Guidance Centers (Nevelési Tanácsadók), which addressed child development and child-rearing problems. When taken together, these three reforms signified a fundamental break with the economic policies, social provisions, and institutional practices of the welfare society.

These reforms also gave rise to a new architecture of need. They signified more than slight additions to the existing welfare apparatus; their effects were more profound than a simple extension of new benefits to the population. These reforms redrew the boundaries of welfare and redefined its terms of inclusion and exclusion. While the societal policies of early socialism took social institutions as the site of re/distribution, the policies of the late 1960s targeted social groups. They were premised on the notion that particular groups had distinct needs that required special assistance. A similar form of targeting occurred at the institutional level. With the introduction of Child Guidance Centers, the institutional welfare apparatus bifurcated and became specialized. It was also infused with professional models that deemphasized clients' institutional positions and highlighted their child-rearing acumen. New welfare practices then arose: domesticity tests to gauge maternal competence, psychological exams to ferret out maternal ambivalence, and personality tests to search for deep-seated emotional problems. In this way, state policies and practices operated in complementary ways to facilitate the emergence of a maternalist subsystem of welfare out of the welfare society.

This argument about the maternalization of welfare adds a new dimension to the existing historiography of the period. Overall, most social scientists view this period as a time of "reconciliation"—the historical juncture when Hungary embarked on a distinctive socialist path. In this period descriptions of Hungarian "goulash communism," "refrigerator socialism," and "mature paternalism" emerged.[1] These metaphors are all premised on the notion of "state" withdrawal from "society." At the economic level, scholars have interpreted the NEM as an attempt to decentralize production and economic decision making. By giving enterprises more influence over production, and workers the ability to change their workplaces, the NEM is said to have accorded Hungarians more power to meet economic needs.[2] At the ideological level, scholars have pointed out that the state backed off of its discourse of "emancipation" in this period.[3] They argue that the socialist state became less interested in overt demonstrations of support and increasingly satisfied with passive acquiescence—a shift embodied in party leader Kádár's overly quoted statement: "Those who are not against us are with us."[4] As a result, it is often assumed that the state retreated somewhat from the private sphere and abandoned direct attempts to transform authority relations in the home.[5]

The feminist literature on late state socialism also adheres to this argument about state withdrawal by focusing on the gender implications of "mature paternalism." There is little consensus about how this withdrawal affected women. Some feminist scholars claim that the state's retreat from the private sphere opened up new possibilities for alliances between men and women.[6] They insist that the sanctioning of the second economy allowed women and men to join forces and to act as a "unit" in the private realm: men used their state jobs to gain access to the second economy, while women used the new child-care policies to stay home and carry out the day-to-day second-economy support work.[7] Thus, the state's retreat is said to have bred solidarity among men and women. According to other feminists, the state's retreat achieved exactly the opposite: it undercut women's autonomy, enhanced the traditional "housewife" role, and released men from family responsibilities.[8] Still other feminists advance similar arguments about the political repercussions of mature paternalism; they claim that the opening up of the private realm infused the emergent opposition with a "defensive privatism" premised on the maintenance of gender hierarchies.[9]

These feminist scholars have made important contributions to gender-blind analyses of mature paternalism, but their arguments are weakened by their acceptance of the narrative of state withdrawal. Although these scholars insert gender into prevailing accounts of late socialism, they do not acknowledge that historical periodizations can change when history is viewed from a gendered lens.[10] When the actual policies and practices of late socialism are analyzed for their gendered meanings, it is difficult to sustain commonly held notions of the state's retreat. Instead, these reforms signified the state's redeployment; they marked an interpretive shift in focus from the organization of social institutions to the meaning of motherhood. By deemphasizing men's contributory roles as family members, this regime redefined who was responsible for familial well-being. By highlighting women's roles as mothers, these social policies feminized care work and reshaped women's identities. And by setting out to rationalize women's child rearing, state institutions entered women's lives in new ways. The difference was not in the level of state intervention. Rather, it was a change in who was regulated and in the kind of gender identities highlighted by the state.

When seen as a period of state redeployment, mature paternalism clearly did not have categorically positive or negative effects on gender relations. As with the welfare society, the maternalist subsystem was a mixed blessing for those it targeted. Whereas the welfare society coupled a broad interpretive terrain with narrow re/distributive practices, the maternalist regime reversed the tendency: it combined a narrower interpretation of need with broader re/distributive practices. As this regime separated mothers' needs from those of other social groups, it codified new maternal rights. As it reprioritized women's identities to highlight the maternal, it fostered a strong sense of maternal entitlement. As it bred divisions between "good" and "bad" mothers, it gave women concrete guarantees. And as it freed men from state scrutiny, it emboldened women to demand new kinds of support. These tensions were inherent in both the social policies and the institutional practices of the late socialist welfare regime.

THE MATERNALIST POLICY REGIME

The social provisions that emerged in the last two decades of state socialism bore a closer resemblance to "welfare policy" in the classic sense of the term than did earlier policies. After decades, during which re/distribution was located in existing economic and social institutions, a distinct sphere of social policy arose in the late 1960s.[11] But plan-related and enterprise-based provisions did not disappear. Rather, they operated alongside a new subsystem of policy. These new policies shifted the site of state re/distribution to national and local governments. Their targets also changed. While societal policies were once aimed at the institutions of work and family, the new social policies narrowed the focus of state welfare. These policies addressed the needs of specific groups and thus resembled the discretionary policies associated with many Western welfare states.

Moreover, the content of these Hungarian policies also resembled that of their Western counterparts. Mothers were one of the first groups to be targeted by the new policy apparatus.[12] As feminist historians have shown, many Western welfare states also had maternalist origins. Early Western social policy arose from the efforts of female activists working under the guise of the "maternal."[13] Throughout North America and Western Europe, female activists claimed special importance as mothers in order to position themselves as the subjects and objects of state building. The social policies they then introduced extended state support to women as mothers—under the rubric either of pronatalism as in France and Germany or of racial anxiety as in the United States.[14] Hungarian social policy was not maternalist in the sense of originating in the work of female activists, but it was maternalist in the sense of providing special support to mothers. In the late 1960s, motherhood became a central eligibility criterion. New labor regulations, leave policies, and income supports treated mothers differently from other social groups. These policies were also accompanied by ideological and discursive practices that emphasized the significance of mothers and granted women distinct "expertise" based on their child rearing.

Despite these similarities, Hungarian policies did differ from Western variants in several respects. Hungarian policies were more expansive and inclusive; they provided more extensive support to mothers. For example, Hungary granted women three years of paid maternity leave, which was longer than that provided under other European policies.[15] Hungary's policies made few distinctions among mothers; they were not linked to income or occupation. In addition, Hungarian policies were premised on labor-force participation. Maternity-leave policies guaranteed women reemployment in their same positions. And before women were eligible for subsidized mothering, they had to spend one year in the labor force. This requirement contrasts with U.S. maternalist policy, which often forbid mothers from working outside the home.[16] It also differs from West European policies, which rarely connected maternal entitlements to wage labor so directly.[17]

Another significant difference between Hungarian and Western maternalist policies was the historical context in which they arose. In the West, these policies signified the first time that women were included in state re/distribution on their own. By bringing women into contact with the state, these policies gave many women their first language of entitlement.[18] But Hungary's maternalist policies arose after decades of state involvement in social life. These policies therefore signified a new type of state engagement with women's lives. Once seen as the responsibility of women and men, child rearing was reinterpreted as an exclusively female domain. Previously recognized as having a variety of complementary identities, women were constituted primarily as mothers. Although motherhood never negated women's roles as workers, it slowly took precedence over them. This reprioritizing emanated from the national and local policy apparatus of late state socialism.

Reprioritizing Women's Responsibilities: National Maternalist Policies

The first sign of the reordering of women's roles occurred in 1965, when the Ministry of Labor formally designated certain jobs as posing a danger to the "lives and well-being of women."[19] A decade earlier, the socialist state had emphasized women's incorporation into jobs previously done by men. Now, these new classifications erected legal barriers to women's employment. Women were excluded from all jobs that involved heavy physical labor, exposure to radiation, or intense vibration.[20] The justification underlying these restrictions was to protect women from work that could impair their reproductive capabilities.[21] At the same time, the Ministry of Labor demarcated certain jobs as being exclusively female. These included nursing, kindergarten teaching, cosmetology, lab assistance, and clerking in specialty stores. With these new classifications, the gender-segregated labor market became codified into law.

In the following year, the list of jobs available to women shortened, and four new categories of forbidden jobs were added. First, women were no longer allowed to work in jobs that could "overstrain" their nervous system. Among other activities, women were prohibited from driving buses with over twelve passengers, cutting stone, or doing mechanized hammering. Second, women were not permitted to work in jobs that exposed them to intense heat, cold, dampness, or fluctuations in air pressure. This restriction precluded women from ship work and from working underground. Third, women were forbidden from working in high places. This prohibition put most construction work beyond their grasp. Finally, they were not allowed to work with substances that could damage their blood, nervous system, or hormones. Hence, jobs related to chemicals, toxins, lead, and nicotine were off-limits to women.[22]

These new labor regulations were significant for at least two reasons. First, they signified a shift in control over labor policy. For decades, enterprise unions had been responsible for securing their employees' working conditions and positions. These laws vested more control in the national Ministry of Labor. Second, these regulations were infused with maternalism. The assumption underlying them was that women had special needs as (potential) mothers and thus had to be protected. In 1972, this emphasis on gender difference was even incorporated into the constitution. The earlier constitutional guarantee of "equal" working conditions was replaced with a pledge to secure "appropriate" work opportunities and conditions for men and women.[23]

In addition to restricting women's access to certain jobs, the regime changed its definition of "appropriate" work opportunities and conditions. By the late 1960s, female workers were thought to be in need of large amounts of time off to devote to child rearing. In late 1967, the centerpiece of the maternalist policy apparatus was born—the GYES. When first introduced, the grant provided six months of support equivalent to the mother's salary and up to two additional years of support at a fixed rate. In 1969 the grant was extended by six months to provide mothers with a total of three years of support.[24] Employers were obliged to reemploy recipients on completion of the leave. To be eligible, women had to be employed full-time continuously for twelve months preceding the birth; members of agricultural cooperatives had to participate in at least 120 days of collective work in the twelve months prior to the birth.[25] These regulations articulated the regime's new emphasis on motherhood rather than wage labor: for every one year of wage labor, women received three years of subsidized mothering.

The GYES program had another key eligibility criterion: it was offered only to Hungarian mothers. Fathers could apply for the grant if they were single parents or if the mother was too sick to care for the children. The grant addressed the "biological and psychological requirements" of motherhood—requirements that fathers presumably did not meet. The exclusion of men was a major point of contention among those formulating the provision. Some participants did resist men's exclusion. Worried that it would reinforce traditional gender roles, they wanted to make the grant a parental right. Ultimately, their arguments lost to policymakers' claims that the "immediate well-being of children and mothers" outweighed the "long-term goal of equality between the sexes."[26] These policymakers also lobbied to extend the grant to mothers for three years, when children's main "oedipal issues" had been resolved.

Overall, most of the scholarly literature on GYES has focused on how the grant solidified a traditional gender division of labor in the workforce and in the home.[27] Yet it is also important to recognize that GYES fostered a strong sense of entitlement in women. For the first time, women had legally codified maternal rights. Because the grant was available to a cross-section of mothers, it did not become a stigmatized form of assistance. Moreover, because the grant was used by diverse groups of women, it was never associated with specific classes. One caseworker, who worked in the Gyámhatóság in the late 1960s, put it best when I asked her about the social connotations of the grant: "GYES was for mothers. I took it, my colleagues took it, and the clients took it. How could I think of it negatively when everyone I knew used it?"[28]

Another reason GYES never became a stigmatized social benefit was that the grant made few distinctions among mothers and thus assumed that mothers had similar needs and required similar support. All mothers, irrespective of their income, occupation, or race/ethnicity, could remain on the grant for three years. And mothers received the same flat-rate stipend while on the grant.[29] From 1967 to 1972, all received 40–60 percent of the average female wage. In the mid-1970s, a three-tiered system was introduced to link benefit levels to family size: mothers with one child received 800 forints per child, those with two children 900 forints per child, and those with three or more children 1,000 forints per child. Until the mid-1980s, these stipends increased slightly with the rate of inflation.

Although the GYES system assumed that mothers had similar needs, women's use of the grants did vary. This variation fell along two key axes. First, there were significant occupational and educational differences in use patterns. Through the 1970s, roughly 14 percent of the female workforce and 6 percent of the national workforce was on GYES at any given moment.[30] Breaking these figures down by economic sector and educational level reveals the different use patterns. Table 6 has these data by industrial sector and type of worker; Table 7 includes data on mothers' use patterns by educational level. Second, the length of time that women stayed on the grant also varied by occupation and education. Professionals and white-collar workers remained on GYES for shorter periods of time, as did those with higher levels of education.[31] There were at least two reasons for these differences. Since professionals and highly educated workers were better paid, they suffered economically from the flat-rate system; they could not afford to remain on the grant for the entire three years.[32] Moreover, although workplaces were required to reemploy women in their previous positions, many women found it hard to make up for lost time or lost opportunities in career advancement. Professionals experienced these losses in

Table 6. Percentage of Labor Force Using GYES by Economic
Sector and Type of Worker, 1970–1978

	1970	1976	1978
Economic Sector			
Industrial	4.8	8	7.6
Agriculture	2.9	4.3	3.9
Transportation	2.1	3.2	3.2
Commerce/trade	4.9	9.1	9.6
Type of Worker			
Manual	3.3	N/A	5.7
White collar	3.7	6.2	5.4

SOURCES: KSH, *A Gyermekgondozási Segélyezés 10 Éve 1967–1976*,
p. 17, and KSH, *A Gyermekgondozási Segély Igénybevétele és Hatásai*,
p. 12.

more pronounced ways and therefore opted to return to work before the
grant had formally expired.[33]

In addition to symbolizing the regime's shift in focus from women's roles
as workers to their responsibilities as mothers, GYES also marked a change
in the site of re/distribution. Prior to GYES, maternity-leave programs were
administered at the enterprise level. After 1968, control was transferred to
the Ministry of Labor. GYES payments were allocated from the central budget (they constituted roughly 2 percent of the GDP in the 1970s).[34] National
officials set eligibility guidelines and benefit levels. They also ensured that
enterprises reemployed recipients. In 1974, a Social Policy Department was
established in the Ministry of Labor to oversee all family policies, including
GYES. As a result, trade unions lost much of their influence. They carried
out policies dictated from above—policies that reflected the maternalist
agendas of demographers and psychologists rather than the work demands
of female employees.

Along with this shift in the site of re/distribution, the administrative
procedures guiding the allocation of maternity leave changed. Soon after the
introduction of GYES, the Ministry of Labor created an appeal system for
women to use if they had trouble with their grants. Women submitted their
appeals to the ministry, in writing or in person. When the ministry could
not resolve a case, it was transferred to the local Gyámhatóság for review.

Table 7. Percentage of Mothers Using GYES by Educational
Level, 1967–1979

Educational Level	1967	1969	1973	1979
Primary	77.3	71.6	81.1	85.9
Secondary	65.3	59.9	76.4	82.9
Higher	34.4	32.6	56.2	68.7

SOURCES: KSH, *A Gyermekgondozási Segély Igénybevétele és Hatásai*,
p. 59; KSH, *A Gyermekgondozási Díj Igénybevétele és Hatásai*, p. 10; and
KSH, *A Nők Helyzetének Alakulása a KSH Adatainak Tükrében 1970–
1981*, p. 67.

Thus, this system vested control over the administration of GYES in national and local state offices. Moreover, the criteria used by these state bodies to assess women's appeals were indicative of the new conception of need that was taking hold. For instance, a study of GYES appeals uncovered the fact that a majority were advanced by women who failed to meet the work requirements or who wanted to stay on the grant continuously for more than one child.[35] Ministry officials had a great deal of discretion in evaluating these appeals, but they seem to have used two main criteria. First, family size was critical: women with three or more children were usually allowed to remain on the grant, even if they had been outside the labor force for years. For instance, one woman was permitted to remain on GYES uninterrupted from 1972 to 1985; after the birth of each of her four children, she applied to continue her grant without returning to work. Each time, her extension was granted. In such cases, officials deemed women's maternal needs so "pressing" that they waived the work requirements.[36]

Second, state officials assessed women's child-rearing practices when evaluating GYES appeals. Women with one or two children who wanted the work requirements waived had to exhibit "appropriate" child-rearing practices. To determine whether they did, the ministry sent Gyámhatóság caseworkers on home visits. Only those women who demonstrated good mothering skills had their appeals granted. As an official wrote about one mother in 1979, "Her work book has expired, but her children develop beautifully and in a clean environment. Her request for a continuation of GYES is granted."[37] Absent from their assessments were detailed accounts of mothers' work lives or performances. In contrast to the criteria used in the period of early state socialism, a strong work record did not help women in their negotiations with state offices. Instead, officials were most concerned with women's ability to perform as competent mothers.

In addition to these new policies, many preexisting social programs took on a maternalist edge in this period.[38] Most important, the system of family allowances (*családi pótlék*) underwent reform to make them more accessible to mothers. Prior to this change, family allowances were paid directly to "heads" of large households employed full-time in state enterprises or cooperatives. In two-parent households, fathers received the allowance attached to their wages. In 1968, the Ministry of Labor changed the work requirements to extend the allowance to students, home workers, and part-time employees. It also offered the allowance to families with two children.[39] As a result, the number of women eligible for the allowance increased by nearly 20 percent.[40] Then, in 1974, the head-of-household provision was replaced by a "primary-caretaker" clause, which allowed separated and divorced mothers to have the allowance attached to their wages. Hence, for the first time, mothers became entitled to family allowances on their own.

In 1974, an appeal system was created through which married women could transfer the allowance to their wages and thus bypass their husbands altogether. As with the GYES appeal system, control over these appeals was vested in national and local governments. But here the chain of command worked in the opposite direction: women submitted appeals to caseworkers, who then transferred them to the ministry. While no reliable data exist on how many women utilized this system, in the two districts of my research, I reviewed twenty-five appeals from the 1970s.[41] The set of maternalist criteria deployed was similar to that used in GYES appeals. Women justified their appeals on the basis of motherhood: they were the ones who actually cared for children. To support their appeals, these women documented their day-to-day child-rearing activities. As one woman argued in 1976, "I clean, cook, and wash for the children. I am their only caretaker."[42] Women like this believed they were entitled to support because of their contributions as mothers. Their sense of entitlement was confirmed by caseworkers. All of the twenty-five appeals were approved on similar grounds: mothers knew what was best for children and needed the resources to secure their well-being. As one caseworker wrote in 1978, "I recommend Mrs. Jenő's appeal. It is obvious that she is the caretaker. She cannot count on her husband. Her responsibilities must be supported."[43]

Taken together, protective labor legislation, child-care leave, and family allowances formed the core of the maternalist policy regime. These provisions trained women how to stake a claim in the welfare apparatus and to emphasize their roles as mothers when couching an appeal. They accorded women a language of entitlement and taught women that, as mothers and caretakers, they had special needs. They also transformed these needs into social rights by guaranteeing women state support for their contributions as mothers. Many women learned a similar lesson about the centrality of motherhood in more direct ways through the local assistance schemes of the era.

Rewarding Good Mothers: Local Maternalist Policies

During the first two decades of state socialism, the main type of discretionary welfare funds administered at the local level was the emergency aid distributed by enterprises.[44] District governments had little say over these funds; caseworkers' influence was limited to writing letters to union officials to convince them of clients' needs. In the late 1960s, this division of labor was reversed when local governments were given their own pool of discretionary welfare funds. Union officials then referred their workers to local governments for assistance. Whereas control over labor regulations, maternity leave, and family allowances moved from enterprises to national state bodies, the administration of discretionary welfare funds shifted from unions to local governments.

Initially, these local funds were quite limited in scope. When introduced in 1969, Occasional Child-Rearing Assistance (Rendkívüli Nevelési Segély) provided clients with financial support up to three times a year.[45] Aside from this requirement, no rules guided the allocation of these funds. Their distribution was left to caseworker discretion. Caseworkers were not even required to conduct home visits or to collect income information from applicants. While no national-level data exist on the use of these funds, in the two districts of my research I found that, in the first four years, caseworkers distributed these funds to approximately 4 percent of their clientele. Of these, roughly 60 percent received assistance once, 30 percent twice, and 10 percent three times. These funds were usually given to mothers to purchase clothing, furniture, or bedding. Home visits were the exception rather than the rule. In effect, caseworkers seemed to use these funds as one-time boosts to their clients' incomes.

This situation changed in the early 1970s. In 1973, according to one caseworker, applications for temporary assistance increased by nearly 30 percent because "word got out" in the large housing estates that there was "money available."[46] In response, the Ministry of Education established a more comprehensive assistance program in 1974, Regularized Child-Rearing

Assistance (Rendszeres Nevelési Segély/RNS). Also administered through local offices, RNS provided on-going income support to families with child-rearing needs. As with the previous program, benefit levels were not fixed. Caseworkers could decide how much aid to distribute and to whom. Yet, unlike the earlier assistance program, the RNS program created a surveillance apparatus to determine eligibility for these funds. Applicants had to submit letters from their children's teachers to verify that they raised them "properly." They were also subjected to home visits in which caseworkers meticulously documented their domestic lives and practices. These investigations fundamentally altered the nature of welfare work in the period and drew caseworkers into the regulation of women's child-rearing practices.

Officially, RNS had only a few eligibility criteria. They were based not on the material resources at applicants' disposal but on the "quality" of the applicant.[47] The RNS rules outlined what kind of a "parent" the applicant had to be. The use of "parent" in the singular indicates exactly whom these funds targeted: mothers. In fact, one of the districts I studied replaced "parent" with "mother" on their assistance applications. According to official regulations, an eligible parent had to keep an orderly flat, remain concerned with her child's development, and exhibit "secure" child-rearing practices. An ineligible parent demonstrated "objectionable" (*kifogasolható*) behavior, "dangerous" (*veszélyes*) child-rearing practices, or "unruly" (*rendetlen*) behavior that caused "negative" social or material circumstances.[48] Clearly, RNS was not aimed at the materially needy. Rather, it targeted "good" mothers and rewarded them for "proper" child-rearing practices.

The forms used by caseworkers to assess eligibility further articulated this maternal emphasis. In effect, these forms were designed to test women's gender practices. They were extremely elaborate, consisting of two or three pages of questions. Most of the questions were open-ended and left considerable room for subjective reflections about applicants. The questions were divided into four categories. In the first category, caseworkers elicited information about the applicant's flat: its size and comfort level as well as subjective evaluations of its quality—its cleanliness, decor, and conduciveness to child rearing. The second category was a set of questions about the "parent." Here caseworkers evaluated the applicant's personality traits. Was the parent diligent and orderly? Was she clean and serene? Could she cook? Was she aware of "modern" child-rearing techniques and domestic practices?

While these questions bred subjective remarks about applicants, caseworker discretion was even more pronounced in the final two categories of questions, which were about applicants' domestic relations. To obtain "accurate" information for the third category, caseworkers conducted short-term participant observation: they showed up at applicants' flats unannounced, usually around dinnertime, to observe family dynamics. This timing enabled caseworkers to examine what the applicant cooked. It also offered caseworkers a first-hand look at how "caring" the mother was with her children. To verify their observations, caseworkers had to complete a fourth set of questions on applicants' relations with their neighbors. Here, they interviewed neighbors about applicants' family lives and domestic practices. Was the family harmonious or in conflict? Was the parent solid and educated? Was she clean and considerate? Did she organize a "peaceful" and "orderly" family environment?

Importantly, these questionnaires excluded a number of key topics. They included few questions about the material resources at applicants' disposal. Except for inquires into their occupations, caseworkers asked no questions about applicants' work lives. Caseworkers seemed almost uninterested in applicants' work histories or work relations. Moreover, there were no inquiries into applicants' extended-family networks. Caseworkers did not ask whether applicants had family members who could support them. In effect, these were domesticity tests, designed to elicit demonstrations of domestic competence. These tests thus accorded caseworkers a new lens through which they interpreted their clientele, the lens of the maternal. And they brought caseworkers onto a new work terrain, the quality control of motherhood.

Initially, the number of RNS recipients was quite low. In the first five years, fewer than half of those who applied for RNS passed its domesticity tests and received aid. In Budapest, from 1975 to 1979, only a few thousand families received this aid. Table 8 has national-level data on assistance cases. The demographic make-up of recipients was quite revealing. In Budapest, over 50 percent of RNS recipients were not employed outside the home; of those who were employed, half were part-time workers.[49] Hence, caseworkers gave preference to women not employed full-time outside the home: while 73 percent of all Hungarian women worked full-time, only 25 percent of RNS recipients were full-time workers.[50]

These re/distributive practices were symptomatic of the narrow conception of need emerging in late state-socialist Hungary. While the previous welfare regime had evaluated clients according to their institutional locations, the maternalist subsystem of welfare gave priority to women's caretaking roles. Protective legislation dictated that women's reproductive roles should determine where they were situated in the labor force; the GYES system gave women three years of subsidized mothering for every year of wage labor. Local child-rearing assistance took this maternal focus one step

Table 8. Number of Child-Rearing-Assistance Cases,
         1975–1986

Year	Occasional Aid	Regular Aid
1975	32,030	3,535
1979	48,103	10,066
1983	62,201	19,689
1986	102,307	22,812

SOURCES: Ágota Horváth, "Egy Segély Anatómiája," pp. 241–243,
and KSH, *Népjóléti Statisztikai Évkönyv*, p. 229.

further, distinguishing between "good" and "bad" mothers and rewarding
"good" mothers with support. These evaluative distinctions then became a
central component of welfare workers' institutional practices.

WELFARE PRACTICES AND THE
GOOD-MOTHER MOLD

At the same time the policy regime underwent reform, important changes
occurred at the institutional level. For the first two decades of socialism, the
institutional welfare apparatus included one main institution, the Gyámhatóság. Without financial resources to distribute, early caseworkers set out
to remake existing social institutions and to integrate clients into them. In
the late 1960s, as the policy apparatus shifted focus to the maternal, welfare
agencies were reconfigured. These offices began to reprioritize women's
responsibilities and to emphasize their roles as mothers. In doing so, they
grounded the maternalization of need in women's everyday lives.

The rise of maternalist welfare practices was the result of two concrete
changes. First, within Gyámhatóság offices, the introduction of new social
provisions profoundly altered the nature of welfare work. Gyámhatóság
caseworkers administered many of these maternalist policies; they educated
clients about the GYES and family allowance systems and processed their
claims. Since both systems targeted mothers, so did caseworkers. With the
introduction of local child-rearing assistance, this maternalist agenda became
firmly located in their work practices. Caseworkers began to use the same
maternalist surveillance techniques when dealing with all sorts of cases,
from divorce to paternity investigations to child protection. Thus, while the

maternalist welfare model entered casework through the new social policies, it eventually permeated all aspects of Gyámhatóság casework.

Second, maternalist welfare practices arose with the creation of a network of new institutions. In 1968, the institutional apparatus expanded to include district-level Child Guidance Centers, which were designed to "modernize" child rearing. Drawing on Western child-development models and the Hungarian psychoanalytic tradition, these centers employed "family experts," who infused the welfare apparatus with their own brand of maternalism. Theirs was rooted less in the dictates of national-level policies and more in their own analytical biases. From Freudian psychoanalysis to developmental theory to functionalist family models, their professional orientations targeted the mother in child and family development. Their institutional practices thus focused on the surveillance, the regulation, and the control of child rearing.

Moreover, with the advent of Child Guidance Centers, the institutional welfare apparatus bifurcated. State actors employed in these institutions assessed clients in different ways, using different techniques to determine who were the "good" and the "bad" mothers. They also approached this intervention differently. Armed with domesticity tests, Gyámhatóság workers used a "carrot-and-stick" approach, rewarding the good and punishing the bad. Family experts deemed this approach overly coercive and took a more educative approach to clients. Despite their differences, these institutions converged to transmit a maternalist agenda to clients and to strengthen the maternalist arm of the welfare apparatus.

From Familism to Maternalism

In the late 1960s, when the government introduced its maternalist policies, the nature and content of Gyámhatóság casework started to change. To a large extent, caseworkers became mediators between clients and national-level social programs. This work required that caseworkers have specialized knowledge; they had to be familiar with the intricacies of these programs' eligibility requirements. To help, Gyámhatóság offices hired a number of "legal advisors" (*jogászok*). As a result, the number of Gyámhatóság employees close to doubled in this period, increasing from three or four per office to six or seven.[51] These offices then began to divide up their work in new ways, separating the bureaucratic work from child protection work. Thus, for the first time, the Gyámhatóság became segmented by work activity and task.

The introduction of this new bureaucratic work also gave rise to a new approach to clients. In the first two decades of state socialism, bureaucratic casework involved the regulation of clients' family forms. After the 1952 Family Law, caseworkers spent an inordinate amount of time documenting formal guardianship. Since this work usually entailed establishing paternity, men were central to Gyámhatóság casework. By the late 1960s, caseworkers had developed efficient procedures to keep clients in compliance with the law. This timing coincided with the rise of new bureaucratic demands related to the GYES and family-allowance appeal systems. Caseworkers' gaze then shifted from fathers to mothers. Once preoccupied with tracking down deadbeat dads, caseworkers began to regulate women's mothering practices.

In this way, bureaucratic caseworkers were carriers of the maternalist agenda at the institutional level. As they entered the Gyámhatóság, they not only brought legal expertise but introduced new criteria with which to assess clients. Since few rules guided their evaluations of GYES and family-allowance appeals, these caseworkers created their own standards to distinguish between the unworthy and the worthy. Initially, their distinctions were not articulated explicitly. Rather, they surfaced in caseworkers' descriptions of successful claimants. They tended to approve women's appeals to transfer family allowances into their names on the same grounds: mothers knew what was best for their children and were committed to securing their well-being. Caseworkers often contrasted mothers' sensitivity to fathers' insensitivity. In appeal decisions, fathers were represented as unresponsive to their children and hence unworthy of state support. As a caseworker wrote about one mother and her husband in 1977, "The father is not using the money in an orderly fashion. The mother will use [the money] to care for the children."[52]

A similar construction of mothers underlaid caseworkers' assessments of GYES appeals. In these evaluations, caseworkers made finer differentiations among women and probed more deeply into their domestic practices. Despite the fact that most women who were denied GYES had failed to meet its work requirements, these women's work histories had little effect on caseworkers' assessments. Instead, their determinations centered on an applicant's presumed devotion to her children. Successful claimants were described in similar terms—as caring, attentive, and committed mothers worthy of "special" treatment. They made financial sacrifices and lived in difficult material conditions to be with their children. And they struggled to secure a "home environment in which children grow and flourish."[53] Unsuccessful claimants were described in diametrically opposite ways. They were perceived to be uncaring, irresponsible mothers; they failed to follow GYES work rules because of their laziness; and they wanted to remain on

GYES continuously because it allowed them to avoid "uncomfortable and demanding activities."[54] Thus, in handling these GYES appeals, caseworkers developed new criteria with which to evaluate mothers.

Until the mid-1970s, caseworkers used these criteria in an informal, ad hoc way. With the introduction of local child-rearing assistance in 1974, these maternal constructions became firmly embedded in Gyámhatóság casework. They were formalized in the domesticity tests used to assess clients' child-rearing abilities. In effect, these tests served as the basis for caseworkers' carrot-and-stick approach. Clients' marks on these tests were the single most important factor determining who received child-rearing assistance; they overrode all evidence of material need. Women who received RNS were defined as unequivocally "good mothers." This label implied a number of attributes. First, they ran orderly, efficient households, and their homes were well decorated. "Her flat was simple but well maintained," wrote one caseworker in 1976. "The furniture was nice and the children had their own beds with blankets. I felt comfortable in the home."[55] Second, they exhibited proper cooking and cleaning skills. "She cooks for the family regularly," reported a caseworker in 1978. "The children are well-fed and I saw no dirt or disorder. She cleans often."[56] Third, they devoted large amounts of time to their children and established "healthy" domestic relations. As one caseworker described a single mother in 1982, "She lives with her sister and her young daughter. She cares for the girl well. She makes sure the girl is clean and always orderly. She pays attention to her schoolwork. Although money is tight, she takes the girl to ballet so she can develop physically."[57]

However, caseworkers consistently denied assistance to women they considered "careless" or "unruly" mothers. These women failed to demonstrate proper gender practices and child-rearing skills. Women who appeared uninterested in domestic upkeep were regularly denied child-rearing assistance. A dirty home, an empty refrigerator, and bad decorating skills were common justifications for rejecting RNS applicants. Women who exhibited behavior "unbecoming of mothers" were also denied support. This category included women who spoke aggressively, drank heavily, and stayed out late at night.[58] In addition, female clients who did not give top priority to child rearing were routinely denied assistance. They were described as "selfish" and "greedy" mothers. One woman prompted concern, despite her cooking and cleaning skills, because of the distribution of rooms in her flat. "The mother received a council flat because of the children, but she has taken the largest room for herself and put the children in the small room. This selfish behavior cannot be supported."[59] Then there was the woman who was scolded in 1977 for her clothing. "The children are dressed in old clothing, and the mother wears only the most fashionable [clothing]. She obviously uses her money for herself and not for the children."[60]

These domesticity tests influenced more than decisions about who received child-rearing assistance; they also shaped clients' institutional fates.[61] Clients' test scores determined how the Gyámhatóság dealt with them. Caseworkers spent more time assisting women they believed to be "good" mothers. Mothers who convinced caseworkers of their commitment to child rearing had deadlines and rules waived for them.[62] Those who demonstrated impeccable decorating, cooking, and cleaning abilities obtained bigger and more heavily subsidized flats.[63] Newly divorced women who exhibited good child-rearing skills were more likely to secure help tracking down deadbeat dads.[64] And women embroiled in divorce disputes who proved they ran "orderly" households elicited favorable custody agreements.[65] Once available to all Gyámhatóság clients, these institutional resources became restricted to the domestically "competent" and maternally "skilled." Through such practices, caseworkers taught women that they could butter up the bureaucratic machine by fitting into a particular mold of mother.

Caseworkers also transmitted this message by negative example. In addition to denying resources to "bad" mothers, caseworkers subjected them to quite punitive practices. Institutionalization was one such practice. In the first two decades of socialism, caseworkers institutionalized a relatively small number of children. They used state care as a last resort, opting instead to place endangered children in extended families. With the introduction of domesticity tests, caseworkers began to center on the nuclear family and to deemphasize the extended family. So when they encountered "problematic" nuclear families, they turned less to extended families and more to state institutions. In these cases, it was as if women and state experts were at war, fighting for control of children and dueling over who was best prepared to raise them. Data on the number of children living in state care reveal that state experts often won these battles. As Table 9 indicates, from 1965 to 1985, the number of children in state care almost doubled: while 1.1 percent of all children were in state care in 1965, this percentage had increased to 2.3 by 1985.

As with most aspects of their work, caseworkers had enormous discretion in deciding when children should be taken from their homes.[66] The most common justification used in the period was that these children lived in "dangerous home environments." For instance, 19 percent of my case sample involved institutionalization; of these cases, 79 percent involved "dangerous home environments." In practice, this was an indirect reference to

Table 9. Rate of State Institutionalization, 1965–1985

Year	Number of Children	Percentage of All Children
1965	33,480	1.1
1975	39,353	1.4
1985	60,949	2.3

SOURCE: KSH, *Népjóléti Statisztikai Évkönyv*, p. 239.

maternal neglect. One thread ran through most institutionalization cases: the mothers had been deemed "incompetent."[67] In their descriptions of these women, caseworkers inadvertently provided a litany of the issues impinging on their lives: of their alcohol problems, their exposure to domestic violence, and their mental-health problems. But caseworkers rarely addressed these problems. Instead, they presented them as contextual information.[68] Caseworkers labeled these mothers "unfit" and used institutionalization to reprimand them. As one caseworker put it in 1977, "The mother does wash and clean, although she cannot cook at all. Her boyfriend lives in the flat with the two little ones, and he causes scandals. He drinks and beats her. Neighbors say her behavior is rhapsodic and unstable. The children are in dangerous circumstances and can be raised in stability [in an institution]."[69]

The Gyámhatóság's focus on clients' mothering skills had interesting implications for its treatment of different groups of clients. One might assume that caseworkers' preoccupation with the maternal would have bred clear class differences in treatment. But it did not. Because caseworkers focused on women's housekeeping and child-rearing practices, middle-class and professional women did not have a clear advantage in these tests. The absence of labor-saving devices and a domestic-service sector made it difficult for these women to use their higher wages to deliver better gender performances. Caseworkers regularly scolded such women for failing to devote enough time to domestic upkeep. Since most middle-class women became clients through divorce and visitation disputes, these reprimands usually surfaced in caseworkers' determinations of custody arrangements. Here caseworkers frequently blamed professional women for being too careerist to devote time to their children. They subjected these women to long lectures about children's needs. Occasionally, they even punished these women with unfavorable custody and visitation arrangements. As one caseworker justified her actions in 1978. "Mr. Benedik wants to extend his visitation to two days a week. He claims his wife is too concerned with her new job as a teacher. She disagrees and says the weekends are her only time to see the children. I found him to be correct and discovered evidence that for her the children are a burden not a pleasure. I recommend that his visits be increased."[70]

At the same time, caseworkers' good-mother mold prompted them to reward women who held less demanding jobs. Caseworkers frequently applauded women who worked part-time, praising them for their commitment to family. They commended many working-class women for rising above difficult material conditions to take care of their families "properly."[71] Over and over, caseworkers extolled women whose flats were modest yet well maintained and whose limited budgets did not stop them from preparing "solid meals."[72] Women who remained on GYES for three years also scored points with caseworkers, who interpreted it as a sign of a mother's commitment to her children. Since industrial workers tended to stay on the grant for its entirety, they often gained leverage in domesticity tests. Hence, because caseworkers' assessments rested on clients' domestic training, the good/bad mother distinction did not fall along clear class lines.

Yet it did correlate quite closely with race and ethnicity. Caseworkers' evaluative criteria had consistently negative effects on Romany, or "gypsy," clients. Because caseworkers were forbidden from stating a client's ethnicity, it is impossible to determine exactly how many Romany clients were deemed bad mothers. But caseworkers often let their biases creep into their case files. From these slips, caseworkers' extreme cultural intolerance surfaced. Caseworkers faulted Romany mothers for not living up to their standards of cleanliness, taste in decor, and culinary accomplishment. "Mrs. Lakatos is an inexperienced mother, even though she has six children," a caseworker wrote of a Romany client in 1975. "Instead of cleaning her filthy flat, she spends her days in the courtyard smoking and complaining about life."[73] Caseworkers were also insensitive to the nonnuclear families of Romany clients. They exhibited disgust at households in which numerous extended kin resided. They were appalled when two or more children slept in one bed. As one put it in 1977, "Gypsies like Mrs. Horváth do not understand that children cannot develop well when surrounded by many others or [when they] share beds with other children."[74] Thus, because of their distinctive child-rearing patterns, Romany mothers were more likely to be labeled as bad mothers and to be subjected to the coercive arm of this welfare apparatus.

Scientific Maternalism and Familial Expertise

In large part, Child Guidance Centers arose as an alternative to this carrot-and-stick approach. Instead of simply rewarding the "good" and punishing the "bad," these centers set out to improve child-rearing practices. Their employees frequently referred to Gyámhatóság workers as "amateurs"—as untrained, uneducated, and unskilled women who were unable to grasp clients' complex problems. "The Gyámhatóság never understood the sources of clients' troubles," a psychologist explained in an interview. "They lacked the background."[75] Child Guidance workers considered themselves experts, equipped with the skills to resolve clients' problems. Indeed, they were better educated than their Gyámhatóság counterparts; most of them had advanced degrees. In the two centers where I did research, they were evenly split between those with university degrees and those with degrees from technical colleges in teaching, pedagogy, or psychology. Despite these differences, their work converged with the Gyámhatóság's in one crucial respect: they also targeted mothers. They believed in child rearing by design and adhered to a scientific mode of raising children with clear prescriptions for mothers.

To a large extent, counselors' maternalism was rooted in their professional training. The first psychologists employed in these offices were trained in the late 1950s and early 1960s; in this period of rebirth for psychology, academics and practitioners reclaimed their psychological tradition. One part of this tradition was psychoanalysis. After decades of practicing underground, psychoanalysts resurfaced and reentered the academy. "It was an exciting time," a psychologist trained in the late 1950s remembered. "Our teachers were famous psychologists just allowed back into the university and eager to pass on all they knew. We used their knowledge in our practical work. It was thrilling."[76] Yet the psychoanalytic tradition transmitted to students was of a particular sort. It was Freudian psychoanalysis, replete with an emphasis on the phallus and oedipal developmental stages. When translated into state practice, this tradition bred a considerable amount of mother blame.

In addition to uncovering the Hungarian psychoanalytic tradition, these early psychologists imported analytical models from the West. Like economists of the period, psychologists had a considerable amount of contact with the West; they attended international meetings and exchanged work with Western colleagues. Through such exchanges, Western theories and models seeped into Hungary. Just as economists imported econometrics and linear modeling from the United States, psychologists adopted personality tests, "world games," standardized intelligence tests, and educational assessments.[77] They also grasped onto functionalist models that conceived of the family as an integrated "system" seeking equilibrium. By using these models, Child Guidance workers differentiated themselves from Gyámhatóság workers. They defined their expertise on the basis of their ability to administer these tests. Since most of these models stressed the role of mothers in personality development and educational achievement, their institutional practices were infused with a form of scientific maternalism.

Although Child Guidance workers distinguished themselves as a group from Gyámhatóság workers, Child Guidance workers themselves were significantly divided. Their work was highly segmented by position and task. At the top of the institutional hierarchy were family psychologists, who had the most education and expertise. They provided behavior counseling to treat children who acted out and psychological counseling to guide children toward healthy resolutions of conflicts. Below them were "pedagogists," who conducted educational counseling to improve children's school performance. Finally, there were "family caretakers" (*család gondozók*), who conducted home visits and reported back to family experts about clients' family lives. Despite their different responsibilities and areas of expertise, all these workers linked children's problems to their mothers and pulled women into the counseling process.

Most of the Child Guidance Centers' clients were recruited through educational work. Every Hungarian family had contact with the centers in this capacity as they conducted the school entrance exams required of all children after preschool or kindergarten. These exams included standardized tests to assess children's verbal and analytical skills, as well as observations to evaluate their "comfort with the collective."[78] Together, these tests determined whether a child was ready for school and at what level.[79] Counselors also interviewed parents (usually mothers) to gather information about their educational level and child-rearing practices. At this point women first experienced this institution's maternalism. In the 132 school exams I reviewed from 1968 to 1985, I uncovered a "GYES effect" on entrance decisions: women who remained on GYES for at least two years were twice as likely as those who took the grants for less time to have their children accepted into school and placed in normal or advanced classes.[80] Counselors regularly applauded the mothers of children who performed well. "Your son did extraordinarily," one counselor told a mother in 1970. "I can see that you stayed with him, played with him, and taught him a great deal at home."[81] Counselors also attributed low test scores to mothers' child rearing. They often told women that their children's slow development resulted from their hasty return to work. "I can see that your daughter has not had much one-on-one contact," a counselor informed a mother in 1973. "This showed in her tests and is the reason why I am keeping her in kindergarten."[82]

In addition to reducing children's early educational problems to their mothers' lack of care, educational counselors blamed mothers for children's learning disabilities later in life. Children with educational difficulties were referred to Child Guidance Centers by their teachers. After an initial meeting, in which counselors diagnosed the nature of the problem, they initiated meetings with the children's mothers. In these meetings, counselors collected information about the mothers' educational background. Counselors then used this information to explain children's slow development. Mothers with little formal education were blamed for transferring their ambivalence about education to their children. As one counselor said to a mother in 1971, "If you show no interest in school, so will the children."[83] Women who had limited involvement in their children's schooling were also scolded. Mothers who could not answer questions about the content of their children's schoolwork or who admitted to devoting less than an hour a day to their children's schooling were reprimanded. "If you do not take his schoolwork seriously you cannot expect Lajos to," a counselor berated a mother in 1979. "His poor marks are understandable to me. Are they to you?"[84]

Educational counselors also looked to mothers to solve their children's school problems. They instructed mothers who were not well educated to make a special effort to encourage their children. As one counselor advised a mother in 1975, "You cannot read well and so Jutka should read to you. This will make her feel special as long as you do not belittle her for her ability."[85] Other mothers were ordered to devote large amounts of time to their children's learning difficulties. Counselors supplied them with materials and instructed them to tutor their children. They also insisted that mothers accompany their children to tutoring sessions, even if it conflicted with their work schedules. As a counselor wrote about one mother in 1976, "This is the third time that Józsi came without a parent. Last time I called to inform the mother of my disapproval. She said she could not take off from work so often. She must be more involved."[86] Fathers were never required to exhibit such concern or to participate in this educational work.

Counselors also targeted mothers as the source of and solution to a wide range of behavioral disorders. These counselors confronted a variety of behavioral problems, such as aggression, attention deficiencies, "destructive feelings," and nervousness.[87] Many of these cases involved young boys who exhibited aggressive or uncooperative behavior at school. When counselors could not detect an underlying learning disability, they blamed the boys' family environment by tracing the boys' anger to neglectful families and interpreting their aggression as pleas for attention. Counselors then looked to mothers to improve family relationships. "His anger will disappear if he is surrounded by love," explained a counselor in 1973.[88] Counselors turned to mothers even when fathers were clearly the source of the problem. For instance, in 1976 two brothers were referred to a behavioral counselor because they were acting out in school. In an initial discussion with the mother, the counselor learned that their father was an alcoholic who often climbed to the top of their high-rise apartment building (lakótelep) and threatened to jump. Instead of calling the father in, the counselor initiated sessions with the mother. In these meetings, the counselor advised her to hide the alcohol or to water it down. In one session, she even suggested that the woman make large dinners to fill up her husband so that the alcohol would not dramatically affect him.[89]

In addition to dealing with children who exhibited uncooperative or anti-social behavior, counselors devoted special attention to the sexual practices of teenagers. This work was highly gendered. Counselors were most concerned with promiscuity and "hypersexuality" (erősen szexuális beállí-tottságú) in teenage girls. Since most girls were referred to these centers by their parents, mothers were involved in this counseling from the onset. And because counselors believed that sexual behavior was passed from parent to child, mothers often became the targets of this counseling. State counselors inquired into mothers' sexual lives. Mothers could not win: counselors blamed both asexual and highly sexual mothers for transmitting pathologies to their daughters. For instance, in 1973 the mother of a "promiscuous" girl argued that her daughter's sexuality was not her fault since "sexual relations with my husband ended years ago." The counselor offered another interpretation: she explained that the girl's behavior was a compensation for what was "missing" from her home.[90] Two years later, the same counselor blamed another mother for the opposite behavior: the client had been married three times and had just moved in with a new man when her daughter began her "wild" sexual behavior. The counselor connected their sexual behavior, warning the mother that if she did not stop her "irresponsible" life, her daughter would remain out of control.[91]

Boys, however, provoked the most concern when they exhibited a lack of interest in girls. These cases also tended to be initiated by mothers, many of whom were frightened that their sons were "sexually distorted." In response, counselors provided interpretations of these "sexual abnormalities."[92] Some counselors adhered to biological explanations, attributing these boys' lack of interest in girls to hormonal or genetic imbalances.[93] More often counselors saw this behavior as rooted in boys' underdeveloped masculinity. To lure their sons to girls, mothers were advised to heighten their sons' masculinity. Usually, they were urged to encourage (or even force) boys to play sports as a way to "alter their hormones" and "draw them to girls."[94] Occasionally, counselors instructed mothers to be less protective of their sons. Theirs was a classically Freudian analysis: smothered by their mothers, these boys were said to be constrained by an unbroken female (maternal) identification and thus unable to view women sexually. The solution? Mothers had to back off and give their sons the freedom to develop "normal" sexual relations.

In addition to their educational and behavioral interventions, Child Guidance Centers conducted a third type of work: psychological counseling. The family experts who performed this work began with elaborate tests to uncover children's psyches. For young children unable to articulate their problems, psychologists administered "world games," in which children built make-believe worlds using small figures.[95] These figures had symbolic meaning, which psychologists analyzed to unearth psychodynamic issues.[96] "Only a trained eye understands what this indicates," a psychologist once remarked as we watched a young boy build his world. "For you he plays, but for me he reveals his innermost dilemmas." For teenagers, psychologists administered exams such as Rorschach tests and the Thematic Appreciation Test. One psychologist defended these tests to me in this way: "Adolescents think that they know everything. With these tests, we show them that we know something. We help them in ways they never knew."[97]

Because of the influence of psychoanalysis on their work, psychologists' interpretations of these tests tended to center on oedipal dilemmas. Small children were diagnosed with phallus-centered problems—castration anxiety for boys, and penis envy for girls. Psychologists transmitted these analyses to mothers, usually with considerable explanation. "Castration anxiety is when your son has a tremendous fear that his penis will be stolen from him," a psychologist once explained to a perplexed mother. "Don't worry. All boys go through it, and it is normal."[98] The high divorce rate in the period created all sorts of familial problems ripe for psychoanalytic interpretation. One of the biggest problems uncovered in this therapeutic work was the effect of absentee fathers on children. Psychologists believed young children became aggressive, violent, despondent, or withdrawn (or exhibited some combination of these effects) after divorce. Their interpretations of these difficulties were strikingly similar: unresolved oedipal conflicts led children to act out. Even here psychologists wove mother blame into their analyses: mothers were at fault for driving men away, for excluding men from parenting, or for not recognizing their children's need for male role models.[99]

One case beautifully illustrates psychologists' interpretive bias.[100] János, a five-year-old boy, was brought to the office by his mother, who was concerned about his bedwetting. A psychologist conducted a world game during which János retreated to the bathroom three times. The psychologist believed this signified castration anxiety. As she wrote in her notes, "The boy repeatedly went to the bathroom in our session to check whether his penis was still there. He fears that it will disappear. This is obviously the source of the bedwetting." She then interviewed János's mother and discovered that the boy's father had recently disappeared from his life. And the boy's grandfather, who had been an important father figure, had recently died. Suddenly, it all made sense to the psychologist. Her diagnosis: "I explained that János is without male role models and he is anxious about his own penis. The mother agreed to do more to keep her son in contact with his father."

State psychologists also attributed adolescents' problems to unresolved oedipal issues. "We know that the extreme egotism demonstrated by Pista can be traced to infancy and a lack of limits," wrote a psychologist in 1975. "We have many layers to uncover to fix his problem."[101] Teen malaise and identity confusion were linked to early experiences. As a prominent child psychologist explained to me, "Identification was a big problem in Hungary, where we had overprotective mothers and absent fathers. Boys never learned to identify with their fathers, and mothers never let them separate. So we got boys, years later, with problems related to the unresolved oedipal stage."[102] Girls were thought to experience problems with their maternal relations and distorted egos. "After months of working with Kati, I discovered that her psychotic mood swings vary with the state of her mother," wrote a psychologist in 1979. "Since her mother is paranoid, Kati's life is uneasy and difficult."[103] Or, as another psychologist described a 1981 case, "Mrs. Denes is a strong and assertive woman. She is raising her daughter to be like her. I advised [the girl's] teacher to intervene."[104] As these analyses reveal, counselors traced teen disorders to inappropriate mothering. Mothers' excessive coddling led to narcissism; their inability to let go caused identity confusion; and their maternal projections put children on emotional roller coasters. Fathers, who also had not fulfilled their oedipal expectations, were absent from psychologists' interpretations.

Once they rendered their interpretations, psychologists set out to resolve children's problems through therapy. These therapy sessions occurred anywhere from one to four times a month and typically ran for about half a year. For the most part, psychologists addressed children's day-to-day problems and gave them concrete advice about the issues confronting them. The gender training embedded in this therapeutic work was palpable. It surfaced most often in the personality traits that psychologists sought to instill in boys and girls.[105] Psychologists regularly promoted stereotypical gender attributes in teenagers. Boys who demonstrated inappropriate male behavior received intensive therapy. In 1975, a fifteen-year-old boy received weekly therapy to treat his "bouts with crying" and "mood swings."[106] In 1976, an eleven-year-old boy was treated for being "too modest" and "unsure" of himself.[107] And, in 1978, a fourteen-year-old boy came to weekly sessions after his father became enraged when he quit playing sports.[108] Girls received counseling when they exhibited different traits. In 1970, a fifteen-year-old, "big, aggressive, fearless girl who does what she likes" underwent therapy to tone down her behavior.[109] In 1972, a fourteen-year-old girl who showed no concern for her appearance was advised to be more "socially desirable."[110] And, in 1980, an eleven-year-old girl who played "rough games" with boys was told to develop female friendships.[111] Thus, this therapy was infused with messages about appropriate gender behavior and attributes.

In some cases, state psychologists coupled this individual counseling with family therapy. In theory, this therapy was to "advise families how to secure a healthy environment" for children.[112] In practice, it became maternal retraining. This work was often done in conjunction with family caretakers. Psychologists deployed family caretakers to assess a family's dynamics and to report back to them. After these visits, many women received communication training. For instance, in one 1970 case, a woman was sent to a counselor by her son's teacher. After a home visit, the family caretaker reported that the woman "arrived home too exhausted to talk to her son." The counselor then instructed her to put a clock on the table every night and to speak to the boy for at least an hour. The family caretaker paid follow-up visits to make sure the mother adjusted her practices accordingly.[113] Mothers were also told to communicate more effectively. Those who yelled at their children were scolded. "When you raise your voice to such an extreme level, you provoke fear in the little one. It is not healthy to frighten her so."[114] At the same time, mothers who seemed too passive were also reprimanded. Psychologists warned that children would not take them seriously if they "whispered."[115] Through this training, mothers were taught to refine their communication skills and to maintain a balance between "yelling" and "whispering."

Psychologists also carried out time-management training with mothers. Often described as "overburdened" and "overwhelmed," mothers were taught to structure their time better and to devote more energy to their children. One family expert developed strict time formulas for mothers, requiring that they spend at least two hours a day interacting with their children. For example, in 1975, when a single mother admitted to this counselor that she was extremely exhausted and depressed, the counselor provided her with a new daily schedule. Instead of instructing her to set aside time for herself, the counselor recommended that she spend all her time with her son; she told the woman to play with her son as a way of relaxing.[116] Other mothers were warned not to become overbearing in order to compensate for the limited time they spent with their children. As one state psychologist explained in an interview, "We confronted so much guilt in our work. Mothers were tortured that they could not be with their children, and they solved this by controlling everything when they were home [in order] to feel involved and important. Of course, this was not healthy."[117] These women were expected to walk a fine line: they had to remain present but not omnipresent, concerned but not controlling.

Finally, in addition to communication and time-management training, some mothers received therapy to address their own psychological "disorders." Many of these clients were women who, despite psychologists' appeals, failed to give their children top priority. So state psychologists set out to treat their "egotistical behavior."[118] Others were mothers who, despite psychologists' lectures, refused to separate from their children. So psychologists taught them how to let go. "This was a struggle," a psychologist revealed. "Mothers were so wrapped up in their sons, they couldn't break [from them]. I had to convince them it was unhealthy. It took years for some to understand. Most never did."[119] And then there were women who, despite psychologists' pleas, refused to develop "close bonds" with their children and exhibited "ambivalence" about their roles as mothers.[120] So psychologists tried to ferret out the source of their maternal ambivalence, often addressing women's feelings of neglect in order to shape them into good mothers.

As in the Gyámhatóság, family experts' institutional practices had interesting class and racial implications. Given these experts' complex psychological models, one might expect that middle-class and professional mothers had an advantage in dealing with these centers. To some extent, these women did mobilize their cultural and educational capital to shape counselors' evaluations. Psychologists frequently described these mothers as "intelligent" and "cultured." These women often gained leverage by engaging counselors in discussions of oedipal issues, child development, and identity formation. Yet counselors did not judge mothers strictly on their ability to speak the language of psychoanalysis or time management. They also assessed mothers according to their willingness to devote large amounts of time to their children. In practice, this type of assessment put many middle-class and professional mothers at a disadvantage. Counselors engaged in ongoing struggles with these mothers to force them to make sacrifices for their families. Educational counselors regularly complained that these mothers "refused" to spend time on GYES or to give children "one-on-one attention." Behavioral counselors faulted these mothers for working too hard or ignoring children's needs. And psychologists constantly berated these mothers for not adhering to their time formulas or prescriptions. So although middle-class women could talk the talk, their inability to translate the talk into practice meant that many of them were deemed "problematic" mothers.

The reverse was true for working-class mothers. They had less cultural capital to wield in these centers. For many of them, the psychologists' discourse must have seemed like a foreign language. Family experts regularly complained that these women were too "simple" to understand their analyses. Educational counselors often blamed them for transmitting educational deficiencies to children. Yet what these mothers lacked in cultural capital, they made up for with their willingness to sacrifice for their children. Family experts applauded these mothers for not placing work over family. Counselors were thrilled that these mothers tended to remain on GYES for the entire time or to work part-time. They appreciated that these mothers accompanied children to appointments and adhered to time formulas more readily than other mothers. As one psychologist said when I asked her about the class character of her work, "Oh, I never treated uneducated women worse. Maybe I even preferred to work with them. They followed my recommendations. The others were difficult. With doctors or teachers it was a struggle. They questioned everything."[121]

Yet these centers' criteria did not transcend ethnic divisions. Family experts' models had consistently negative effects on Romany women, who were at a complete disadvantage in these offices. Counselors saw them as culturally deficient and unwilling to accept "modern" child-rearing techniques.[122] Romany mothers who were illiterate and unable to tutor their children were called "ineffective."[123] Those who yelled at their children were said to be "uncaring."[124] Those who administered physical reprimands were deemed "cruel."[125] Because Romany women had more children than non-Romany Hungarians, it was more difficult for them to devote one-on-one time to children. This practice infuriated family experts. Moreover, Romany women were more likely to question these experts' models; many characterized theories of castration anxiety and penis envy as "crazy" or "ridiculous."[126] These responses further enraged family experts, prompting them to deem Romany mothers "hopelessly incompetent."[127] Hence, while family experts' good/bad mother distinction may have transcended class divisions, it fell neatly along ethnic lines.

SEGMENTING THE WELFARE APPARATUS AND NARROWING THE CONCEPTION OF NEED

During the final two decades of state socialism, a specialized welfare apparatus arose out of the welfare society. At the policy level, the site of state re/distribution became less diffuse. Social provisions linked to the economic plan were coupled with new policies administered through national-level ministries and departments. At the local level, benefits controlled by enterprises were accompanied by new district programs. By the late 1960s, locales had access to their own income-maintenance funds and thus relied less on those under the purview of trade unions. Hence, this period was marked by the emergence of a targeted subsystem of social policies and a new cohort of policy experts trained to administer them.

A similar form of specialization occurred in the institutional welfare apparatus. As the welfare terrain bifurcated, the segmentation among and within agencies heightened. On the one side was the Gyámhatóság, carried over from the previous regime, albeit in altered form. Although these agencies continued their bureaucratic and child protection work, they took on new duties connected to discretionary welfare programs. As different workers carried out child protection and eligibility work, segmentation within Gyámhatóság offices increased. On the other side were Child Guidance Centers, formed largely in response to the perceived deficits of the Gyámhatóság. The division of labor in these centers was even more pronounced; these offices included those with educational, behavioral, and psychological expertise. Thus, as social provisions became more differentiated, welfare agencies became more segmented; as the policy apparatus became more targeted, the institutional apparatus fragmented.

These processes of specialization then gave rise to a narrower conception of need. There were three levels to this interpretive narrowing. First, the social policies of the period were less institutional or collectivist in orientation. They separated mothers' needs from those of other social groups. Labor policies emphasized the differences between male and female workers; policymakers created a feminine sphere of labor policy that forbid women from performing work that could impair their reproductive capabilities. With time, mothers' special needs were codified into their own subsystem of welfare policy; they were given time off from work and new material support. In the process, the welfare system became increasingly segregated by sex. Men were not thought to have such familial responsibilities; their contributory roles as family members were deemphasized and even negated. In effect, this policy apparatus cordoned off women's needs as mothers: it separated women from men and extended support to women as mothers.

Second, once women's needs as mothers had been separated out, welfare institutions stepped in to segment maternal needs further. At this level of interpretive narrowing, state agencies broke the maternal into smaller parts for treatment. In doing so, they ascribed new meaning to the categories of gender; they redefined what constituted "appropriate" female behavior. Armed with new surveillance techniques, Gyámhatóság caseworkers judged women's domesticity to uncover who required better housekeeping skills and who needed to become more attentive. Child Guidance counselors were even more skilled at this maternal categorization. They zeroed in on who needed to spend more time with children, who required communication training, and who needed to work on their psyches. But all these state actors missed the larger institutional context surrounding mothers—that is, their integration into and satisfaction with the institutions of work, the nuclear family, and the extended family. Placed at the center in the previous regime, women's institutional well-being now fell outside the state's purview. The segmentation of welfare work gave rise to a narrower understanding of women's identifications; welfare workers' specialized practices led them to view their female clientele through the more limited lens of the maternal.

Third, with this segmentation, new distinctions surfaced among mothers. In this final level of interpretive narrowing, state agencies targeted individual action and behavior. Using new evaluative criteria, they developed a good-mother mold to classify individual clients. This classification further inscribed appropriate gender attributes. On one side of the divide were women who delivered impeccable gender performances. Their housekeeping skills, communication abilities, and psychological composition all met state actors' high standards. And they were treated accordingly, routed through the "good-mother" track, which was replete with rewards. On the other side were women who failed these domesticity tests. Unable to fit into ideal family models or psychological profiles, they were deemed problematic mothers. As a punishment, they were routed through the "bad-mother" track and subjected to new forms of intervention. In short, there were three moments to the maternalization of need: the cordoning off of the maternal, the breaking down of different parts of the maternal, and the disentangling of the maternally worthy from the unworthy.

Hence, as in the welfare society, there was a tension between the interpretive and the re/distributive underpinnings of this regime. Yet, in the maternalist subsystem, the re/distributive expanded while the interpretive contracted. As this system grew to include new welfare policies and agencies, it became less collective and more specialized. As it accorded women new kinds of benefits, it segregated by sex. As it extended new forms of entitlement to mothers, it conceptualized their needs in more limited ways. And as it codified new maternal rights and guarantees, it bred new surveillance techniques and evaluative distinctions among women. Amidst these tensions Hungarian women struggled to grapple with the state's expectations of them. Faced with a welfare apparatus that targeted and treated them in new ways, women experienced a contraction in their room to maneuver. In response, they developed new strategies to resolve these tensions and to protect themselves in everyday life.

4. Strategies of Expansion
Possibilities and Limitations

The maternalism embedded in the late socialist welfare regime was a mixed blessing for Hungarian mothers. This regime embodied contradictory tendencies that presented both limitations and possibilities for those it targeted. To a large extent, the regime's limitations were outgrowths of its interpretive narrowness: as the boundaries of inclusion and exclusion were redrawn, entire social groups moved outside the sphere of state regulation. The welfare apparatus then became increasingly segregated by sex. Although women were the primary recipients of state assistance in the welfare society, their spouses had been subjected to considerable state scrutiny. In the mid-1960s, the state's focus narrowed to encompass the nuclear family and one primary person in it, the mother. In the process, fathers fell outside the bounds of scrutiny. If a family was doing well, the mother was to be rewarded; if a family was having trouble, the mother was to be blamed. In effect, the social conception of need narrowed to exclude the paternal and to accentuate the maternal. This shift had profound consequences for female clients. With their mothering practices under a microscope, female clients found it harder to shield themselves from stigmatization than they had in the past.

This interpretive narrowing then led to a contraction of the space within which female clients could maneuver. At the discursive level, the terrain on which needs claims could be advanced became more confining. The welfare society had accorded clients a plethora of rhetorical possibilities for claims-making. Clients could stake claims on the basis of their roles as workers, parents, spouses, and family members. These claims were weighted equally; none of them negated or took precedence over the others. With the rise of the maternalist welfare apparatus, these discursive possibilities were limited. Claims based on women's roles as wives or as extended kin were no longer explicitly acknowledged. This regime also instituted a new ranking of recognized needs: social policies gave women three years of subsidized mothering for one year of wage labor, while welfare workers rewarded those who emphasized their mothering over all else. With fewer rhetorical possibilities and a more rigid ranking of acceptable claims, the discursive space surrounding female clients contracted.

Along with this discursive narrowing, clients' practical maneuverability was constrained. In the welfare society, women maneuvered among their social roles to increase their level of integration; the regime's collective focus enabled them to negotiate their different institutional demands and responsibilities. This maneuverability was undermined with the rise of welfare maternalism. Instead of scrutinizing existing institutions, state actors subjected women's mothering to higher levels of surveillance. Women then found it more difficult to connect their different social responsibilities and to illuminate the many issues impinging on their lives. Moreover, as welfare work became increasingly specialized, clients were broken into smaller pieces for treatment. This segmentation further obscured women's multiple needs and the ways in which they intersected in everyday life. As a result, clients became more confined in their institutional maneuvering.

At the same time as the maternalist subsystem of welfare interpreted need in narrower terms, it also extended new resources to mothers. Although this regime did highlight one primary social position, it re/distributed a series of new benefits to those who occupied this location. The GYES and family-allowance systems provided extensive material support for caretaking and established new channels through which women could demand state assistance. Because these policies were based on women's contributions as mothers, they essentially constituted social rights; they were remuneration for women's work as mothers.[1] These provisions also made few distinctions among mothers: all mothers received the same flat-rate payments for the same amount of time. In this way, maternalist policies undercut some of the re/distributive inequalities that had plagued the welfare society. For the most part, access to national-level benefits did not require bureaucratic connection. As a group, mothers were entitled to assistance and could make general claims to state support.

The power of these resources should not be underestimated. As many Western feminists have argued, maternalism can be an empowering discourse for women.[2] Historically, it has been the central idiom through which women have secured state assistance. By proclaiming special importance as mothers, women have gained access to the state, both as policymakers and as claimants.[3] Moreover, women have often achieved this access by forging group identities and connections among diverse groups of mothers.[4] In Hungary, many women seemed to experience the empowering moment of the maternal. Welfare workers expressed a new sense of urgency; firmly ensconced in their professional niches, they seemed convinced of the importance of their maternal mission. And many clients seemed emboldened by their new maternal entitlements: these guarantees enabled them to make legitimate demands on the state and accorded them a sense of social significance.

Furthermore, in Hungary this maternal discourse proved to be flexible and malleable. In their institutional interactions, female clients found ways to expand the confines of the maternal to articulate other needs and desires. They enlarged the state's interpretive parameters in two ways to expose needs once recognized in the welfare society. First, they linked their needs as mothers to their needs as wives. Faced with state actors who were not inclined to problematize male behavior, female clients struggled to pull men back into view, reminding welfare workers that good mothers needed supportive and involved fathers. In doing so, they mobilized state actors to gain leverage in their domestic power struggles. Second, women strategized with this maternalist discourse to raise a wider range of needs. With their needs as workers deemphasized, many female clients maneuvered to force an acknowledgment of the connection between work and family; they discussed how the double burden exhausted them and how they often felt emotional turmoil and depression. By couching these problems in maternal terms, women redirected welfare workers' focus to the conflict between work and family. In the process, they formed bonds with caseworkers to mitigate the isolation they felt as mothers. Instead of remaining in the confines of the maternal, female clients strategized with their maternal resources to defend their interests as wives, workers, and women.

Yet access to these maternal resources was not equal. As in the welfare society, women's ability to utilize state resources varied. Unlike the welfare society, which linked maneuverability to institutional location, the maternalist subsystem of welfare structured women's strategic possibilities along the good/bad–mother divide. This chapter traces how this institutional tracking operated and how it structured clients' maneuverability.[5] It reveals how those women defined as "good" mothers worked the prevailing needs talk to meet their needs as wives and as women. Yet it also shows how the success of women deemed to be "bad" mothers was more contingent. Those who could deflect blame onto their husbands carved out space to defend themselves as wives, while those who could not shift blame were subjected to punitive welfare practices. Thus, although both groups of women struggled to expand the confines of the maternal, only some were successful. Their struggles reveal the possibilities and the limitations of welfare maternalism.

PROVING AND USING COMPETENCY:
THE GOOD-MOTHER TRACK

In the mid-1960s, as the welfare apparatus became more specialized, it instituted new techniques for classifying its clientele. Whereas early socialist welfare agencies rarely collected data on their clientele, late socialist agencies compiled complex statistical analyses of their caseloads. From these data, it is possible to piece together a picture of their clientele, as well as their modes of categorization. The number of clients connected to district offices rose steadily during this period. The caseloads of both Gyámhatóság offices I studied increased from 6,000–7,000 clients per year in 1968–1975 to 8,000–10,000 clients per year in 1975–1985. Over half these cases were on-going and involved regular contact. Child Guidance Centers' caseloads were smaller, although they also increased. From 1968 to 1974 the two Centers I studied drew in 300–400 clients yearly; by the late 1970s they recruited 500–700 new clients. Put another way, roughly 15 percent of the residents in these locales had contact with welfare offices, with 7–9 percent maintaining regular contact.[6]

With this influx of clients, welfare workers began to catalogue their caseloads in new ways. In particular, they began to differentiate between competent and incompetent mothers. Competent mothers were women who did not require intervention to alter their child rearing. In the Gyámhatóság, competent mothers raised their children in "healthy" environments; if they had material problems, they were not related to "irresponsible" behavior. From 1968 to 1975, such women constituted roughly 65 percent of the clientele in the offices I studied; from 1975 to 1985, the percentage dropped to 55 percent.[7] In Child Guidance Centers, "good" mothers were those who did not need help improving their child rearing, time management, or communication. Through the 1970s, they constituted approximately 77 percent of the centers' caseloads; by the early 1980s, the percentage dropped to 68.

Clients defined as competent mothers shared a few important characteristics.[8] First, they were more likely to be at home full-time. In this period, roughly 27 percent of Hungarian women remained outside the paid labor force, while 52 percent of those defined as good mothers were not employed outside the home—36 percent of them were on GYES, 11 percent were housewives, and 5 percent were on disability pensions. Second, the good-mother label was linked to a woman's embedment in the nuclear family—

83 percent of these clients were married, 14 percent divorced, and 3 percent never married. Third, although good mothers who were employed occupied a wide range of occupations, the majority worked in light industry or administration. Finally, good mothers were ethnically homogeneous; it was rare to find a Romany woman defined as a good mother. Thus, the typical good mother was white, married, and on (temporary) leave from her industrial or administrative job.

Given their structural positions, good mothers had a series of distinct needs.[9] Those who did not work outside the home faced unique problems managing their status as full-time mothers. Financially, they confronted new burdens. Because GYES did not pay them their full salaries, they experienced a decline in their standard of living. And since the Hungarian wage structure was still premised on a two-wage-earner family, these women often had a hard time making ends meet. As a result, by the mid-1980s, approximately 22 percent of those on GYES were "at risk" of slipping into poverty.[10] In addition to their material problems, many full-time mothers expressed feelings of isolation and confinement. In meetings with caseworkers, they frequently discussed how they missed working outside the home. Their yearning was not only material: they also missed their colleagues at work and their sense of belonging to the collective.[11]

In addition, good mothers who were not employed outside the home had a series of needs as family members. Many of them experienced a loss of domestic bargaining power after they became full-time mothers. In part, the loss was economically motivated: since they contributed less to the family budget, their ability to control their families' resources had been undermined. This loss of control then affected the division of labor in their homes. Now at home full-time, these women confronted new difficulties getting their husbands to participate in child rearing. Time-budget studies confirm that mothers who were not employed outside the home spent an average of nine hours per day on domestic upkeep, while their husbands averaged only half an hour.[12] Hence, during this period the domestic division of labor became its most unequal.

Further exacerbating these women's domestic troubles was the large increase in alcohol consumption in this period: from 1968 to 1985, alcohol consumption increased by 70 percent, and the number of registered alcoholics nearly doubled.[13] Approximately 90 percent of alcoholics were men, the majority of whom were married.[14] In fact, by the mid-1980s, alcoholism had become such a serious problem that the population continually ranked it as the second most pressing social issue in public-opinion surveys—more serious than housing shortages, crime, or health problems.[15] In welfare offices, many women complained about the day-to-day repercussions of such trends and their inability to curtail their husbands' drinking. Their sense of powerlessness must have been heightened by their feelings of isolation; with fewer social contacts, their ability to regulate their husbands' behavior was curtailed further.

Good mothers who worked outside the home had a series of pressing needs of their own. As workers, they confronted an increasingly segregated labor market. Following the introduction of protective labor policies, women began to be channeled out of heavy industry and into light industry. Many of them were then shut out of the occupations and enterprises that provided more extensive benefits. Thus, although women's labor-force participation continued to grow in this period, the gender wage gap remained unchanged. Moreover, this occupational segregation occurred at a time of increased consumption. In this era of "refrigerator socialism," social expectations around consumption were growing. Hence, Hungarians had new access to household appliances, automobiles, and televisions at precisely the time when women were least able to afford such items on their own.[16]

In addition to their needs as workers, many of these mothers expressed needs as women. In welfare offices, they often admitted to feeling exhausted and overwhelmed. Stories of fatigued and overworked mothers resounded throughout this welfare apparatus as women continued to face difficulties balancing their work and family demands. On average, women reported spending less than two hours a day relaxing, as compared to men's four hours.[17] All this fatigue took its toll on women's emotional well-being. From 1967 to 1986, the number of Hungarians who sought help from psychiatric institutions more than doubled; the majority of these new patients were women.[18] In this way, many good mothers experienced threats to their material, familial, and emotional welfare. And they often turned to welfare institutions for help in grappling with these problems.

Passing the Tests

Before female clients could articulate any of these needs, they had to demonstrate their maternal worthiness. To pass this test, clients mobilized everything at their disposal. Since the Gyámhatóság and Child Guidance Centers administered somewhat different tests, clients' strategies varied slightly by institution. The Gyámhatóság's domesticity tests required that clients perform for caseworkers directly, usually during home visits. An overwhelming majority of Gyámhatóság clients had to give such performances; only those with simple, bureaucratic problems were exempt from these investigations. To gain the most from these tests, clients used them for two purposes—to exhibit their domestic skills and to bond with caseworkers. Only by achieving both ends could clients exert some influence over their institutional trajectories.

Since most home visits occurred in the evening, caseworkers usually arrived as women prepared the evening meal. Thus, the first topic of conversation between caseworkers and clients tended to revolve around food. This was the first part of the domesticity test. "When I entered Mrs. Horváth's flat, the joyous smell of paprika potatoes filled the air," a caseworker noted in 1970. "The family had just sat down for dinner. . . . It was well prepared."[19] As discussions of cooking ensued, effective clients mobilized their gender capital to impress caseworkers. Women frequently gave caseworkers tastes of what they were cooking.[20] They also shared cooking ideas and recipes. What was the best way to make stuffed cabbage? What about *palacsinta* (crepes)? Beef stew? Women who were not cooking could compensate by serving caseworkers something to eat or drink. Serving food gave clients the chance to exhibit the items in their cupboards. As clients performed, they had to be careful: if they admitted to consuming goods that caseworkers could not afford, they could be frowned on; if they served expensive meat or vegetables, they could provoke envy. The key was to impress, but not to intimidate, caseworkers.

After the food discussions, home visits usually included tours of clients' flats. On these tours, clients exhibited items "necessary" for child rearing, including children's beds, clothing, and toys. Clients also had to demonstrate their housekeeping skills. As they toured their flats, clients often commented on their cleaning regimens. "On Saturday mornings she cleans the common space, and the boys do their room," a caseworker once recounted. "Then they go to the cinema as a reward."[21] Women also pointed out their decorating skills. "There were fresh flowers on the table," a caseworker recounted in 1979. "Mrs. Varga replaces them regularly. This is a good idea, and the flowers gave the flat a healthy feeling."[22] Or as another caseworker put it in 1972, "Her flat was small yet tasteful. I am convinced they live in an orderly and well-maintained manner."[23] Here, clients drew caseworkers into housekeeping discussions. How could they divide up the rooms to give children their own space? How could winter bedding be transformed into summer bedding? "She has adorable beds made up for the girls," a caseworker wrote with admiration in 1971, "with matching comforter and pillow covers that she replaces in the summer . . . an excellent idea. . . . The girls are well cared for."[24]

Gyámhatóság home visits frequently included demonstrations of the fruits of clients' maternal labor. In addition to discussing children's activities and hobbies, mothers often had their children perform for caseworkers. For instance, in 1975 a woman had her son play Ping-Pong on the kitchen table to reveal how well he played.[25] Others brought out school projects to show to caseworkers. In 1970, at his mother's urging, a twelve-year-old boy gave a caseworker a short lecture about the origins of the Hungarian language. His mother was quick to note that he received the best grade in his language class.[26] Effective clients drew caseworkers into these child-rearing discussions. Did they have children? What were their talents? Again, the strategy was to prove domestic competence while establishing a maternal bond with caseworkers.

Clients connected to Child Guidance Centers strategized in similar ways, although their performances occurred in a different setting. Since home visits were fairly uncommon, counselors' assessments took place in the context of a formal interview. In these office interviews, mothers had to provide in-depth knowledge about their children's lives. Counselors expected mothers to recall the details of their children's births—from complications during pregnancy to children's precise birth weights. They also demanded that mothers know all about their children's schooling, friends, and extracurricular activities. And counselors bombarded mothers with questions about their level of involvement in their children's lives. Mothers were to know exactly how much time they devoted to different child-rearing activities. "One hour we walk, shop, and talk," a mother confidently recounted in 1972. "Then one hour for play. Then we cook and eat. After this, two hours of schoolwork and the Esti Mese and bed."[27] This kind of regimented child-rearing program impressed counselors; they interpreted it as evidence that these mothers adhered to a "philosophy" of child rearing. "She plans everything," a counselor wrote in 1977. "The children have order and stability."[28]

Although these initial interviews were critical parts of the centers' maternal tests, these assessments did not end there. Throughout the counseling process, mothers had to maintain consistent gender performances. Because counselors expected mothers themselves to bring children to counseling sessions, good mothers made it a point to contact counselors before and after each session. In this way, they demonstrated their on-going commitment to their children. "The mother asked me for an update after Judit's sessions," an educational counselor noted in 1980. "I am encouraged by her concern."[29] Others impressed counselors with reports of children's involvement in extracurricular activities. In 1975, a mother sent a list of the educational classes she had taken her son to.[30] In 1977, a mother called her counselor to inform her of the sports programs she had enrolled her hyperactive son in.[31] One mother perfectly articulated the new maternal focus in a 1970 letter: "I am happy to inform you of a special arrangement I secured with my workplace. On those days when I leave work early to take Béla to his therapy, I come to work early too. It was difficult to secure, but I do this to help my son."[32]

Gaining Domestic Bargaining Power

After these clients had pledged allegiance to the maternal, they were in a position to speak of a wider range of needs. Most often, they extended their recognized roles as mothers to gain bargaining power in their homes. Female clients appropriated three general strategies to protect their interests as wives: they used the good-mother label to secure special financial resources, to regulate male behavior, and to change the division of labor in their homes.

The main material reward available to "good" mothers was the child-rearing assistance distributed by Gyámhatóság offices. To gain access to these funds, female clients strategically mobilized their maternal skills. On home visits, applicants linked their ability to maintain "proper" mothering practices to these financial resources. As they took caseworkers on tours of their flats, they discussed how their domestic upkeep would be even better if they had more money. In their kitchens, they remarked that they could feed their children healthier food if they had the resources. "I do all I can to give the little ones the nutrients they need," a mother explained in 1969. "With a few extra forints, I could offer meat occasionally; children need meat, you know."[33] When they discussed recipes, female clients talked about how they longed to cook with "real" ingredients. As one mother joked in 1976, "My boys know it as stew, not beef stew, because they have never seen meat in it. This is a tragedy."[34] Clients also showed caseworkers their children's rooms and pointed out that they could furnish them better with more money. In 1977, a mother who had devoted two months' salary to new beds for her sons complained that the boys had already outgrown the beds.[35] In 1979, another woman made a similar argument about housekeeping. As her caseworker wrote, "Her flat is immaculate. The mother works hard at this and dreams of life with a vacuum cleaner or a clothes wringer. She would have time to make the home more orderly and warm."[36]

Female clients also mobilized their maternal capabilities to secure material assistance from their children's fathers. Divorced clients could obtain this support directly from their ex-husbands' wages. But those who were not formally divorced from these men or who did not know their whereabouts needed special assistance. And while caseworkers in the welfare society eagerly tracked down deadbeat dads, welfare workers in this regime were reluctant to do such investigative work. They found these cases too complicated and time-consuming.[37] Until the mid-1970s, caseworkers tended to deal with these cases by foot-dragging. After the introduction of RNS in 1974, caseworkers began to allocate RNS as a replacement for child support. This solution was disadvantageous for clients: RNS benefits not only were lower than child-support payments but were also less stable and placed clients under constant surveillance.[38] As a result, many female clients pleaded with caseworkers to squeeze child support out of their ex-husbands. Their pleas were usually centered around their needs as mothers. Clients regularly complained that they needed more money to survive. "Raising two boys on one salary is impossible," wrote a divorced mother who received RNS instead of child support in 1979. "I do all I can, but the home will suffer; the boys will suffer."[39] During home visits, these clients complained about the uncertainty of RNS, arguing that it left them in insecure material situations and unable to plan ahead for their children. Eventually, their appeals proved effective; with enough pleading, most of them convinced caseworkers to devote the time to secure their child-support payments.

These pleas for child support lead to the second strategy used by good mothers—linking the maternal and the paternal to regulate male behavior. Female clients often drew welfare workers into their family lives in quite intimate ways in order to exert control over their husbands. In doing so, they strategically connected their maternal abilities to the existence of caring fathers. They established this link by discussing how difficult it was to raise children without paternal involvement. Most often, their goal was simply to get fathers more involved in child rearing. This was an objective particularly for those "good" mothers not employed outside the home. Many of them traced their husbands' lack of involvement to GYES, claiming that their husbands had withdrawn from the household after they went on GYES.[40] Quite often, women coupled these complaints with requests for advice from caseworkers. As one woman wrote to the Gyámhatóság in 1976, "He is absent in every way. I have no one to turn to. . . . Please advise me, for the children's sake."[41]

In Child Guidance Centers, female clients frequently connected the maternal and the paternal in their psychological counseling. When confronted with psychologists' lectures about oedipal dilemmas, many mothers pointed out that this analysis was based on high levels of paternal involvement. Some mothers defended themselves against accusations that they were overprotective by claiming to compensate for absent fathers. In response to a counselor's explanation of her son's oedipal issues, one Romany woman exclaimed in 1970, "Identification problems! His father is never at home and when he is, he is drunk." Did the counselor have any ideas about how to cope with *that* problem?[42] Other mothers pointed out that counselors' analyses rested on the compatibility of parental roles. As a mother once wrote to her psychologist, "If I understood you correctly, his father is a role model. If this does not work and he refuses? What happens then?"[43] Instead of letting psychologists retain an exclusive focus on the maternal, these mothers widened the analytical lens to include men's oedipal responsibilities.

For the most part, the clients' goal was to obtain advice about how to get men more involved in child rearing. Yet female clients also strategized to pull state actors into their actual domestic struggles. These clients positioned welfare workers as educative threats, prepared to scold an unruly husband or father. Clients told caseworkers about their husbands' verbal abuse. They recounted how their husbands humiliated them in front of the children and thus undermined their maternal authority. In doing so, they convinced caseworkers to help curb this verbal abuse. "He calls me a whore in front of the little ones," a woman reported to her caseworker in 1975. "They have no respect for me as a result." On subsequent visits, the caseworker inquired about this abuse and scolded the man for his language.[44] Or as another client exclaimed in 1979, "Communication training! Talk to him about communication. Ask him why he calls me a prostitute and why he screams about his penis and semen in front of the children."[45] The counselor then alerted the family caretaker, who raised the issue with the man on her later visits.

Female clients who were subjected to physical abuse also used state actors as educative threats to curb their husbands' violence. They connected this abuse to their ability to mother, arguing that it was extremely difficult to keep an orderly house amidst excessive alcohol use or domestic abuse. These women convinced welfare workers that, to protect their maternal capabilities, the caseworkers had to lecture their husbands. In these lectures, women had welfare workers pose material threats by warning men that their behavior could lead to the withdrawal of support. This tactic was particularly useful for the husbands of RNS recipients. Well aware that their eligibility for RNS rested on their gender practices, these women threatened to change their performances if men failed to stop their abusive behavior. This was the tactic used by a woman in 1979 who warned her husband that she could not continue to uphold "such high domestic standards" if he continued his drinking. As the caseworker wrote about her husband, "He is aware of the consequences. He understands this must change."[46]

A Gyámhatóság case from the 1970s was indicative of this use of caseworkers.[47] The Szellő case began in 1972 when a woman contacted the

Gyámhatóság after she heard brutal fights in a neighboring flat. On the initial home visit, Mrs. Szellő impressed the caseworker with her domestic abilities; her flat was impeccable and her children well cared for. Over tea, Mrs. Szellő admitted that her husband beat her on a nightly basis. She knew the children heard, and this "tormented" her. The caseworker responded by writing a letter to her husband and informing him that "state authorities" disapproved of his behavior. All was quiet for two months, but then the beatings began again. Mrs. Szellő wrote a letter to her caseworker, explaining that she was overcome with fear. The caseworker stepped up the control: she visited Mr. Szellő and lectured him about his abuse. This warning frightened him for six months; then the beatings resumed. This time the caseworker called him to the office and subjected him to an onslaught of threats. To preempt further beatings, the caseworker sent Mr. Szellő letters, reminding him of their "discussion." The case closed in 1975 with no new beatings reported.[48]

Finally, in addition to obtaining material rewards and keeping their husbands in check, good mothers appropriated welfare workers to secure a more equitable domestic division of labor in their households. On their own, caseworkers would not have problematized arrangements where mothers did all the domestic work. In fact, they tended to view such arrangements favorably, especially when they bred "orderly" households. Although some clients also preferred to remain solely responsible for domestic upkeep, others found this division of labor unfair. And they searched for ways to change it, often turning to welfare workers for help. In the Gyámhatóság, the largest group of clients to use caseworkers in this way were women at transitional points in their lives. For instance, married women returning to work after long stays on GYES frequently looked to caseworkers for such assistance. They expressed concern that their return to work would adversely affect their family lives. To assuage their fears, these women asked caseworkers to educate their husbands about their new demands. Importantly, these appeals were couched around women's maternal roles. Clients were careful to point out that they were not shirking their responsibilities. On the contrary, they were protecting their mothering and enhancing their maternal competence.

Another group of Gyámhatóság clients who turned to caseworkers for this kind of help were newly separated or divorced women who continued to reside with their (ex)husbands. Their old family rules had broken down without giving rise to new ones. In the transition, these women had lost much of their domestic leverage. For clients who could convincingly argue that their maternal capabilities rested on the creation of equitable domestic relations, welfare workers intervened to set household boundaries and financial responsibilities. "I am on the list for my own council flat, but it will take years," one client wrote to a caseworker in 1970. "Until then my husband does everything to disrupt family life. He drinks and brings women to the flat at all times of the night. How can I raise children in such an environment?" To assist her, the caseworker divided up their three-room flat, giving the man a small room in the back of the flat.[49] In 1976, another woman claimed that her ex-husband regularly kicked the family out of the flat in his drunken rages. Her caseworker divided up the flat and devised a contract that gave the man access to certain rooms. Although the contract was not legally binding, it enabled the woman to demand reentry into the flat when her husband kicked her out.[50]

Gyámhatóság clients who were not formally divorced from their husbands had caseworkers draw up agreements to solidify each partner's financial obligations. These women tended to be in particularly vulnerable positions since they could not legally demand child support from their husbands. Instead, they used caseworkers' contracts to collect monthly support. One woman found her contract so useful that she desperately came to the Gyámhatóság in 1978 after her husband had destroyed her copy in a drunken rage. The caseworker calmed her: "I told her how he [her husband] is very silly. Does he think I cannot draw up a new one?"[51] Although these financial contracts were not legally binding, they were functional. They enabled women to bargain with stubborn husbands. One caseworker put it best when I inquired about these contracts: "Oh no, they were not supported by the court. This would have taken years. No, much of our work was like this. Back then clients were afraid of us. We were the big *tanács,* so the papers worked."[52]

Mothers connected to Child Guidance Centers strategized in more subtle ways to alter the gender division of labor in their homes. They often appropriated the centers' child-rearing recommendations to devote more time to their children and less to household tasks. In doing so, they forced their husbands to take over more of the domestic burden. Clients used counselors' time formulas to coerce their husbands to become more active in the household.[53] For instance, some claimed that they could not do the shopping on days when they transported their children to counseling sessions.[54] Others used the centers' tutoring sessions to disengage from household demands. Take this home-visit report written by a family caretaker in 1977: "I arrived at the home at 6:30. The mother was in the back working with the boys while the father was heating up the food. When I asked her about it, she said he did this since the therapy started."[55] Although these clients never overtly challenged the centers' focus on the maternal, they maneuvered within it to place domestic responsibility on their husbands.

Securing Personal Well-Being

In addition to mothers who extended the maternal focus to encompass their needs as wives, others redirected it to highlight their needs as women. This refocusing was even more difficult to secure. While the link between the maternal and the familial was fairly straightforward, the connection between clients' needs as mothers and as women was more tenuous. It implied a discursive stretch that raised new questions about women's fulfillment and happiness. It was also a riskier link for women to make. By voicing such problems, these clients jeopardized their status as competent mothers. They admitted to limitations that could have easily been construed as evidence of maternal inadequacy. Despite these risks, many clients did articulate concerns they had as women and carved out help to resolve them.

The most common problem raised by these clients was their extreme exhaustion. Faced with multiple demands, they admitted to feeling overwhelmed. They were engaged in a constant juggling act, which had taken its toll. They felt older; they tired more easily; and they were more forgetful. "Mrs. Juhász looks fifty but she is only thirty-four," a counselor wrote about one such woman in 1971. "With three teenage sons and her work in the hospital, she moves all the time. This is apparent."[56] Such exhaustion was particularly acute for mothers whose children had behavioral problems. "Even before Gábor was arrested, life was difficult; now it is unbearable," a mother wrote to her caseworker in 1980. "The court dates, the probation officers, and the regulation—I feel like an overcooked potato, ready to come apart."[57] Others revealed bouts with depression. They told stories of being too depressed to leave their flats. They admitted to crying regularly. And they spoke of a general sense of malaise and melancholy. Of course, they always connected their discontent to their child-rearing capabilities by expressing concern that their exhaustion or depression would make them less attentive mothers.

In order to ensure that these confessions did not breed maternal blame, clients often drew parallels between their experiences and those of welfare workers. Did they feel tired too? Were they strained by their work and family demands? They asked state actors how to best organize their chaotic lives.[58] The conversations that ensued sometimes seemed like state-socialist versions of "feel-good psychology," with counselors encouraging women to focus on the positive aspects of their lives.[59] In 1979, a client even turned a routine home visit into a counseling session. The home visitor arrived at

Mrs. Gombár's flat late in the evening. Visibly exhausted, Mrs. Gombár instructed the caseworker to sit down for tea. Mrs. Gombár then discussed her difficulties straddling work and family. As the caseworker recalled the incident in an interview, "I remember I was impressed. I thought, wait, sometimes we are not so different, I mean, from the clients. There we were, both tired and eager to return to our families. So we talked."[60] Or as a state psychologist explained in an interview, "I cannot say that I never saw similarities with the women I helped. This is normal, part of the process. Maybe even more with me because I also worked and had a family and struggled for sanity. We were not the same, and I had more education to [help] understand. But there were similarities too and I felt them."[61]

Implicit in many of the interactions between caseworkers and mothers were clients' sense of isolation and desire to form social bonds that could undercut feelings of confinement. These problems surfaced most often in Child Guidance Centers. In fact, they arose so often that counselors gave them a name, calling them symptoms of the "GYES syndrome" or the "child-care neurosis."[62] These names were indicative of who was most likely to experience such isolation: new mothers and women on GYES. In meetings with counselors, these women regularly admitted to difficulties adjusting to their position as full-time mothers. They expressed surprise at their loneliness and detachment. "I go all day without talking to a single adult," one young mother told a counselor in 1982. "My poor husband, when he comes home, all I do is talk. I exhaust him."[63] They also missed their colleagues at work. "I take the baby to my workplace every week," explained a mother on GYES. "They like to see him develop, and I like the company. Some days I stay all day."[64] A few mothers admitted that their loneliness led them to become overprotective. For instance, while talking to a state psychologist in 1977, a mother on leave from her job as a public-transit worker had an epiphany: she realized that she "regulated" her young children to replace the "sense of control" she once had at work.[65]

Given the prevailing discourse of the maternal, counselors rarely encouraged these mothers to end their isolation by returning to work. Instead, most mothers received advice about how to deal with their "neuroses." Women who resided in workers' hostels were advised to seek out activities arranged by the hostel child-care center.[66] Women who lived in large housing complexes were referred to local cultural centers (*művelődési házak*). Child Guidance Centers often posted announcements of collective activities in their waiting rooms.[67] As one psychologist explained in an interview, "It was difficult for mothers in a big city like Budapest. When I had my children in my old village, I never felt lonely, and everyone knew everyone. . . .

Some housing estates in the city tried to reproduce this feeling with local shops and centers and gathering places. I always encouraged mothers, especially the new ones, to use these facilities."[68]

Mothers who were working often extracted concrete institutional resources from welfare workers to ease their burdens. Once provided to a wide range of women in the welfare society, these practical resources were extended to a select group of women in this period: those who could demonstrate that such assistance would improve their mothering abilities. For such women, caseworkers helped to secure better child-care arrangements. Women who spent hours transporting their children to and from remote child-care facilities could activate caseworkers to intervene with "higher" authorities in control of district facilities. As an educational counselor wrote in 1971, "The time the mother spends on buses, trams, and metros could be used more productively as quality one-on-one time with Jutka [her daughter]."[69] To help her, the counselor placed Jutka in a district kindergarten. Others had state actors push their kids into coveted after-school programs by arguing that it eased their work loads and made them better mothers.[70] For these clients, the rewards were quite tangible: better child-care and housing arrangements.

For others, this maternal maneuvering resulted in the establishment of on-going support networks. In the early 1970s, both of the Child Guidance Centers I studied held support groups for women. Initially, these groups targeted new mothers and single parents. With time, they expanded to include all mothers. Center psychologists held meetings two to four times a month. Attendance appeared to be good; these groups attracted twenty to thirty mothers. Although psychologists did not keep records of group discussions, their institutional summaries listed the topics they covered. They included discussions about entertaining children, grappling with depression, dealing with sibling rivalry, and maintaining orderly flats. As one counselor recalled in an interview, "In 1974 I ran the new mothers' group. The women had much energy and many dilemmas. They taught each other from their experiences."[71] Another counselor recounted the evolution of one of her groups: "The new-mother group became the toddler group. The toddler group became the kindergartners' mothers' group. This made my work much easier."[72]

Quite likely these groups made women's lives easier too by enabling mothers to connect with women who had similar problems. Many of these women seemed to have nowhere else to turn; therapists for adults were almost nonexistent, and state mental-health facilities were extremely punitive. By voicing common concerns and arriving at workable solutions, these mothers formed social bonds. In this way, female clients excavated yet another resource once available in the welfare society—a sense of social integration and connection. Although their excavation work had to be done under the rubric of the maternal, it ended up providing them with the maneuverability they needed to defend their personal well-being.

THE RISE OF MATERNAL STIGMA: THE BAD-MOTHER TRACK

For women located on the other side of the good/bad–mother divide, the limitations of the maternalist subsystem were far more apparent. While "good" mothers could strategize to meet a multiplicity of needs, those defined as "bad" mothers were more vulnerable. In the two districts of my research, welfare workers labeled a surprisingly large number of clients as maternally incompetent. Until the mid-1970s, roughly 20 percent of the Gyámhatóság's clientele were deemed "dangerous" parents; 10 percent were thought to be so "incompetent" that their children were institutionalized; and 5 percent were said to be so "irresponsible" that they were denied child-rearing assistance.[73] Thus, "bad" mothers constituted 35 percent of all Gyámhatóság clients. By the early 1980s, the percentage had increased to 45. Child Guidance Centers were only slightly more tolerant. In the 1970s, they identified 23 percent of their clients as requiring serious familial intervention. By the early 1980s, the number had risen to 32 percent.

Clients defined as bad mothers were demographically similar to each other in several respects. First, they were more likely to be employed outside the home. Roughly 80 percent of these clients were in the paid labor force on a full-time basis.[74] Second, these clients tended to be located at the lower and the upper echelons of the labor force. Approximately 60 percent of those defined as bad mothers worked as unskilled laborers or assistants; the remaining 40 percent were split between skilled workers and professionals. Hence, these mothers usually fell into one of two income groups: although the majority of them lived just around the subsistence level, roughly 25 percent had incomes higher than the average. Finally, bad mothers were ethnically diverse and consisted of many Romany women.[75]

This group of clients also had a wide range of needs. Like many good mothers, these women faced a number of work-related problems. Yet, unlike good mothers, who often needed help managing their (temporary) status as full-time mothers, these clients needed assistance with their existing work positions. They tended to work in jobs with limited flexibility: those employed as unskilled laborers had little bargaining power in their workplaces, while those with professional jobs claimed that their careers made it hard to juggle their family demands. Moreover, the former group faced particularly pressing material needs. In contrast to good mothers, whose material difficulties often resulted from stays on GYES, this group of mothers suffered on-going financial constraints. They bore the brunt of the gender-segregated labor market: they suffered most from the era's protective labor policies. Since these women often worked as unskilled laborers or assistants, few had skills to market in the burgeoning second economy; they were located in the 30 percent of the population that was unable to bolster their incomes by participating in "after-hours" work in the nonstate sector.[76] As a result, these women experienced real pauperization; many were located in the 15 percent of the population that had slipped into poverty in the late 1970s.[77]

Accompanying their material needs, women defined as bad mothers had domestic needs as wives. The majority of them were married at the time of their contact with welfare institutions: roughly 70 percent lived with their spouses, 25 percent were divorced or separated, and 5 percent had never married. Like good mothers, these clients also complained about their lack of domestic power. But, unlike good mothers, whose limited domestic power was due to their (temporary) economic dependence, these clients' unequal domestic relations were less economic or less temporary in nature (or both). On the one hand, professional women were not economically marginal in their households. Instead, they had problems managing their dual-career families; they tended to be married to other professionals and found it difficult to convince their spouses to make sacrifices for the family. On the other hand, poor women who were defined as bad mothers experienced more permanent forms of powerlessness. Their economic marginalization meant that they could not survive on their wages alone, and they were therefore highly dependent on a male wage, which often translated into other forms of dependence. Unable to make it on their own, many were forced to remain in relationships they found unfulfilling and dangerous. In welfare offices, these women frequently spoke about feeling trapped—about how they had no choice but to stay with men who abused alcohol or threatened them physically.

Finally, women labeled as bad mothers had needs that were not reducible to their roles as workers or wives. These women spoke often about serious mental-health problems, incapacitating emotional disorders, and alcoholism. It is unclear whether they experienced these problems more or simply lacked the resources to obscure them. Yet a series of studies conducted in the 1970s indicated that such problems seemed more pervasive among these classes of women. For instance, a 1976 study of 1,051 industrial and agricultural workers found that women with lower levels of education reported much higher rates of alcohol consumption.[78] Similarly, a 1977 study of 323 female alcoholics uncovered a higher incidence of alcohol abuse among lower- and working-class women; while 13 percent of the alcoholics surveyed were professionals or skilled workers, 61 percent were semiskilled or unskilled workers.[79] Whether or not these kinds of problems were actually more acute in lower- and working-class communities, they did surface far more often in these women's interactions with welfare workers; such problems were therefore at least more visible, and potentially more pressing, for these mothers.

Despite the severity of their problems, these clients had trouble utilizing state resources. While good mothers maneuvered through the maternalist welfare apparatus, bad mothers were more confined in their movements. Their institutional trajectories were rockier from the onset. They had a harder time passing welfare workers' domesticity tests, and their failure to do so left them more vulnerable to the coercive arm of this welfare apparatus. To protect themselves, some clients developed strategies to redirect the punitive arm of the state onto their husbands. Those who could not gain maternal redemption through paternal condemnation faced state scrutiny on their own. They were then subjected to levels of surveillance and humiliation unparalleled in the welfare society.

Failing the Test

Many clients' difficulties with the maternalist welfare apparatus surfaced in their initial contact with it. These women had trouble delivering the kind of gender performance expected of them. Some of them were simply unaware of what was required. Welfare workers' domestic standards were not entirely obvious; these women did not walk into clients' flats and demand a specific performance. Instead, they sent subtle clues of what they were looking for—clues that many of these women failed to interpret. These misunderstandings were particularly common in the late 1960s and early 1970s, when clients tended to appeal for state aid on the basis of their roles as workers. When caseworkers asked about cooking, these women shifted the conversation to their work lives. Who could think of cooking after long days at work? Who had the energy to clean after they had worked so diligently at the workplace? Rather than engaging in discussions about housekeeping, these clients boasted about their work achievements. As one client explained in the hope of impressing her caseworker in 1969, "I am simply a cleaning woman; I know this. Yesterday the head of the workplace came to me, pulled me aside, and said we have the cleanest place in the enterprise and thanked me especially—a job well done."[80] Imagine the shock women like this experienced when they were scolded for being too preoccupied with work. As a woman wrote to the Gyámhatóság in 1971 after her child visitation was restricted, "I work too much? What does this mean? I do what is required of me, no more than this."[81]

Other clients misread welfare workers' evaluative criteria by appealing for state assistance on the basis of their material deprivation. Such appeals were particularly prevalent among RNS applicants, who, in an attempt to bolster their applications, exposed their severe material problems. Since they were applying for financial aid, they assumed that they had to exhibit deprivation. They showed caseworkers their empty cabinets, remarking that they did not have the money to keep them well stocked. They pointed out how their flats had few amenities and were decorated with old furnishings. And they explained that their children were forced to sleep in the same bed and had few toys to play with. By showing caseworkers how poor they were, these women inadvertently provided welfare workers with the evidence needed to deny them assistance. These clients were shocked when caseworkers rejected their applications because of their "unstable" home lives.

Of course, some clients were aware of the good-mother mold but simply could not fit into it. These women lived so far from welfare workers' ideals that they could not adjust their behavior to put on a good gender performance. For instance, many poor women found themselves unable to fulfill welfare workers' expectations because of their work schedules.[82] With little control over their work hours and little ability to negotiate with their supervisors, they had limited flexibility. To make matters worse, some of them worked the night shift, which made it quite difficult to remain involved in their children's lives. They were at work when their children were at home; they were at home when their children were in school. Quite often, they were also at work when caseworkers came calling. Their domestic competence was therefore tested in their absence, and, as a result, they had little control over state evaluations. They were also more vulnerable to having caseworkers believe their husbands' or neighbors' accounts of their mothering practices—accounts that often emphasized their limits and failures as mothers.

Finally, some female clients could not fit the good-mother mold because of serious social problems. Alcoholism was by far the most common problem constraining these women. As a caseworker wrote about one such client in 1979, "Mrs. Jenő is obviously an alcoholic, and it shows on her face. She admitted to me that she wastes her salary on *pálinka*. This explains the household disarray and the absence of food."[83] Not surprisingly, these women rarely performed well on the Gyámhatóság's domesticity tests. Some were never at home when caseworkers came calling. Others were intoxicated during their performances, slurring words and staggering through tours of their flats. Both types of behavior enraged caseworkers, leading them to deem these women "incompetent" or "irresponsible." In addition, these clients rarely maintained the high level of involvement in their children's lives that counselors required of them. In their interviews, they infuriated counselors by failing to provide "basic" information about their children's school progress, hobbies, or friends. They also angered counselors by refusing to adhere to their child-rearing regimens or to keep their appointments. This behavior prompted state counselors to interpret them as "neglectful" and "disorderly" mothers.

One exceptional case from the Child Guidance Center exemplifies the concrete ways that female clients failed these domesticity tests. Although the case was initiated in 1980, counselors still spoke about it some fifteen years later. Known as the "pig case," it had become a symbol of the maternal pathologies of the period.[84] The case began when young Tamás was referred to the center because of his antisocial behavior at school. State counselors immediately conducted a "world game" in which Tamás exhibited "aggression" and a "fixation with animals." In her interview with his mother, Mária, the counselor became concerned that Tamás's troubles were rooted in his family environment. Because Mária seemed to be drunk and could not keep "one line of thought," the counselor deemed her a potentially "dangerous" mother.

On subsequent visits, the counselor learned that Mária lived in a garden house with her husband, an alcoholic who was in and out of state treatment facilities. When Mária began to miss her meetings and "refused to cooperate," she was defined as a "neglectful" parent. A home visit was then ordered, a visit that sealed the counselor's evaluation. The family caretaker found wine bottles strewn throughout the house and "no food in sight." But the real problem surfaced in Tamás's room. There the caretaker discovered a chicken in the closet and a pig in the bed. As Mária explained that her son loved the pig, Tamás jumped in: "Mommy lets me sleep with it when I'm good. I hug it all night." Appalled, the counselor used the occasion to reflect on the state of Hungarian motherhood: "A pig in the bed. Imagine how our families have decayed. In this disgusting house of complete disorder, there was a sweet little boy. This boy sleeps with dirty farm animals. Imagine."

Maternal Redemption through Paternal Condemnation

After clients like these failed welfare workers' domesticity tests, they were placed on the bad side of the maternal divide. With this positioning, a different set of welfare practices kicked in—practices that were far more punitive than those experienced by good mothers. Welfare workers often refused to assist these clients. Clients embroiled in divorce or custody battles were punished with unfavorable decrees or custody recommendations. Those who sought financial support were denied RNS. And those who wanted general child-rearing support were rejected until they stopped their "inappropriate" behavior. In contrast to good mothers, who came out of domesticity tests with new resources, these clients had fewer institutional possibilities. Under the coercive arm of the welfare state, these clients had little room to maneuver.

Most of these clients were aware that they fell on the bad side of the maternal divide. Punitive welfare practices did not operate in subtle ways; they directly encroached on women's lives. Hence, clients who had other resources immediately broke off contact with the welfare apparatus. Sensing danger, they took their punishment and ran for cover. This was the strategy used by most professional mothers: these women accepted welfare workers' unfavorable custody decrees or educative lectures and never contacted these agencies again. Other clients appeared to be unable or unwilling to break contact with these offices. Instead, they struggled relentlessly to gain some institutional leverage.

Primarily, these mothers tried to gain this leverage by challenging welfare workers' maternal expectations. They attempted to contextualize their mothering practices and to prove that welfare workers' requirements were not realistic. Some submitted letters from their workplaces to inform welfare workers of their schedules and responsibilities.[85] Others had neighbors or relatives visit these agencies to explain the many demands placed on them.[86] Still others sent welfare workers letters from doctors to confirm that they suffered physical or mental illness.[87] For the most part, these strategies failed to work; welfare workers held to their rigid maternal standards. Occasionally, they expressed pity for these clients, commenting that their plights were "unfortunate."[88] But the label remained: they were "incompetent" mothers unable to care for their children properly.

Although bad mothers could not strategize themselves out of compliance with welfare workers' maternal standards, they could gain some institutional leverage if they were willing to shift blame. The most successful strategy available to these women was maternal redemption through paternal condemnation. They convinced welfare workers that while they accepted the good-mother mold, they could not fit into it because of uncooperative husbands. Female clients used several tactics to deflect blame onto men. Many of them argued that their husbands' "laziness" forced them to work harder to support the family. For instance, in 1978 an RNS applicant who had been defined as a "marginal" mother defended herself by asserting that she needed help because her husband refused "to work the hours [necessary] to support us."[89] In a 1979 case, a woman who was accused of being a "workaholic" shifted blame onto her spouse, explaining that she would happily cut back her work hours, but her husband's "laziness" made this impossible.[90] Or, as another woman put it in 1981, "Yes I know the little ones need their own beds. Talk to him about it because he will only work part-time and finds no way to do overtime or increase his wages. We do not have the money to buy anything."[91] These clients claimed that their good maternal intentions could not be actualized because of paternal laziness.

In addition, bad mothers blamed their husbands for creating domestic turmoil, which undermined their maternal abilities. They agreed with welfare workers that their households were far from the ideal, but they attributed the problems to their spouses. For example, in 1974 a woman who applied for financial support left wine bottles lined up in front of her door. After her caseworker tripped over the bottles, the client inundated her with stories of her husband's drinking and how it inhibited her from keeping an "orderly" house.[92] Clients also blamed male violence for the disintegration of their households. One woman continued to initiate home visits for months after her children were institutionalized. On these visits, she provided caseworkers with evidence of domestic violence and suggested that her husband be put under state care instead of the children.[93] In 1979, another woman had her neighbor visit the Gyámhatóság to inform caseworkers how impossible it was for her to maintain a peaceful family life with a "brutal husband."[94] Or take this counselor's 1980 summary of a female client:

> Mrs. Szücs remembers a time when she was normal and her neighbors recall . . . also . . . when they [she and her husband] were young and the children were small and the fights with her husband were not so frequent and brutal. Then she kept the flat orderly and concerned herself with the children. Now, with the daily fights, she disappears into the flat for days and does not even leave to do the shopping. The depression is chronic, perhaps psychopathic, now.[95]

By advancing such arguments about their husbands, many clients could redeem themselves in the eyes of welfare workers. In this way, these clients used their husbands in qualitatively different ways than good mothers did.

While good mothers also drew on their spouses' behavior to gain support, they did so under the guise of maternal competence; they had welfare workers intervene to improve their already commendable mothering practices. Clients defined as bad mothers, however, struggled to redirect the punitive arm of the state away from themselves and onto their spouses. Theirs was a more defensive, even desperate, strategy. This difference had important implications for the institutional resources available to them. Having constituted men as the source of the problem, welfare workers were willing only to help these women control their spouses. Clients could then secure three kinds of weapons: they obtained punitive tools to control men at home; they had welfare workers punish men themselves; and they had their spouses forcibly removed from their homes.

Clients' ability to utilize these weapons depended on welfare workers' evaluations of their problems. These weapons fell along a scale of severity; and welfare workers distributed them according to the presumed depth of clients' problems. Those clients whose families had deteriorated but had not yet decayed were allowed to administer the paternal punishment themselves. Welfare workers provided women with the punitive tools and let them decide how to use them. For instance, caseworkers often gave clients copies of negative home-visit reports. Clients then mobilized these documents when fighting with uncooperative husbands. "Look what the *tanács* has said about us," one woman exclaimed to her husband in 1980 as she handed him a copy of the home-visit report describing them as "irresponsible."[96] RNS applicants who had been denied assistance appropriated their rejections in similar ways: they used them to convince husbands that their abusive behavior had economic consequences. As a caseworker wrote in 1980, "Mrs. Szabó made it clear to Mr. Szabó that they will receive no aid until his drinking stops. He knows he must stop."[97] Clients also used welfare workers' threats of institutionalization as domestic ammunition. In 1969, one woman asked that her son be temporarily institutionalized so she could prove to her husband that his abusive behavior had consequences.[98] By appropriating the punitive arm of the state for their own ends, these women regulated and exerted control over their husbands.

Other clients had less flexibility in deciding how to deal with problematic husbands. Welfare workers believed that these women's problems were too severe for them to resolve on their own. Instead of allowing clients to determine the kind of intervention that these men needed, welfare workers guided the control. Generally, these women had called on welfare workers to address extreme male violence. In 1970, a woman pleaded for help in ending her husband's "destructive" and "brutal" life-style.[99] In 1977, another woman begged a state counselor to stop her husband from disappearing for days at a time.[100] Once called on, state actors set their own agendas. Gyámhatóság caseworkers frequently used the police and the courts to scare these men. They warned "lazy" men that they could be labeled "publicly dangerous work avoiders" and imprisoned; they arrived at the homes of abusive men with policemen or lawyers.[101] Counselors also used the threat of hospitalization to frighten men, referring abusive men to mental-health institutes for "exploratory exams."[102] Occasionally, they recommended that these men do short stays in Ministry of Health facilities to force them to change.[103]

When welfare workers' threats failed to alter male behavior, they forcibly removed men from their households. By the time a case reached this stage, it had moved outside of the woman's control. Hence, it is impossible to tell whether women approved of these removals. Their consent was more or less irrelevant: welfare workers had decided that familial well-being could not be secured if the men remained in the household, so they had them taken away. In alcohol-abuse cases, for example, welfare workers deemed men with alcohol problems "public disturbances" and reported them to the police. In 1978 a caseworker had one such man imprisoned for over a year.[104] In 1981, another man was jailed for six months.[105] Counselors advised ministry officials of men in need of treatment for alcoholism. Although welfare workers never brought these men in for counseling, they "redeemed" the mothers by condemning the fathers.

Yet the strategy of maternal redemption through paternal condemnation also obscured a number of critical issues. It effectively enabled welfare workers to avoid other problems confronting female clients. Although clients could carve out punitive tools to control their husbands, they could not obtain resources to address other needs. They received no help with their work lives; they were unable to secure assistance with their own alcohol problems; they did not get support to deal with their own mental illness; and they obtained little help in healing the wounds of years of male violence. Unlike good mothers, who expanded the confines of the maternal to expose their feelings of exhaustion and depression, bad mothers had no such maneuverability. The most they received were institutional weapons to use against their husbands. Otherwise, they were left to their own devices to grapple with the problems confronting them in everyday life.

The Unredeemable and the Punishable

Although maternal redemption through paternal condemnation was a confining strategy, it did afford clients some maneuverability. For those bad mothers who were unable or unwilling to deflect blame, life was even more difficult. Many of these clients were incapable of shifting blame: they lived alone or could not convince welfare workers to attribute their family problems to their spouses. Others seemed unwilling to use this strategy of deflection; even though they lived with abusive men, they refrained from drawing these men into their dealings with welfare workers. Left unshielded, these clients were subjected to extreme humiliation and degradation.

This humiliation took several forms. In their meetings with welfare workers, women withstood an onslaught of attacks on their maternal worthiness. These interactions had an almost voyeuristic quality to them, with welfare workers encouraging women to give concrete accounts of their lifestyles. They lured clients into revealing details of their failings as mothers. On home visits, welfare workers continued to probe until these women divulged everything from the intricacies of domestic abuse to their drinking patterns to their sexual practices. Once they had their evidence, the barrage of assaults began. Caseworkers labeled these women "disgraceful," discursively marking them as "other." Welfare workers never held back: "When I come to your house, I feel sick," a caseworker informed one mother in 1976.[106] From case files, it is difficult to tell how women reacted to this humiliation. Given the depth of their "othering," it is likely that many reacted as this woman did in a 1971 letter:

> Comrade, I could say nothing when you came calling and I welcomed you into my flat. I did not expect you to come, but I offered all you asked of me. I hid nothing, and I realize that my family is not ideal. With respect, I must say that the language you used was unnecessary. Please, I do not want to offend, but this was not how I imagined our authorities to speak. I have been crying since I heard these words from you, a responsible figure.[107]

Quite often, the humiliation experienced by these women devolved into public displays of degradation. Once they had elicited all their damning stories, welfare workers shared this information with clients' neighbors. In their interviews with neighbors, caseworkers frequently retold stories of clients' domestic turmoil. They notified neighbors about these women's domestic incompetence—how they never cooked, bathed their children, or cleaned their flats. They recounted these women's drinking patterns. And they provided windows into their marital relations. "The neighbor thought he heard the couple fighting," a caseworker wrote in 1976. "I told him he was correct and that the husband puts the wife in a closet where she screams until he lets her out. He was appalled."[108] Clients often resisted these public displays and frequently asked welfare workers not to involve "outsiders" in their family problems. They complained that their neighbors treated them with disrespect after learning about their problems. But their requests were rarely granted. The public marking was part of their punishment; the collective othering was retribution for their maternal incompetence.

The punishment inflicted on these clients not only included verbal assaults but also had practical effects. Bad mothers' applications for child-rearing assistance were consistently rejected, as were their requests for help tracking down deadbeat dads. They rarely received favorable decisions in divorce and child-custody disputes; they were more likely to leave marriages with few material resources and less likely to have full custody of their children. Such treatment was couched as a punishment for their "problematic" mothering. As one caseworker put it in an interview, "Some clients were stupid. They refused to care for their children, [and] their flats were in disarray, but they demanded exclusive custody of the children. They asked for contracts that gave them all of the contact with the kids. They were so surprised when I told them what I thought and gave *them* very little contact with the children. Well, they deserved it."[109]

Other women were punished through bodily interventions. It was not uncommon for welfare workers to send these women for medical and psychiatric exams. The goal was to uncover whether they had biological or neurological disturbances that explained their "abnormal" behavior. For instance, in 1979 one woman underwent four neurological exams in an attempt to trace her "neuroses to chemical or hormonal inconsistencies in her organism."[110] These tests frequently led to the distribution of medications to alter their behavior.[111] Clients who showed no sign of improvement after drug therapy were hospitalized. Overall, I uncovered six cases of hospitalization from the period. Forcibly removed from their households, these women were placed in psychiatric institutes and Ministry of Health facilities. They were all defined as "dangerous" to their families and "uncooperative" with welfare workers. As a caseworker wrote about one such woman in 1978, "Because of her drastic behavior and bad mental condition, it is our professional opinion that she be taken away from her family and hospitalized. "What was her drastic behavior? The client had enraged caseworkers by refusing to cook or clean for her family and by escaping from her house nightly, during which time she "wandered" around the city alone.[112]

Although these intrusions into clients' bodies were extremely invasive, the ultimate punishment inflicted on them was the institutionalization of their children. The number of mothers who received this punishment was not insignificant; by the mid-1980s roughly 20 percent of Gyámhatóság cases I studied involved institutionalization.[113] Officially, all institutional-

ization cases were to be temporary. In practice, mothers had extreme diffi-
culty getting their children released. In contrast to the situation in early
socialism, when caseworkers used state facilities to give women the time to
establish better living conditions, welfare workers in this regime used institutionalization as a punishment. They inflicted it on women who had been
marked and dehumanized through extreme levels of surveillance. Because
these women received little help, it was nearly impossible to disrupt the
negative constructions of them and to have their children returned.

Roughly 21 percent of the institutionalization cases in my sample ended
with the children released from state care. These cases involved exception-
ally resourceful mothers who struggled to resolve their problems on their
own. Some left Budapest to return to their villages, where they had more
social support. This was the route taken in 1971 by a woman whose children
were put under state care because of her extreme depression.[114] It was also
the solution used in 1979 by a woman whose son was institutionalized
because of her alcohol abuse.[115] Other clients left abusive spouses to marry
more "responsible" men. In 1978, a woman deserted her violent husband for
a "calm" and "quiet" man almost twice her age.[116] Another woman, after
years of dealing with her husband's alcoholism, deserted him in 1981 for a
colleague's brother and a "beautiful life."[117]

Yet these clients were anomalies. Far more common were those who spi-
raled into decline after their children were institutionalized. Devastated by
the removal of their children, they experienced the worsening of their problems. Depressed clients isolated themselves and exhibited self-destructive
behavior. "She said she rarely leaves the flat now," a caseworker wrote about
one such woman in 1971. "When she goes into public and sees children she
cries."[118] Women with alcohol problems drank more, often losing their jobs
or getting into trouble with the police. For instance, after her children were
institutionalized in 1973, one woman was arrested twice for drunken public
disturbances.[119] Another moved from workplace to workplace when her son
was taken away in 1980, eventually landing in jail for stealing alcohol.[120]
Women who lived with violent men became more vulnerable to male
attacks without the shield of their children. Instead of stopping these downward spirals, caseworkers saw them as evidence of these women's incompetence. They used such problems to support continued institutionalization.

Some of clients' downward spirals ended in tragedy. Mrs. Boza was one
such client, and her case highlights the underside of the maternalism of the
period.[121] The case began in 1972, when Mrs. Boza came to the Gyámhatóság to apply for a new flat; she lived with her husband and two children
in a one-room flat. On a home visit to assess her application, her caseworker

detected problems. She agreed that the flat was too small but faulted Mrs. Boza for doing "nothing" to improve it. The children slept in one bed in the same room as their parents, which the caseworker deemed "unacceptable." Yet the real problem was the evidence of alcohol abuse. "There was no food in the house," the caseworker wrote. "Empty bottles littered the flat. The money goes for alcohol." She then interviewed a neighbor who told stories of Mrs. Boza's incompetence—how she worked part-time so she could maintain her drinking, how the children were not fed properly, and how she used the language of a "prostitute." This interview prompted a series of home visits in which caseworkers probed further into Mrs. Boza's domestic practices and discovered more signs of alcohol abuse. After one visit, a case-worker cornered a neighbor who described Mrs. Boza as "out of control." In a telling comment, the caseworker wrote, "Mr. Boza comes home each night and beats his wife. Even this does not help because he leaves the next day and she begins again."

With this report, the Boza case shifted from a simple housing complaint to a case of maternal neglect. Mrs. Boza received a letter stating that the Gyámhatóság had decided to institutionalize her children. She resisted the decision, but her husband was quoted as saying it was a "good decision" because his wife was not a "proper mother." Two months after the initial home visit, the Boza children were placed in an institution for neglected children. Mrs. Boza then became extremely depressed and refused to leave her flat. On a follow-up visit, the caseworker discovered that three of Mr. Boza's male relatives had moved into the flat and slept in the same room as the couple. She reprimanded Mrs. Boza: "How could she let this happen? Her home is now completely unfit for children." Over the next year, Mrs. Boza took leave from her job. According to neighbors, she did so because of her drinking. At the end of 1973, Mrs. Boza was arrested for sleeping intox-icated in a park. Her children were then moved to a remote children's home, and she was informed there was "no chance" her case would come to an end in the near future. In early 1974, the Boza case did in fact end. One morn-ing, while the men were at work, Mrs. Boza entered the kitchen, shut the door, turned on the gas stove, and inhaled. She was dead by the time the men returned from work in the evening.

STATE REDEPLOYMENT AND THE CONTRADICTIONS OF HUNGARIAN MATERNALISM

From the perspective of women like Mrs. Boza, it is difficult to sustain the prevailing narrative about the "retreat" of the late socialist state. Instead, in this era the boundaries of state intervention were redrawn. Primarily, these boundaries shifted to encircle mothers. After mothers were cordoned off in their own subsystem of welfare, they had more state apparatuses to deal with: they had to adhere to standards set by caseworkers, home visitors, educational counselors, psychologists, and family caretakers. And they had to do so by voicing their appeals in one primary register, the discourse of the maternal. Once accorded numerous rhetorical possibilities for claims-making, female clients were now expected to highlight their identities as mothers. The measurement devices used to survey their mothering practices also multiplied. Women had to demonstrate everything from domestic expertise to time management to communication skills. In addition, clients confronted new classifications for separating the worthy from the unworthy. No longer positioned according to their institutional locations, clients were defined by the good-mother mold. Faced with this classification scheme, clients developed new strategies to defend a wider range of interests.

For those women located on the good side of the maternal divide, the discourse of the maternal proved to be malleable and flexible. They worked it to link their experiences as mothers to those of welfare workers. Once they had demonstrated that they fit the good-mother mold, these clients carved out a series of material resources. By linking the maternal to the paternal, they forced men to become more involved in their families; they curbed their husbands' verbal and physical abusive; and they altered the division of labor in their homes. Also, women defined as good mothers successfully struggled to have welfare workers address their needs as women; they elicited help grappling with their feelings of exhaustion and depression. Although these clients were discursively confined to the maternal, they took advantage of their maternal position. In the end, they experienced the possibilities inherent in this subsystem of welfare.

Clients who fell on the other side of the maternal divide encountered fewer possibilities. Unable to fit the good-mother mold, these female clients had a difficult time establishing collusive relationships with caseworkers. They were then vulnerable to the coercive arm of the welfare apparatus. Their only way out was to seek maternal redemption through paternal condemnation. Clients who were able to deflect blame then had access to the institutional tools to control men at home or to punish men via welfare workers. But clients who were unable to deflect blame were left without even these resources. Marked and "othered," these women were subjected to degrading welfare practices. They experienced public displays of humiliation; they withstood interventions into their minds and bodies; and they had their children taken away. The most resourceless and troubled, these clients received little assistance grappling with their problems. If anything, their troubles worsened as their room to maneuver contracted.

These gender strategies illuminate both the possibilities and the limitations of Hungarian maternalism. They also underscore the tension between the interpretive and the re/distributive underpinnings of this welfare regime. This tension was of a qualitatively different sort than the one that plagued the welfare society: here the re/distributive expanded, while the interpretive narrowed. This regime solidified new maternal guarantees, but it also feminized the welfare sphere. This apparatus provided women with a sense of entitlement, but it also gave rise to evaluative distinctions among mothers. This subsystem offered some women the tools to form collusive relationships with state actors, but it subjected others to new forms of punishment. Thus, as this welfare regime became specialized and introduced new modes of scrutiny, client maneuverability contracted. Within the maternalist apparatus, it became harder for all women to negotiate their different demands and desires. And it became nearly impossible for some women to utilize the welfare apparatus to resolve their everyday problems.

This contraction in client maneuverability not only was significant for what it revealed about past welfare practices but was also a sign of what was to come when the welfare system was reformed yet again at the end of the state-socialist period. Once instituted, the surveillance techniques began to encroach on larger groups of clients. They extended beyond those defined as bad mothers to reach a wider range of women. The social distance separating clients and welfare workers expanded further, and the punitive institutional practices encompassed more of the client population. The limited resources that some clients appropriated under the guise of the maternal then began to evaporate. As a result, female clients soon found themselves defending their identities as mothers in an attempt to salvage the repertoire of maternalist strategies.

Part 3

THE LIBERAL WELFARE STATE, 1985–1996

The Dynamics of Change: Professionalization and Globalization

According to prevailing mythology, 1989 marked a major turning point in Hungarian welfare development. That year is thought to be the grand historical marker, the moment when the processes of democratization and marketization restructured the system of re/distribution. On the one hand, democratization is said to have opened up the state to new political contests over what the population needed and to new forms of citizen involvement in satisfying those needs.[1] On the other hand, marketization is thought to underlie welfare restructuring. According to this logic, once the government became committed to a market economy, it began to see the causal links among high welfare expenditures, soft budget constraints, and economic collapse.[2] And once Hungary entered the world economy, the government was forced to recognize the deleterious effects of expansive entitlement systems and to scale back its welfare expenditures.[3]

While democratization and marketization certainly placed new pressures on the state, it is historically inaccurate to reduce welfare reform to a consequence of these processes alone. The privileging of 1989 has obscured the complex reform dynamics initiated under state socialism—dynamics that propelled new groups into policy formulation and prompted a reconceptualization of need. In the mid-1980s, key assumptions about which sectors of the population were most in need changed. Until this point, the Hungarian welfare regime recognized the needs of specific social groups and erected a subsystem of welfare to provide women special benefits as mothers. With time, the maternalist welfare discourse was dislodged by a new language of welfare. This new needs talk emphasized the problems confronting the poor. It also gave rise to new practices—concrete ways to reconfigure assistance

so it would reach the materially needy. And this needs discourse was articulated by groups of professionals who made inroads into the state prior to
the "system change" of 1989.

Hungarian sociologists were the first to pose a challenge to the late state-
socialist welfare regime. In many ways, their role in these reforms was similar to the role played by psychologists two decades earlier. Like psychologists, Hungarian sociologists had a rocky route back into the academy.
Through the 1960s, sociologists remained marginal to the academy, and
numerous constraints were placed on their scholarship. Research on social
problems and class structure was clearly off-limits. Many sociologists who
pushed these limits had their work destroyed and opted to publish "underground." Others were banished from the academy or left the country altogether. A few sociologists were able to address these topics within official
boundaries by conducting social surveys of income distribution, work patterns, family composition, and child-rearing practices.[4] These studies were
quite descriptive in nature; they rarely extended beyond survey data to analyze what their findings revealed about social life under state socialism.

In the late 1970s, some sociologists began to carve out the space to conduct analyses of social problems and class divisions. Many did so through
stratification studies that documented the social implications of the second
economy and limited market mechanisms.[5] These sociologists found a dual
system of stratification developing in Hungary. At the top were new entre-
preneurial classes with access to second-economy goods, services, and
incomes; at the bottom were those without the skills or resources to secure
second-economy incomes.[6] Sociologists revealed that those without skills or
resources, who constituted over 30 percent of the population, experienced
pauperization in the late 1970s. They also discovered new inequalities surfacing among Hungarian families. They found that female-headed households and urban families had begun to slip into poverty in the early 1980s.[7]
All these findings sensitized sociologists to the plight of the materially
deprived and prompted them to search for palliative measures.

Other sociologists came to similar conclusions through their research on
working-class and Romany communities. For instance, in the 1970s sociologist István Kemény conducted studies of poverty among the Hungarian
Roma. Working with a number of young sociologists, Kemény set out to
uncover the living conditions and life circumstances of the Romany population. Through interviews, these sociologists encountered the extreme
poverty plaguing Romany communities. They found families living without
access to the most basic necessities, such as food and shelter. The research
papers resulting from the study provided the first concrete analyses of

socialist deprivation.[8] They indicted the welfare apparatus for allowing the "neediest" to fall through cracks in the system, with their social problems unresolved. To fill the cracks, some of these researchers created a poor-relief organization, SZETA (Szegényeket Támogató Alap). Primarily, SZETA conducted charity work—distributing money, food, and clothing to the needy.[9] Yet SZETA also acted as a pressure group that lobbied local governments.[10] While the bulk of its lobbying efforts were on behalf of individual clients, they also exerted pressure on local-government officials to create new policies designed to protect the impoverished more broadly.

While SZETA pressured local officials, other sociologists set their sights on revamping the policy sphere—often with the support of the party/state. In the 1980s, sociologists were increasingly permitted to hold conferences and to publish research on poverty and material deprivation.[11] Many of them even received financial backing from government ministries and research institutes.[12] For instance, in the early 1980s, a group of researchers from the Institute of Sociology was commissioned to study the existing welfare system and to recommend areas for reform.[13] Headed by Hungary's most prominent welfare scholar, Zsuzsa Ferge, the Social Policy Research Group prepared a series of reports that documented cracks in the existing welfare system and outlined proposals for reform.[14] First, they called for more centralized control over re/distribution through the creation of a new Ministry of Welfare. Second, they proposed major increases in expenditures, including the expansion of universal entitlements and the creation of new income-maintenance programs. Because these researchers were themselves influenced by SZETA, they also criticized existing welfare institutions for their "preoccupation with mental hygiene."[15] They then pushed for the introduction of poor-relief agencies to treat poverty directly. As Hungarian sociologist Géza Gosztonyi phrased it, at this time "science and power" came together and paved the way for the reform of the welfare system.[16]

Gosztonyi's formulation underscores the dual motivations behind sociologists' appeals. On the one hand, their work was clearly oppositional; it was an attempt to use social-democratic politics to critique actually existing state socialism. Most of these social scientists were firmly embedded in the emergent democratic opposition, which at that juncture was still committed to social justice. As they studied poverty, these sociologists raised issues that remained outside officially accepted discourse and sought to protect vulnerable social groups. In doing so, they did not strive to introduce a liberal welfare state based exclusively on poor relief. Instead, they mobilized West European and Scandinavian welfare models to imagine a system that coupled comprehensive entitlements with poor relief. In many respects, they raised these issues at great personal risk, unsure whether they would be silenced or reprimanded by the authorities.

On the other hand, these sociologists' political commitments should not deflect from a recognition of the professional interests they had in these reforms. By proclaiming themselves as the "knowers," sociologists became those with the expertise to formulate the policies of a discretionary welfare system. By claiming the role of the "expert," they carved out influential positions for themselves as analysts and policymakers. Hence, although sociologists were clearly concerned about the fate of the impoverished, their reform maneuvers were also propelled by their own professional interests.

As sociologists formulated their proposals for revamping the welfare system, another group of professionals was busy developing their own reform agenda. As in the late 1960s, when psychologists and economists converged to push for welfare reform, sociologists shared the 1980s' reform stage with liberal economists. Like their predecessors, these economists made a direct link between economic and social policy. Yet while their predecessors used maternalist policies to alleviate economic problems, this new generation of economists viewed such policies as economically debilitating. In part, this shift was due to their particular views of economic reform. In the earlier period, reform economists imagined a mixed system that combined market mechanisms with centralized planning. By the 1980s, such economists started to equate economic democracy with full-scale marketization.[17] They had come to view market relations as "nonhierarchical"; thus, they maintained that marketization would breed economic equality and justice.[18] They had also come to believe that dynamic economies were based on the "clashing of economic interests" outside the state sphere; thus, they were convinced that centralized planning had to be abolished fully.[19] In effect, their reform agenda began to center on freeing up market relations and forcing the state to pull back from the economy.[20] Their agenda proved to be quite influential: many reformers constructed their arguments while working in government institutes, often with the explicit support of sectors of the party/state.[21]

Reform economists also formed their ideas about the emancipative role of the market while participating in the democratic opposition.[22] Like sociologists, economists were quite active in the opposition; they wrote in samizdat publications and attended "underground" seminars and lectures. Through such exchanges, these groups were exposed to one another's reform agendas. In fact, sociologists and economists frequently worked together in the period. For instance, the 1986 social-policy-reform study, *Turnabout and Reform*, included work by economists that linked democratization to marketization and foreign investment.[23] In some respects, economists' and sociologists' reform agendas were consistent: both saw the need for redistributive shifts and the targeting of state assistance.[24] Yet, in other respects, their agendas differed: while sociologists remained committed to social entitlements and guarantees, economists expressed antipathy to such state intervention. In effect, economists' commitment to marketization led them to view the "needs" of the economy as antithetical to an expansive welfare system.[25] For them, successful market reform became contingent on reducing state expenditures and narrowing eligibility criteria.[26] Their formula was clear: having a redistributive system based on a "principle of need" was the best way to harden soft budget constraints and to increase economic efficiency and growth.[27]

Hence, by the mid-1980s, these two homegrown reform discourses had begun to take root. Given their different views on the fate of social entitlements and protections, they were engaged in something of a discursive struggle to define the precise terms of reform.[28] The stakes heightened in the late 1980s, when another welfare discourse seeped into Hungary through its increasingly porous borders—the discourse of need articulated by the International Monetary Fund (IMF) and the World Bank.[29] In this respect, Hungary was in a unique position in the region. Hungary joined the IMF earlier than any other East/Central European country: it joined in 1982, while Poland did not join until 1986 and Czechoslovakia until 1990. Thus, international agencies exerted more control earlier on in Hungary. Their influence on the direction of the Hungarian economy is well documented: immediately after Hungary joined the IMF, prices were liberalized and new reform plans were unveiled.[30] In the subsequent decade, international agencies stepped up their policing of the Hungarian economy in an attempt to guide it toward liberal capitalism. And these agencies also wielded control over the shape of the welfare-reform debate. Armed with neoliberal theory and Western mythologies about how welfare states "should" operate, representatives from the IMF and World Bank issued numerous social-policy reports urging Hungarians to develop restrictive eligibility criteria. These reports unleashed a series of all-too-familiar arguments: they claimed healthy economies could not work with "encompassing" entitlement criteria; they spoke incessantly about the debt to provoke fears of economic decay; and they proposed that welfare would become more "humane" through poverty programs and means tests.

To bolster their claims, these international agencies began to appropriate the work of local social scientists. Because of the IMF's unflagging commitment to structural adjustment programs, it was not reliant on local research;

when it did use this work, it drew on economists' ideas to bolster its "liberal internationalist" policies.[31] Representatives from the World Bank proved to be more responsive to the work of Hungarian social scientists. But even theirs was a selective appropriation: they ignored sociologists' commitment to social entitlements, while grasping onto their ideas about poor relief. These agencies drew on sociological analyses of the bureaucratic privilege embedded in the socialist system to call for a targeted welfare system. Without clear income tests, they argued, the welfare system would continue to operate according to informal bargaining, which disadvantaged the poor.[32] These agencies also pointed to studies that suggested universal eligibility criteria were advantageous to wealthy Hungarians, who could afford to pay "market price" for subsidized goods and services.[33] In this way, these agencies cleverly presented their proposals as "welfare with a human face." By replacing expansive entitlement criteria with more restrictive ones, they argued, the truly "needy" would receive a larger piece of a smaller pie.[34]

While international agencies mobilized Hungarian poverty research to plant their welfare agendas in local soil, the reverse was also true: Hungarian social scientists mobilized international poverty discourses in their own political struggles. Initially, they used global agencies quite strategically. For instance, immediately after Hungary entered the IMF in 1982, numerous opposition leaders secured permission to travel abroad—at least in part because the government feared reprisals from international agencies.[35] Similarly, Hungarian sociologists and economists frequently appropriated these agencies' poverty discourse to bolster their critique of state socialism and to argue for a discretionary subsystem of poor relief.

As time went on, this global poverty discourse began to penetrate Hungarian expert systems and to shape their reform agendas. There was a material basis to its discursive power: these international agencies extended coveted financial resources to support local research and teaching. Many of Hungary's most prominent welfare experts joined these agencies' payrolls. For example, the Hungarian Institute of Sociology conducted several policy studies for these agencies—studies that indicted universal welfare programs for failing to halt social displacement and deprivation at the local level.[36] The Social Research Institute provided regular installments of quantitative data on welfare expenditures—data that charted how Hungarian expenditures were on the increase and how inconsistent they were with Hungary's level of development.[37] International agencies also recruited individual social scientists to conduct studies of social assistance, urban poverty, and redistributive trends.[38] All these projects produced findings that echoed the policy orientations of their funders: they concluded that welfare universalism was ineffective in addressing material deprivation and lacked solidarity with the poor and needy.

In the post-1989 period, international agencies began to subsidize new research and educational institutions. For this effort, a wider array of agencies entered the picture, including UNICEF, the European Union, the Organization for Economic Cooperation and Development, and the International Labor Organization.[39] In 1989, Hungary's first school of social work opened in Szekszárd, and the first degree-granting Department of Social Policy and Social Work was founded at Eötvös Loránd University in Budapest. This department relied so heavily on international support that the department chair held the title "European Union Chair of Social Policy." Over a dozen other schools of social work then sprouted up; their curricula included required courses on poverty regulation. To further inundate local expert systems, international agencies funded conferences and meetings on welfare reform, which they often called "technical-assistance programs." These meetings were organized in similar ways: Western experts gave opening speeches on the theory and practice of the targeted welfare state; workshops in which Hungarians learned to administer such programs followed. The information transmitted in these meetings always flowed in one direction, from Westerners to Hungarians. The goal was clear: to teach Hungarians the tools of the welfare-state trade and to bring them in line with Western modes of welfare capitalism.

As Hungarian social scientists conducted these research projects, taught in these educational institutions, and attended these conferences, their commitment to universal entitlements waned. When they first attacked the socialist welfare system, they did so with a genuine commitment to social guarantees and a concern for the impoverished. With this social-democratic critique, social scientists made inroads into the state. But the state they made inroads into was itself crumbling, which left social scientists feeling "needy" themselves. So when global police arrived in the late 1980s, bearing gifts of financial support, many social scientists accepted their offerings, all strings attached. They had an interest in accepting: it gave them access to resources rapidly evaporating in the Hungarian state and academy. It also enabled them to carve out places for themselves in the welfare apparatus. They had finally evolved into the "experts" they strove to become under state socialism; they had gained the ability to design and administer the programs of a newly materialized welfare state.[40] In the process, they lost their interest in defending universal entitlements. As a result, they ended up planting the seeds for the growth of a liberal welfare state out of the previous materialist welfare apparatus.

5. Materializing Need
The Regulation of Poverty and the Stigmatization of the Poor

Beginning in the late 1980s, social scientists, economists, and representatives of the IMF and World Bank engaged in a series of discursive exchanges over the direction of Hungarian welfare development. These exchanges had concrete institutional effects on the welfare apparatus. Out of policy studies came new proposals for the introduction of means-tested programs. Out of schools of social work came new cadres of welfare workers trained to regulate poverty. And out of international conferences came new casework models. Once organized around a series of maternal entitlements, the welfare apparatus was reconfigured to target and treat the materially deprived.

These structural changes in the welfare state are not unique to Hungary. Nor have they gone unnoticed in the scholarly literature on Eastern Europe. After decades of neglecting the welfare state or reducing it to the economic structure of socialism, area specialists have begun to examine regional welfare patterns. Like accounts of the postsocialist transition more generally, this welfare scholarship is quite descriptive in nature. These scholars have focused on the redistributive shifts currently under way in the region. Using large-scale statistical surveys, many scholars have uncovered strikingly similar redistributive trends in the region. They have revealed how, with the end of full employment, unemployment rates skyrocketed across East/Central Europe.[1] They have unearthed how, as class structures became stratified, income distributions bifurcated.[2] They have discovered how, as price subsidies and socialized services disappeared, poverty rates soared.[3] And they have uncovered how, as welfare universalism and social entitlements became a relic of the past, large sectors of the working class and the Romany population experienced new levels of deprivation.[4] Thus, the redistributive portrait these scholars have painted is quite bleak: across the region, welfare restructuring has wreaked havoc on the material lives of particular social classes and ethnic groups.

In addition, feminist scholars of Eastern Europe have added women to the list of the losers in the welfare-state transition. Feminists have shown that East European women currently have access to fewer state benefits—from child care to maternity leave to food subsidies to child-rearing support—than they did in the past.[5] As the state stopped assuming many of its prior responsibilities, reproduction became privatized; as a result women's work loads increased and their sense of well-being decreased.[6] Feminists have also found that, with the narrowing of social and political guarantees, women have become increasingly marginal to a shrinking state sphere.[7] In effect, feminist scholars have shown that state retrenchment in the region has caused a contraction in women's opportunities for social citizenship.

At the same time as these analysts point to similar outcomes of state restructuring, others have exposed important variations among East European welfare trajectories. These scholars have outlined the organizational make-up of regional welfare regimes; many have borrowed comparative frameworks from Western welfare scholarship, particularly Gøsta Esping-Andersen's model of the "three worlds of welfare capitalism."[8] From this perspective, scholars have found regional examples of all three regime varieties.[9] For example, the Czech Republic bears a close resemblance to a social-democratic regime because of its low unemployment rate, limited use of means tests, and expansion of citizenship-based rights.[10] Examples of corporatist regimes abound in the region; because of their heavy reliance on church, family, or personal networks, the Polish and German welfare regimes are thought to have strong corporatist undercurrents.[11] And one does not have to look far for an example of a liberal welfare regime; with its shrinking entitlement sphere, extensive use of income tests, and heavy reliance on the market, Hungary exemplifies such a regime. Hence, these regime classifications show that although their outcomes may be similar, East European countries differ in the centrality of the state, the family, and the market in their redistributive systems.

Of course, not all scholars are content with simply describing regional patterns of welfare redistribution. Instead of looking to the present to chart the dynamics of transition, they look to the future to prescribe where these transitions should eventually end. Their desired endpoints are clear: the reduction of social expenditures and the overall shrinking of the state sphere.[12] In effect, these scholars prescribe formulas to bring Eastern Europe in line with dominant modes of welfare capitalism. To reduce expenditures, they argue that states must adhere to more restrictive eligibility criteria and a more consistent "principle of need." To protect the economy from soft budget constraints, they claim that states must relinquish their commitment to social entitlements. And to secure a reduction in size, they maintain that states must apply stringent income and means tests to social programs.[13]

Despite their different emphases, both descriptive and prescriptive accounts of welfare restructuring share two crucial limitations. First, as they center on the present or the future, what gets lost is the past—that is, what welfare reform signifies to a population accustomed to a system of social entitlements and protections. Second, both descriptive and prescriptive analyses focus almost exclusively on the scope of the redistributive apparatus. Although this apparatus is important, underlying these quantitative shifts in size were equally profound changes in the social architecture of need. In contemporary Hungary, the boundaries of welfare were redrawn yet again; this time they were reconfigured around particular social classes. As the maternalist subsystem of welfare crumbled, motherhood was dislodged as a central eligibility criterion. With this shift, all needs talk was confined to the material. The bureaucratic regulation of the impoverished became the modus operandi of the welfare system. Once linked to recipients' contributions as mothers or workers (or both), eligibility came to be based on recipients' financial problems. In the process, the welfare system's interpretive focus shifted from familial integration to poverty regulation.

This chapter examines the concrete manifestations of these shifts at the policy and institutional levels. It traces changes in the policy sphere to the mid-1980s, when major reforms reconfigured the eligibility criteria underlying assistance programs. These transformations culminated in the mid-1990s, when the policy apparatus was subjected to income tests. Accompanying these policy shifts were alterations in the nature of welfare work. Now positioned as piece-rate workers armed with surveillance tools, welfare workers have become increasingly distanced from clients. Out of this separation have emerged mythologies about the "new" welfare client—myths that imbue welfare practices with stigmatizing tendencies that have never before characterized the welfare system.

LIBERAL WELFARE POLICIES: TARGETING AND TREATING POVERTY

Before the mid-1980s, neither income nor social class directly influenced access to state support in Hungary. When state distribution moved from the enterprise to the national and local governments in the late 1960s, recipients' family form and maternal abilities largely determined eligibility. At the national level, all families with the same number of children received the same family allowance; all mothers were given the same flat-rate maternity-leave grant. Even local-level child-rearing assistance was distributed without much concern for applicants' material circumstances. These eligibility requirements were made possible by these programs' funding structure: the maternity-leave and family-allowance programs were financed directly from the central state budget, while child-rearing assistance was supported by centralized subsidies given to local governments.[14]

In the mid-1980s, the target, the site, and the financing of state redistribution all changed. First, welfare policy began to target different social classes. Initially, this targeting was achieved with income tests, through which those with low incomes gained access to special benefits. With time, income tests were coupled with means tests that required applicants to reveal the material resources at their disposal. These tests were first applied to local child-rearing assistance (RNS) in the late 1980s. By the early 1990s, they were used in all local income-support programs. And, by the mid-1990s, national-level benefits had been subjected to income tests. As a result, the targets of state assistance shifted to the materially needy.

Second, accompanying changes in the targets of state welfare were alterations in the sites of redistribution. While the maternalist regime vested control in national and local governments, the liberal welfare regime bolstered the role of local governments. From 1983 to 1993, the number of Hungarians who received some form of child-rearing assistance increased by over 1,000 percent.[15] In the mid-1980s, local governments also created a series of new poor-relief programs to provide temporary aid to poor families in transition. By the early 1990s, local governments administered over twenty different poor-relief programs. As these local programs expanded, national programs underwent major cutbacks.

Third, the financial relationship between the national and local governments changed. Whereas the maternalist regime centralized welfare funding, the liberal regime decentralized it. The 1990 Local Government Act and the 1993 Social Act created a new financial division of labor between the national and local governments.[16] These acts established a complex system through which the national government covered some programs and local governments took responsibility for others. For example, funding for unemployment compensation, family allowances, and maternity leave came from the national budget. Yet funding for the more than twenty other poor-relief programs came almost exclusively from local governments, as did the financing for services like child care.[17] The national government exerted little influence over the development of such programs. And it did not offer much financial assistance to support them. It did, however, provide "block grants" to locales. The amount of these transfers was minimal and depended on a variety of factors, including a locale's number of inhabitants, poverty rate, percentage of inactive earners, and tax base.[18]

To justify the localization of welfare funding, policymakers claimed that locales had to have the ability to meet the needs of their specific populations. They argued that since the economic transition would affect locales differently, districts needed the flexibility to decide how to respond to particular forms of dislocation. In reality, the results have been far less sanguine: localization resulted in profound variation in the assistance provided to residents in different districts. Almost ironically, wealthier districts offered more extensive support to their residents, while poorer districts were more strapped financially.[19] Budapest's twenty-one districts differed according to the number of times their residents received support, as well as the amount of that support. In Budapest's District One, which is quite small and relatively well off, residents were allocated three times more social assistance than the Budapest average.[20] Thus, with the decentralization of funding, welfare policies took on a more explicit class character. Recipients' access to state support became dependent on how much money they earned, where they lived, and the median income in their neighborhoods.

In this way, the policy reforms enacted in Hungary were more complex than simple changes in benefit levels. Instead, they signified shifts in the targets of welfare, the site of redistribution, and its financial underpinnings. Eventually, these shifts displaced motherhood as a key eligibility criterion. Yet these changes were not carried out all at once. Rather, they surfaced through a series of protracted reforms that were first initiated in the late state-socialist period.

Late State-Socialist Policy Reform

The first sign of the shift from the maternal to the material occurred in 1985, when maternity-leave grants (GYES) were linked to recipients' income. Since its inception, GYES had consisted of flat-rate payments given to all mothers, regardless of their income. This flat-rate system was disadvantageous to middle-class and professional women, whose salaries were significantly higher than the fixed payments. As a result, these women stayed on the grant for shorter periods of time, which prompted two sets of concerns. First, many sociologists linked use patterns to rising inequalities among families. In their poverty studies, sociologists argued that GYES rates widened the social distance separating middle-, working-, and lower-class families.[21] Flattening out these use patterns, they claimed, could undercut the stratification among families. Second, GYES use patterns also concerned a vociferous group of populist writers. For them, these patterns threatened the well-being of the Hungarian nation by creating a situation in which the country lost "intellectual capital."[22] These writers argued that GYES rewarded "the undeserving and the deserving equally" and thus taught Hungarians that "being lumpen pays."[23]

Partly in response to these concerns, the GYES system was reformed in the hopes of increasing middle-class women's usage. In 1985, GYES was broken into three separate provisions. The maternity-leave grant (Gyermekágyi Segély) ran for six months after childbirth at a rate equivalent to the mother's previous salary. Then mothers were given a choice. They could opt to stay on GYES and receive a flat-rate payment for two and a half more years. Or they could go on the new child-care grant (Gyermekgondozási Díj/GYED), which paid them 75 percent of their previous salary for two years and flat-rate payments for an additional six months. The goal of this new provision was to entice more middle-class women to use the grant, thus flattening out the class differences associated with it.[24] Hence, for the first time since its creation, the maternity-leave system was linked to recipients' income.

Immediately following these changes, more women did begin to use the maternity leave grant. In 1979, 83 percent of those eligible for the grant used it; by 1986, this percentage had risen to 89.[25] Moreover, as Table 10 indicates, the introduction of GYED did end up luring more white-collar workers to take maternity leave. What is more, as Table 11 indicates, the introduction of GYED affected the amount of time that mothers stayed on the grant. In particular, white-collar workers remained on the grant longer after the introduction of GYED. Although GYED did prompt white-collar workers to use the grant for longer periods of time, it did not convince them to have more children. As Table 12 indicates, the birthrate rose only slightly in 1985 and then trailed off to its pre-GYED levels.

While these GYES reforms sought to increase middle-class women's usage, all subsequent policy reforms were designed to exclude the middle class and to target the "needy." The first policy to undergo such reform was RNS. Once distributed on the basis of domestic competence, in the mid-1980s these funds were transformed into poor-relief benefits. It is not entirely clear why this program was targeted first.[26] One possible explanation is that the RNS reforms resulted from the practical work of groups such as SZETA. In its lobbying efforts, SZETA exerted pressure on district-level welfare offices and advocated for the materially deprived, many of whom had been denied RNS assistance. Thus, these activists challenged the discre-

Table 10. Percentage of Mothers Using GYES/GYED by
Occupational Group, 1967–1986

Year	Manual Workers	White-Collar Workers
1967	78	63
1973	83	73
1979	88	79
1986	93	85

SOURCE: KSH, *A Gyermekgondozási Díj Igénybevétele és Hatásai,* p. 8.

Table 11. Length of Time on GYES/GYED by Occupational
Group, 1979 and 1986

Length of Time	Manual Workers, %	White-Collar Workers, %
1979		
Up to 1 Year	15.5	29.5
Up to 2 Years	21.9	28.2
More Than 2 Years	62.6	42.3
1986		
Up to 1 Year	9.0	14.5
Up to 2 Years	18.6	27.1
More Than 2 Years	72.4	58.4

SOURCE: KSH, *A Gyermekgondozási Díj Igénybevétele és Hatásai,*
pp. 14, 53.

tionary nature of welfare distribution and pushed for more clearly defined
eligibility criteria.[27] An alternative explanation is that RNS reforms were
the result of local officials' exposure to the social problems confronting their
residents.[28] Government officials worked in the same building as the
Gyámhatóság; they saw clients' problems on a daily basis. According to
many caseworkers, these experiences prompted officials to create new policies to assist the materially deprived. As the head of a Gyámhatóság
explained in an interview, "The poverty was worse. We all saw it, and the

Table 12. Hungarian Birthrate (per 1,000), 1984–1990

Year	Birthrate
1984	11.8
1985	12.2
1986	12.2
1987	11.9
1988	11.4
1989	11.9
1990	12.1

SOURCE: KSH, *Time Series of Historical Statistics, 1867–1992*, p. 148.

leaders upstairs saw it too. [It was] very visible, even in our waiting rooms, which these officials passed by each day. Everyone knew it was time for something else."[29]

Initially, this "something else" was income tests. In the mid-1980s, applicants for local child-rearing assistance were subjected to income formulas. The timing of the introduction of these tests varied by district. In one of the districts of my research, the tests surfaced in 1984; in the other district, they arose in 1986. These tests profoundly altered the nature of redistribution. All applicants for these funds were required to submit income documentation to be evaluated by a new cadre of eligibility workers. When eligibility workers were suspicious of the documentation, applicants had to submit letters from their employers. Caseworkers then calculated applicants' real income; only those with monthly incomes below the subsistence level were eligible for assistance.

With time, more questions were added to the income tests, and, as a result, they were essentially transformed into means tests. At first, these questions were designed to control for applicants' second-economy work and to weed out applicants whose official incomes were low but who bolstered them with unofficial work. Caseworkers required applicants to submit bank statements and accounts of their savings. Applicants also had to provide lists of valuable household items, including electronics, automobiles, and telephones. Home visitors were deployed to check on applicants' accounting and to calculate the resources at their disposal. Recipients also underwent follow-up investigations up to three times a year to determine whether their disposable income had changed. These rules applied to clients who caseworkers found to be domestically "competent," as well as those

Table 13. Number of Child-Rearing-Assistance Cases,
1987–1995

Year	Regular Assistance	Occasional Assistance
1987	39,081	194,997
1990	80,000	782,000
1993	289,000	2,341,000
1995	384,565	2,080,183

SOURCES: Zsuzsa Ferge, "A Magyar Segélyezési Rendszer Reformja II," p. 33, and KSH, *Népjóléti Statisztikai Évkönyv*, p. 245.

considered "incompetent." Thus, within only a few years, poverty tests had displaced domesticity tests as the key method for distributing local welfare benefits.

As Table 13 shows, the number of clients who received this aid increased following this shift. Although these rates are clearly a reflection of the socioeconomic changes of the period, they are also indicative of just how discretionary the allocation of these funds had been in the previous decade. Once means tests took the place of domesticity tests, caseworkers ended up distributing more assistance.

While these changes in the RNS program were indicative of the regime change under way, the real symbol of this shift was the creation of unemployment benefits. Although full employment had not been realized in practice, it was the pillar of the prior welfare regimes; the welfare society and the maternalist welfare state rested on employment for all. This commitment to full employment was not officially abandoned until 1987, but in the mid-1980s the government enacted a series of policies that effectively undermined it. In 1983, district employment offices were established to assist those without work.[30] These facilities were set up even though the official unemployment rate remained minuscule until the early 1990s, as Table 14 indicates. By 1985, these offices were administering a "retraining benefit" to update the skills of those without work. This program reached a small slice of the population; the year it was introduced, only eight thousand workers received the benefit.[31]

The following year, the first official unemployment benefit was created. The name of the program was as convoluted as its eligibility requirements: The "Extended Waiting Period before Terminating Employment" program

Table 14. Unemployment Rate, 1990–1996

Year	Percentage Unemployed
1990	0.8
1991	4.1
1992	11.0
1993	13.4
1994	12.0
1995	11.1
1996	10.5

SOURCES: World Bank, *Magyarország*, p. 11, and KSH, *Magyarország*, p. 8.

covered groups of at least ten workers made "redundant" simultaneously. The program provided six months of support at full pay and an additional six months at a means-tested rate. Not surprisingly, the program reached few workers: during its first year, only 332 workers received this assistance.[32] In 1987, a program of "jobs for public utility" was founded for those who were unemployed through "no fault of their own." Just as this new scheme got off the ground, another unemployment benefit was introduced. Like its predecessors, this benefit was highly restrictive; it excluded first-time job seekers and those who had been unemployed for over a year. So although employment offices registered eighteen thousand unemployed workers in 1989, less than one-fifth of them received unemployment compensation.[33]

These small, incremental changes chipped away at the principle of full employment. With the Employment Act of 1991, this principle was abolished entirely. This legislation embodied the key elements of the welfare regime emerging in Hungary. First, the benefit was not a universal entitlement; instead it targeted the "truly needy." Second, it was extended only to those who had paid into the system by working for at least one year prior to their termination. The length of time that workers could remain on the grant varied from 180 days to two years, depending on their work history. Third, benefit levels were income tested and linked to claimants' prior wages. They also varied by educational level. First-time job seekers with at least a secondary education were granted 75 percent of the minimum wage, while those without high school degrees were given 15 percent.[34] Fourth, benefit levels were quite stingy; they failed to put recipients above the subsistence level. Finally, in order to receive this benefit, claimants had to seek employment. Employment officers checked up on recipients' diligence and withdrew support from the "undeserving" or "uncooperative."

After its introduction in 1991, unemployment compensation underwent numerous revisions. In 1992, the government imposed an eighteen-month time limit on benefits: for the first twelve months, recipients got 70 percent of their previous wages, while for the remaining six months, they received only 50 percent of their wages. In 1993, these rules changed yet again: time limits were shortened to twelve months, and recipients were given 75 percent of their previous wages for only four months.[35] Then, in 1994, the national government mandated that local governments introduce assistance programs to cover the "long-term" unemployed. The resulting policy supported recipients for an additional six months as long as they agreed to engage in forty hours of collective work every week.[36] Although all these programmatic shifts altered the size of the program, they did not revise the basic principles underlying the 1991 legislation.

In this way, unemployment legislation was a symbol of the demise of an old and the rise of a new conception of need. It marked an end to the most basic social need acknowledged under state socialism—the need for stable, secure employment. By abolishing the state's long-standing guarantee of a job, this legislation dismantled the main pillar of the Hungarian entitlement system. The program also signified a new mode of welfare allocation: by distributing benefits according to income and educational level, it codified new eligibility criteria. It also solidified new surveillance techniques to separate the worthy from the unworthy. Although this discretionary welfare model arose in late socialism, with time it encroached on what remained of the maternalist policy apparatus.

The Bokros Plan and Beyond

After the storm of welfare reform in the late 1980s, there was calm. Or, more precisely, there was calm at the national level. At the local level, the storm of reform had only begun. Beginning in the early 1990s, local governments created a plethora of new supplementary assistance programs. These programs varied by district: some locales offered a wide range of programs, while others provided few. Yet most districts offered their residents some version of "transitional aid" (Átmeneti Segély) for families undergoing serious economic changes; "flat-upkeep assistance" (Lakásfenntartási Segély) for those in need of help maintaining their flats; "medical support" (Közgyógyellátási Segély) for those unable to pay for medicine; "nursing grants" (Ápolási Segély) for those who cared for sick or elderly relatives; and "funeral grants" (Temetési Segély) for those unable to pay for the funerals of deceased relatives. By the mid-1990s, over twenty new local-level assistance programs operated to cover several million Hungarians. Although their size and scope varied, these programs shared one important feature: they were all means tested and extended only to the materially deprived.

With the creation of these new policies, the economic base of state social-ism metamorphosed into a local-level subsystem of targeted welfare provi-sions. Full employment was replaced by unemployment compensation; standard-of-living guarantees turned into transitional social assistance; sub-sidized housing was transformed into income-tested flat-maintenance sup-port; and medical subsidies were replaced by means-tested medical assis-tance. As Table 15 indicates, the number of Hungarians who relied on these targeted programs was not insignificant.[37] Of course, the key feature of these new programs is that they extended past social protections only to particular social classes: 100 percent of RNS recipients and 98 percent of transitional-aid recipients lived below the official subsistence level.[38] Hence, by the mid-1990s, a new logic of assistance had permeated the local-level welfare apparatus.

However, this assistance logic had yet to take hold at the national level. Two key remnants of the socialist welfare system—family allowances and maternity-leave grants—made it through the mid-1990s relatively unscathed.[39] To a large extent, this inaction was due to the political orienta-tion of the first postsocialist government. Comprised of a coalition of Christian conservatives and moderate nationalists, the Antall-Boross gov-ernment proclaimed a commitment to "God, Family, and Homeland."[40] Although it is questionable just how devoted the government was to national familism, this ideological commitment did constrain its budgetary agenda. Given its promise to protect the family and the reproduction of eth-nic Hungarians, the government opposed all cuts to existing maternalist programs.[41] In effect, the government's parliamentary majority created a buffer around these programs; it shielded them from attacks by the liberal opposition and by agencies like the IMF and World Bank.

Almost ironically, this buffer crumbled with the Socialist Party's (MSZP) victory in the 1994 parliamentary elections. Eager to revamp its image, the MSZP quickly distanced itself from its state-socialist predecessors and entered into a governing coalition with the liberal Alliance of Free Demo-crats. This political makeover prompted the MSZP to abandon its prior com-mitment to social justice as overly idealistic and outdated. It also led the

Table 15. Number of Recipients of Local Assistance Programs, 1990–1995

Type of Program	1990	1993	1995
Transitional Aid	807,000	1,847,000	2,080,183
Unemployment Compensation	—	1,000,600	220,000
Flat-Upkeep Support	—	54,300	182,121
Medical Assistance	—	273,000	461,909
Funeral Support	3,000	13,400	14,332

SOURCES: István Harcsa, *Szociális Ellátás az Önkormányzatoknál (A Kísérleti Adatgyűjtés Tapasztalata)*, pp. 24–25, 54, 63; Zsuzsa Ferge, "A Magyar Segélyezési Rendszer Reformja II," p. 33; and KSH, *Népjóléti Statisztikai Évkönyv*, pp. 237, 245.

party to embrace the liberal discourse of economic restructuring and to pledge allegiance to the formulas dictated by the IMF and World Bank. The MSZP promised comprehensive, yet cautious, economic reform. It agreed to bring inflation and the budget deficit under control. And it vowed to reduce the state sector. These promises quickly drew the Socialist government into the business of welfare reform. During its first year in office, the MSZP planted the seeds: it held numerous public forums on the fate of the entitlement system and published political manifestos to explain why Hungary's high expenditures were not sustainable. In newspaper and television interviews, government officials argued that Hungary needed a more equitable welfare system that reflected its new class divisions. The application of a consistent "principle of need," they claimed, would allow state support finally to reach the poor and the needy.

Until early 1995, the government considered using the tax system to reform state redistribution. Levying new taxes on the state benefits received by high-income groups would have allowed entitlement programs to remain universal on the surface, but they would have been taxed away for the upper and middle classes. Yet many government officials concluded that this approach did not go far enough. For instance, then Finance Minister Lajos Bokros vociferously argued that a reformed tax system was insufficient to reduce the state sector and called for a comprehensive reform of all entitlements. And on March 14, 1995, the Hungarian government unveiled the "Bokros Plan," a collection of reform proposals designed to dismantle the remaining entitlement programs.[42] It achieved this dismantlement by applying income tests to the family-allowance and maternity-leave systems. In its initial form, the plan set income cut-offs so low that it would have shut out large sectors of the lower and working classes from these programs.[43]

The Bokros Plan sparked a contentious public debate. The political battle lines were quickly drawn. On one side was a coalition of liberal and socialist politicians who applauded the plan as "brave" and "courageous."[44] In parliamentary debates, members of both parties defended the plan by appropriating a discourse of economic need: social expenditures had to be brought down to secure a "healthy" economy, while welfare universalism had to be abolished to ensure economic "growth."[45] As a Socialist MP put it in a parliamentary speech, "The plan is in the economy's interest. Because of this, it is in all of our interest."[46] This was a classic formulation: austerity in the present would breed prosperity in the future.[47] Not only would the plan guarantee economic development, but it would facilitate Hungary's entrance into the European Union. Over and over, politicians claimed that universal entitlements had become globally extinct and that income tests were the international norm. As another MP argued in a parliamentary speech, "The plan is a critical step toward liberalism. We cannot forget this. It moves us closer to integration with the liberal OECD countries and to Europe as a whole."[48]

The political defense of the Bokros Plan was not limited to the floors of Parliament. Socialist and liberal politicians flooded the media with arguments to justify the plan. Here, too, they appealed to the "needs" of the economy and European integration. Yet a new justification surfaced in these public appeals: politicians advanced class arguments about the redistributive fairness of welfare targeting. The day the plan was announced, Prime Minister Gyula Horn appeared on television to point out that new social divisions had surfaced in Hungary—divisions that, he reasoned, necessitated new policies aimed at those in need. Suddenly, politicians uncovered a plethora of wealthy women whom they accused of abusing the existing welfare system. In interviews, government officials drew on such mythical figures to drum up support for their reform package. In a newspaper interview, female MP Andrea Szolnoki's remarks exemplified this strategy: "Two well-paid doctors do not deserve a family allowance. In their budget it is a drop in the ocean. But poor parents should receive more support. This differentiation is necessary."[49]

Overall, public protest over the plan was limited, despite the fact that a poll taken after the plan's announcement revealed that 63 percent of Hungarians thought these cuts posed a "danger."[50] Instead, opposition to the plan developed in three stages. First, in Parliament, conservative politicians adamantly resisted the plan. While socialists and liberals defended it in the name of the Hungarian economy, these politicians challenged the plan in the name of the Hungarian nation.[51] Some of them interpreted the plan as representing a loss of national sovereignty; they argued that it had been imported from abroad and accused the government of acquiescing to international demands. Others insisted that the plan amounted to "national suicide"; they claimed that it unduly burdened the middle class, which they saw as the backbone of the nation. Still others forecasted a "tragic end to the family"; they argued that the plan discouraged the desirable "Christian middle class" from reproducing. In this way, although reproduction and motherhood occasionally surfaced in this rhetoric, the aim was not to reestablish the social contributions of mothers; instead, motherhood was deployed as a trope to bolster a nationalist (and even racist) agenda.[52] Yet because these political conservatives constituted a parliamentary minority, they exerted little influence over the shape of the Bokros reforms; they would have to wait four years, until one of their parties gained parliamentary control, for their arguments to be reflected in the policy sphere.

Second, once it became clear that the plan had the necessary parliamentary support, the opposition directed itself at the Constitutional Court. The court was then inundated with appeals from doctors, lawyers, and social scientists. Using a clause from the constitution that guaranteed the state's protection of families, these groups tried to have the plan deemed unconstitutional. In effect, they argued that a constitutional right to family protection implied broad material support for all families, which the Bokros plan violated by targeting certain income groups. Hence, until the summer of 1995, the welfare debate was essentially a constitutional debate about the meaning of family protection. Opponents of the plan had good reason to have faith in this strategy: the Hungarian Constitutional Court was an unusually activist court, known for it broad, and often radical, juridical interpretations. In fact, the court's 1995 ruling did validate the right to family protection and women's right to self-determination. Yet it stopped short of linking these rights to material guarantees, thus determining that the essence of the Bokros Plan was constitutional.[53]

Third, as it became clear that the plan would be implemented after this court ruling, opponents turned their attention to setting acceptable eligibility cut-offs. Social scientists played a highly visible role at this stage. For nearly a year, they had been studying the projected effects of the Bokros Plan. In doing so, they linked the issue of welfare reform to larger debates about the subsistence level.[54] In journal and newspaper articles, they challenged the official social minimum and advanced new calculations of a more realistic poverty line. They then argued that the Bokros Plan should reflect their calculations. For instance, based on the revised minimums included in Table 16, roughly 60 percent of the population lived at or below the poverty line in 1994. Since the Bokros Plan's cut-offs were 15,000 forints per person, it would have denied social benefits to up to 40 percent of the population, many of whom were "needy." Thus, these sociologists argued for higher income cut-offs on redistributive grounds.

After over a year of debate and negotiation, the Bokros Plan went into effect on April 15, 1996. Although its income cut-offs were higher than those initially proposed, the plan did dismantle the two remaining maternalist welfare programs. First, it income-tested family allowances, thus making them available only to certain classes of families. This change affected huge numbers of Hungarians: in 1995 family allowances reached 1.5 million Hungarian families to support over 2.5 million children. After 1996, only those two-parent families with monthly incomes below 19,500 forints per person remained eligible for the allowance until their child's sixth birthday.[55] For single parents, the cut-off was 23,400 forints per person. To keep the allowance, recipients had to undergo income reviews. If their monthly income fell above the cut-off, they were denied further support.

Second, the plan restructured the system of child care grants (GYES/GYED). The Bokros plan abolished GYED, the grant that had been linked to mothers' income in 1985.[56] Once entitled to three years of support, Hungarian women were granted 180 days of maternity leave. This change also affected large numbers of women: in 1994 over 150,000 Hungarian mothers had been supported by GYED. The plan also subjected GYES recipients to income tests. Only those women whose income fell below the family-allowance cut-off of 19,500 forints per person were eligible for an additional year of support at a fixed rate. Mothers were required to update their income data regularly; those whose monthly income exceeded the cut-off while on the grant were denied further assistance.

In the years following the introduction of the Bokros reforms, analyses of its effects proliferated. Most of them evaluated the plan through a redistributive lens. Not surprisingly, liberal economists and sociologists interpreted the plan as a redistributive improvement; they argued that it finally channeled state assistance to the needy. They also applauded the plan for putting Hungary on the road to having a smaller state sector, which they believed would be economically advantageous in the long run.[57] Yet even those social scientists who had been opposed to the plan slowly began to jump aboard the reform bandwagon.[58] Some became convinced that a financially strapped state could not be expected to maintain a strong entitlement system. Others began to see that these reforms would not cut as deeply as

Table 16. Estimated Social Minimum by Household Type, 1995 (in forints)

Household Type	Monthly Family Income	Monthly Income per Person
Single Mother with 1 Child	39,476	19,738
Single Mother with 2 Children	52,282	17,427
Two Parents with 1 Child	57,226	19,075
Two Parents with 2 Children	70,924	17,731
Two Parents with 3 or More Children	84,512	16,902

SOURCE: Zsuzsa Ferge, "A Magyar Segélyezési Rendszer Reformja II," p. 28.

initially projected; according to most estimates, roughly 20 percent of the population was cut from family allowances, as opposed to early estimates of 40 percent.[59] Many social scientists began to reason that, given Hungary's new class divisions, perhaps it was "morally offensive" to distribute limited state resources to the financially secure. They also began to argue that, given the redistributive inequities of the past, perhaps welfare targeting was an improvement: at least it ensured that state funds would go to the truly impoverished. One local government official articulated this reasoning best when he justified the plan to me in an interview: "It is a simple principle. Give to the poor and not to the rich. This is basic. But, because of our socialist past, we have a hard time understanding it. We will learn."[60]

Yet there is another lesson to be learned from the Bokros reforms. They not only limited the scope of welfare redistribution but also advanced an important interpretive agenda. Structurally, the reforms moved family allowances and maternity leave out of the entitlement sphere and into the realm of social assistance; they thus linked the future of these programs to the fluctuations of parliamentary politics.[61] These reforms also altered the terms of state assistance by prioritizing social class over other social positions. The message was clear: child rearing was no longer considered a social responsibility deserving remuneration; women were no longer guaranteed compensation for their maternal labor; and claims to state assistance were no longer framed around one's contribution as a worker, mother, or family member. In short, these reforms taught women that they would be recognized only as "needy" individuals and that their "neediness" would be conceptualized in strictly material terms.

These interpretive shifts were not simply abstractions. In addition to marking a conceptual break with the foundations of the socialist welfare system, these policy reforms had practical effects. Once institutionalized, they transformed the experience of welfare. With the introduction of targeted programs, a new division of labor surfaced in welfare institutions; with the entrance of means tests, welfare work took on an assembly-line quality; and with the introduction of new surveillance techniques, welfare workers and clients became increasingly distant from each other. As a result, a series of new stereotypes about the pathologies of Hungarian welfare clients arose.

DISCRETIONARY WELFARE PRACTICES: TESTING, ASSISTING, AND JUDGING THE NEEDY

As with the policy apparatus, the first major reshuffling of welfare institutions occurred in the late socialist period. The historical convergence was striking. In 1985, the same year the GYES system underwent reform, the institutional apparatus was restructured. Here, too, social scientists were at the forefront of the reorganization. After years of faulting existing welfare agencies for being too punitive or too preoccupied with mental hygiene, a group of social scientists and lawyers appealed to the Ministry of Education to establish "experimental" institutions to confront social problems.[62] From the outset, they were clear about how they diverged from those who supported the prevailing institutional models: they wanted to shift the institutional focus to the social problems engulfing adults and families; they sought to introduce a poor-relief model of welfare work; and they wanted to build voluntary, service-centered agencies without formal control over clients. In 1985, the ministry granted them twelve institutions to be run on a trial basis. The name of these institutions was emblematic of their "alternative" approach: they called themselves Family Support Service Centers (Család Segítő Szolgálat Központok).[63] While these centers were to be evaluated after five years, the review never happened. Instead, in the years following their creation, the centers sprouted up in local governments across the country. By 1991, over one hundred centers operated in Hungary, twenty in Budapest alone.

The advent of these centers immediately prompted reorganization in the institutional division of labor. Given Family Support Service Centers' tumultuous birth, this restructuring was contentious; it prompted anger from both sides of the institutional divide. On the one side, the Child Guidance Centers saw the establishment of their new counterparts as implying that they had not done their job properly.[64] State counselors and psychologists also worried that these centers would increase the competition for scarce resources.[65] As a result, they erected barriers between their institutions. Counselors deemed the centers "illegitimate" and "ungrounded."[66] In one Budapest district where these agencies shared a building, counselors built a concrete wall to cordon off their offices. As a social worker explained to me in an interview, "They despised us and feared we would contaminate them. At one level it was funny, at another [level] very tragic."[67] After a series of professional battles, Child Guidance Centers conceded the familial sphere to their rivals and limited their work to children. "Maybe it was better," a psychologist revealed in an interview. "We never liked the other work anyway. We were trained to deal with children, and now we finally use this expertise."[68]

On the other side, the Gyámhatóság was equally distressed by the centers' emergence. Caseworkers continually referred to this new cadre of state actors as inexperienced. "They were all a bunch of intellectuals over there," a caseworker explained in an interview. "They knew it all from the books. They came in with their models and arrogance and never asked us what we thought. They could do it better. Well, they had their heads in their butts."[69] As the pillar of the Hungarian welfare apparatus, the Gyámhatóság could not cede control to these new institutions; it was forced to coexist with them. As a result, the welfare apparatus bifurcated yet again. According to the Family Support workers, it split between their "alternative" approach and the Gyámhatóság's "punitive" model. Gyámhatóság workers saw the split as a division between their "effectiveness" and Family Support Service Centers' "inexperience." This split was epitomized in the titles each institution gave to workers. In the Gyámhatóság, there were caseworkers (*fő/előadók*), child-welfare workers (*gyermek védelmi munkások*), and eligibility workers (*asszisztensek*). In Family Support Service Centers, there were just social workers (*szociális munkások*). "We are social workers because we are different," one center worker explained to me. "We do what no one does. We don't control; we help socially."[70]

But names can be deceiving. However rigidly these agencies policed their borders and insisted on difference, their work shared an essential feature: they collapsed clients into one category of claimants—the materially deprived. In doing so, they grounded the materialization of need in clients' everyday lives.

Casework as Piecework

Not all the changes in welfare practices were attributable to this institutional reshuffling. In the mid-1980s, internal changes carried out within Gyámhatóság offices profoundly altered the nature of welfare work. In order to administer the new assistance programs under their control,

Gyámhatóság offices expanded. By the late 1980s, the number of Gyámhatóság employees in the districts I studied had increased by nearly 50 percent.[71] These new workers were channeled into an even more specialized division of labor: caseworkers were responsible for child protection, while eligibility workers handled legal and policy-related cases. These two broad categories of workers were broken down further as caseworkers were classified according to their skill level and experience. Moreover, in this period, home visits were separated from office work and often contracted out to temporary workers not regularly employed in the Gyámhatóság. Home visitors received lists of clients to report on. Since they were paid on a per-visit basis, they tried to make as many visits as possible on a given outing.[72] As a result, caseworker/client interactions were transformed. In the office, they became more specialized and limited in scope; outside the office, they became more rushed and disengaged.

The nature of caseworker/client interactions also changed with the introduction of new procedures for evaluating clients. Beginning in the mid-1980s, local governments instituted new guidelines for caseworkers. First, they limited the number of visits required for different cases. For instance, caseworkers had to conduct two visits per year for recipients of occasional child-rearing assistance and four visits per year for recipients of regularized aid. Second, local governments created standardized questionnaires for workers to use on these visits. These were closed-ended instruments comprised of multiple-choice questions and with only a small space for comments about applicants.[73] Third, the focus of these investigations also changed. Questions about clients' domestic skills were removed, as were inquiries into their domestic relations. In their place were questions designed to gauge clients' level of material need. In addition to gathering income data, welfare workers determined the value of applicants' flats and furnishings. These questions effectively transformed caseworkers' old domesticity tests into poverty tests.

Initially, these poverty tests were to be used only when administering financial assistance. Yet, as with domesticity tests, these poverty tests eventually permeated most Gyámhatóság work. Whereas domesticity tests shaped how caseworkers treated a client, poverty tests determined whether caseworkers dealt with a client. Welfare workers used these tests to forge a clientele; they took on only those who demonstrated material need. Women were regularly shuffled out of these offices when found to be living in good financial conditions. One home visit comes to mind. Mrs. Szabó was referred to the Gyámhatóság in 1995 by her son's teacher. When we reached her flat, located in an elite area of Budapest, Mrs. Szabó had us sit down for coffee.

She then recounted story after story: how her husband left her for his secretary; how she was fired from the Ministry of Culture because of her communist background; and how her family banished her because they could not deal with her "nervousness." Her words literally floated by the caseworker, who sat drinking her coffee and calculating the value of Mrs. Szabó's expensive furnishings. After learning how large her disability pension was, the caseworker abruptly got up, walked out of the flat, and dropped the case. On the way back to the office, she turned to me and asked, "What was that woman about? Please, I have clients who can't even feed their kids. What did she want from me?"

A similar filtering process characterized the work in Family Support Service Centers. All their clients came to the office voluntarily, often on a walk-in basis. Social workers always greeted new visitors with a litany of questions about their income. Using this information, they made the necessary calculations to determine whether the visitor was eligible for additional state support. These calculations then determined who became clients. Those found to be eligible for new support became clients, and social workers helped them navigate through the maze of new welfare regulations. Those who were impoverished but had been denied aid also became clients as social workers helped to appeal their decisions. And those who lived in difficult material conditions but were ineligible for state aid also became clients: social workers gave them handouts or food packages (or both). Social workers encouraged all other visitors not to bother them with "frivolous" problems. I encountered countless instances when social workers acted like Gyámhatóság caseworkers, dropping cases and shuffling people out of the office after deeming them materially secure. One social worker who had been employed in a Family Support Service Center since its inception explained the priorities to me in an interview:

> Listen, we have limited resources and we make choices. This is not complicated. Today, in the waiting room, I had two women whose child-rearing assistance was cut, a woman whose husband lost his job, a woman whose heat was turned off, and a lonely woman who wanted to talk. Who do you think I helped first? Who do you think waited all afternoon until I got to her at the very end of my shift?[74]

The poverty tests employed in these offices also influenced how welfare workers dealt with those who became clients. With time, these tests accorded state actors an increasingly narrow lens through which to view their clientele. As caseworkers used these tests, they began to restrict themselves to clients' material problems. In the mid-1980s, caseworkers appropriated the new office division of labor to shield themselves from clients with domestic conflicts. They sent such clients on wild goose chases, continually referring them to different workers and institutions for help. In 1986, a female client who sought assistance dealing with her abusive husband went through a string of caseworker referrals until she gave up and turned to the police.[75] By the time of my fieldwork in the mid-1990s, caseworkers had developed elaborate ways to avoid what they called "long-winded clients." Some caseworkers ran to the bathroom when they saw these clients coming. Others hid in neighboring offices until these clients disappeared. In one office, two caseworkers established their own "rescue system": whenever one of them got stuck with a long-winder, she kicked the adjacent wall, prompting the neighboring caseworker to come over with an "emergency" to end the meeting. As one of them remarked after a successful rescue mission, "You think she [the client] would learn. I don't want to hear about every fight with her husband. What does she think I can do?"

Caseworkers coupled these avoidance tactics with strategies to reduce all their clients' problems to material issues. Such reductionism was most apparent when state actors interacted with clients who had domestic problems. Approximately 32 percent of my sample involved some sort of domestic violence—abuse that caseworkers rarely addressed. Instead, caseworkers found ways to turn this violence into a material problem. "Don't talk about the fights with your husband," a social worker once advised a client who was applying for public assistance. "Just tell them that your husband lost his job and you have no heat. That's the real problem."[76] A good example of this reductionism was the case of a young Romany woman who came to a Family Support Service Center in 1994, ostensibly for help paying an overdue utility bill. As her meeting with the social worker progressed, she began to remove her clothing to show us the scars and cigarette burns covering her body. By the end of the meeting, she had broken down in tears and begged for help. To assist her, the social worker provided a few hundred forints for medicine to treat her wounds and a referral to a local soup kitchen.

Caseworkers also collapsed clients' child-rearing problems into material issues. Whereas in the maternalist regime "child protection" encompassed a range of domestic conflicts, by the late 1980s caseworkers defined it in strictly material terms.[77] A caseworker who began work in the 1980s defined it in this way: "Child welfare is saving children from poverty and the dangers of it. What else could it mean? Children are healthy and secure when they have food, a home, and clothing."[78] In practice, this definition meant that caseworkers dismissed clients whose child-rearing problems were not accompanied by poverty. As with their handling of domestic violence, caseworkers rejected the requests of materially secure mothers. "I am sorry, I cannot help you," a caseworker once told a woman seeking help on behalf of her delinquent son. "You have the resources to deal with the problem, so try a probation officer." Client appeals not framed in material terms fell on deaf ears. "Did you hear me?" one Romany woman exclaimed as her caseworker measured the size of her flat. "I said that he goes to those prostitutes on Rákóczi Square. This is dangerous for the little one, with all the diseases. Are you writing this down?" The caseworker rolled her eyes as she pretended to write something down.

Clients with both child-rearing concerns and material problems had their child-rearing concerns reduced to material problems. Caseworkers attributed all sorts of child-rearing difficulties to material deprivation. In doing so, they ignored other issues impinging on mothers' lives. As a caseworker analyzed one mother's situation in a 1986 case file, "The mother is angry and abusive with her son because, since his birth, the family has slid into poverty."[79] Caseworkers frequently linked juvenile delinquency, rebellion, and poor school performance to low family income. In one 1991 case, a welfare worker even attributed a teenage girl's sexual promiscuity to her family's poor material circumstances. As she wrote in her case notes, "Five people live in one room. There is no bathroom in the flat so they use the collective one in the building. . . . The girl escapes this with her irresponsible and disorderly behavior with older boys."[80]

Caseworkers viewed poverty as the source of a variety of other social problems in addition to domestic conflicts and child-rearing difficulties. For example, they saw poverty as the underlying cause of alcohol abuse. As the head caseworker in one Gyámhatóság office theorized in an interview, "In Hungary there are many alcoholics because we are such a poor country—not like the United States. We drink because our lives are so miserable. . . . Yes, this worsened since the system change because more people are poor and very miserable."[81] It was not uncommon for clients with alcohol problems to come staggering into these offices, looking for someone to talk to. They rarely found sympathetic listeners. "How many forints do you spend on *pálinka*?" a social worker quizzed one such client. "Imagine, if you had that money, you would not be here." As a caseworker once told me when I asked her how she assisted such clients, "Well, we never give them money. You know where it will go. We have special food packages for them, so they get the nutrients they need." Caseworkers dealt with clients who had psychological problems or emotional troubles in similar ways. They collapsed these clients into one main category, the materially needy. And they interpreted all their needs through one primary lens, the lens of the material.

This narrow interpretation of need then shaped the assistance extended to clients. Beginning in the mid-1980s, state actors assisted their clients in one of three general ways: they provided clients with money and material goods; they trained clients to "survive" poverty; or they placed the children of clients with severe material problems in state care. Most often, they distributed financial assistance to clients and assumed the money would solve their problems. The kind of poor relief administered by welfare workers varied somewhat by institution. The Gyámhatóság had the most to give: they had occasional and regular child-rearing assistance, as well as twenty other income-support programs at their disposal. Once used as a reward for "good" mothers, these funds became the central way that caseworkers dealt with their clients. As Table 17 reveals, there was a large increase in the number and proportion of clients receiving child-rearing assistance in one of the offices I studied; by 1992, almost three out of four clients in this office had been defined as "needy" or materially deprived.

The allocation of poor relief worked somewhat differently in Family Support Service Centers. Each center had its own stash of emergency funds, food, and clothing. Few rules regulated the distribution of these resources; clients were not entitled to any of them. In theory, social workers were to allocate this aid to pay for child care, utilities, or funerals.[82] In practice, they used these funds to resolve other issues. Approximately 80 percent of the interactions I observed in these centers involved the transfer of material goods.[83] More specifically, they involved negotiations over clients' "neediness." Since social workers could not give money to everyone, they developed their own allocative criteria. These standards combined clients' objective material circumstances with their performance skills. All clients had to muster up evidence of material need. In addition, they had to deliver a good "needy" performance: they had to appear sympathetic but not pathetic. The overwhelming majority of clients came out of these negotiations with a few hundred forints, a food package, or supermarket coupons. Those who gave particularly effective performances found these exchanges quite lucrative: in 1992, the szegénytelep center gave four of its clients 100,000–120,000 forints, which amounted to 65 percent of the average Hungarian wage. One married couple received a total of 165,000 forints, slightly less than the average yearly income.[84]

In these poor-relief negotiations, welfare workers often provided another kind of assistance—poverty-survival training. Social workers took on small caseloads of clients whom they taught how to "survive in poverty."[85] For many, this training involved learning how to make the most of negotiations with other state officials, especially Gyámhatóság eligibility workers. Here

Table 17. Szegénytelep Child-Rearing-Assistance Cases,
1985–1992

Year	Number of Cases	Percentage of All Cases
1985	384	5
1989	1,070	18
1991	4,384	61
1992	5,010	71

SOURCE: Szegénytelep institutional summaries, 1985–1992.

social workers embarked on what can best be termed "client packaging": they taught clients how to represent themselves in order to secure assistance. Social workers conducted role playing with their clients: "Now pretend I am an assistance officer. How would you explain your problem to me?" In these exercises, social workers critiqued clients' language and tone of voice. "Anger will not work," one social worker told a Romany client. "They don't like that over there." Social workers also instructed clients how to pass Gyámhatóság poverty tests. They explained how means tests worked and how failing them would result in the withdrawal of assistance. "You receive aid now, but that will change if you are not prepared," a social worker lectured a client in 1994. "But do not lie because that will get you cut from support."

Social workers' poverty training also included lectures about how to live more "productively." Many social workers provided clients with resource-management training. "Some clients don't realize they are poor," a social worker once explained to me. "They spend money like they had jobs. Then they come in here when they run out [of money]." So social workers taught these clients to "economize" and "budget," showing them how to calculate their monthly expenses and to shop for discounted products. In the early 1990s, social workers regularly warned clients about price increases. "I explained to Mrs. Horváth that the price of bread, milk, and sugar will go up at the start of the year," a social worker wrote in 1991. "I told her to budget for this."[86] In 1993, one center posted flyers notifying clients that utility subsidies had been cut. Others were counseled about changing their lifestyles. Clients with alcohol problems were routinely lectured about its connection to poverty. Here social workers tried to instill new "values" in their clients, such as morality, piety, and frugality. As one social worker put it, "If more clients lived [according to these values], they would not be in such terrible conditions."[87]

Gyámhatóság caseworkers rarely engaged in such counseling; it was too time-consuming. Instead, caseworkers took another approach with clients whose problems remained unresolved after the receipt of poor relief: they placed their children in state care. Once used to punish "bad" mothers, institutionalization became the central way that caseworkers dealt with clients who had severe material problems. Although the number of children placed in state care remained steady during the 1990s, the grounds for institutionalization changed. In the hundreds of cases I reviewed from this period, I uncovered few references to clients' domestic competence. Caseworkers had little to say about clients' maternal practices; they paid little attention to clients' child-rearing skills. Yet caseworkers offered elaborate accounts of clients' material conditions and inability to provide basic necessities for their children. Poverty had become the main justification for removing children from their homes. For instance, from 1990 to 1995 the overall number of "endangered children" close to doubled; of the new cases, 94 percent were defined as "materially" (*anyagilag*) endangered. Statistical data collected by these offices provide further evidence of this shift: in 1984, 29 percent of the children placed in state care were said to be materially endangered; by 1992, this percentage had increased to 87.[88]

In large part, this shift in the grounds for institutionalization was connected to the rise of new surveillance techniques and practices. Approximately 90 percent of the institutionalization cases I reviewed began as RNS assistance cases. While on follow-up visits to assess eligibility for further support, caseworkers became dismayed by clients' "persistent" material problems.[89] Armed with poverty tests, caseworkers elicited detailed information about clients' material lives. This information was then used to institutionalize their children. Roughly 41 percent of the institutionalization cases I reviewed cited "inappropriate housing" as the reason for removing children from their families. "Did you see how they lived?" a caseworker once exclaimed to me after a home visit. "Six people in one room. Of course I will take the children. How could they imagine otherwise?" The income data collected by caseworkers was used in similar ways. Approximately 39 percent of the institutionalization cases I studied quoted "low wages" as a justification for placing children in state care. As one caseworker put it in a 1990 case, "With those wages, it is impossible to support three children. They are lying about their income, or they live in terrible poverty. Either way, the children must go."[90]

Accounts like these were indicative not only for what they included but also for what they excluded. In their evaluations, caseworkers were attentive only to clients' material conditions. They failed to consider the ways clients struggled within difficult material conditions to ensure their children's well-being. This filtering process became clear as I accompanied caseworkers on home visits. On these outings, I watched as evidence of clients' everyday struggles literally fell outside caseworkers' view. For example, I encountered Mrs. Lakatos, a young single mother who lived with two other families and who struggled to pay extra rent so her daughter could have her own bed. I met Mrs. Kovács, a mother of three whose small flat became overcrowded after she recruited two elderly aunts to live with her and take care of her children when her enterprise child care was cut. I listened to Mrs. Alma explain how, despite her cramped flat, she kept the family's dogs because they made her sons happy. I observed as Mrs. Kemény outlined how she used her savings to build a wall in her flat to cordon off her abusive husband and to shield her children from his abuse. And I sat in awe as Mrs. Sebő recounted how she went to an elite area of the city to search the trash bins for clothing and household items. But these struggles never made it into caseworkers' evaluations. Instead, they were deemed "material-endangerment" cases; they all ended with the institutionalization of these women's children.

While it is tempting to blame caseworkers for this reductionism, its source was deeper. In contemporary Hungary, the boundaries of welfare were redefined in monetary terms. The resulting discursive silences were deafening: stories of unruly and violent men resounded throughout this welfare apparatus, but were never heard; confessions of maternal isolation and exhaustion were voiced repeatedly, but went unacknowledged; and cases of extreme mental illness and alcohol abuse loomed large in these offices, but remained unaddressed. This silencing was maintained by the specialized organization of casework. Caseworkers became border guards, policing the new lines of inclusion and exclusion. They worked on an assembly line, using poverty tests to determine who was needy and who was not. These working conditions also left welfare workers with less room to maneuver and less opportunity to connect with clients. From this separation arose all sorts of mythologies about the new Hungarian "welfare cheat."

Pathologized Welfare Clients

Welfare workers employed in the Gyámhatóság and Family Support Service Centers were frustrated with their work; they complained incessantly about how theirs was a thankless job. In part, their frustration stemmed from their working conditions. As they sat in their collective offices, processing case after case, Gyámhatóság caseworkers often admitted to feeling like alienated, piece-rate workers. The overwhelming majority of them had no particular commitment to welfare work. Instead, most of them had become caseworkers almost by accident: they needed work and somehow ended up as caseworkers. With little formal casework training or background, they felt overwhelmed. Their feelings of alienation may explain the extremely high turnover rate among caseworkers: on average, Gyámhatóság workers lasted two to four years before moving on to other types of office work.[91] In fact, the few caseworkers who stuck it out for more than a decade exhibited the most dissatisfaction with their work. They regularly commented on how their work used to be different; they reminisced about a time when they had more control. "Before, everything was normal, the clients too," an older caseworker explained in an interview. "Now the whole situation is insane, very crazy."[92]

Social workers from Family Support Service Centers expressed similar antipathy toward their work. Like their Gyámhatóság counterparts, a minority of them had planned to become social workers: in a 1997 survey of social workers, 54 percent reported that they had become social workers "by chance"; an additional 36 percent claimed that they were drawn to social work because of a general interest in "helping" or "listening to" people.[93] They were also quite frustrated by their working conditions: they admitted to feeling powerless; they felt unable to deal with the problems confronting them; and they claimed to have little connection to or sympathy for their clients. As a young social worker summarized the situation in an interview:

> I left the university and came here so I could help. This is what the name of the center says we do. Now it seems so crazy. I'm a fireman. Really, I put out fires, but I save no one. The secret is that I do not even want to save them anymore. It is not possible and too tiring. Anyway, they don't want to be saved. It's all a game. We all pretend to help but the fires get bigger and bigger. [94]

In addition, welfare workers' own sense of economic vulnerability and fear of falling must have exacerbated their frustration. Most welfare workers were lower- or working-class women, only one step above their clients in the class hierarchy.[95] Thus, while they faced difficult material conditions, they had become ineligible for the social-assistance programs they oversaw. In effect, the new welfare boundaries they policed excluded women like themselves; the poverty tests they administered disadvantaged women whose lives were similar to theirs. Welfare workers seemed aware of this disparity and frequently referred to it in their interactions with clients. As they distributed child-rearing assistance, caseworkers noted that they could use extra money to raise their kids; as they allocated housing maintenance funds, they mentioned that their flats needed repair and renovation.

Such comparisons became more prevalent after the introduction of the Bokros Plan. These reforms cut many welfare workers from maternity benefits, which ended up widening the social distance separating them from clients. In late socialism, welfare workers and clients had been connected to the social-policy apparatus on similar terms: their contributions as mothers linked them and entitled both to state support. After the Bokros Plan, few policies joined them. One caseworker described this distancing best when she explained the Bokros Plan to me: "I don't know what the clients complain about; with their income they are sure to get support. Mothers like me will be harmed. If I do not have my baby in the next year, *I* will be without support, not *them*."

Hence, the liberal state situated welfare workers and clients on opposite sides of the welfare divide. The barriers separating them were many; the bridges connecting them were few. Not surprisingly, this situation bred contempt for the "other." While welfare workers in the maternalist regime also engaged in punitive welfare practices, they did so with only a portion of their clientele. In the contemporary welfare apparatus, these practices extended to the entire clientele, encroaching on those once shielded and protected as "good" mothers. This shift did not occur immediately. Beginning in the mid-1980s, welfare workers began to use a new language when writing about their clients. This shift was clearest in RNS assistance cases. Caseworkers had always used a hostile tone when describing those women who had been denied aid. But, in the 1980s, they began to adhere to the same tone when describing successful applicants. They wrote about these women's flats as "dirty," "disorderly," and "disgusting." They called these women "primitive," "uneducated," and "scandalous." And they questioned these women's morals, ethics, and life-styles. From their descriptions alone, it was impossible to determine whether a client's application had been approved or denied. The only difference was the client's income.

By the time of my fieldwork in the mid-1990s, welfare workers' contempt had devolved into a full-scale stigmatization of their clientele. This contempt surfaced in numerous ways. Most common were those caseworkers who read new meanings into their clients' appeals for assistance. They began to interpret them as evidence of individual pathology and defect. These interpretations soon gave rise to the icon of the "welfare cheat" and a new language to describe her. She was a lazy, uncultured, simple, and disorderly woman. She was a woman who could not be trusted. She was a

woman capable of forging income documents or hiding electronics in clos-
ets. All these agencies had institutional archives of stories to support this
image: home visitors who found expensive household goods hidden under
beds or in neighboring flats; caseworkers who discovered fake work records
or unreported income; and clients who came to the office covered with fine
jewelry. Caseworkers then used these stories to explain client poverty.
"Clients are different today," one older caseworker revealed in an interview.
"They lie, cheat, and steal. Even the Hungarians do this now. Terrible."[96]
Once reserved for Romany clients, the myth of the "welfare queen" loomed
over all clients. Whatever their ethnicity, all clients were thought to be
potentially pathological and capable of extreme deception.

Quite often, this image of the "welfare cheat" was coupled with mythologies about clients' aggressive behavior. Most caseworkers believed their
clients were capable of outrageous acts of violence. All the welfare institutions I studied employed "security guards." In the Family Support Service
Centers, they were male social workers trained to "keep order." In the
Gyámhatóság, they were policemen who wielded weapons. When I asked
about the need for these guards, welfare workers told me these men
"herded" and "tamed" their clientele. They stood outside the agency doors,
blocking the entrance and deciding whom to let in. They escorted clients
into the office and watched over their meetings with welfare workers. To
intimidate potentially aggressive clients, these men walked through the
office, asking, "Is everyone all right?" or "Does everyone feel safe?" When
clients got angry, these men forcibly removed them from the office. In
effect, clients had become in need of continual surveillance. As a female
client once screamed as she was removed from the Gyámhatóság, "She has
taken my children away; why do I need to be taken away too? You would
also be upset; am I not allowed to be angry?"

Caseworkers' defensive attacks on their clients frequently descended
beyond their presumed personality traits to penetrate their physical bodies.
The sight, the smell, and the feel of clients' bodies were common topics of
conversation among caseworkers. Many caseworkers used animal metaphors to describe their clients, referring to them as cattle and pigs. Caseworkers called those days when assistance applications were due "slaugh-
terhouse days" because of the large number of clients who gathered outside
Gyámhatóság offices to submit applications. Even more demeaning were the
constant remarks that caseworkers made about clients' appearances. They
regularly made fun of deformities in their clients' bodies. "Was that person
human? Man, woman, or beast?" a caseworker once joked about a client.
They also came up with degrading names for clients. There was the "tooth-

less one," a woman whose front teeth had been knocked out by her husband and who could not afford replacements. There was the "legless one," a woman who lost part of her left leg in a "domestic accident" and could not pay the medical costs to repair it. There was even the "voiceless one," an elderly man who suffered from throat cancer and spoke through a device attached to his mouth. In a 1989 case, a particularly poetic caseworker used the metaphor of a "battlefield" to describe a client's body: "She works on Rákóczi Square. [This is] appropriate. Bruises all over, like a war, . . . tattoos on the skin, like mines, . . . and the mouth of a soldier."[97]

Moreover, caseworkers spoke incessantly about the "smell" of their clients. They berated clients for not washing regularly. "I used to wash before work," a caseworker once remarked. "Then I realized that it's no use, so now I clean myself as soon as I return from work." Another caseworker told the office a story about how her two sons once remarked that she smelled like a "zoo" when she arrived home from work. While her story provoked hysterical laughter among her colleagues, it prompted the clients in the room to drop their heads in embarrassment. Then there was the caseworker with whom I rode the metro to work each day. When we exited the metro station, located over three blocks from the office, she began to talk about how she could smell her workplace. To deal with the odor, she brought air freshener to the office. She kept it by the door and continually sprayed it around to rid the office of the "sickening smell" of poverty.

Given their disgust with the sight and smell of clients, welfare workers avoided physical contact with clients' bodies. In effect, clients became "untouchables"—contaminated bodies not to be felt. The workers' desire to avoid physical contact may have been another reason for the male security guards: these men handled and touched the contaminated. When situations arose that necessitated physical contact with clients, welfare workers called in the guards to do the dirty work. One time an elderly client lost her balance and fell to the floor of a Gyámhatóság office. Unable to get up, she was forced to lie on the floor until a security guard arrived to help her. It was clear that the caseworkers feared physical contact with the client. Another caseworker articulated this fear to me explicitly when she once saw me touch a client. The client's son had been institutionalized, and she came to beg for his return. After a caseworker rejected her appeal, the woman wandered around the office, eventually ending up at my desk. As she sat crying, I touched her hand in an attempt to comfort her. The caseworker looked on, mortified. I was immediately reprimanded: "Never touch a client. Wash your hands immediately because you never know what you can get from them." Thus, the pathologization of the Hungarian welfare client was complete; it had extended beyond their personalities to encompass their physical bodies.

CONFINING WELFARE WORKERS AND WELFARE RECIPIENTS

Beginning in the 1980s, the Hungarian welfare system underwent a series of profound changes. At the redistributivetive level, the percentage of the population eligible for state assistance declined. With the end of universal entitlements, the size of the redistributivetive pie shrank. Accompanying these reforms was an interpretive shift. Once structured around the "needs" of social institutions and then of mothers, the welfare apparatus was reoriented to target and treat the materially "needy." Once conceptualized in societal terms and then in maternal terms, the prevailing definition of need was materialized. Thus, this period saw a narrowing in the confines of welfare. After decades of tension between the redistributive and the interpretive, these two levels were synchronized: the liberal welfare state was consistent in its allocative and interpretive narrowness.

The materialization of need was a discursive construct in the broadest sense; it implied a reorganization of both the language and the practices of welfare. Understanding the precise dynamics of this reorganization can offer insight into the workings of welfare liberalism. Hungarian welfare liberalism had both local and global roots. It sprouted up locally, in the late socialist period, as social scientists instituted reforms to target state assistance at the truly needy. In the early 1990s, with global police watching over them, national-level policymakers set out to make the welfare apparatus consistent with the blueprints of the IMF and World Bank. Since these blueprints involved the decentralization of welfare, local governments were granted more authority over benefit allocation. As the site of redistribution shifted, so did its targets. Preferences were given to the middle class in the GYES system; then preferences were given to the impoverished in local-government schemes; finally, all those not materially needy were expunged from national policies. In the process, the nature of eligibility was transformed. Previously connected to recipients' social contributions, state assistance was now based on recipients' inability to contribute.

If local officials and global police were the key architects of this new welfare regime, welfare workers were its construction workers. Theirs was not an easy assignment. With the rise of a new division of labor within and among institutions, working conditions worsened. Welfare workers became classified according to the particular tasks they performed. Cases were segmented and broken into their smallest parts. Speed was emphasized, and engagement with clients was frowned on. The tools of the trade were limited to the distribution of poor relief, poverty-survival training, and institutionalization. In effect, casework became piecework, and clients became income calculations. A gulf then began to separate welfare workers and clients. Their interactions were confined to brief encounters of material surveillance. Welfare workers heard the appeals of only certain classes of women and only those framed in poverty terms. They avoided all complications and shielded themselves from clients who slowed down the production process. In short, welfare workers helped to build a welfare apparatus that undercut their own room to maneuver and ability to find satisfaction in their work.

These changes in the organization of casework were coupled with equally important shifts in the content of welfare work. Caseworkers became border guards: they policed the boundaries of inclusion/exclusion to determine who was in need. Of course, the maternalist welfare apparatus had also operated in dichotomous terms. But whereas welfare workers in the previous system bifurcated clients into "good" and "bad" mothers, the mythologies that arose in the liberal regime encompassed the entire client population. And, in the liberal state, inclusion in the welfare apparatus implied a process of othering unparalleled in the previous regimes. Welfare workers believed their clients were capable of extreme acts of deception and violence. They saw their clients as out of control and in need of taming. They marked clients' bodies with the smell and the feel of poverty. In effect, the punitive tactics once used against a segment of the client population encroached on the lives of all clients. The modes of stigmatization designed to punish bad mothering practices were elaborated to penetrate clients' mental and physical being.

In this way, while the liberal welfare regime constrained welfare workers, it was also confining to clients. Whereas the previous welfare regimes encompassed both possibilities and limitations, the liberal welfare state was more consistently limiting. Most broadly, it excluded a group of women who were materially "secure." For them, the liberal welfare regime signified a series of losses: these women lost valuable state resources and tools to utilize in their everyday lives. Yet even for those who remained included, this welfare state was confining. This regime not only provided them with fewer resources but also interpreted their needs in narrower, more reductionist terms. As a result, the liberal welfare state marked a contraction in clients' room to maneuver and prompted them to develop new strategies of excavation to protect their well-being.

6.   Strategies of Excavation
Inclusions and Exclusions

When scholars evaluate the contemporary Hungarian welfare state, they tend to use one of two lenses. First, many assess it through a political lens to argue that the population has benefited from the "democratization" of the state sphere and the end of "bureaucratic state collectivism."[1] Although these scholars acknowledge that welfare funding has dried up since the 1980s, such concerns are tempered by their belief in the power of democracy. At the policy level, they see new space for contests over whose needs will be met by the state.[2] With the ability to elect political representatives and to form nongovernmental organizations, Hungarians are said to have the means to interject their conceptions of need into a once-closed political sphere. At the institutional level, scholars note a flourishing of self-help and charity initiatives from "below."[3] With the creation of a nonstate, human-services sector, Hungarians are thought to have become proactive in the defense of their needs. In short, these scholars adhere to a classic ideological formulation in which the expansion of political citizenship breeds new forms of social citizenship and in which the extension of political rights enlarges social rights.

Yet when we move from political ideology to empirical reality, it is clear that this lens obscures as much as it illuminates. Indeed, Hungarians now elect their political representatives. However, these politicians instituted reforms that dismantled social entitlements and guarantees. Indeed, Hungarians can now form political organizations. However, they have not launched any large-scale mobilization to contest welfare reform despite the fact that a majority of them claimed to be "endangered" by reform.[4] Indeed, the human-services sector has expanded. However, it remains financially strapped and limited in influence.[5] Of course, democratization is not insignificant, but democratization alone has not given Hungarians more space to articulate their interests; it has not created a more responsive welfare apparatus or a more participatory needs talk.

Second, other scholars evaluate the liberal welfare state through a redistributive lens. Although they acknowledge that many Hungarians became ineligible for state benefits as entitlement criteria were narrowed, they interpret this narrowing as economically imperative.[6] They argue that the state could not continue to maintain social expenditures that paralleled those of Western Europe and Scandinavia. They claim that the state could not continue to work with encompassing eligibility criteria that subjected it to soft budget constraints. And since redistributive choices had to be made, it was best they privileged the economically vulnerable.[7] Thus, these scholars present welfare targeting as both economically and socially just: those who can afford to pay "market price" for goods and services should be forced to do so, while the poor and the needy should receive larger pieces of the redistributive pie.

Like democratization analyses, this redistributive argument rests on a selective interpretation of social reality. From the perspective of macrolevel expenditures, welfare targeting may be defensible; if we look only at who gets what material resources, perhaps it is fair to channel limited state funds to the materially deprived. Yet when we move from statistical aggregates to life experiences, this redistributive argument becomes less sustainable. First, it underestimates the costs of welfare targeting for those excluded from the state sphere. By reducing all social needs to material deprivation, this argument obscures a variety of other problems confronting the population. As I reveal in this chapter, women who have been excluded from the welfare apparatus have a plethora of needs as workers, mothers, wives, and family members—needs that are arguably social responsibilities but that remain unmet in the state sphere. With such privatization, these women are forced to resolve their problems without public support. Welfare targeting has thus had profound effects on these women's everyday lives and maneuverability.

Second, the redistributive defense of welfare targeting overestimates the gains made by the poor. In relative terms, the liberal welfare state does indeed distribute more funds to the materially needy. But, in absolute terms, this group has experienced profound material losses: they have lost guarantees to employment, to basic necessities, and to overall security. Moreover, welfare states are responsible for more than the redistribution of material benefits. They also provide clients with other practical and discursive resources. At this level, clients have experienced additional losses. The materially deprived now enter the state on entirely new terms: their inclusion is based on what they lack financially rather than on what they contribute socially. With this shift, the included have fewer ways to stake claims to state assistance. They are also more constrained institutionally and have a harder time forming collusive relationships with welfare workers. Moreover, the conditions of assistance have changed: new mythologies swirl around clients to heighten their subjective sense of stigmatization. The liberal state has therefore dramatically altered the nature of assistance for those it targets and treats.

This chapter examines the liberal welfare state from a more encompassing lens than that used for the two just described. Instead of centering only on who gets which political and material benefits, I emphasize the redistributive and interpretive effects of welfare targeting. Drawing on the 210 case files I analyzed and the hundreds of cases I observed directly, I paint a picture of the liberal state's two institutional trajectories: the tracks to exclusion and to inclusion.[8] Through these institutional processes, some women were channeled out of, and others into, the welfare sphere. Although their dynamics were different, both tracks were characterized by practical and discursive losses. Moreover, although these losses had different implications for the excluded and the included, both groups responded by reasserting the maternal: the excluded used the maternal as an offensive strategy of reinclusion, while the included used it as a defensive strategy of destigmatization. Thus both groups excavated past identities as mothers to gain leverage in the present and to disrupt welfare workers' limited preoccupation with the material.

THE NEWLY EXCLUDED

From an examination of case files alone, it would appear that only impoverished women came into contact with contemporary welfare offices. Whereas case files from the previous welfare regimes included clients from different socioeconomic classes, case files from the new regime encompassed only the materially needy. Yet it would be a mistake to interpret these files as representative of the interactions in welfare agencies. Unlike socialist welfare offices, which employed tests to determine how clients were treated, welfare institutions now deployed tests to decide who became a client. This is a key difference between the liberal welfare apparatus and its predecessors: in the liberal welfare state, tests worked as exclusionary mechanisms. In my ethnographic research, I discovered that a fairly diverse group of women showed up in welfare offices, but only some of them left paper trails. Approximately 20 percent of the interactions I observed in these offices involved such silencing—that is, they involved women whose problems were deemed too "frivolous" for welfare workers to take on formally.

Although my information about these excluded women was limited, they seemed to share a few demographic characteristics. Most generally, they were not impoverished. But they also were not materially secure. The poverty tests used by these offices were based on the official subsistence level, which was so low that it captured only the very poor. Thus, income tests failed to include many lower- or working-class women who had suffered severe material losses since the 1980s. These women tended to have jobs in the manufacturing or service sectors. Those who were unemployed or on maternity leave had spouses with decent wages. These women's flats were usually in relatively good shape and were located in the better parts of Budapest. And they tended to have smaller families, with two children at the most. In short, these women were just holding on to a decent standard of living: they were one job, one pregnancy, or one crisis away from a slide into poverty.

When such women came to welfare offices, they rarely sought material assistance. Instead, they had other issues to resolve—from registering children to setting custody or visitation rights to exchanging their flats. As they grappled with such bureaucratic issues, these women frequently voiced additional needs. Some of their needs were new to the transition period, while others were not so new. As workers, they expressed concerns about the stability of their jobs. In the 1990s, the official unemployment rate soared, jumping from 0.8 percent in 1990 to 13.4 percent in 1993 to 11.1 percent in 1995.[9] Put another way, from 1992 to 1997, 46 percent of all Hungarian households had at least one unemployed member.[10] In addition, Hungary remained the only East European country where female unemployment lagged behind male unemployment; in 1995, 10 percent of Hungarian women were unemployed, compared with 12.7 percent of Hungarian men.[11] This disparity was due largely to women's willingness to rebound quickly from bouts of unemployment. Yet, as a result, women often moved into less lucrative sectors of the labor force. For instance, there was a huge increase in women employed in the service sector: over 70 percent of women were employed in this sector, up from 46 percent in the early 1980s.[12]

In addition, the nature of the workplace had changed. Many workplaces simply disappeared; from 1990 to 1995, 1.4 million registered workplaces vanished.[13] With privatization, few of the existing firms offered subsidized goods and services to their workers. By the mid-1990s, only a small minority of workers received social services at work: 22 percent received medical care, 9 percent subsidized goods, 9 percent subsidized recreation, and 3 percent subsidized transportation.[14] As work-based provisions disappeared, female workers devoted more of their salaries to covering household expenses. Moreover, they did so as the real value of their wages fell by roughly 6 percent every year from 1989 to 1995.[15] These problems were exacerbated by the persistent gap between women's and men's wages; the average female wage remained roughly 66 percent of the average male wage.[16] In welfare offices, women often referred to such problems: yes, they were fortunate to have work, but their positions had become more vulnerable and unstable.

Alongside their problems as workers, these women confronted new difficulties balancing work and family. As mothers, they experienced new impediments to child rearing. Not only had they lost social benefits through their workplaces, but many had become ineligible for state maternity leave and family allowances. When combined with the end of subsidies for child-rearing goods and services, these new constraints, they felt, hindered their ability to mother "properly." Some even spoke of feeling forced to choose between work and motherhood for the first time in their lives. Although a new domestic-service sector surfaced, it remained out of reach for most of these women; they were more likely to be the providers than the users of such services. They also continued to be the main service providers in their own homes. Despite the increased availability of consumer goods and services, women now devoted 20 percent more time to shopping and cleaning than they did in the late 1970s.[17] Much of this new time was spent searching for cheaper goods and instituting cost-cutting domestic practices.[18] Moreover, the division of household labor had changed little since the 1980s. On average, women still did three quarters of the housework and spent three times more time than men on child care.[19] When they met with welfare workers, women complained incessantly about this situation: with everyone in their families working harder, their husbands had become more disengaged as fathers, leaving them to shoulder the domestic burden under difficult conditions.

In addition to their needs as members of families in transition, women voiced domestic needs that had echoed through the welfare apparatus since their mothers' and grandmothers' time. As in the past, alcoholism created serious problems for many women. Yet ample evidence indicates that these problems had worsened since the 1980s. From 1984 to 1993, the number of alcoholics more than doubled in Hungary, rising from 4.3 percent of the population in 1984 to 9.8 percent in 1993.[20] An overwhelming majority of

these alcoholics were men; in 1993 there were three times more male alcoholics than female alcoholics.[21] In addition, according to even the most conservative estimates, over 25 percent of Hungarian men drank at "dangerous" levels, compared with 9.2 percent of women.[22] In welfare offices,
women often complained about their husbands' drinking patterns. Experi-
entially, many of them believed their spouses' drinking had worsened in
recent years because of the stress of economic vulnerability. Thus, they
looked to welfare workers for help dealing with their needs as wives of alcoholic men.

As in the socialist period, domestic violence surfaced in a large number of
the interactions in contemporary welfare offices. Because of the lack of reliable historical data, it is hard to gauge whether domestic violence had in fact
worsened. Yet anecdotal evidence suggests that it had: newly established
battered-women shelters reported a large increase in the number of women
seeking help;[23] a Hungarian women's magazine, *Nők Lapja*, ran a series of
articles on new levels of domestic violence.[24] Moreover, in the first systematic study of domestic abuse, Hungarian law professor Krisztina Morvai
uncovered important inconsistencies in the nature of abuse, particularly in
the public's response to it.[25] State authorities, from the police to the courts
to welfare workers, became less likely to intervene in domestic conflicts or
to remove violent men from their homes.[26] Many of the women in my sample experienced the results, just as new processes of exclusion minimized
their needs and privatized their problems.

Processes of Exclusion

Despite their relative economic security, many of these women arrived in
welfare offices with work, family, and emotional problems. It was not
entirely clear why they turned to welfare institutions for help. Perhaps
some of them had utilized the institutions in the past. Others may have had
nowhere else to turn and came to welfare agencies as a last resort.[27] Yet they
rarely found what they were looking for. In the 1990s, the boundaries of
welfare were redrawn. With this redrawing, the kinds of problems these
women faced effectively fell outside the bounds of acceptable needs claims.
Unable to demonstrate material need, these women were pushed to the
other side of the welfare divide; their problems were deemed too trivial to
warrant caseworker attention.

Women received this message in a variety of ways. Most often, they
encountered welfare workers who avoided or ignored their problems.
Welfare offices were always overrun with clients. On arrival in these offices,
clients registered with intake officers by providing their names, addresses,

and the nature of their problem. Women with nonmaterial problems were routinely placed at the bottom of waiting lists. They sat in overcrowded rooms for hours, watching as women with assistance claims were waved past them. On those rare occasions when the agencies were not full, welfare workers often fled when they saw these women coming; they retreated to the bathroom, to lunch, or to "closed" meetings with colleagues. Such avoidance tactics followed these women into their meetings with welfare workers. Some women confronted welfare workers' rescue system—that is, their meetings were abruptly interrupted by "emergencies" that welfare workers had to attend to immediately. Others received referrals to different agencies or to church groups; effectively they were sent on wild goose chases around the welfare system. In one Gyámhatóság, caseworkers even created mythical workers to deflect long-winders—workers who either did not exist or who came in so infrequently that they were impossible to contact. The message to these women was clear: they should look elsewhere to resolve problems in their work and family lives.

Those women who did not get the message through caseworker aloofness experienced more direct tactics of exclusion. They were made to feel guilty about using up welfare workers' time and energy. These women told stories of depression, isolation, and domestic conflict to the faces of uninterested caseworkers. Their stories were regularly interrupted as welfare workers launched into lectures about the meaning of true neediness. In these lectures, women had their problems trivialized. Indeed, it must be terrible to work such long hours, but did they know that the majority of clients had no work at all? Of course, it was unfortunate that their spouses withdrew from the household, but at least their partners were working. And, yes, it was a pity that they spent hours searching for affordable household items, but at least they could provide food and shelter for their children. In these speeches, women found themselves compared with more materially deprived clients. They did not fare well in the comparison; their problems were deemed less urgent and less pressing than those of the impoverished. Again, the message was clear: these women's problems fell outside the new parameters of welfare.

It would be too simplistic to blame welfare workers' lack of training or inflexibility for these exclusions. Rather, they were rooted in the new borders that had formed around the welfare apparatus. This new situation became clear toward the end of my fieldwork. After observing hundreds of instances in which welfare workers simply ignored women's pleas for domestic help, I made my only intervention into their welfare practices: I brought in advertisements for two nonprofit organizations created by and for women. The first was a battered women's hot line run by a feminist group; the second was a telephone service that dealt with women's problems. I gave these groups' flyers to welfare workers in all the agencies I studied. But I never saw a welfare worker use these referrals. In one office, I found the flyers in a trash can; in another office caseworkers used them as scratch paper. As I concluded my fieldwork, I asked welfare workers why they had not used the service referrals. Their answers were the same: they were welfare workers, not counselors or therapists. Over and over, they told me that such problems fell outside their "domain." Once again, the message was clear: new lines of exclusion had shut out those who were not impoverished.

With these realignments, the newly excluded lost all sorts of discursive and practical resources. Their room to maneuver in the welfare apparatus contracted to the point of immobility. Discursively, they had fewer rhetorical possibilities for claims-making. As acceptable modes of argumentation for aid were limited to poverty claims, these women were left speechless. Their social contributions as workers, mothers, and family members no longer gave them the right to speak. An office interaction between an elderly woman and a social worker exemplified this discursive silencing. After waiting for hours, Mrs. Nagy entered a Family Support Service Center, only to be greeted with a litany of questions about her available material resources. As the social worker made her way down the long list of questions, Mrs. Nagy explained that she just wanted a "sympathetic ear." Perplexed, the social worker continued down her list. Mrs. Nagy then recounted her difficult life with stories about abusive husbands, disrespectful children, and hostile relatives. At times she made little sense, but her loneliness and depression were apparent. As her stories went on, the social worker began to do paperwork and make phone calls for other cases. When Mrs. Nagy left, the social worker admitted that she had "tuned out" as soon as she learned of Mrs. Nagy's large salary as a secretary. "Her talk was like background music from the radio," the social worker explained. In effect, Mrs. Nagy's income had curtailed her ability to speak or to be heard.

For similar reasons, women like Mrs. Nagy found themselves unable to squeeze practical tools out of welfare institutions. Although few of these women sought material assistance, they did seek strategic help—someone to phone an inflexible workplace, to lecture a recalcitrant spouse, to scold a rebellious child, or to threaten a violent husband. However, they rarely got such assistance. Instead, they were told to use their own resources. After one woman explained that her husband had thrown their television set out the window in a drunken rage, she was advised to use her own savings to fix the window and to buy a new television. Another woman, in response to stories about how she feared leaving her daughters alone with her alcoholic husband, was instructed to hire a baby-sitter to assuage her fears. Thus, when these women did extract advice from welfare workers, it always steered them away from state services and toward private solutions.

Of the hundreds of instances of exclusion I encountered in these welfare offices, one case exemplified the disjuncture between what some women sought and what they got from welfare institutions. I first met Mrs. Kaltner in 1994.[28] By her appearance alone, one could tell that Mrs. Kaltner had peasant origins: she had a round face, a robust body, and often wore makeshift babushkas, especially in the summer. The first in her family to move to Budapest, Mrs. Kaltner arrived in the early 1970s to attend the university. She recalled those years as particularly difficult; without the support of her relatives, she felt lonely and depressed. In retrospect, she believed her emotional difficulties were the reason she quickly jumped into a marriage with a maintenance worker at her university. "I suppose I should have examined him more closely," she remembered. But she agreed to marry him after only a few dates and then had three children in succession. Amidst these pregnancies, she finished her degree and landed a job in a major textile company. The job came with many benefits and a salary twice that of her husband's.

Mrs. Kaltner's contact with the Gyámhatóság began in the late 1970s, when she visited the office to register her third child. When a caseworker asked whether her husband was the boy's father, Mrs. Kaltner remarked, "Yes, unfortunately." Her response prompted a conversation about the man and how "difficult" he was. Even though she was the main breadwinner, he refused to do anything around the house and often became "aggressive." The caseworker then agreed to "visit" her husband and admonish him about his behavior. On this visit, the caseworker described Mr. Kaltner as a "typically" bad father and husband. Although he did not drink, he complained incessantly about his wife. Yet the caseworker had only good things to say about Mrs. Kaltner. She applauded Mrs. Kaltner's domestic skills and ability to secure a "stable" environment for her small children. As a reward, the caseworker helped Mrs. Kaltner on an on-call basis. Whenever her husband needed a lecture, Mrs. Kaltner called on the caseworker. This situation went on for about three years, with Mrs. Kaltner occasionally using the caseworker to quell domestic conflicts and to scold her husband when he acted out.

Mrs. Kaltner's contact with the Gyámhatóság then ceased for over ten years. It was unclear why; nobody ever asked her. In 1994, she resurfaced. Her earlier caseworker had retired, and she was assigned to a young caseworker. I recall her first visit vividly. It was a hot summer day, and everyone in the office was in a particularly bad mood. With sweat pouring from her babushka, Mrs. Kaltner recounted story after story of her husband's abuse. He controlled her every move in the household. He told her what to cook, what to wear, and where she could go. He even forbid her from visiting with colleagues after work. With each new story, the caseworker became increasingly annoyed. After Mrs. Kaltner referred to her job as an accountant, the caseworker interrupted her to ask for income data. When she learned that Mrs. Kaltner earned over 50,000 forints, the caseworker glared at me and rolled her eyes. Within minutes, she rose from her desk and informed Mrs. Kaltner that time was up. She had other clients waiting: "If you must, you will need to come back another day."

Despite the cold reception, Mrs. Kaltner did return to the office, sometimes as often as twice a week. Each time, she came with new stories of abuse. Some of her accounts were wrenching, like the time her husband locked her in a room for the weekend because she failed to buy the ingredients for his favorite meal. Or the time he ordered their children to tell her how obese she was. Yet the caseworker was never moved by these stories. Instead, she deemed Mrs. Kaltner a long-winder and hid in neighboring offices or retreated to lunch when she saw her approaching. When she could not avoid Mrs. Kaltner, the caseworker used the office's rescue system to escape, kicking the adjacent wall to prompt a colleague to come over with an "emergency" to end the session. Mrs. Kaltner was then left alone with me, telling her stories of violence. As the caseworker once apologized to me, "I am sorry that you get stuck with her. You must be bored. You can walk out too."

These avoidance tactics went on for weeks before Mrs. Kaltner confronted her caseworker. One afternoon, Mrs. Kaltner was telling a new story about her husband. The week before he had stolen part of her paycheck, sold many of her cooking utensils, and purchased a new television set. He then banished her from the room when he was watching it. "He hides the remote control so I cannot turn it on when he is gone," Mrs. Kaltner explained. The caseworker had had enough. She kicked the adjacent wall so hard that we all heard. When her colleague came over to disrupt the meeting, Mrs. Kaltner protested. A fight ensued. "This is very rude," Mrs. Kaltner said. "I am not going to leave this time. I need help." The caseworker snapped, "Help? With the remote control? Jesus, you make more money than my boss, and no one I know has a remote-control TV." Mrs. Kaltner retorted that she wanted advice not financial assistance. Furious, the caseworker got up, opened the door, and screamed that she had clients without homes, without jobs, and without heat. She informed Mrs. Kaltner that she would call her if ever a time came when she could deal with "remote-control problems." Embarrassed, Mrs. Kaltner lowered her head, walked out of the office, and never returned.

Strategies of Reinclusion

When confronted with these institutional processes of exclusion many women like Mrs. Kaltner relinquished their desire for state assistance. They simply disappeared from these institutions, with few traces or paper trails. As a result, it was quite difficult to assess how they resolved their problems; it was impossible to track them down or to determine whether their private resources proved sufficient. Yet other newly excluded women did not disappear so quietly. They stayed around to contest their dislocation. They tried to redraw the boundaries of welfare to include their needs and problems. Interestingly, these women waged their struggle on similar terms: they reasserted a sense of entitlement based on motherhood. When their appeals for domestic assistance were ignored or rejected, they drew on their needs as mothers. Having learned to utilize their positions as mothers to protect themselves in the past, they strategized to salvage this identity. In effect, they returned to the idiom of the maternal to contest their exclusion from the liberal welfare state.

This reassertion of maternal entitlement surfaced differently in various contexts. During office visits, women mourned the loss of their previous social significance as mothers. When they were subjected to elaborate poverty investigations, they questioned the limited scope of welfare workers' inquiries. "Why do you need evidence of my mother's pension?" a young woman once snapped. "Isn't it enough that I am a single mother with two kids?" Along these lines, some women attempted to reinsert maternal skill as a criterion for state assistance. They asked eligibility workers why they paid attention only to "my husband's salary" or "my family's income." Wasn't it important that they struggled to raise their children properly? While fighting with a caseworker, one woman even argued that GYES recipients should not be held to the same standards as others since they had chosen not to work "for their children's sake." By advancing such arguments, these women tried to expand the prevailing eligibility criteria to include their contributions as mothers.

On home visits, women's demonstrations of maternal competence were even more pronounced.[29] As home visitors hurried through their flats, many women tried to persuade them to slow down. They pulled out the accouterments of the old domesticity tests: offering home visitors food and drink, showing them pictures of family outings, or discussing their children's problems. The goal was clear: by exhibiting good mothering skills, they hoped to butter up the bureaucratic machine. Although such exhibits may have worked in the past, they were futile in the present. Caseworkers rarely documented their accounts. In fact, this strategy may even have hurt some women since caseworkers usually found their tactics annoying and distracting. "Wasn't that woman crazy?" a caseworker once asked me after a home visit in which we were inundated with stories about the woman's cleaning and cooking routines. "I am writing that she is insane, totally crazy."

Since Family Support Service Centers distributed their resources in an entirely discretionary manner, women in these offices drew on their maternal competence to an even greater extent. Nearly all of them pleaded for help on the basis of their roles as mothers. They could return to work after only a few weeks at home with their newborns, but they would jeopardize their children's health and well-being. They could continue to live in fear of their husbands' violent outbreaks, but they would be inattentive mothers. And they could remain depressed and isolated, but they would set a horrible example for their children. As "good" mothers, they claimed to deserve safe, secure family lives. In advancing such arguments, these women also strove to insert maternal criteria into center poverty tests; they attempted to expand the nature of eligibility to include the quality of their mothering. Yet they were no more successful than women connected to the Gyámhatóság. Social workers responded by reasserting their material standards. It was nice that these women were committed mothers, but were they poor?

Perhaps the clearest example of this maternal strategizing was these women's utilization of the fruits of their maternal labor. Women brought children of all ages to the Gyámhatóság and Family Support Service Centers. Waiting rooms seemed like playgrounds, with children running around and screaming. Mothers chased them, warning them not to get dirty before they saw the caseworkers. Once inside the office, mothers drew on their children to show that they were "good" mothers deserving of help. Some pointed out how their children were well maintained and well behaved. They reminded welfare workers that it had become more expensive to feed children and more difficult to shield them from negative influences. Others brought in school records and reports to prove they were responsible mothers. "Look how my son writes his name," said one client whose income was just above the cut-off for assistance. "I taught him this." One female client even had her son sing and dance in the hopes of bolstering her appeal to exchange her flat. However, like their arguments about maternal competence, these maternal demonstrations rarely worked. Welfare workers just stared at these women, perplexed by the "strange" things they did to get assistance.

In this way, women rarely gained concrete resources from their strategies of reinclusion; their maternal maneuverings did not yield the support they sought. But they did provide these women with a position to speak from, a language of entitlement. With this maternal discourse, these women refused to be silenced. They did not stop talking about the larger context in which they mothered. They continued to describe the abuse plaguing them in their everyday lives. They did not refrain from discussing their feelings of isolation and exhaustion. And they insisted that resolving these problems was the state's responsibility. In the process, these women asked tough questions of welfare workers: Why was it important whether they had televisions or VCRs? And why wasn't it important if they felt disconnected or depressed? Why was it relevant how much money they lived on? And why wasn't it relevant that they lived amidst violence? Hence, although the contemporary welfare system was full of silencing, it was not silent. While new groups of women were excluded from the state sphere, they did not go quietly. The discourse of the maternal emboldened many of them to remain noisy and to contest the institutional processes that pushed them outside the new confines of welfare.

THE INCLUDED

At the same time the welfare system instituted new mechanisms to siphon off some women, it also created new forms of inclusion. Starting in the late 1980s, there was a large expansion of the "welfare rolls." National-level data reveal how dramatic the increase was: from 1985 to 1995, the number of recipients of some form of child-rearing assistance increased by over 1,000 percent. Put another way, during this period, 25 percent of the population applied for some kind of social assistance from welfare institutions; 18 percent of the population received aid.[30] These trends are deceiving if interpreted without an appreciation for the qualitative shifts in the nature of welfare work. Clearly, caseloads did not increase by 1,000 percent. Instead, a new homogeneity characterized caseloads: to become a client, one had to demonstrate material need. Whereas those with family problems once constituted the bulk of caseloads, such cases were largely excluded; impoverishment was now the thread that linked caseloads. Hence, although welfare offices did experience an expansion in their caseloads, the real story lies in the shifting nature of cases—that is, in the terms of inclusion.

Because welfare institutions collected data on their active clientele, it is possible to construct a demographic portrait of this group of women. From their case files, I discovered that many of them had been socially marginalized and defined as "bad" mothers in the late state-socialist period. Yet the parallels between these groups go only so far: roughly 50 percent of active clients who had been connected to welfare institutions in the socialist period had been considered "good" parents. Basically, these clients were lower- and working-class women who had suffered a major setback in the 1990s. Some of them struggled with bouts of unemployment. Others had spouses who had been laid off. Others were divorced. Still others confronted serious social problems. But these women all shared an inability to mobilize private resources or personal networks to halt their slide into poverty.

Given their socioeconomic positions, these women had a series of pressing material needs. Perhaps most immediate were their needs as workers. Although 46 percent of the population experienced some form of unemployment from 1992 to 1997, the percentage was much higher for clients of welfare institutions. Approximately 62 percent of active cases in the two districts of my research involved unemployment.[31] In large part, this higher rate was due to the fact that many female clients had been employed in those sectors hit the hardest by economic reform. From 1993 to 1996, unemployment displaced 13 percent of those employed in the manufacturing sector and 17 percent of those in construction—two sectors that absorbed much of the lower and working class.[32] The availability of new forms of public aid did not provide much of a material buffer. From 1993 to 1996, roughly 70 percent of those who lived below the social minimum received some form of poor relief; 40 percent of them received more than one type of assistance.[33] Yet even those clients who pooled all the available poor relief were still unable to bring their families above the poverty line.[34] These clients' needs as workers were of the most basic sort; very simply, they needed employment.[35]

In addition, many of those connected to welfare institutions had officially recognized jobs and thus were part of a relatively new social phenomenon in Hungary: a large group of working poor. Over 30 percent of my case sample consisted of employed clients who could not bring their families above the minimum subsistence level. This percentage is consistent with national-level poverty data. In 1994, 25 percent of the employed fell below the social minimum,[36] with 35 percent of unskilled workers, 24 percent of skilled workers, and 19 percent of office workers living below this level.[37] The material needs of the Hungarian working poor were not dissimilar to those of their Western counterparts: they were also in need of work that paid a livable wage and that was accompanied by social benefits.[38] Of course, the key difference was that many of these Hungarians had had such work in the not-so-distant past. Thus, they experienced their material deprivation in both relative and absolute terms.[39]

The plight of the working poor was exacerbated by the fact that the material environment surrounding their work lives had worsened since the 1980s. With the end of price subsidies, many basic necessities fell outside their reach. For example, state expenditures on housing had declined dramatically since the 1980s: while the government devoted 6 percent of the GDP to housing in 1989, by 1994 the percentage had dropped to 1.4.[40] In effect, those who did not enter the transition period with stable, preferably council, housing confronted serious problems. In 1991, occupants of state rentals and co-ops were given the option to purchase their flats at an extremely low price; 52 percent took advantage of the opportunity.[41] As a result, the Hungarian rate of home ownership became one of the highest in the world. Yet its rental sector was one of the smallest; while 18 percent of Hungary's housing stock were rentals in 1990, the percentage had fallen to 6 by 1996.[42] In effect, those who were unable to purchase a state flat in the early 1990s were shut out of the housing market. Many of them were forced to reside in extremely poor-quality housing without the most basic amenities.[43] Others were compelled to join their relatives in already cramped flats. Still others were forced onto the streets; by the most conservative estimates, fifteen thousand Hungarians had become homeless since the 1980s, while another four hundred thousand were at risk of becoming homeless.[44]

Yet even those Hungarians fortunate enough to secure stable housing faced extreme difficulties maintaining their households. From 1991 to 1994, utility prices increased by roughly 300 percent.[45] For large sectors of the population, heat became a luxury in the winter; for some, electricity became a luxury all year round. So did providing stable meals for their families: from 1989 to 1995 food prices more than quadrupled.[46] And, with the end of subsidies for children's clothing, toys, entertainment, and care, raising children became an extremely expensive endeavor. Families living at or below the subsistence level found it hard, if not impossible, to pay "market price" for goods and services essential to the maintenance of their households.

These material problems were especially acute for clients who were raising their children alone. The proportion of single-parent households rose steadily—from 10 percent in the mid-1980s to over 15 percent in the mid-1990s.[47] Put another way, in 1983 the illegitimacy rate was 8.3 percent; by 1993, it had increased to 17.6 percent.[48] In many respects, sole mothers were hit hard by economic marketization and privatization; over 40 percent of them lived in poverty.[49] The network of social support once available to them largely evaporated. With housing privatization, these women could no longer rely on preferences in the allocation of council flats. And they could not count on receiving special benefits through their workplaces. In short, with the withdrawal of public support for child rearing, sole mothers faced a series of urgent needs as parents and caretakers.

At the same time, not all clients' problems were reducible to their material deprivation. In times of economic scarcity and vulnerability, the division of labor within households can undergo profound transformation. In welfare offices, many clients revealed that the power relations in their homes had been reconfigured. Some women claimed that as their families slid into poverty, they lost domestic bargaining power. In their resource-constrained households, men had taken control of economic decision making. "He says that only he can decide where every forint goes," explained one female client. "Because only he sees the larger future and picture." Other women confronted the opposite pattern: their husbands left the entire household planning and budgeting to them. They interpreted this division of labor as equally unjust; it required that they strategize and work magic to keep afloat. When funds became tight or ran out at the end of the month, their husbands became furious: "One week all we had to eat was [instant] potatoes. He was so angry, [he] yelled, and disappeared for days." Hence, like their predecessors in the previous welfare regimes, many female clients continued to have needs as wives and as members of families undergoing complex power shifts.

Moreover, like many newly excluded women, female clients faced serious threats to their physical well-being. Some of these threats came from the same source: 32 percent of the active case files I reviewed involved domestic violence. These clients often bore the signs of abuse all over their bodies—from bruises to burns to missing teeth to broken limbs. They were quite forthcoming about who had perpetrated this violence. "I got these [bruises] last week when Fradi lost," a client declared. "He was angry because he lost money on the game."[50] Or, as another female client recounted, "Every Tuesday night I get a few hits. I don't know why he chooses this night, but it is always the same." Many clients also made a connection between male violence and alcohol abuse. Their accounts frequently began with their husbands' heavy drinking and ended with physical assault. "I know when his favorite pub closes," a client once explained to me. "I always make sure the children are in bed, and I prepare for what I get when he returns."[51]

Finally, many female clients experienced new threats to their emotional well-being. Of course, emotional distress was not itself a product of the transition period; clients in the previous welfare regimes also expressed feelings of isolation, loneliness, and depression. Yet, in contemporary welfare offices, these expressions took on a new sense of urgency; clients described feeling too depressed to leave their flats or to care for their families. On the whole, emotional distress engulfed more women after the 1980s: while 23 percent of the population complained of "neurotic disorders" in 1983, the percentage increased to 38 in 1995.[52] Similarly, the percentage of the population that sought treatment for psychological problems increased by 30 percent during the 1990s; the number of women who sought help for depression rose by 50 percent.[53]

Although emotional turmoil plagued Hungarians from multiple social strata, some evidence indicates that it affected the impoverished more acutely. According to mental-health surveys, emotional distress, anomie, and alienation were more pronounced among the poor. For example, those who lived below the social minimum were twice as likely to report feeling "powerless" as those in other income groups. They were three times more likely to report feeling incapacitated by nervousness and anxiety. And they were three times more likely to report feeling "overwhelmed" by life itself.[54]

The Limitations of Inclusion

Clearly, when women like these surfaced in welfare institutions, they had a series of complex needs. Their problems intersected in complicated ways; they were the combined result of economic vulnerability, familial conflict, social marginalization, and emotional turmoil. Unlike women defined as "materially secure," these women did not have welfare-office doors closed on them. After all, they were from the social strata that policymakers had promised to help; they were the impoverished, who, social scientists claimed, would benefit from welfare restructuring. Yet few female clients saw themselves as beneficiaries of the transition. Unlike policymakers and social scientists, these women rarely evaluated their situations in relative terms, as compared with those of the newly excluded. Rather, they assessed their lot in absolute terms. The comparison left them wanting. They expected the state to provide decent work and affordable basic necessities but instead received a bit of poor relief. They expected stable housing but instead received meager funds for flat upkeep. And they expected help improving their domestic lives but instead received lectures on how fortunate they were to remain eligible for state programs. In addition, they were put on assembly lines and processed by welfare workers who often deemed them "untouchables." From such experiences, the limitations of the liberal state must have seemed more apparent than its benefits.

Of course, this was not the experience of all welfare clients. Some seemed satisfied with the terms of their inclusion. Perhaps they came to welfare offices with lower expectations; perhaps they had resigned themselves to expect less from the welfare system. Whatever the reason, these clients simply sought temporary boosts to their incomes and were relatively content with the material handouts. They seemed grateful when welfare workers provided them with small amounts of money. And they seemed appreciative when social workers distributed food packages or supermarket coupons. These clients also seemed relatively unaffected by the treatment they experienced when obtaining such support. They looked untroubled by the welfare myths swirling around them or the assembly-line quality of welfare work. In effect, they received what they wanted—a bit of financial help or material support.

Given the nature of my data, it is close to impossible to determine what proportion of clients were content with the assistance they received. Yet, from my case-file analysis and participant-observation research, I found such clients to be in the minority. Far more common were clients who expressed dissatisfaction with the terms of their inclusion. They felt limited by the kind of assistance available to them, as well as by the conditions under which they received it. These clients had much higher expectations for the welfare system. As numerous social scientists have revealed, the Hungarian population remained quite "state-centered"; public-opinion surveys showed that a large majority of Hungarians still looked to the state to ensure their overall well-being. For instance, polls indicated that 91 percent of Hungarians surveyed believed that the state should subsidize prices; 89 percent saw it as the state's responsibility to secure full employment; 81 percent held the state responsible for reducing inequality; and 78 percent thought it was the state's duty to investigate how each and every wealthy person got rich.[55] The attitudes of most Hungarian welfare clients were consistent with these findings. They came to welfare offices in the hopes of improving their lives. They knew a bit of poor relief wouldn't cut it: their problems were too complicated to be resolved with a few hundred forints. These clients had higher expectations and felt constrained when welfare institutions failed to meet them.

Clients did not reject the available poor relief, but, at the same time, they demanded more comprehensive and less fleeting help. More specifically, unemployed clients regularly sought assistance finding work. These women told stories of unsuccessful employment searches; they repeatedly discussed how their skills had become obsolete. "I am an excellent metal carver," one woman explained to her social worker. "[I'm] the best woman my [shop] steward saw do the job. Now the factory has closed, and there is nowhere to go." While women from previous generations advanced such claims in order to transform caseworkers into employment officers, contemporary clients experienced no such transformation. Throughout my time in these offices, I saw only one welfare worker find work for a client. And she did it more out of fear than out of concern for the client's well-being. One of the only male clients in the office, Mr. Kapos often came into the Family Support Service Center to demand money and food packages. After being confronted with his aggressive tactics, a social worker called a friend who worked in a local restaurant. With some cajoling, she convinced her friend to hire Mr. Kapos as a busboy. Later, I asked the social worker why she went out of her way for Mr. Kapos. She was honest: "He scares me. I just wanted him out of here." The most her other clients received were referrals to employment offices and a bit of poor relief.

Clients who were employed encountered similar limitations on what they could expect from welfare institutions. They also came to these offices with a host of work-related problems. These clients protested that their low wages kept them below the poverty line. They complained about inflexible supervisors. They described terrible working conditions—rooms without ventilation and long work hours without breaks. Again, these were issues that women from their mothers' and grandmothers' time had addressed in welfare institutions. But when contemporary welfare workers encountered such appeals, they simply threw up their hands in bewilderment. "What did that woman want me to do about her boss?" a caseworker once asked about such a client. Most likely, clients like this wanted a bit of mediation—someone to advise them about how to improve their work lives or to intervene to rectify their work problems. What they got instead was a bit of poor relief, a food package, or supermarket coupons.

Although clients' appeals as workers were not addressed to their satisfaction, at least they were acknowledged. Because clients established discursive links between their material deprivation and their work lives, welfare workers listened to them. Such links were more difficult for clients with domestic problems to make. Many clients came to welfare institutions seeking help with their child-rearing or caretaking responsibilities. They often discussed how disconnected they felt as mothers. They told stories of how they were too depressed to leave their flats. As a caseworker wrote about one such woman, "She sits in her bathtub all day, cries, and listens to music. How strange."[56] Overwhelmed by the demands placed on them, some female clients began to drink too much: "Neighbors say that she leaves the flat only to buy alcohol. She confirms that she drinks too much on occasion."[57] Other female clients felt unprepared to deal with the new threats to their children's welfare. They claimed to lack the time and the know-how to grapple with juvenile delinquency, rebellion, and drug use. "I see other boys in the building sniffing glue," one woman remarked to a caseworker. "How to protect my son from such behavior?" Whereas the maternalist regime gave assistance to some women with these kinds of problems, the rewards of this regime were limited to poor relief. Yet the punishments for some clients remained the same: in the two districts of my research, approximately 10 percent of such "needy" mothers had their children taken away from them and institutionalized in state facilities.[58]

Similar limitations awaited clients who sought help negotiating power relations with their spouses. When female clients advanced needs they had as wives, they hit an impenetrable discursive barrier. As they applied for public assistance, these clients often interjected comments about needing help controlling their husbands. For instance, instead of simply answering questions about their spouses' income, some women suggested that their husbands be called in to provide such information. "Honestly, I do not know his salary," a client once responded to her caseworker. "He refuses to tell me. Maybe he will tell you." And while welfare workers had them there, could they ask their spouses why they refused to contribute to the household budget? Why they spent so little time with the children? Why they drank away their pay? Rather than picking up on such cues, welfare workers usually told clients to bring in their spouses' work documents on their next visit.

Female clients' attempts to involve welfare workers in their domestic conflicts were even more pronounced on home visits. On those rare occasions when welfare workers entered clients' turf, these women struggled to carve out practical tools for dealing with these men. "Yes, the flat is clean, and this is completely because of me," one client remarked as we entered her apartment. "When he [her husband] is home, he sits there, he smokes, he drinks, and he threatens me and the children." Or as another client remarked as we toured her flat, "Officially, this is the children's room. I stay here now also . . . [as] protection from his outbursts." Whereas welfare workers in the previous regime would have picked up on these appeals— rewarding "good" mothers with help and punishing "bad" mothers with coercion—these welfare workers remained silent. They took notes on clients' valuables, calculated the size of clients' flats, and then scurried off to the next address on their list.

In addition to clients who felt limited by the assistance available to them, other clients seemed more troubled by the conditions under which they received it. These clients complained incessantly about having to beg for state aid. They frequently told me that they dreaded coming to welfare offices because caseworkers made them feel "embarrassed" and "ashamed." They despised the means tests administered by welfare agencies. As they were forced to detail their material resources in these large, collective offices, they appeared humiliated and vulnerable. "This is unnatural, very unnatural," one woman repeated as she listed her family's resources to an office full of other clients and caseworkers. Occasionally, clients contested these poverty investigations as a waste of time and pointed out that they could have used the time they spent tracking down income documentation to search for employment.

For some female clients, the new forms of stigmatization accompanying this surveillance constrained them the most. Clients were aware of the mythologies looming over them. They knew that welfare workers told jokes about them; they could recite the degrading names caseworkers had for them. Thus, many clients spent as little time as possible in welfare offices. As a female client once remarked to her friend as they left the Gyámhatóság, "I always feel dirty here. They are so despising." Clients also realized that welfare workers constructed them as welfare cheats. They therefore became visibly embarrassed when bombarded with inquiries into their "true" level of material deprivation. They often came to welfare offices with their heads down, whispering answers to caseworkers' loaded questions about the "real" ways they supported their families. Since the simplest omission or the most benign mistake on their part could get them deemed a "welfare cheat," clients regulated their own behavior with a new intensity. If they were not careful or slipped up only one time, they could find themselves on the track to exclusion and expelled from the welfare system altogether.

Just as Mrs. Kaltner's experience illuminated the dynamics of exclusion, one case truly exemplified the dynamics of inclusion—and their devastating consequences. Mrs. Zsigó, or Vilma as she preferred to be called, was the oldest of four children raised by a single mother in a poor area of Budapest.[59] Vilma's father died when she was young, and her mother had to support the family alone. Vilma dropped out of school when she was sixteen years old and joined her mother at a local bottle factory. In 1988, when her mother remarried a man who drank too much, Vilma decided to move out. Around this time Vilma met Miklós, a young man who worked in a nearby metal factory. Vilma was immediately attracted to his "crazy ways." She knew that Miklós came from a troubled family; his father was an abusive alcoholic who had forced Miklós to quit school and go to work when he was young.

Although Miklós was "difficult," she married him in 1988, and they moved into a one-room flat. After her two sons were born, they received a two-room council flat. Vilma recalled this period fondly, as her family got by quite well on a combination of Miklós's wages and her child-care grant.

Few of the details about Vilma's past surfaced in her initial meetings with welfare workers. Her case began in 1993, when she came to her local Family Support Service Center after Miklós lost his job. In her first meeting, Vilma answered her social worker's questions about her income and was told she could receive "help" in the form of food packages and occasional money. Vilma then came in each Friday to pick up this aid. She rarely asked for anything more. On one occasion, she requested help paying an overdue utility bill. It had been a cold winter, and, without the old subsidies, the bill was higher than usual. She received the money to pay the bill. Another time she asked for advice about what to do once her GYES grant expired; she was referred to a district employment office.

In these interactions, Vilma made no mention of the bruises and scars that covered her face. She was never asked about them; she never raised the issue. Then, on one hot summer day, Vilma came to the office wearing a short-sleeve shirt that exposed the bruises and burns covering her arms. Now out in the open, Vilma nervously referred to them as the "marks" of her husband. On subsequent visits, Vilma described the beatings Miklós inflicted on her, which had worsened since he lost his job. To make extra money, Miklós had begun to play music. Consequently, he stayed out late and drank more. When he returned home, fights would erupt. "At least he does it at night," Vilma remarked. "So the children do not see." Her social worker listened as Vilma recounted these stories but rarely added anything. After one particularly chilling account of a beating, the social worker responded, "Oh men, they are crazy." Another time her social worker offered to help Miklós find a job. But nothing ever came of it. Other than this empty offer, Vilma received no counseling and no referrals to a battered-women's shelter.

Shortly after Vilma opened up, the center ran out of welfare benefits. The social worker referred Vilma to the Gyámhatóság, explaining that there was "nothing left for [her] here." Given Vilma's low family income, her social worker instructed her to apply for RNS; Vilma followed her instructions and applied for aid. A home visit was made to assess Vilma's eligibility. During the visit, a problem was discovered: Miklós owned expensive musical instruments that put their disposable income over the assistance cut-off. If he didn't sell the instruments, Vilma would be denied aid. This threat prompted a series of fights between Vilma and Miklós. Apparently, he won

the fights since Vilma was given only occasional aid. This assistance provided less than half of what RNS offered and had to be reapplied for every
few months. Without other options, Vilma took the assistance.

Over the next year, when Vilma came to the Gyámhatóság to reapply for
aid, her bruises became more visible, as did the signs of severe alcohol abuse.
Vilma's body became thinner and thinner, and her face puffier and puffier.
Home-visit reports documented her decline. Caseworkers noted that her
flat was increasingly empty, with few furnishings, household items, or food.
They described how empty alcohol bottles "littered" the flat and how the
"stench of decay and dirt" permeated the home. School reports complained
that Vilma's children came to school hungry, unbathed, and in dirty clothes.
Yet nothing was done to halt this slide. Vilma's family income remained low,
so she continued to receive occasional welfare assistance.

When Vilma lost her job in late 1994, her life decayed further. Rumors
began to circulate that she had turned to prostitution. Apparently, a caseworker had seen Vilma standing at Rákóczi Square, a notorious gathering
place. "She was wearing a short skirt and prostitute boots," he reported,
"with that look of trouble on her face." Vilma's caseworker immediately
called her into the office and confronted her. She threatened to withdraw
Vilma's assistance if she did not stop her "illegal activities." Bombarded by
accusations, Vilma sat there, with her head down, denying the charges.
Clearly deflated, she was being "hit" from all sides, but received help from
no one.

I saw Vilma last in 1995. Her body was emaciated, bruised, and battered.
She had come to the Gyámhatóság to place her children in an institution for
neglected children. She remembered me from her days at the Family Support Service Center. As she filled out the necessary paperwork, she turned to
me and nervously remarked, "I had no choice. At least I won't have to come
here and see them [the caseworkers] anymore."

Strategies of Destigmatization

In many respects, Vilma was just the kind of client that the liberal state was
supposed to help. Poor and vulnerable, she fit the model of the newly targeted "needy individual"; after all, it was her material deprivation that kept
her in the system. Yet, instead of enjoying the fruits of inclusion, many
women like Vilma experienced a downward spiral. They lost domestic
power; they became more depressed and isolated; they were beaten more
regularly; and they became more materially deprived. When they tried to
voice these problems, their appeals fell on deaf ears. When they attempted
to activate welfare workers in these struggles, they got little response. In

effect, their inclusion in the welfare apparatus was premised on a selective silencing. If they spoke of financial hardship, they were heard. But if they spoke of their battles with spouses, children, or themselves, they were ignored—often with devastating consequences.

These shifts in the terms of inclusion did not affect groups of docile, passive women. These women had developed opinions about their needs and how they should be met. A few of these clients saw their new dislocation as bound up with the new political economy of welfare. "This is how they always said it worked under capitalism: nobody will care for the poor," one client half-jokingly said to me. These clients were also politically astute in their analyses of what welfare targeting would eventually devolve into. They argued that future welfare funding would always be in jeopardy since the government was more likely to cut programs destined for the poor than to cut other programs. For instance, in 1994, one district reduced the amount of child-rearing assistance. A number of clients immediately interpreted this reduction as proof of the government's disregard for policies supporting the poor. One client made this argument to me in 1995, the day the Bokros reforms were introduced. She asked about the welfare reforms under way in the United States since she had heard they were similar to the Bokros Plan. I then explained how they were different—that the cuts in the already targeted AFDC program paled in comparison with those being made in Hungary. She quickly corrected me: "You pay attention. This was the first step. Next they will cut more. It will not be so different."

More common than clients who advanced long-term, structural explanations for their dislocation were those who strategized to carve out a bit more room in which to maneuver in the short term. Interestingly, the form of their strategizing was strikingly similar to that of the newly excluded: these clients also highlighted their social contributions as mothers. But unlike the newly excluded, who appropriated the maternal to gain reentry into the welfare apparatus, female clients utilized the maternal to change the content of the assistance they received. Theirs was a more defensive strategy; they used the maternal as a shield against pathologization. Like many excluded women, some clients may have retreated to the maternal because of past welfare experiences. For them, the rise of the liberal welfare regime engendered a return to state socialism. For others, motherhood may have been the only place to turn; it may have been the only contributory identity they could use to counter myths about their deficiencies. Whatever its source, many clients used the idiom of the maternal to contest their losses and expand their room to maneuver.

Their maternal strategizing took several forms. First, clients often appropriated their identities as mothers to connect with welfare workers and to close the social distance separating them. It was as though these clients believed that they could undermine the mythologies swirling around them by forming personal relationships with the myth makers. Initially, I was quite confused by the flood of questions clients asked caseworkers. Wasn't it supposed to work the other way? In my observations, I often learned more about welfare workers—where they were from, whether they were married, and whether they had children—than about clients. At first, I interpreted clients' questions as a tactic to deflect attention from themselves. With time, I realized the objective was to form collusive relationships with welfare workers and eventually to draw into view more of their own lives.

Clients usually raised questions about welfare workers' lives when they had been denied assistance or when their appeals for help went unrecognized. At these junctures, clients connected their experiences as mothers to the experiences of welfare workers. In doing so, clients attempted to show welfare workers that they both struggled with common problems and shared dilemmas. This was the strategy used by an RNS recipient in 1994, when her aid was threatened after a home visitor discovered she owned a new television and VCR. The caseworker interpreted these possessions as a sign that the woman was a "welfare cheat." Instead of explaining how she purchased the electronics, the client turned the tables on her caseworker. Did she have children? Didn't she feel better knowing her children were safely at home in front of the TV and not roaming the streets of the city?

Another client used a similar strategy of identification with the mother of a social worker at a Family Support Service Center. The client's ex-husband refused to pay child support for their three children. Instead of forcing him to pay, the Gyámhatóság gave her RNS, which was insufficient to support the children. So she came to a Family Support Service Center to ask a social worker to intervene. When the social worker hastily responded that this was not her job, the client retorted, "Are you a mother?" The social worker defensively replied that she was too young to have children. The client continued, "Well, that's why you don't understand. What about your mother? Was she divorced?" After the social worker reluctantly admitted that her mother was divorced, the client immediately drew parallels. Imagine if her father had not supported her. Would this have been fair? What would her mother have done? Her strategy was clear: she connected her experience to her social worker's life in order to challenge the social worker's refusal of help.

Prior to the introduction of the Bokros Plan, clients also used the family-allowance and GYES programs to connect to welfare workers. For instance, in 1994 a Gyámhatóság client used her family allowance to shield herself from stigmatization. She had come to the office to apply for RNS, and her eligibility worker was giving her a hard time. As they filled out the paperwork, the caseworker made nasty comments about all the assistance that the client received; she berated her for failing to remember the exact amount of these benefits. When they reached the question about her family allowance, the client claimed that she could not recall the amount. After noticing the caseworkers' pictures of her children on her desk, the client said, "You have children too. Do you know how much we receive for two children?" Her question was doubly loaded. By using "we" she tried to destigmatize the assistance she received. And by turning the question back on the caseworker (who could not recall the amount of her allowance), she undermined the caseworker's accusations of ineptitude. Other clients made more explicit policy connections between themselves and caseworkers. For instance, two caseworkers employed in one Gyámhatóság were pregnant. Clients often asked about their pregnancies and plans for child-care leave. They then discussed their experiences on the grant, prompting a conversation about a policy they shared. As a client once joked about one of these caseworkers after she went on leave, "I hope her husband is well paid. Maybe she will come in after me, sitting on my side of the desk this time."

Second, in addition to mobilizing their experiences as mothers to connect with the myth makers, female clients used maternalist arguments to challenge the myths themselves. Many clients explained their material deprivation by referring to the high cost of raising children. They were not poor because of individual defects. Rather, they were committed mothers forced to live in a difficult material situation in order to be with their children. "We were in a good material condition before the baby," one client remarked to her caseworker. "But since then we have fallen." In the office, as clients listed their income sources, they often contextualized these data by informing caseworkers of their child-rearing costs. It was not their fault that they struggled so hard: the conditions of child rearing had worsened, and they suffered the consequences. On home visits, as caseworkers toured their barren flats, clients further contextualized their situation. In response to caseworkers' disapproving looks, they explained that they could not afford to furnish their flats or buy children's toys without state subsidies. To counter caseworkers' disparaging comments about their "disorderly life-styles," clients described how hard they worked to raise children. "Avoid work?" one client exclaimed when her caseworker accused her of being lazy. "I have four children, and I work more than in any job I had as a clerk. Then I sat all day, and now I do the hardest work, without pay."

Other clients appropriated the products of their maternal labor to disrupt caseworkers' myths about their defects and pathologies. Like many newly excluded women, clients regularly brought their children to welfare offices. Yet they utilized their children for slightly different ends; they used their children as extensions of themselves to challenge stereotypes of their "out-of-control" behavior. When accused of leading disorderly lives, many clients immediately pointed out how well they raised their children. For instance, a client once came to the Gyámhatóság wielding a home-visit report that labeled her a "drunken," "uneducated," and "simple" woman. Furious, she responded that if it were true, she would not have been able to raise two healthy girls. To prove her point, she had her two small daughters by her side, dressed in new clothes. Clients who were deemed violent and aggressive also used their children as myth disrupters. While male security guards hovered around them and surveyed their every move, these women tightly grasped their babies. They often picked up their babies once the surveillance began, using them as shields and as reminders that they were mothers, not murderers. One client articulated this response explicitly when her caseworker referred to her as "brutal." The client picked up her baby and held him across the desk, challenging the caseworker to examine him for signs of abuse. If she were so aggressive, wouldn't he bear the markings? If she were so brutal, where was the evidence?

Female clients also appropriated their children to confront constructions of their "untouchable" nature. Clients seemed well aware of the physical distance that welfare workers insisted on maintaining with them. Although a few clients tried to bridge this distance by forcing physical contact with caseworkers, most achieved this contact through their children. Babies were particularly useful here. Even the most hardened caseworker could soften when confronted with a baby. Clients knew they could and thus encouraged caseworkers to reach out to their infants. "Go ahead and hold him," an extremely poor RNS recipient once prodded her caseworker. "I just washed the blanket, and it is clean." Clients also pushed their small children into contact with caseworkers. "Give the nice lady a kiss, she has helped us," a RNS recipient once said to her daughter. Or, as another encouraged her son, "Shake the nice man's hand and thank him for letting your sister come home to us." Few caseworkers could resist such gestures, which provoked approving smiles in mothers. Although they themselves could not be touched, watching their children come into contact with state actors seemed to please many female clients.

Third, female clients used similar strategies when they had been denied access to the fruits of their maternal labor. Clients whose children had been placed in state care regularly appealed these decisions in maternal terms. They struggled to convince caseworkers that poverty was not the same as maternal neglect. These exchanges constituted some of the most painful moments in my fieldwork; these women mobilized everything at their disposal to have their children returned. For instance, one mother, after letting us into her dark basement flat, immediately put out a plate of cookies. She then explained that they were her son's favorite cookies, and even though she had little money, she always brought them to him at the children's home. Then there was the recently divorced mother of four whose two sons had been institutionalized because of material deprivation. As she walked us through her barren flat, she nervously explained that she had been forced to sell most of her furnishings to pay the utility bill. Then she proudly opened a small closet to reveal two boxes of toys that belonged to her sons. She claimed she would never sell the toys; even though she needed the money, she knew that her boys would come home one day. One female client articulated this maternal response best after her two daughters had been removed from school without her consent and then institutionalized. Enraged, she came storming into the Gyámhatóság. "These are my babies, I am their mother. How could you take them like this from me? Without asking? You did not even inform me. I clean them, I feed them, and I take them to school. Then you take them away. Yes, we are in hard times now, but I am not the devil. I am the mother. Well, what does this mean?" When hearing such accounts, caseworkers seldom budged; all the cookies, toys, and confessions of love could not deflect their attention from clients' material conditions.

FAILED STRATEGIES AND NEW WELFARE REALITIES

During the 1990s, Hungarian welfare clients were promised many things from many different groups. International police from the IMF and World Bank promised them "welfare with a human face." Economists and sociologists promised them a welfare system that was more sensitive to the needs of the vulnerable. Welfare scholars promised them new possibilities for identity formation and interest articulation. Instead they got a welfare apparatus plagued with new patterns of exclusion and inclusion. They confronted new forms of targeting that channeled some of them out of the welfare system altogether. They faced new institutional processes that redefined the acceptable needs claims for those remaining in the system. In effect, the liberal welfare state fostered and fueled social divisions among the potential client population. In doing so, it caused new experiences of loss for both the excluded and the included.

Perhaps most pronounced were the losses of the newly excluded. Despite their relative material security, these women faced a host of problems: as workers they felt vulnerable; as mothers they felt overwhelmed; as wives they felt powerless; and as women they felt lonely. Whereas these problems were once defined as social issues, they were now privatized. When some of these women came to welfare offices for help, they were silenced and treated as though they spoke a foreign language. Others were made to feel guilty for usurping caseworkers' time. Still others were advised to turn elsewhere for help—to the market to resolve work problems and to private networks to grapple with domestic turmoil. In short, as these women were banished from the state sphere, they lost their access to a variety of practical resources.

As the contemporary welfare apparatus established new entrance requirements, it also set a new needs talk for those it admitted. Tighter borders formed around state welfare. Only those from certain income groups gained access to this realm, and all they had access to was poor relief. Although some clients seemed content with this material support, most clients sought additional assistance: as workers, they sought help finding employment; as mothers, they sought help providing for their children; as wives, they sought help grappling with domestic turmoil; and, as women, they sought help struggling with emotional distress. Yet these practical resources largely evaporated around them, as did the discursive resources that would have enabled them to stretch the welfare borders. Their inclusion in the welfare apparatus was based not on what they contributed socially but on what they lacked financially. New constructions of their neediness formed around them; new mythologies about their pathological character and contaminated bodies were soon to follow. The result was a contraction in their room to maneuver in everyday life.

When confronted with these losses, neither the excluded nor the included reacted by launching public protests. Instead, as generations of women before them had done, they set their sights on caseworkers in an attempt to manipulate them and to protect themselves. And they did so in similar ways: by reasserting their social significance as mothers. Given their institutional positions, these two groups used the maternal for different ends. The excluded excavated the maternal as an entrance ticket, while the included used it as a defensive strategy of destigmatization. Despite these differences, both groups drew on the maternal in an attempt to extend the boundaries of welfare and to improve the conditions of state assistance.

Yet intentions do not always coincide with outcomes. Although this excavation work enabled women to critique the new system, it did not have the desired institutional outcomes. The excluded were unable to open up new channels for inclusion. For the most part, their strategizing had little effect on the conditions of welfare allocation. When it had an effect, it was not the desired one: instead of leading to an inclusive welfare apparatus, it prompted caseworkers to reassert their material criteria adamantly. The same was true of client strategizing. At best, their strategies left welfare workers perplexed by the "strange" things that clients did to get assistance. Yet these strategies could also exacerbate clients' problems by inclining welfare workers to attack them as "overdemanding" or "crazy." Thus, although the discourse of the maternal gave women the ability to speak, it did not lead to concrete institutional changes.

Herein lies a critical difference between clients' strategies of the present and those of the past. The welfare society and the maternalist welfare state encompassed both possibilities and limitations. Within them, clients worked the prevailing needs talk to carve out resources for use in their everyday lives—that is, to enhance their institutional integration, to gain domestic power, or to secure their own sense of well-being. Yet the contemporary strategies resulted in no such gains. Few women left welfare offices feeling more integrated, powerful, or secure. In part, their inability to disrupt the current welfare regime was connected to the weapons they wielded. Theirs were largely ineffective weapons, premised on welfare models and forms of entitlement that had been thoroughly discredited. Moreover, the welfare regime these women were up against was arguably more impenetrable than its predecessors. It was premised on a poverty discourse that failed to acknowledge multiple needs; it rested on surveillance techniques and disciplinary practices that pathologized and stigmatized. In the liberal welfare regime, clients not only experienced a loss of concrete resources but also lost the space for effective contestation and reconstruction.

In this way, the Hungarian transition story offers insights into the relationship among political, civil, and social rights. It challenges the assumption that an expansion of political citizenship necessarily breeds new forms of social citizenship. Precisely the opposite occurred in Hungary: as political rights expanded, social rights contracted. Similarly, this story calls into question the blind faith so often placed in civil society—that is, the belief that societal well-being is a natural outgrowth of the enhancement of civil society. During the 1990s, the terrain of civil society grew, and new space opened up outside the formal state sphere. But, because of the profound changes within the state arena, some social groups faced difficulties utilizing this new civic space. Redistributive changes heightened their sense of deprivation and fear of falling. Such disenfranchisement certainly mitigated against the mobilization of women, the poor, and the Roma in civil society. Interpretive changes further impeded such mobilization. Now stripped of their contributory identities, on what basis could such groups launch large-scale public protests? Now constituted as needy individuals, with what language could such groups claim a collective, public voice? Thus, instead of looking to the realm of civil society for the pill that will cure all social ills, one must interrogate the exclusions and inclusions within the state sphere. As this transition story reveals, without strong social rights many Hungarians remain unable to utilize fully their new civil and political rights.

Conclusion
Welfare Lessons from East to West

In 1994, the Eötvös Lóránd University in Budapest held a memorable conference on welfare reform. Funded by a series of international foundations, the conference brought together prominent welfare scholars from Eastern Europe, Western Europe, and North America. The Westerners arrived with complicated welfare theories and models. Few of them had ever been to Hungary, and thus they began their speeches by rejoicing in how "exciting" it was that Hungary had finally been "opened up" to international comparison. The world was filled with examples for Hungary to learn from, and they were there to provide a sampling of these possibilities. Some analysts offered up liberal welfare models and questioned whether Hungary was willing or able to emulate them. Others used these models to warn Hungarians of the dangers awaiting them: the lessons to be learned from the West were negative ones not to be followed. Following these speeches, Hungarian social scientists responded with celebratory comments about their new access to the global world of welfare. After decades of "exclusion" from the international welfare state trade, they were eager to make up for lost time. Indeed, there was much to be learned. And they were grateful that their Western colleagues had come to help decipher these lessons.

While Hungarian social scientists can certainly learn from the comparative work of Western scholars, the reverse is also true: a number of important lessons can be gained from the history of Hungarian welfare. In the rush to compensate for Hungary's fifty years of "exclusion," few of these lessons have been acknowledged. In this book, I attempted to excavate them. As I made my way through a half century of Hungarian welfare history, I maintained two dialogues. The first was perhaps the more explicit one: I challenged scholars of Eastern Europe to reject the overly simplistic dichotomy between the "socialist past" and the "capitalist present" and to resist the temptation of homogenizing the socialist part and blindly celebrating the capitalist part. Both these conclusions emanate clearly from my reperiodization of Hungarian welfare regimes and my theorization of their succession. The second, more implicit dialogue extended beyond the East European context to offer broader lessons and insights that can inform Western welfare state theory and politics.

Over fifty years, Hungary organized its welfare system in three different ways. Embodying distinct sets of policies and practices, these welfare regimes articulated contrasting conceptions of need: they shifted from a focus on the institutional to a preoccupation with the maternal to an emphasis on the material. This kind of diversity in welfare forms is unique. When welfare scholars seek to understand state variation, they are often forced to conduct cross-national comparisons. Yet Hungary's history of welfare experimentation enabled me to draw broad, comparative lessons from a single case study. These include a conceptual lesson about how to analyze welfare states, a feminist lesson about how different states regulate the social relations of gender, and a political lesson about how welfare states can become stigmatizing social spaces.

THE LAYERED STATE: ANALYZING WELFARE REGIMES

Throughout this book, I deployed the concept of a "welfare regime" to structure the historical analysis. My use of this concept diverged in important ways from the traditional usage. For regime analysts like Esping-Andersen, the term encompasses a collection of redistributive policies that link the state, the market, and the family.[1] By contrast, I employed the term to unpack the complex of apparatuses that constitute the state itself. In this way, as I embarked on a historical ethnography of Hungarian welfare, I advanced an alternative approach to the study of the state. This approach views the state as layered with national and local institutions. It also exposes how these state levels constantly interact and transform each other. Instead of taking the welfare state as a uniform body, this layered approach examines the state as a bundle of institutions linked through relations of mutual determination.

The first type of layering I uncovered was a layering of state policies and practices. I discovered that state institutions are shaped by national-level social policies and concrete, local relations to clients. Over the course of its development, the Hungarian welfare system was reformed on both levels. The key components of these welfare regimes were articulated in the policy apparatus and in the organization of welfare work. There was a striking compatibility between these state layers in all three regimes. In the early socialist period, state policies and agencies deflected welfare responsibilities back onto the social institutions that generated them: societal policies attempted to strengthen and rebuild the institutions of work and family, while welfare workers acted to enhance clients' institutional integration. In the late socialist period, state policies and agencies targeted women as a means of supporting families: maternalist policies funneled special resources to women as mothers, while welfare workers developed casework techniques to regulate women's mothering practices. Finally, in the contemporary period, state policies and agencies emphasized the bureaucratic regulation of poverty: means-tested policies targeted the materially needy, while welfare workers treated the impoverished. Hence, the state layers of policy and practice operated in complementary ways over this fifty-year period.

Although these policies and practices formed constellations that fit together in patterned ways, their relationship was not a simple causal one. Rather, there was an affinity between particular policy modes and institutional arrangements; these state levels reinforced each other. For instance, it would be far too simplistic to attribute the societal focus of the early socialist welfare regime to its economic policies alone. While they were important, other factors were determinant at the local level, including the lack of segmentation within agencies and the limited resources at caseworkers' disposal. The same is true of the late socialist regime. Although it would be tempting to reduce this regime's maternal focus to its social policies, other processes shaped welfare workers' maternalism, including the specialization within and among agencies and the professionalization of welfare work as a whole. In fact, local-level maternalism developed beyond what the social policies dictated: it made all sorts of evaluative distinctions among mothers, which eventually filtered back into the social policies of later decades. The interaction between policies and practices is equally apparent in the contemporary period. The introduction of income and means tests clearly altered the nature of welfare work; it transformed casework into piecework and welfare workers into eligibility workers. Yet this new organization of casework then channeled back to influence policy. Welfare workers ascribed new meaning to poor relief and interpreted it as "marked"; they "othered" recipients as defective and pathological. Thus, instead of establishing a causal hierarchy between these state layers, I exposed how policies and practices are bound up in relations of mutual determination.

Obviously, the precise form and content of these state layers are specific to Hungary. Yet my findings regarding state layering and mutual determination have theoretical significance for Western welfare state scholars. These findings highlight the importance of examining multiple state realms when analyzing modern welfare systems. They suggest to scholars that they use a wide lens in order to understand fully how welfare states operate. It is not sufficient to analyze only social-policy apparatuses. These policies must be implemented, administered, and grounded in the lives of real people; they must be combined with and integrated into actual institutions. By setting the conditions of state redistribution, this filtering process can ascribe new meaning to policies themselves. Furthermore, it is at this filtering stage that clients confront state constructions of welfare. Clients experience these constructions as mediated by welfare workers; they encounter the message through the messengers. The interconnectedness of Hungarian policies and practices therefore offers a broad lesson to welfare state scholars by pointing to the theoretical insights gained when one investigates how different state realms are combined, integrated, and experienced by clients.

In addition, my historical study uncovered a second form of state layering. Welfare states are made up not only of layers of policies and practices but also of redistributive and interpretive apparatuses. My conceptualization of a "welfare regime" highlighted both state roles. In doing so, I further expanded traditional approaches to the study of the state. Just as most political sociologists restrict themselves to policy analyses, they tend to view state provisions as purely redistributive in nature. They look to policy structures to determine where different regimes locate their key redistributive mechanisms—in the market, in the family, or in the state.[2] And they examine the size of policy apparatuses to gauge how much states redistribute and who gets which resources. Yet welfare states regulate much more than material relations. They survey a multitude of other social relations, including relations between women and men, parents and children, and husbands and wives. In the process, states ascribe meaning to a variety of social roles; they define the "appropriate" behavior of workers, parents, spouses, and family members. In effect, states engage in a considerable amount of boundary work, interpreting the terms of inclusion and setting the borders surrounding social institutions. Thus, in analyzing welfare state development, it is essential to unearth how each state layer evolves over time, or, in Nancy Fraser's terms, to link the state's role as "need satisfier" to its role as "need interpreter."[3]

This dual focus is especially important to maintain in view of the fact that these state layers do not always develop in consistent ways. It is possible for a welfare state to combine a large redistributive apparatus with a narrow interpretation of need. The reverse is also imaginable: a welfare state could couple broad interpretive structures with restrictive redistributive practices. In fact, I uncovered both patterns in the Hungarian welfare system. The early socialist regime was characterized by a tension between the redistributive and the interpretive. This regime operated with an expansive conception of need: it held entire institutions responsible for social well-being and recognized multiple social identities. Yet it was plagued with redistributive inequalities and an abysmal record of distributing political rights. The opposite pattern characterized the late socialist regime. Here the redistributive apparatus expanded to include new social policies, welfare agencies, and forms of entitlement. But the interpretive underpinnings of this regime narrowed to encircle only some social groups and to acknowledge only a limited repertoire of maternal identities. A similar tension plagued the contemporary welfare system. In the 1990s, Hungarian welfare expenditures soared, and the welfare rolls burgeoned. But the state now worked with its narrowest definition of need, material deprivation.

Given these developmental inconsistencies, the story I told in this book would have been quite different if I had limited myself to one of these state layers. Had I followed the traditional sociological route and traced only redistributive developments, my story would have been one of progressive expansion. It would have begun with a resource-strained system riddled with redistributive inequalities, moved on to a more generous system comprised of extensive family benefits and social guarantees, and concluded with a bloated system characterized by huge expenditures. Had I tracked only the interpretive, I would have told the opposite story, a story of the progressive narrowing of interpretations of need as the state shifted focus from the institutional to the maternal to the material. It would also have been a story of the progressive reduction in the identities acknowledged by the state, an account of a welfare apparatus that first recognized clients as workers, parents, spouses, and family members, then saw them as workers and mothers, and finally reduced them to needy individuals. Because I maintained a focus on both the redistributive and the interpretive, I told all these stories. And I wove them together into one narrative that emphasized the twists and turns of welfare and the simultaneous expansion of and contraction in state apparatuses.

Thus, there are clear empirical payoffs to approaching the state as a layered, interactive entity. Again, although the precise contours of the layering I uncovered are specific to this study, they do have broader theoretical implications. They suggest that while the size of a state's redistributive apparatus clearly matters, so too does its interpretation of need; while it is critical to ask "who gets what" in a given welfare state, it is equally important to interrogate the terms of inclusion and exclusion. For instance, throughout Western Europe and North America, massive reforms are rearranging state welfare structures. Both opponents and proponents of these reforms have focused on their redistributive consequences—on how time limits and work requirements will affect recipients' material well-being. Without a doubt, these are critical questions to investigate. Yet they should not obscure the equally profound interpretive shifts accompanying these reforms. In fact, these redistributive and interpretive changes may very well be in tension. In the process of scaling back the state, these reforms may end up encoding a broad conception of need—an interpretation that targets a range of social institutions and acknowledges new client identities. Of course, it remains to be seen whether welfare reform will have these unintended effects. But the conceptual point holds: this layered approach to the state can provide new insights into the dynamics of welfare reform cross-nationally and into the inconsistent, and even contradictory, nature of state development.

THE GENDERED STATE: EVALUATING WELFARE REGIMES

This historical study of Hungarian welfare not only exposed the layered quality of state welfare regimes but also evaluated and assessed these regimes. With this evaluative agenda, I entered the tricky terrain of "state effects," a terrain where many social scientists fear to tread. Their reluctance is quite understandable: when researchers evaluate the effects of state welfare regimes, they are often forced to confront their scientific leanings and commitments. The evaluations I ended up with in this study clearly reflected my sociological biases. First, as a feminist sociologist, I filtered this historical account through a gendered lens. Because I see welfare politics as always infused with some form of gender politics, I would argue that gender is a critical lens through which to assess state welfare regimes. But it is only one of many evaluative lenses; other researchers, working with other lenses, might have drawn different conclusions from these historical data. Second, my analytical focus on welfare policies and practices and on state redistribution and interpretation shaped my evaluative criteria. Given this focus, I was not content with an assessment of the redistributive outputs of national-level policies. Instead, I emphasized how different state forms encoded specific relations of domination and how those relations shaped women's ability to maneuver against the state. In effect, I sought to explicate the dialectics of domination and resistance in each welfare regime.

As I developed this dialectical approach, I entered into a dialogue with other feminist scholars of the state. Since the 1980s, feminist state theory has evolved into one of the most exciting subfields of political sociology. Unlike other state scholars, feminist theorists have not shied away from taking an evaluative stance on different modes of welfare development. In fact, most feminist scholars evaluate state gender regimes in similar terms: they assess the extent to which states promote female dependence or independence. Early feminist work on the state assumed the state's role in securing female dependence—either on individual men ("private patriarchy") or on men as a collective embodied in the state ("public patriarchy").[4] More recent feminist work rejects the simple assumption of state patriarchy and develops sophisticated ways to assess the gendered effects of state welfare. For instance, many feminists have adjusted the criteria used by regime analysts to account for gender; they propose that we examine the extent to which states de/commodify women and enable them to form "autonomous" households.[5] In effect, they have constructed new categories to compare the paths of dependence and independence set by welfare states.

These new classificatory schemes have added nuance both to feminist and to nonfeminist analyses of state development. Yet, as Nancy Fraser and Linda Gordon argue, the continued preoccupation with in/dependence obscures as it illuminates: these overloaded terms tend to deflect from the social interdependencies that states secure and regulate.[6] The historical findings of this study corroborate their argument. Instead of acting to secure women's dependence or independence, the successive Hungarian welfare regimes linked women to different social realms. In early socialism, state policies and practices formed links among the workplace, the nuclear family, and the extended family. In effect, they channeled women and men into the state sphere and then redirected them back out into better-integrated institutions. In late state socialism, these links narrowed. Rather than strengthening women's ties to existing institutions, this regime tightened the grip of state experts; it channeled women into the state sphere, enmeshed them in professional discourses, and released them as "better" mothers. And in the contemporary period, the state largely expected women to make their own links. By closing the door to large numbers of women and offering minimal assistance to those let in, the state effectively forced women to turn to private networks like the nuclear family and the market. In this way, state dominance did not operate in the dichotomous terms of dependence and independence. Rather, it worked through the formation of social interdependencies by deciding whom to draw in, where to channel them, and which social relations to target and treat.

These channeling processes then shaped the array of gender identities acknowledged by the state. As welfare states negotiate social interdependencies, they recognize different gender categories; as states direct women to specific social institutions, they highlight certain social positions. For instance, the early socialist state's focus on institutional arrangements fostered an appreciation of women's many identities: its policies and practices viewed women as workers, mothers, spouses, and family members. And it weighted these identities equally. When the late socialist state focused narrowly on the mother/child dyad, it solidified a new ordering of identities: it constituted women primarily as mothers and secondarily as workers. It also created a new ranking of maternal identities, defining some women's maternal identifications as praiseworthy and others as pathological. Finally, as the liberal welfare regime restricted itself to poverty regulation, it collapsed all identities into one—the materially deprived. This progressive reduction in the number of recognized gender identities should be seen as a mode of state control. By closing off a range of possible identifications, these regimes construed women's needs and desires in increasingly limited terms. The implications are clear: instead of restricting themselves to an analysis of dependence and independence, feminist scholars may find it theoretically more powerful to view state gender regimes as working through the social links and identities accentuated by welfare states.

Yet this reconceptualization of state dominance begs the critical question: How do women fare in these different welfare regimes and modes of state regulation? In addressing this question, this book offers perhaps its most important contribution to feminist state theory. Overall, as feminists have deconstructed state gender regimes, they have paid inadequate attention to the varied responses these regimes provoke in women themselves. To the extent that feminist scholars explore women's reactions to state control, they tend to treat women as abstractions. As Diane Sainsbury put it, the goal has been to disentangle how the "ideal recipient" fares in different welfare systems.[7] But women have complicated relationships to welfare policies and practices, relationships that are difficult to recognize when they are treated as abstractions. Female clients often react to welfare provisions in unexpected ways; they frequently defend social relations that feminist scholars might find troubling in the abstract.[8] Yet such responses must be taken seriously in order to arrive at a full understanding of the gendered underpinnings of different welfare regimes.

In this study, I built these responses into my conceptual framework by analyzing what I termed "client maneuverability,"—the discursive and practical space available for clients to defend their own interests. At the discursive level, I theorized that welfare states shape maneuverability by demarcating the rhetorical possibilities for claims-making; they define how participatory the prevailing needs talk can be, whether it can be stretched, and, if so, in what direction. At the practical level, I theorized that welfare states frame maneuverability by extending concrete tools to clients— resources that affect clients' ability to connect their different needs and to protect their interests. Moreover, I conceptualized both types of maneuverability as closely bound up with the nature of state domination. By setting forth an array of recognized identities, welfare states structure female clients' strategic possibilities and capabilities.

When I applied this framework to the Hungarian case, I found a startling result: from the inception of Hungarian state socialism to the present, there was a progressive reduction in both forms of client maneuverability. Over this fifty-year period, the discursive terrain on which clients could frame their assistance appeals shrunk. In early socialism, women connected to the welfare system encountered a fairly broad discursive space. Perceived to have a multiplicity of identities, women could couch their claims as workers, mothers, spouses, and family members. As the welfare system began to recognize fewer identities, this discursive space narrowed; as women's social roles were broken down, female clients were permitted to speak in limited idioms. Hungarian women linked to the maternalist welfare state experienced such narrowing. Acknowledged primarily as mothers and secondarily as workers, these female clients had a harder time voicing their concerns as wives or family members. In the contemporary state, this silencing reached new levels. Identified only as needy individuals, female clients found it close to impossible to raise any issue not reducible to the financial. Hence, as the overall number of recognized identities shrunk, the discursive space surrounding clients contracted.

At the same time, the number of available identities also determined women's practical maneuverability. Over time, as the Hungarian welfare state recognized fewer gender identifications it chipped away at the concrete resources at clients' disposal. For instance, because the welfare society saw women as multiply situated, it enabled female clients to mobilize state resources to resolve a variety of issues: they appropriated state actors to improve their work and family relations, to connect their many responsibilities, and to make their lives more manageable. This practical maneuverability contracted when the welfare system was based on more limited gender constructs. As the maternalist regime reduced the number of recognized gender identities, its clients had to struggle to draw welfare workers into their work or domestic relations. Seen mainly as mothers, female clients had a harder time negotiating their demands and protecting themselves in everyday life. In the liberal regime, women's practical maneuverability was reduced further. By collapsing all clients' identities into one, the materially needy, this regime offered its clients little more than poor relief. Female clients now found it impossible to convince welfare workers to mediate power relations in their homes, to scold abusive spouses, or to mitigate their own feelings of isolation. Hence, just as clients' discursive maneuverability contracted over time, so too did their ability to carve out practical tools for use in their everyday lives.

Of course, these findings concerning client maneuverability do not imply that women were "better off" in Stalinist Hungary. Rather, they suggest that women were better able to act on their own behalf in welfare systems that acknowledged multiple gender identifications. When provided with a number of possible roles to identify with, clients had more discursive tools to articulate their needs and desires. When clients could draw from a repertoire of identities, they had more practical resources with which to negotiate their demands and responsibilities. Thus, another broad lesson can be learned from the Hungarian case: the number of identities recognized by the state appears to be correlated with the degree of client maneuverability. Welfare systems premised on multiple identities and social roles tend to give clients more room to maneuver.

THE STIGMATIZING STATE: DECONSTRUCTING WELFARE LIBERALISM

The relationship between state form and client maneuverability is even more complex if we consider variations in the kind of identities acknowledged by welfare states. Here we reach a final set of insights to be drawn from the Hungarian case—insights into how and why welfare states become stigmatizing social spaces. In many ways, this book told a story of the rise of welfare stigmatization. Unlike welfare state scholars who treat stigmatization as an inherent, albeit unfortunate, part of the welfare state, I revealed that such dehumanizing connotations must be created. I also argued that the reasons for such associations are not reducible to the size of the state or the stinginess of its programs. In the Hungarian case, welfare stigmatization was intricately linked to the terms of inclusion and entitlement. As the welfare system drew in clients on the basis of what they lacked as opposed to what they contributed, welfare took on negative connotations. And as the welfare terrain became increasingly stigmatized, further constraints were placed on client maneuverability.

One of the unique qualities of the first two Hungarian welfare regimes was their relatively low level of stigmatization. In part, this lack of stigmatization was due to their expansive client base: both regimes cast their regulatory nets wide enough to encompass a variety of social institutions or social groups. Perhaps even more important, these regimes accentuated clients' positive identities; they drew in clients based on their social significance. The early socialist welfare society emphasized clients' contributions as workers and family members; it supported women's and men's attempts to fulfill their social responsibilities. While the late socialist welfare system narrowed its focus, it still construed clients in positive terms, bestowing social importance on women as mothers and linking state support to their valued roles as child-rearers. This emphasis on clients' social contributions then shaped the interactions between welfare workers and clients. State actors were able to draw parallels between their lives and their clients' lives; they were likely to form collusive relationships with women who shared a common cause; and they were disinclined to "other" their clients as "pathological." Similarly, clients used their positive identifications to develop a sense of entitlement and to make new claims on the state: in the welfare society women extended the state's focus on institutional form to include content, while women in the maternalist state expanded the confines of the maternal to encompass the familial. By linking clients' inclusion to their social contributions, these regimes undercut stigmatization and enhanced maneuverability.

The contemporary welfare system reversed this pattern. With the rise of welfare liberalism, state institutions closed their doors to all but a few, and they were not the privileged few. Clients were no longer brought into the state sphere because of their social contributions. The state drew them in on the basis of what they lacked; inclusion in the welfare system now rested on the demonstration of material limitations. The connotations associated with "welfare" thus changed: welfare clients were equated with the materially deprived. It did not take long for welfare workers to view clients as mentally, psychologically, and physically deprived as well. With few policies connecting welfare workers and clients, it was no longer clear what these women shared. As the social distance separating the two groups widened, clients' subjective sense of stigmatization heightened. Discursively marked as "other," clients' silencing intensified and their negotiating power weakened.

From this analysis, a final political lesson emanates from the Hungarian case. The history of Hungarian welfare provides a powerful indictment of welfare liberalism. Through the lens of the East, it is possible to gain new insight into the workings of a welfare model that has prevailed in the West for decades. This lens illuminates how the dehumanizing connotations of "welfare" are not inherent to the construct itself but must be invented. It also reveals how such inventions are sustained through the size of the welfare apparatus and through its terms of inclusion. Because welfare liberalism operates with a narrow repertoire of recognized identities, it draws in relatively small sectors of the population under the rubric of "welfare." And because welfare liberalism links inclusion to deprivation, it accentuates recipients' limitations as opposed to their social contributions. Hence, the stigmatizing undercurrents of liberal welfare states may be rooted less in their puny size and more in the narrowness of their gender constructs; in other words, welfare stigmatization may have less to do with the stingy amount that liberal states redistribute and more to do with their failure to value women's social contributions and responsibilities.

The political implications of this analysis are clear: for welfare politics to be transformative, it must be linked to feminist politics. And this feminist politics must be informed by a comparative understanding of how welfare states can enable and constrain female clients. At this historical moment, the version of welfare liberalism surfacing in Hungary is ascendant on a global scale. It is engulfing the welfare states of North America, Western Europe, and Scandinavia. It is dismantling these states' entitlement systems and replacing them with policies aimed at the bureaucratic regulation of poverty. Clearly, any politics of resistance to this welfare model must include a fight to retain or expand the scope of existing social provisions. For those committed to improving women's lives and to keeping the state a safe, unstigmatized space, the battle must extend beyond the size of state policies to encompass their content. Primarily, the material reductionism that underlies welfare liberalism must be attacked. At the same time welfare policies and practices must be made sensitive to the value of women's social contributions. Only by waging welfare politics based on the recognition of women's multiple identifications, needs, and desires will we be able to build welfare states that provide clients with the most discursive and practical space in which to maneuver.

Methodological Appendix
Historical Excavation in an Era of Censorship

When I first conceived this research project, I imagined that it would be a clear comparison of the state-socialist and postsocialist Hungarian welfare systems. I envisioned that I would employ two main research methods—interviews with state actors from the socialist period and participant observation in the contemporary period. Soon after I began the research in 1993, it became apparent that this methodological approach had to be extended. My initial interviews with welfare workers and government officials raised more questions than they answered. Those employed in the current welfare system had little information about previous welfare practices. Over and over again, these respondents told me that no welfare institutions or social workers existed in Hungary prior to the mid-1980s. Respondents who had in fact worked in the socialist welfare system offered only vague accounts of how it operated. Few could recall details about their institutional practices. Instead, they fell back on generalizations about the nondemocratic character of state socialism as a whole.

In effect, these interviews elicited ideological commentary on state totalitarianism. While revealing, such commentary did not provide me with the kind of data I needed to comprehend the actual workings of Hungarian welfare. As I interviewed welfare workers in their offices, surrounded by archives of case files dating back to the 1950s, I realized that the contents of these historical records had been censored. Eventually, I concluded that in order to gain a full understanding of state-socialist welfare I would have to crack open these documents and mine them for their lost meanings.

Hence, after the first few months of my research, this project became more complicated than I had initially anticipated. By the time I left the field in 1995, I had collected three main types of data. First, I conducted eighteen months of fieldwork in the three key Hungarian welfare institutions.

Second, I interviewed thirty-one welfare workers, state psychologists, local government officials, and policymakers connected to the Hungarian welfare system from the early 1950s to the mid-1990s. Finally, I carried out extensive archival work on state-socialist welfare practices. This archival research involved two types of data. It included a review of 1,203 case files from Gyámhatóság, Child Guidance Centers, and Family Support Services. It also encompassed a study of enterprise documents from five factories in the Csepel region of Budapest from 1948 to 1968. All these data, except those from the enterprise study, were collected from October 1993 to April 1995. The enterprise analysis was carried out while I was on a follow-up research trip in 1996.

As I expanded the project's methodological scope, I narrowed it geographically. I quickly realized that my analysis of welfare practices had to be limited to specific locales. Since I came to this realization once the research began and because all my research contacts were in Budapest, I decided to do my institutional study in two Budapest districts. This geographical narrowing made the project manageable, but it also raised new concerns about the generalizability of my findings. Clearly, I did not want to limit my conclusions to Budapest. To make my findings more generalizable, I sought two districts with demographic profiles consistent with national patterns. Thus, I chose two districts with populations around 100,000 since, according to government statisticians, this was the preferred administrative-district size across Hungary. At the same time, I also wanted the districts to differ in the composition of their populations; such differences would allow me to compare welfare institutions working with diverse populations and would ensure that my research findings were as reliable as possible.

STARTING FROM "BELOW": THE ETHNOGRAPHY

I began the research ethnographically, working in Family Support Services in one of the districts, szegénytelep. This agency became my research "base"; from it I mapped out the larger welfare structure and connected to other agencies. My entry into this office was surprisingly smooth. It was made possible by an acquaintance I had in the agency, Karolina, who laid the groundwork for my study. To facilitate my entry, she arranged for me to give a presentation about my research to the entire welfare office. I outlined my research goals before a group of fifteen social workers. While most of them were perplexed as to why a sociologist from the United States wanted to study their work practices, they quickly incorporated me into the agency's day-to-day activities. I attended staff meetings, observed social worker/client interactions, and socialized informally with the office's employees. In exchange for their help, I taught English to a group of social workers twice a week. In these classes, I learned an enormous amount about their backgrounds and feelings about their work—information I would have never gained had I only observed their interactions with clients.

There were two constraints put on my work in this institution. The first came from me: I insisted that social workers obtain informed consent from clients before I observed their meetings. Initially, social workers were reluctant to obtain consent; they believed it would limit my access to clients. As it turned out, all the clients agreed to let me observe their meetings. Second, the head of the agency granted me access to the center under the condition that I not contact clients outside the office. Although I understood his concern for confidentiality, I worried that this restriction would limit my research. Yet it did not turn out to be an impediment. Social workers often left me alone with their clients as they completed paperwork or other tasks. I could thus talk with clients and elicit their perspectives on the assistance they received. The head social worker gave me approval to use these conversations as long as they occurred within the confines of the office.

My entrance into the district Gyámhatóság was rockier. This institution was far more difficult to penetrate. I vividly recall my first visit to the office: within an hour, I was cycled through a series of caseworkers, all of whom looked at me with blank faces as I explained my research. Although I did not realize it at the time, I was "processed" through the institution like a client, shuffled among caseworkers who wanted nothing to do with me. In a desperate attempt to end the cycle, I turned to a former Gyámhatóság caseworker then employed in the Family Support Services center where I was conducting my research. Zsuzsa walked me over to the Gyámhatóság, introduced me to each caseworker, and asked them to assist me. After her introduction, I was allowed to sit in a small chair and watch caseworkers interact with clients. Eventually, these women warmed up to me. Within a month, they gave me my own desk. The physical layout of the office was conducive to ethnography; it consisted of three large rooms that housed three to four caseworkers. Because no barriers separated caseworkers' desks, I could observe multiple interactions simultaneously. Midway into my fieldwork, caseworkers began to take me on home visits. And I spent every Friday afternoon with one caseworker as she made her weekly home visits.

Once I became rooted in these two offices, I set out to extend my research to a second district, ipartelep. My entrance into this district's agencies was also relatively smooth, especially in the Gyámhatóság because there was a direct link with the szegénytelep office; Kati, one of the szegénytelep caseworkers, had recently migrated there. Kati facilitated my transition to this new office and helped me secure the necessary approvals for my research. My entrance into the ipartelep Gyámhatóság was also easier because I already knew a great deal about these institutions and could fit into them more readily than I had in the past. I made fewer mistakes in my initial interactions with these caseworkers. For instance, when I made my first contact with the szegénytelep caseworkers, I asked them what university they had attended. My question was met with cold stares, so I corrected myself by asking them what vocational school they had gone to. Again, no response. At that time, I had no idea that Gyámhatóság caseworkers rarely had more than high school degrees. This blunder proved to be difficult to overcome: many caseworkers believed I was a "clueless intellectual" and thus kept their distance for months. When I entered ipartelep's Gyámhatóság, I knew to avoid such errors and thus was integrated more quickly and fully into the institution.

In contrast to the many links that existed between Family Support Services and Gyámhatóság offices, Child Guidance Centers were more isolated. The fact that there were few overlaps among those working in these centers and other welfare institutions made it difficult to gain access; I could not mobilize my fieldwork connections to help pave my way. Instead, I drew on contacts I made in my interviews to gain entry. Early in the research, I interviewed two of the most prominent Hungarian family psychologists—women who had essentially designed these centers in the 1960s. At my request, they called their colleagues working in these offices to support my research. Within weeks, I was given permission. Overall, my work in these agencies was more constrained; confidentiality was a more pressing issue here since the psychologists worked with children and counseled them about quite sensitive topics. And because, by the time of my fieldwork, these centers had abandoned their work with mothers to focus on childhood disorders, my observations of their practices were more limited. My research centered on these institutions' case files, although I also attended staff meetings and had ongoing discussions with the psychologists before and after their counseling sessions.

While gaining access to and acceptance in all these welfare institutions was a struggle, the fieldwork itself was even more difficult. When I began the research, I thought of myself as a "hardened" ethnographer. I had just completed grueling ethnographic research in the California juvenile justice system and felt confident that I could handle anything I encountered in Hungary. But that research did not prepare me for the Hungarian welfare system. In effect, I worked in the center of a crumbling welfare state. Displacement and dislocation were omnipresent. On a daily basis, powerlessness and frustration surrounded me. On one side were the clients, clearly struggling to keep themselves afloat. It pained me to see them face discursive and practical losses and confront their inability to carve out the resources necessary for their own well-being. On the other side were the welfare workers—women who were frustrated by work they found unfulfilling. It was difficult to watch them lash out defensively at their clients as they became increasingly powerless. Many of these women became good friends of mine; I knew they were not malicious or mean-spirited. Yet when confronted with abysmal working conditions, they reacted in understandable, although not commendable, ways. At the everyday level, there was no one to blame. There were few clear-cut "bad" guys. Instead, there was just a great deal of pain and suffering.

RETREATING INTO THE PAST:
THE ARCHIVAL RESEARCH

When confronted with the pain of the present, like many clients, I sought refuge in the past. Initially, I did not do so by choice. After months of ethnographic work, I realized I had to examine the case files lining the office walls. My requests to review these records were approved on one condition: I had to conduct the archival work in the offices. Because of the highly sensitive nature of these documents, government officials required that my work be supervised. Government archivists recorded every case file I reviewed; they transferred these files to welfare workers who then passed them on to me. I was not allowed to remove the documents from the offices. And I was forbidden from photocopying them. As a result, I carried out this archival research while I did the participant observation.

At first, I was displeased with this arrangement; I worried that it would be too distracting to conduct archival work amidst the chaos of these agencies. But, in the end, the situation proved to be a blessing. It allowed me to compare past and present in an ongoing way. As I sat surrounded by silencing and read accounts of a time when clients could voice a variety of problems, the difference between past and present became stark. Moreover, conducting my archival work amidst caseworkers also gave me the chance to elicit their reactions to earlier welfare practices. I often recounted case histories for welfare workers in order to see how they would respond to their predecessors' approaches. In fact, through these exchanges I became aware of just how much the past had been censored: welfare workers knew almost nothing about how their institutions had once operated; they were stunned and amazed by the accounts hidden away in their own archives.

One incident perfectly illustrates this silencing of the past and the stereotypes it bred. In szegénytelep, the arrival of the first box of case files, from the 1950s, piqued caseworkers' interest. As I dusted off the dirt covering the file box, a young male caseworker rushed over to see what was inside. We opened the box together and found a stack of about seventy-five pages held together by a rubber band. Zsolt shook his head in disgust. "Imagine, all those papers for one case. This was a terrible time in our history. They controlled with an iron fist and interrogated everybody." His comment prompted a discussion among caseworkers about how intrusive the socialist state had been. As they talked, I sifted through the papers and discovered that the box actually contained twenty different cases that averaged three to four pages each. After I informed the caseworkers of my finding, their interpretation immediately changed. As one of them remarked, "Exactly, no one cared back then. Those officials did not waste their time [assisting clients]. They did not care about protecting families or children."

Like these caseworkers, I also assumed that my archival research would confirm the prevailing "line" about the invasive socialist state. I expected to find little variation within the socialist period. And I anticipated that this early Hungarian socialist state would work with narrow understandings of clients' problems—understandings dictated by and filtered through the prevailing ideology. Yet soon after I began the historical excavation, I realized that the case files told a different story. They articulated variation in state-socialist welfare practices. They revealed that early state actors' conceptions of need were more expansive than those of the welfare workers surrounding me. These files transmitted their accounts so meticulously that they were hard to dismiss. In this way, the state-socialist fixation with bureaucracy was advantageous for me. Caseworkers constructed extremely detailed descriptions of each case. They regularly gave verbatim accounts of their conversations with clients. And they always saved their correspondence—from written requests to official decisions to client letters to home-visit reports. All these records were typed and filed chronologically. The story they told could not have been better packaged and prepared.

Since I was not inclined to accept the surprising story emanating from these case records, I began to question my sample itself—perhaps I was just examining a select set of cases written by particularly zealous groups of welfare workers. As a result, I became methodical about my sampling procedures. Because caseworkers catalogued their files by family name, I could not draw my sample on the basis of the clients' sex. Instead, I insisted on a random sample of files. Throughout the research, I made only two attempts to shape my sample. First, I sought consistency in my sample size for each district. I sampled roughly one hundred cases from each institution, in each district, for each decade under examination to ensure that my findings were not biased toward a particular institution or district. Second, I strove to make my sample consistent with these offices' caseloads. For the welfare society, this goal was close to unattainable since this Gyámhatóság did not keep institutional summaries of its caseload. Yet for the two later regimes, I was able to use these offices' yearly overviews of their caseloads to guide my sampling. For instance, the Gyámhatóság classified their cases into three categories—bureaucratic cases, child-protection cases, and institutionaliza-tion cases. When gathering my sample, I made sure that my case break-downs were consistent with the agencies' rates. This sampling procedure allowed me to trace the shifting definitions of different types of cases. It also increased the likelihood that my data were representative of the offices' caseloads and that the patterns I uncovered reflected the agencies' welfare practices.

There are obvious limitations to working with historical data like these since case-file data can be riddled with problems of reliability. Because they are constructed by welfare workers themselves, they are subject to all sorts of biases. In many ways, they are a reflection of state actors' perspectives rather than "objective" accounts of the workings of welfare institutions. In my study, this problem was not as acute as it could have been because of the way I analyzed the records. Instead of taking them as neutral accounts of "reality," I examined them as constructions; I read the files as interpretive acts. In effect, I studied the biases inherent in the records; I took the filter-ing processes represented in these accounts as data themselves.

In particular, I first analyzed these case files for what they revealed about caseworkers' constructions of need. I approached this work inductively, let-ting the case files reveal the important categories of analysis and patterns of practices. When I read these files, I recorded who was targeted in a given case—the mother or the father, the wife or the husband, the nuclear or the extended family. I also unearthed how welfare workers interpreted the prob-lem at hand. With time, I found consistencies in the accounts. I then began to center on whether a client's problem was thought to be work-related, family-related, poverty-related, or some combination of the three. More-over, within these broad categories, I developed more precise ways to classify caseworkers' interpretations. If the problem was work-related, I examined whether the issue was finding the client work or improving his or her work life. If the problem was family-related, I investigated whether the spouse, the parent, or extended kin were at issue. And if the problem was poverty-related, I focused on the type of material deprivation. Finally, as I charted these different case trajectories, I documented the mode of regulation—that is, how welfare workers set out to treat the problem at hand. Did they seek social integration? Were they educative or punitive? Did they provide counseling? What kind? Directed at whom? Did they hand out material assistance? To whom? With what connotations? In short, at this level, I analyzed these records as data on caseworkers' constructions and interpretations of need.

I also drew on case files to reconstruct a picture of client maneuverability in each welfare regime. This analysis of client strategizing was facilitated by the particular methods welfare workers used to complete their files. Unlike U.S. social workers, Hungarian welfare workers regularly provided verbatim accounts of their exchanges with clients. Particularly in the first two welfare regimes, caseworkers constructed elaborate records of office interactions and home visits. Their records often included hundreds of pages of legalistic forms and records of conversations signed by the clients themselves. These files also included all the letters written by clients. Because of the absence of telephones in state-socialist Hungary, much of the contact between welfare workers and clients consisted of letters. Moreover, a number of caseworkers I interviewed claimed that clients preferred to couch their appeals in written form. They believed the *tanács* (local government) building, which housed the Gyámhatóság as well as the local police and secret services, intimidated clients. As a result, when they could, clients opted to write to welfare workers.

Caseworkers' verbatim accounts and clients' preference for letter writing enabled me to hear client voices in these case files. I then had the data to view socialist welfare practices from the perspective of clients. Had the case files consisted only of caseworkers' accounts, it would have been impossible to examine these regimes from "below" or to trace patterns of client maneuvering. But through caseworkers' transcripts of client responses, I could explore how different clients related to caseworkers' constructions. Did clients accept their need interpretations? Did they contest caseworkers' understandings of their problems? Did they counter them with their own interpretations? Client correspondence was even more helpful here than the transcripts. Through their letters, I could explore clients' concrete responses. Did they remain within the bounds of the prevailing needs talk? Or did they stretch it? In what direction? With what outcome? Hence, from the case records, I uncovered clients' modes of strategizing.

UNDERSTANDING THE HISTORICAL CONTEXT:
THE INTERVIEWS

In many respects, the interviews I conducted were designed to supplement my ethnographic and historical findings. Once I discovered that I could not obtain concrete information on welfare practices through these interviews, I began to use them to address a series of broader, more contextual issues. The interviews were not entirely standardized; my questions varied according to whom I was interviewing and at what stage I was in the research process. Overall, I conducted thirty-one interviews with respondents who fell into three main categories. First, I did sixteen formal interviews with welfare workers—eight with Gyámhatóság caseworkers, four with Child Guidance Center counselors, and four with Family Support Services social workers. These interviews provided me with information I could not have gotten from my fieldwork or case-file study. With past workers, I asked questions about the organization of their institutions—how their work was structured, divided up, and regulated. I also inquired about the relationship among institutions and their connections to different state actors. In addition, these interviews included questions about welfare workers' backgrounds, institutional trajectories, and views of clients. From these discussions, I constructed a broad picture of the nature of past welfare practices and the larger institutional context surrounding welfare workers.

Second, I conducted eight formal interviews with local-government officials and policymakers. Here too my goal was to gain information about the larger welfare structure. I used these data to investigate how and why particular institutional arrangements arose. For instance, I probed these officials to determine who created the domesticity tests and means tests that so altered the nature of welfare work. At the same time, I also inquired into the origins of key social provisions. Through such questions, I gained insights into the concrete dynamics of policy formulation and the different social groups involved in welfare reform. In fact, from these interviews I arrived at my arguments about the causes of the policy changes—that is, how the battles among professionals in the 1960s gave rise to maternalist policy and how the struggles of sociologists and economists in the 1980s paved the way for a liberal policy regime. Since little has been written about these issues, my interviews provided me with a unique perspective on the nature of Hungarian policymaking and reform.

Finally, I carried out seven in-depth interviews with Hungarian academics and welfare-state scholars. Although I consulted many social scientists throughout the research process, I initiated formal interviews with those who seemed most knowledgeable about welfare development. Overall, these interviews centered on the policy sphere, the area where these respondents' expertise was the greatest. Like policymakers, these academics provided invaluable insights into the timing of and impetus behind many key policy shifts. Most of them had been active participants in the building of the maternalist and liberal welfare regimes and thus gave first-hand accounts of the debates underlying these reforms. Moreover, these academics had extensive knowledge of the eligibility criteria for different provisions. The information they provided enabled me to develop a larger framework within which to understand the concrete changes I was observing through case records and the ethnography. In this way, these interviews with social scientists guided my policy analysis: they provided me with critical information about policymaking and references to the most useful secondary sources on the Hungarian welfare system.

RETURNING TO THE FIELD:
THE ENTERPRISE ANALYSIS

When I left Hungary in April 1995, I believed that this ethnographic, archival, and interview research would yield the data necessary to analyze the development of Hungarian welfare. For the most part, I was correct; from these data, I constructed a new periodization of Hungarian welfare, explicated its policy and institutional underpinnings, and unearthed its different gender constructs. Yet as I began to write up my findings, I realized that my own biases about the site of state welfare had blinded me to the re/distributive role played by enterprises in early state socialism. I then became aware of a critical omission in my data: I had not collected any material on the allocative practices of state-socialist enterprises. Their importance in early socialist re/distribution was unquestionable: they surfaced repeatedly in Gyámhatóság case files, as caseworkers maintained close connections with enterprise officials. Since I could not make an argument about the role of enterprises without concrete data, I returned to Hungary in the summer of 1996 to conduct a study of enterprise re/distribution.

Initially, I planned to collect these data from enterprises located in the districts of my research. Yet after interviews with the staff at the Hungarian National Archives, I concluded that it was more essential to study enterprises with the most complete set of records. According to the archivists, the comprehensiveness of enterprise collections varied tremendously. And two of the largest factories in the districts of my research appeared to have incomplete records. But the collection from a complex of five factories in the

Csepel region of Budapest was almost entirely intact. Because Csepel played an instrumental role in the 1956 revolution, archivists claimed that their enterprise records were closely guarded by the authorities and thus were well maintained. As a result, I decided to focus my enterprise study on this complex of five Csepel factories.

As was not possible in my archival work with Gyámhatóság case files, I was able to order copies of these enterprise records. Doing so was enormously helpful given the limited amount of time I had to review these documents in Hungary. My analysis focused on three areas. First, I reviewed the documents from the Social Policy Department from 1948 to 1968. They included records on all benefits-in-kind and benefits-in-cash distributed by enterprise officials. Second, I examined the complete set of trade-union records, including reports on working conditions, labor control, and emergency-funds distribution. Finally, I studied the entire set of workers' hostel records. This was definitely the most time-consuming part of the research; these documents numbered in the thousands and consisted of detailed accounts of the lives of hostel residents. Yet they were also the most revealing materials. They provided a unique window into the concrete workings of enterprise re/distribution and its effects on workers' everyday lives.

Because I conducted the enterprise research after I analyzed the other data, I approached it more deductively. When collecting the case-file and ethnographic data, I proceeded inductively, drawing my regime types, concepts, and categories from the data themselves. By the time I did the enterprise study, I had already constructed my regime periodization. Hence, I went into the enterprise study with a clear sense of what I was testing: I wanted to evaluate whether enterprise re/distribution operated with societal criteria and, if so, which ones. Overall, the enterprise analysis confirmed my arguments about the workings of the welfare society. It solidified my sense that early socialist re/distribution targeted social institutions. It also bolstered my claims about the regime's familial underpinnings and focus on social integration. In this way, I ended the research with a deductive analysis that enabled me to test my research findings and conclusions.

Notes

INTRODUCTION

1. David Stark and László Bruszt, *Postsocialist Pathways: Transforming Politics and Property in East Central Europe*, p. 3.

2. See Robert Deacon, *Global Social Policy: International Organizations and the Future of Welfare*, and "Social Policy, Social Justice and Citizenship in Eastern Europe"; Zsuzsa Ferge, "Recent Trends in Social Policy in Hungary," and "Social Citizenship in the New Democracies: The Difficulties of Reviving Citizens' Rights in Hungary"; Toni Makkai, "Social Policy and Gender in Eastern Europe"; and Rudolf Andorka and István Tóth, "A Jóléti Rendszer Jellemzői és Reformjának Lehetőségei."

3. See János Kornai, *The Economics of Shortage;* Iván Szelényi, "Urban Inequalities under State Socialist Redistributive Economies"; and Iván Berend and György Ránki, *The Hungarian Economy in the Twentieth Century.*

4. See Iván Szelényi and Róbert Manchin, "Social Policy under State Socialism: Market Redistribution and Social Inequalities in East European Socialist Societies," and Ferenc Fehér, Ágnes Heller, and George Márkus, *Dictatorship over Needs.* In addition, some scholars have broken this period into two distinct eras, arguing that the "classic socialism" of the immediate postwar period evolved into "consolidated socialism" following the Hungarian revolution of 1956. See Szonja Szelényi, *Equality by Design: The Grand Experiment in Destratification in Socialist Hungary.*

5. See János Kornai, "Paying the Bill for Goulash Communism"; Ákos Róna-Tas, *The Great Surprise of the Small Transformation;* László Bruszt, "Without Us but for Us? Political Orientation in Hungary in the Period of Late Paternalism"; and Gil Eyal, Iván Szelényi, and Eleanor Townsley, *Making Capitalism without Capitalists: The New Ruling Elites in Eastern Europe.*

6. See Stark and Bruszt, *Postsocialist Pathways;* Eyal, Szelényi, and Townsley, *Making Capitalism without Capitalists;* Susan Gal and Gail Kligman, eds., *The Politics of Gender after Socialism;* and József Böröcz and Ákos Róna-Tas, "Small Leap Forward: Emergence of New Economic Elites in Hungary,

Poland, and Russia." For a critique of this "plurality" approach, see Michael Burawoy, "Neoclassical Sociology: From the End of Communism to the End of Classes."

7. See Gail Kligman, *The Politics of Duplicity: Controlling Fertility in Ceausescu's Romania;* Gal and Kligman, *The Politics of Gender after Socialism;* Susan Gal, "Gender in the Post-socialist Transition: The Abortion Debate in Hungary"; Katherine Verdery, "From Parent-State to Family Patriarchs: Gender and Nation in Contemporary Eastern Europe"; and Sharon Wolchik, "Reproductive Policies in the Czech and Slovak Republics."

8. As in the productive realm, there was variation within this early reproductive regime. Most notably, following Stalin's death, abortion policy was liberalized in many countries of the region, although centralized surveillance of women's bodies remained. For more on the "thaw" of the mid-1950s, see Kligman, *The Politics of Duplicity,* and Wolchik, "Reproductive Policies in the Czech and Slovak Republics."

9. For an analysis of historical continuity and discontinuity, see Michael Burawoy and Katherine Verdery, eds., *Uncertain Transition,* chap. 1.

10. See Stark and Bruszt, *Postsocialist Pathways,* and David Stark, "Path Dependence and Privatization Strategies in East Central Europe."

11. See Szonja Szelényi, Iván Szelényi, and Winifred Poster, "Post-Communist Political Culture in Hungary."

12. Notable exceptions to this elite focus in the Hungarian context include Michael Burawoy and János Lukács, *The Radiant Past: Ideology and Reality in Hungary's Road to Capitalism;* Martha Lampland, *The Object of Labor: Commodification in Socialist Hungary;* Zsuzsa Gille, "Cognitive Cartography in a European Wasteland: Multinational Capital and Greens Vie for Village Allegiance"; and Miklós Haraszti, *A Worker in a Workers' State.*

13. I thank Martha Lampland for drawing out this connection for me.

14. Burawoy, "Neoclassical Sociology."

15. For a similar conception of the welfare state, see Nancy Fraser, *Unruly Practices.* Also, for an explication of different conceptions of the welfare state and their implications for historical analysis, see Lynne Haney, "Engendering the Welfare State" and "Feminist State Theory: Applications to Jurisprudence, Criminology, and the Welfare State."

16. Many scholars have documented this propaganda in the East European context. See Kligman, *The Politics of Duplicity;* Joanna Goven, "The Gendered Foundations of Hungarian State Socialism: State, Society and the Anti-politics of Anti-feminism"; Éva Fodor, "Power, Patriarchy, and Paternalism: An Examination of the Gendered Nature of State Socialist Authority"; and Victoria Bonnell, *Iconographies of Power.*

17. For more on this concept of the "loosely coupled system," see John Hagan, "The Everyday and the Not So Exceptional in the Social Organization of Criminal Justice Practices"; Ruth Horowitz, *Teen Mothers: Citizens or Dependents;* and Haney, "Feminist State Theory."

18. See Gosta Esping-Andersen, *The Three Worlds of Welfare Capitalism,* and Ann Orloff, "Gender and the Social Rights of Citizenship."

19. It is quite difficult to translate the name of this institution into English. The closest translation would be Child Protective Services since the Gyámhatóság had the legal authority to remove children from their homes and to place them in state care. Yet, as I describe in this book, the Gyámhatóság did much more. It also carried out all the bureaucratic work related to the family, acted as an employment agency, and counseled parents about their child rearing. I will therefore use the agency's Hungarian name when discussing it.

20. For a fuller discussion of these oppositions, see Haney, "Feminist State Theory."

21. See Julia Adams, "Feminist Theory as Fifth Columnist or Discursive Vanguard: Some Contested Uses of Gender Analysis in Historical Sociology."

22. For an overview of the development of this field, see Ann Orloff, "Gender in the Welfare State."

23. Esping-Andersen, *The Three Worlds of Welfare Capitalism.*

24. See Orloff, "Gender and the Social Rights of Citzenship," and "Gender in the Welfare State"; Siv Gustafsson, "Childcare and Types of Welfare States"; and Julia O'Connor, Ann Orloff, and Sheila Shaver, *States, Markets, and Families.*

25. See Diane Sainsbury, ed., *Gendering Welfare States,* and Diane Sainsbury, *Gender, Equality, and Welfare States;* and Barbara Hobson, "Solo Mothers, Social Policy Regimes, and the Logics of Gender."

26. Fraser, *Unruly Practices.*

27. See Robin Muncy, *Creating a Female Dominion in American Reform, 1890–1935;* Theda Skocpol, *Protecting Soldiers and Mothers;* Linda Gordon, *Pitied but Not Entitled: Single Mothers and the History of Welfare;* Seth Koven and Sonya Michel, eds., *Mothers of a New World: Maternalist Politics and the Origins of Welfare States;* and Gisella Bock and Pat Thane, eds., *Maternity and Gender Policies: Women and the Rise of the European Welfare State, 1880–1950.*

28. See Susan Pedersen, *Family, Dependence, and the Origins of the Welfare State: Britain and France, 1914–1945;* Alyssa Klaus, *Every Child a Lion: The Origins of Maternal and Infant Policy in the U.S. and France, 1890–1920;* and Gwendolyn Mink, *The Wages of Motherhood.*

29. See Linda Gordon, *Heroes of Their Own Lives;* Regina Kunzel, *Fallen Women, Problem Girls: Unmarried Mothers and the Professionalization of Social Work, 1890–1945;* Joanne Goodwin, *Gender and the Politics of Welfare Reform;* Lynne Haney, "Homeboys, Babies, Men in Suits: The State and the Reproduction of Male Dominance"; and Renee Monson, "State-ing Sex and Gender."

30. Fraser, *Unruly Practices,* chap. 7.

31. See Kunzel, *Fallen Women, Problem Girls;* Gordon, *Heroes of Their Own Lives;* and Haney, "Homeboys, Babies, Men in Suits."

32. See Haney, "Engendering the Welfare State," for a more elaborate discussion of these analyses.

33. See Robert W. Connell, *Gender and Power.*

34. See Júlia Szalai, "From Informal Labor to Paid Occupations: Marketization from Below in Hungarian Women's Work," and Kligman, *The Politics of Duplicity.*

35. These names translate into "poor locale" and "industrial locale," respectively.

36. Központi Statisztikai Hivatal (hereafter referred to as KSH), *Statisztikai Évkönyv* (1995).

37. World Bank, *Magyarország*, p. 11.

38. Gábor Kertesi and Gábor Kézdi, *A Cigány Népesség Magyarországon*, p. 323.

39. Ibid., p. 323.

SOCIALIZING NEED

1. For detailed accounts of Hungary's postwar economic ruin, see Sándor Balogh, *Nehéz Esztendők Krónikája, 1949–1953: Dokumentumok*; Zoltán Baksay, *A Munkaerőhelyzet Alakulása és a Munkanélküliség Felszámolása Magyarországon, 1945–1949*; Iván Berend, *A Szocialista Gazdaság Fejlődése Magyarországon, 1945–1968*; and Zsuzsa Ferge, *Fejezetek a Magyar Szegénypolitika Történetéből.*

2. For more on this postwar model of reconstruction, see Iván Pető and Sándor Szakács, *A Hazai Gazdaság Négy Évtizedének Története, 1945–1985*; Sándor Balogh, *A Magyar Népi Demokrácia Története, 1944–1962*; and Mark Pittaway, "Industrial Workers, Socialist Industrialization, and the State in Hungary, 1948–1958."

3. For more on these ideological campaigns, see George Hodos, *Show Trials: Stalinist Purges in Eastern Europe, 1948–1954*; Nigel Swain, *Hungary: The Rise and Fall of Feasible Socialism*; Lampland, *The Object of Labor*; István Fehérváry, *Börtönvilág Magyarországon, 1945–1956*; Tibor Dessewffy and András Szántó,*"Kitörő Éberséggel" A Budapesti Kitelepítések Hiteles Története*; and Sándor Balogh and Ferenc Pölöskei, eds., *Agrárpolitika és Agrárátalakulás Magyarországon, 1944–1962.*

4. See Robert Deacon, *Social Policy and Socialism*; Szelényi and Manchin, "Social Policy under State Socialism"; and Kornai, "Paying the Bill for Goulash Communism."

5. Zsuzsa Ferge, *A Society in the Making: Hungarian Social and Societal Policy 1945–1975*, p. 13.

6. Ibid., pp. 20–22.

7. See Barbara Einhorn, *Cinderella Goes to Market: Citizenship, Gender, and Women's Movements in East Central Europe*; Chris Corrin, *Superwomen and the Double Burden: Women's Experience of Change in Central and Eastern Europe and the Former Soviet Union*; Júlia Szalai, "Some Aspects of the

Changing Situation of Women in Hungary"; Verdery, "From Parent-State to Family Patriarchs"; and Mária Adamik, "Feminism and Hungary."

8. See Sharon Wolchik, *Women, the State, and Party in Eastern Europe;* Goven, "The Gendered Foundations of Hungarian State Socialism"; Bonnell, *Iconographies of Power;* and Andrea Pető, "As He Saw Her: Gender Politics in Secret Party Reports in Hungary during the 1950s."

9. Goven, "The Gendered Foundations of Hungarian State Socialism," p. 23.

10. For detailed accounts of the MDP's rise to power, see Sándor Balogh, *Parlamenti és Pártharcok Magyarországon, 1945–1947;* Balogh, *A Magyar Népi Demokrácia Története;* Bennett Kovrig, *Communism in Hungary: From Kun to Kádár;* István Tóth, *A Nemzeti Parasztpárt Története, 1944–1948;* and Pittaway, "Industrial Workers, Socialist Industrialization, and the State in Hungary."

11. See Kligman, *The Politics of Duplicity.*

12. Balogh, *Nehéz Esztendők Krónikája,* p. 132.

13. *Családjogi Törvények* (hereafter CsJT), p. 30.

14. Deacon, *Social Policy and Socialism,* p. 201.

15. This rule would apply when the man had inherited property from his family and hence did not share ownership with his wife formally. It is also important to note that it often took years for divorced mothers to secure state flats on their own. Hence, by giving women access to their husbands' property, this provision effectively provided women with stable housing after divorce.

16. CsJT, p. 49.

17. Ibid., p. 68.

18. Ibid., p. 66. When a child's father was "unknown" or the mother was unwilling to reveal his identity, local child-protection offices became the child's paternal guardian.

19. This percentage varied according to the number of children and the father's salary. See Ferge, *Fejezetek a Magyar Szegénypolitika Történetéből.*

20. CsJT, p. 98.

21. The image of Hungarian men in this portrait was rather unbecoming. They appeared as being most in need of regulation and control. They came across as property owners, unwilling to voluntarily cede resources to their (ex)wives; as potential deadbeat dads, reluctant to acknowledge or support their offspring; and as overall shirkers of domestic obligations, unable to commit to women or to care for their families. Hence, the 1952 Family Law constructed a view of the family in which men's domestic duties and responsibilities had to be fixed and codified into law in order to protect the well-being of women and children.

22. In fact, this is one reason Hungarian societal policies are rarely recognized as a form of re/distribution. Most welfare-state scholars conceptualize social provision in limited terms, as distinct income-maintenance or support programs for specific social groups or families. Because the Hungarian policies of this period were not administered through a separate policy apparatus, and

since they targeted social institutions (rather than groups or individuals), they are often overlooked in the existing literature.

23. In this chapter, I adhere to the definition of economic planning advanced by Szelényi and Manchin—that is, the centralized process through which the revenues of individual firms were appropriated to the state budget and reallocated as government grants, subsidies, or handouts in the spheres of production and reproduction. Szelényi and Manchin, "Social Policy under State Socialism," p. 107.

24. See Kornai, *The Economics of Shortage*.

25. This connection between centralized re/distribution and soft budget constraints was the result of several factors. It led to a situation where firms were placed in a hierarchical relationship to the center and where their accumulation of resources depended on their bargaining position with the center; this position was itself shaped by the firm's profitability, size, political connections, and ability to fulfill parts of the plan. For more on the relationship between planning and soft budget constraints, see Burawoy and Lukács, *The Radiant Past*, and Szelényi and Manchin, "Social Policy under State Socialism."

26. Kornai, *The Economics of Shortage*, p. 36.

27. See Kligman, *The Politics of Duplicity*, and Lampland, *The Object of Labor*.

28. Szelényi, "Urban Inequalities under State Socialist Redistributive Economies."

29. Ibid., p. 82.

30. Szelényi and Manchin, "Social Policy under State Socialism," p. 104.

31. In his early work, Szelényi argued that centralized re/distribution created a system in which "primary" social inequalities resulted from bureaucratic privilege and position. Thus, he saw the introduction of the market, via the second economy, as a way to counter these inequalities. Later, he discovered that the market had created its own forms of "secondary" inequalities, which were related to one's access to skills, goods, and services. He then called for a more discretionary "welfare state" to address the secondary inequalities of the market. For the development of these arguments, see Szelényi and Manchin, "Social Policy under State Socialism."

32. Ferge, *A Society in the Making*, pp. 88–89.

33. The Hungarian term was *közveszélyes munkakerülés*. In the early 1950s, work avoiders could be subjected to prison terms ranging from eight days to two months. For a discussion of these police campaigns and the selective enforcement of these policies, see Róna-Tas, *The Great Surprise of the Small Transformation*, and Pittaway, "Industrial Workers, Socialist Industrialization, and the State in Hungary."

34. Phineas Baxandall, "Reinventing Unemployment in Hungary: Politics, Pensions, and Patterns of Work," and Pittaway, "Industrial Workers, Socialist Industrialization, and the State in Hungary."

35. According to Ferge, this provision was introduced because state restructuring in 1954 led to the "release" of a number of state employees. This provi-

sion was designed to cushion them during this transition; hence, it was modified once this shift was completed. According to Ferge's data, only a few hundred Hungarians ever used these benefits. Ferge, *A Society in the Making*, p. 91.

36. In Hungarian, the phrase is "Nyolc óra munka, nyolc óra pihenés, nyolc óra szórakozás." It subsequently became the source of jokes, parodies, and songs.

37. For more on the first five-year plan, see Pittaway, "Industrial Workers, Socialist Industrialization, and the State in Hungary."

38. Ibid., p. 150. Put another way, from 1949 to 1960, industrial employment increased by a total of 14 percent; the percentage of skilled workers in the labor force increased by 5 percent; and the percentage of unskilled and semi-skilled workers rose by 10 percent. Rudolf Andorka and István Harcsa, "Long-Term Modernization of Hungarian Society," p. 26.

39. For higher estimates, see Ferge, *Fejezetek a Magyar Szegénypolitika Történetéből*.

40. For a fuller discussion of the abortion politics of the period, see Gal, "Gender and the Post-socialist Transition"; Goven, "The Gendered Foundations of Hungarian State Socialism"; and Kligman, *The Politics of Duplicity*.

41. From 1953 to 1956, the Hungarian birthrate was fairly high, at 21–25 births per 1,000, but it dropped by 50 percent at the end of the 1950s. KSH, *Time Series of Historical Statistics, 1867–1992*, p. 148. This decline in birthrates was one of the main reasons for the erection of a maternalist subsystem of welfare in the mid-1960s. I discuss this change in welfare regime more fully in the introduction to Part Two.

42. Pittaway, "Industrial Workers, Socialist Industrialization, and the State in Hungary," p. 180.

43. In spite of this decree, throughout the 1950s, women were legally permitted to remain outside the paid labor force if "somebody else could provide for them." Ferge, *A Society in the Making*, p. 89.

44. KSH, *Time Series of Historical Statistics, 1867–1992*, p. 37.

45. Goven, "The Gendered Foundations of Hungarian State Socialism," p. 30.

46. KSH, *A Nők Helyzete a Munkahelyen és a Családban* , pp. 9–10.

47. Pittaway, "Industrial Workers, Socialist Industrialization, and the State in Hungary," p. 181.

48. Goven, "The Gendered Foundations of Hungarian State Socialism," and Martha Lampland, "Biographies of Liberation: Testimonials to Labor in Socialist Hungary."

49. Lynne Haney, "From Proud Worker to Good Mother: Gender, the State, and Regime Change in Hungary."

50. Lampland, "Biographies of Liberation."

51. Goven, "The Gendered Foundations of Hungarian State Socialism"; Mária Márkus, "A Nő Helyzete a Munka Világában"; and Ferge, *A Society in the Making*.

52. Ferge, *A Society in the Making*, p. 164. Interestingly, the percentage falling into the lowest quintile remained unchanged at 7 percent in both 1931

and 1962. See also Pető and Szakács, *A Hazai Gazdaság Négy Évtizedének Története.*

53. These data on official income rates are limited in that they do not account for additional sources of income available to those in particular occupations. Nor do they control for the resources gained from participation in the informal economy. Unfortunately, since the second economy was not legal in this period, there are no reliable data on such alternative sources of income.

54. Income data from 1950 and 1955 are only somewhat reliable. According to many historians, there were extreme drops in real income from 1951 to 1954—drops that the government wanted to obscure. See Pittaway, "Industrial Workers, Socialist Industrialization, and the State in Hungary"; Goven, "The Gendered Foundations of Hungarian State Socialism"; and Balogh, *Nehéz Esztendők Krónikája.*

55. KSH, *Statisztikai Évkönyv* (1961) and *Statisztikai Évkönyv* (1962).

56. In other words, they were used to determine whether it was possible to tinker with wage levels in order to flatten out differences among various family forms or whether these changes could best be achieved via special family supports. Ferge, *A Society in the Making.*

57. Another reason is that so much of the scholarly work done on the 1950s and early 1960s is ideologically motivated—set on proving the extreme hardship of the era or the progress made during it. This ideological bent makes it even more difficult to assess the actual living standard of the population. For some of the best work on the material realities of the period, see Balogh, *Nehéz Esztendők Krónikája;* László Gál, *Szociálpolitikánk Két Évtizede;* and Andrea Pető, *A Munkások Életkörülményei Magyarországon az 1950-es Években.*

58. Andorka and Harcsa, "Long-Term Modernization of Hungarian Society," p. 35.

59. Gál, *Szociálpolitikánk Két Évtizede,* p. 189.

60. Ibid., p. 192; Ferge, *A Society in the Making.*

61. Variations in subsidies were especially prevalent for those goods and services distributed by enterprises. As I describe in the next section, enterprises often linked the availability of subsidized goods to their workers' family sizes.

62. See Balogh, *Nehéz Esztendők Krónikája,* and Pető and Szakács, *A Hazai Gazdaság Négy Évtizedének Története.*

63. Pető, *A Munkások Életkörülményei Magyarországon az 1950-es Években,* p. 159; and Rudolf Andorka and István Harcsa, "Consumption," p. 87.

64. While my focus here is on basic foodstuffs, another big area of centralized price subsidies was medicine. From 1950 to 1960, state expenditures on pharmaceutical subsidies increased by over 400 percent. Put another way, by 1960, 7 percent of all centrally subsidized benefits-in-kind were for medicine—more than the amount allocated for state nurseries. Ferge, *A Society in the Making,* pp. 242–243.

65. KSH, *Az Élelmiszer Fogyasztás Alakulása Magyarországon,* and KSH, *Budapest a Szocializmus Útján 1950–1960.*

66. Andorka and Harcsa, "Consumption," p. 88.

67. In particular, in the early 1950s, coffee consumption dropped to 50 percent of its prewar levels, and tobacco consumption declined by 60 percent. Pető, *A Munkások Életkörülményei Magyarországon az 1950-es Években,* p. 162.

68. Ibid., p. 53; KSH, *Az Élelmiszer Fogyasztás Alakulása Magyarországon;* KSH, *Budapest a Szocializmus Útján;* and KSH, *Statisztikai Évkönyv* (1961).

69. KSH, *The Standard of Living,* p. 197, and Pető, *A Munkások Életkörülményei Magyarországon az 1950-es Években,* p. 58.

70. Andorka and Harcsa, "Consumption," p. 87.

71. Gál, *Szociálpolitikánk Két Évtizede,* p. 76; and Ferge, *A Society in the Making,* p. 105.

72. Ferge, *A Society in the Making,* p. 105. According to Ferge, these differences between nurseries and kindergartens were due to the fact that kindergartens were more costly to operate: their teachers had to be better educated and trained. This was one reason the Hungarian government opted to give mothers a three-year maternity-leave grant in the 1960s.

73. Personal and political connections also seemed to play a role in childcare placement. According to Ferge (ibid., pp. 255–256), by the early 1960s, over 80 percent of managers and professionals had secured kindergarten placements for their children, while only 40 percent of unskilled workers had their children placed in state-run centers.

74. This preference became clear in my review of case files from the period, as women often asked caseworkers to help them transfer their children to district facilities so their husbands and extended kin could take over some childcare responsibilities.

75. Deacon, *Social Policy and Socialism,* p. 201.

76. Council flats also came with a series of guarantees and rights. Eviction was outlawed in 1950, except in extreme cases of neglect. Also, occupancy rights could be passed across generations as long as the new occupant had lived in the flat for at least one year prior to inheriting it. For more on the housing issue, see ibid. and Szelényi, "Urban Inequalities under State Socialist Redistributive Economies."

77. In addition, a fourth kind of housing was allocated by individual enterprises—temporary and permanent workers' hostels, which are discussed in the next section.

78. According to Deacon, employers often paid this deposit for their employees, especially for managers. Deacon, *Social Policy and Socialism,* p. 204.

79. In this period, the interest rate hovered around 2 percent; ibid.

80. If families failed to (re)produce the agreed-on number of children, they lost their subsidies and were forced to pay back those they had already received.

81. Deacon, *Social Policy and Socialism,* pp. 203–204.

82. Ibid., p. 205, and Ferge, *A Society in the Making,* p. 295.

83. Ferge, *A Society in the Making,* p. 294.

84. In addition, cultural facilities were centrally subsidized in this period. Subsidies for "socialized entertainment" constituted a quite large portion of the national budget, as much as nurseries and kindergartens. The network of the-

aters, cinemas, and museums expanded from 1950 to 1965; the number of theaters doubled and the number of cinemas tripled in this period. Because admission to these facilities was also heavily subsidized, attendance increased significantly. Yet, what is particularly interesting about the existing data on use
patterns is that they tended to be reported by family. For instance, one 1959
study even compared cultural use patterns of families with those of employed
and unemployed women. Statisticians reported that families with working
women attended the theater three times as often and the cinema twice as often
as families in which women were not employed outside the home. They then
used this finding to conclude that the "cultural situation" in families with working women was "significantly higher" than that in families of "housewives."
KSH, *A Nők Helyzete a Munkahelyen és a Családban,* p. 18.

85. For more on the 1956 revolution and the role of the industrial working
class, see William Lomax, ed., *The Hungarian Workers' Councils of 1956,* and
György Litván, *The Hungarian Revolution of 1956: Reform, Revolt, and
Repression 1953–1963.*

86. Berend and Ránki, "A Magyar Iparfejlődés a Felszabadulás Után," p. 192.

87. Baxandall, "Reinventing Unemployment in Hungary," p. 9.

88. István Kollár, *The Development of Social Insurance in Hungary over
Three Decades,* p. 45.

89. Gál, *Szociálpolitikánk Két Évtizede.*

90. Kollár, *The Development of Social Insurance in Hungary over Three
Decades,* p. 48.

91. Ferge, *A Society in the Making,* pp. 114–115, 155–156.

92. Gál, *Szociálpolitikánk Két Évtizede,* p. 137.

93. I chose to examine historical documents from this collection of Csepel
factories for a number of reasons. Most important, their enterprise records from
1949 to 1962 have remained relatively intact—in large part because of the special role played by Csepel factory workers in the 1956 revolution: they formed
workers' councils quite early on, and once the revolution was underway, they
were some of the first to strike and to occupy factory buildings. As a result, after
the revolution, all their enterprise records were sealed in the national archives,
where they remained until the 1990s. According to national archivists, preserv-
ing the records made the document collection from these factories the most
comprehensive in the country. In addition, I also chose this complex of enterprises because it included a mixture of factories. There were two metal factories,
two iron factories, and one light-industry factory in the sample. Thus, their
employees included an unusual mix of men and women. For more on my analysis of these enterprise records, see the Methodological Appendix.

94. Csepel Vas és Fémművek, 5-1921/11.

95. Csepel Vas és Fémművek, 5-1921/188.

96. Csepel Vas és Fémművek, 77-193301/60–201.

97. For instance, in the Csepel factories I studied, subsidized cultural activities were held an average of three times a week. They included ballet, poetry
readings, Shakespearean plays, and operas. While it is quite likely that for the

most part the upper echelons of the workforce took advantage of such cultural events, enterprises also showed films to their workers at heavily subsidized rates. For instance, in 1954 this complex of Csepel factories showed 257 films. Of them, 109 were Western, 78 were Hungarian, and 70 were Soviet. (They even showed Charlie Chaplin's *The Great Dictator*, translated into Hungarian.) Csepel Vas és Fémművek, 55-200112.

98. In the six Csepel factories I studied, these trips occurred every weekend from June to August to allow all workers the opportunity to participate.

99. Kollár, *The Development of Social Insurance in Hungary over Three Decades.*

100. See Szelényi and Manchin, "Social Policy under State Socialism." In fact, Szelényi used this finding to argue that the abolition of subsidies would have been advantageous to the poor. As he put it, "If people had to pay market price for their vacation homes, then the higher income groups would lose their subsidies and the inequality ratio between the poor and the rich would decline" (p. 104).

101. Similar patterns characterized other "fringe benefits" distributed through firms, such as access to company automobiles. Ferge, *A Society in the Making*, p. 140.

102. For an account of hostel living conditions, see Pittaway, "Industrial Workers, Socialist Industrialization, and the State in Hungary."

103. Központi Népi Ellenőrzési Bizottság (hereafter KNEB), *Lakáshelyzet.*

104. Ibid., p. 154. More specifically, this study found that 37 percent of those residing in enterprise housing were workers with children, 31 percent were married couples, and 36 percent single men. The relatively high proportion of single men was due to the fact that they applied for such housing in much higher numbers.

105. Ibid., p. 45.

106. Csepel Vas és Fémművek, 103-22001/30–100.

107. Csepel Vas és Fémművek, 103-22001/10–209.

108. Csepel Vas és Fémművek, 103-22001/109–188.

109. Csepel Vas és Fémművek, 103-22001/222.

110. Csepel Vas és Fémművek, 103-22001/302–394.

111. Kollár, *The Development of Social Insurance in Hungary over Three Decades*, p. 40.

112. Ferge, *A Society in the Making*, p. 215. What is more, for a family with three or more children, the allowance was 35 percent of the average wage.

113. In 1962, the government extended maternity leave to twenty weeks for both categories of female workers.

114. Gál, *Szociálpolitikánk Két Évtizede*, p. 122.

115. These sick days were paid at rates hovering around 20–30 percent of the average wage.

116. Csepel Vas és Fémművek, 39-2201/20–302.

117. Csepel Vas és Fémművek, 39-2201/62.

118. The only real division in these offices was between "principal" case-

workers (*főelőadók*) and regular caseworkers (*előadók*). The principal case-workers tended to be more experienced and often oversaw particularly difficult cases. They also tended to be better educated. While 70 percent of all caseworkers had the equivalent of a high school degree, over half of the principal caseworkers had advanced degrees. As a result, principal caseworkers were slightly better paid. In 1960, regular caseworkers averaged 1,000–1,500 forints per month while principal caseworkers often made over 2,000 forints. KSH, *Társadalmi Szolgáltatások, 1960–1971*, p. 42. When one compares these wages with the income data presented in Table 5, it is clear that both types of state workers were fairly well paid. They made more than skilled workers and only slightly less than engineers.

119. Országos Gyermek és Ifjúságvédelmi Tanács, *A Gyermek és Ifjúságvédelem Mai Helyzete*.

120. Gyámhatóság institutional report #08110: 7.

121. Gyámhatóság case #08102: 19.

122. Gyámhatóság case #013991: 11.

123. Gyámhatóság case #081290: 23.

124. Gyámhatóság case #081992: 76.

125. Gyámhatóság case #013220: 109.

126. These visits were especially prevalent in divorce cases: Gyámhatóság cases #013221: 11, 08393: 126, 0135512: 74.

127. Gyámhatóság case #01320: 120.

128. Gyámhatóság case #013441: 73.

129. Goven found similar cases in her study of the activities of the Communist Party's women's organization. She discovered that, in this period, political activists often set out to force men to participate in the household. In a few cases judges lectured Hungarian men about the need to "help" their wives with the housework. Goven, "The Gendered Foundations of Hungarian State Socialism."

130. Gyámhatóság case #08165: 59.

131. Gyámhatóság case #013444: 123.

132. Author's interview #08112: 3.

133. In her study of the Communist women's organization, Goven discovered a similar preoccupation with the determination of paternity. In its political writings, this organization made it clear that the state "hurries to the aid of the deserted mother" and that "punishment awaits those irresponsible and unprincipled men" who refused to fulfill their familial obligations. While Goven traces this preoccupation with paternity to the ideological regime of the period, I also see it as an outgrowth of legal regulations instituted by the 1952 Family Law. Goven, "The Gendered Foundations of Hungarian State Socialism," p. 40.

134. Gyámhatóság case #083414: 22.

135. Gyámhatóság case #08112: 34.

136. Gyámhatóság case #013221: 11.

137. Gyámhatóság case #08112: 66.

138. But these cases weren't limited to such changes. Most began in this way

and then extended to other issues. Only approximately 15 percent were limited to guardianship changes.

139. Gyámhatóság case #013662: 108.
140. Gyámhatóság case #013221: 78.
141. Gyámhatóság case #081102: 120.
142. Gyámhatóság case #013220: 91.
143. Gyámhatóság case #013110: 48.
144. Gyámhatóság case #013110: 40.
145. Gyámhatóság case #08991: 82.
146. Gyámhatóság case #08100: 20.
147. Gyámhatóság case #08119: 30.
148. Gyámhatóság case #013110: 51.
149. Gyámhatóság case #08100: 19.
150. Gyámhatóság case #08221: 143.
151. Gyula Illyés, *The People of the Puszta.*

STRATEGIES OF INTEGRATION

1. For examples of this "totalitarian" theory applied to the Hungarian case, see Fehér, Heller, and Márkus, *Dictatorship over Needs;* György Konrád, *Antipolitics;* and Szalai, "From Informal Labor to Paid Occupations."

2. See Lampland, "Biographies of Liberation"; Gal and Kligman, *The Politics of Gender after Socialism;* and István Rév, "The Advantages of Being Atomized."

3. Fehér, Heller, and Márkus, *Dictatorship over Needs.*

4. See Goven, "The Gendered Foundations of Hungarian State Socialism," and Kligman, *The Politics of Duplicity.*

5. For classic formulations of this argument, see Kenneth Jowitt, "Soviet Neo-traditionalism: The Political Corruption of a Leninist Regime," and Andrew Walder, *Communist Neo-traditionalism.*

6. See Iván Szelényi and György Konrád, *Intellectuals on the Road to Class Power;* Miklós Haraszti, *A Worker in a Workers' State;* and Burawoy and Lukács, *The Radiant Past.*

7. See Szalai, "Some Aspects of the Changing Situation of Women in Hungary"; Adamik, "Feminism and Hungary"; Corrin, *Superwoman and the Double Burden;* Einhorn, *Cinderella Goes to Market;* and Ferge, *A Society in the Making.*

8. Verdery, "From Parent-State to Family Patriarchs," and Kligman, *The Politics of Duplicity.*

9. Goven, "The Gendered Foundations of Hungarian State Socialism," p. 76.

10. For more on the notions of "private" and "public" patriarchy, see Carol Brown, "Mothers, Fathers, and Children: From Private to Public Patriarchy"; Mary McIntosh, "The State and the Oppression of Women"; and Eileen Boris and Peter Bardaglio, "The Transformation of Patriarchy: The Historic Role of the State."

274 / Notes to Pages 63–70

11. Martha Lampland, *The Object of Labor*, and "Standards for Stalinists: The Science of Socialist Production in Hungary, 1948–1953."

12. For a similar argument about the nature of control in the period, see Pittaway, "Industrial Workers, Socialist Industrialization, and the State in Hungary."

13. I focus on these two groups of clients because of their different positions in the welfare society—differences that then allowed me to illuminate the forms of maneuverability characteristic of this regime.

14. KSH, *A Nők Helyzete a Munkahelyen és a Családban*, p. 8.

15. KSH, *Statisztikai Évkönyv* (1966), p. 174.

16. For the most detailed account of these difficulties, see Ferge, *Fejezetek a Magyar Szegénypolitika Történetéből*, and *A Society in the Making*.

17. KSH, *A Nők Helyzete a Munkahelyen és a Családban*, pp. 10–12, 16.

18. For instance, in 1961, 31 percent of all Hungarian households had washing machines, 15 percent vacuum cleaners, and 10 percent hot-water heaters. KSH, *Háztartásstatisztika*, p. 24.

19. Ibid., pp. 44, 45, 55.

20. Rudolf Andorka and István Harcsa, "Deviant Behavior," and Béla Buda, "Ethnographic Perspectives on Alcohol Use and Abuse."

21. For example, the number of cirrhosis deaths was 5 per 100,000 in 1950; by 1965 it had risen to 9.8 per 100,000. Buda, "Ethnographic Perspectives on Alcohol Use and Abuse," Table 5.7, and Andorka and Harcsa, "Long-Term Modernization of Hungarian Society," p. 45.

22. KSH, *Az Alkoholizmus Kifejlődésének Tényezői*, pp. 115, 136.

23. Csepel Vas és Fémművek 44-7760/69.

24. Csepel Vas és Fémművek 21-3310/21.

25. Ibid.; Csepel Vas és Fémművek 12-332/19.

26. Csepel Vas és Fémművek 14-1121/90.

27. Unfortunately, there are no reliable national-level data on these contests. In my research, I reviewed three contests from the sample of Csepel factories. In all of them, married women with children gained access to more vacations than did other groups. In one factory, married women with children were only 28 percent of the workforce, but they constituted 48 percent of those who went on these vacations.

28. Csepel Vas és Fémművek 5-1060/10.

29. Csepel Vas és Fémművek 63-3392/12–13.

30. It is not clear how many factories had such allowances since they were not centrally mandated. All five of the Csepel factories I studied had such funds for their workers.

31. Csepel Vas és Fémművek 39-11210/30.

32. Csepel Vas és Fémművek 22-3321/23.

33. Csepel Vas és Fémművek 65-22201/30.

34. Gyámhatóság case #08110: 39.

35. Gyámhatóság case #089911: 12-1.

36. Gyámhatóság case #01317: 22-3.

37. Gyámhatóság case #08993: 204-7.
38. Gyámhatóság case #01320: 117.
39. In addition, the legitimacy of their needs claims may have been related to enterprise officials' and caseworkers' identification with these women. These state actors tended to be women, most of whom also faced difficulties combining work and family. Moreover, the nature of "social work" in this period enabled state actors to see these parallels between their lives and their clients' lives. As a result, they may have been less inclined to ascribe individual blame to their clients' requests for assistance.
40. Gyámhatóság case #01311: 102-2.
41. Gyámhatóság cases #13001: 12, 8001: 111, 8012: 9, 13012: 10.
42. Gyámhatóság cases # 013221: 11, 08112: 39, 08112: 48.
43. These material issues were rarely raised in the workplace. In the Csepel records I reviewed, I found no evidence of female workers raising such problems with shop stewards or managers. Female workers may have avoided such issues for fear they would have had an adverse effect on their work assessments. This silencing may also relate to the fact that many enterprise officials were men and thus less trustworthy confidants. I thank Michael Burawoy for this insight.
44. Gyámhatóság case # 01300: 12-111.
45. Gyámhatóság case #08702: 102.
46. Gyámhatóság case #01302: 11.
47. Gyámhatóság case #01001: 111-12.
48. Gyámhatóság case #08006: 59.
49. Gyámhatóság case #013221: 109.
50. Gyámhatóság case #08011: 10.
51. Gyámhatóság case #013002: 9.
52. Gyámhatóság case #08001: 69.
53. Gyámhatóság case #013442: 35.
54. Gyámhatóság case #013221: 124.
55. Gyámhatóság case #08119: 105.
56. Gyámhatóság case #08001: 99.
57. Andorka and Harcsa, "Long-Term Modernization of Hungarian Society," p. 45.
58. Ibid.
59. These claims were particularly prevalent in the pre-1956 Ratkó period. Since abortion was illegal and birth control quite inaccessible, many women were forced to have children by men they hardly knew.
60. Gyámhatóság case #01301: 109-12.
61. Gyámhatóság case #01301: 111-30.
62. These economic reforms not only legalized certain sectors of the second economy but also gave workers the ability to change workplaces. These reforms are discussed in Part Two of this book.
63. Gyámhatóság case #08990: 12.
64. Gyámhatóság case #08110: 59.
65. Gyámhatóság case #013001: 129.

66. Csepel Vas és Fémművek 65-22202/6.
67. Gyámhatóság cases #013001: 149, #08110: 109, #08119: 203.
68. Gyámhatóság case #013001: 112.
69. Gyámhatóság case #013022: 170.
70. Gyámhatóság case #08001: 101.
71. Gyámhatóság case #08192: 66.
72. Gyámhatóság case #01344: 133.
73. Gyámhatóság case # 08220: 81 (special collection).
74. Gyámhatóság case #013441: 37.
75. Gyámhatóság case #013001: 110-121.
76. Interestingly, in these interactions the relationship between the socialist state and its clients most resembled the image portrayed in the feminist literature: here the state became women's fathers, spouses, and family members. Instead of suggesting that these positionings revealed the state's desire to encroach on all spheres of life, these data indicate that they were also rooted in single mothers' interests. Without a doubt, these relations were infused with paternalism. But, to a large extent, single mothers maneuvered within this paternalism; they dealt with the state in familial terms to protect their own well-being.
77. Gyámhatóság case #08129: 11.
78. Gyámhatóság institutional summary, 1955, document #0811: 199-22.
79. Gyámhatóság case #0132210: 99.
80. Gyámhatóság case #081132: 70.
81. These requests were particularly prevalent in the decade following World War II because of the large number of Hungarian men lost in the war.
82. Gyámhatóság case #13001: 175.
83. Gyámhatóság case #013221: 90.
84. Gyámhatóság case #080098: 13.
85. Gyámhatóság case #081123: 76.
86. Gyámhatóság case #013442: 54.

THE MATERNALIST WELFARE STATE, 1968–1985

1. More specifically, from 1954 to 1962, the birthrate fell by nearly 50 percent, dropping from 23 births per 1,000 in 1954 to 12.3 in 1962. Goven, "The Gendered Foundations of Hungarian State Socialism," p. 133.
2. See Aladárné Mód, "Születésszám és Életszínvonal," and András Klinger, "A Társadalmi Rétegenként Differenciált Termékenység Alakulása Magyarországon."
3. See Henry David, *Family Planning and Abortion in the Socialist Countries of Central Europe*, and András Klinger, B. Barta, and G. Vukovich, *Fertility and Female Employment in Hungary*.
4. Goven, "The Gendered Foundations of Hungarian State Socialism."
5. For an analysis of this Romanian regime, see Kligman, *The Politics of Duplicity*.

6. Gal, "Gender in the Post-socialist Transition," pp. 261, 270.

7. Kligman, *The Politics of Duplicity.*

8. The Czechoslovak state also gave women the right to take two and a half years of unpaid maternity leave. For more on these policies, see Wolchik, "Reproductive Policies in the Czech and Slovak Republics"; Martin Mácha, *Social Protection in the Czech Republic;* Mitchell Ornstein, "Transitional Social Policy in the Czech Republic and Poland"; and the Czechoslovak Ministry of Social Affairs, "Czechoslovakia."

9. For more on these Soviet policies, see Linda Cook, *The Soviet Social Contract;* Bernice Madison, *Social Welfare in the Soviet Union;* and Vic George and Nick Manning, *Socialism, Social Welfare, and the Soviet Union.*

10. Klinger, Barta, and Vukovich, *Fertility and Female Employment in Hungary.*

11. For these data on growth rates, see Andorka and Harcsa, "Long-Term Modernization of Hungarian Society," p. 26, and Pető and Szakács, *A Hazai Gazdaság Négy Évtizedének Története,* pp. 595, 599. For a discussion of the dynamics of growth, see Berend, *A Szocialista Gazdaság Fejlődése Magyarországon, 1945–1968,* and Iván Berend and György Ránki, *Hungary: A Century of Economic Development.*

12. For more on these exchanges, see Joanna Bockman, "Economists and Social Change: Science, Professional Power, and Politics in Hungary, 1945–1995."

13. The literature on the NEM is enormous. For the best work in English, see ibid.; Róna-Tas, *The Great Surprise of the Small Transformation;* and Berend and Ránki, *The Hungarian Economy in the Twentieth Century.*

14. János Tímár, "Economic Reform and New Employment Problems in Hungary."

15. Ferge, *A Society in the Making,* and Deacon, *Social Policy and Socialism.*

16. See István Bálint, "Baleseti Veszély és Egyéni Veszélyeztetettség"; István Bálint and Mihály Murányi, "Pszichológiai Tényezők Hatása a Könnyűipari Balesetek Megoszlására"; and István Bálint and Tibor Hódos, "Futószalagon Dolgozó Ruhaipari Munkások Neurózisának Vizsgálata."

17. Interview with Dr. Judit Karczag, April 28, 1994.

18. See Hedvig Just-Kéry and Ferenc Lénárd, "A Gondolkodási Műveletek Előfordulása Kiscsoportos Óvodásoknál a Szervezett Foglalkozások Keretében"; László Réti, "Az Iskolaérettség Pszichológiai Vizsgálata"; Lucy Lieberman, "A Családi Csoportterápia Néhány Problémája"; Pál Gégesi, "Zárszó"; and Ferenc Lénárd and Erzsébet Bánlaki, "Az Érzelmek Felismerése Arckép Alapján 7–17 Éves Korban."

19. See György Majláth and Imre Pick, "A Bűnöző Anya Szerepe egy Fiatalkorú Banda Bűncselekményeiben"; Tamás Kolosi and György Majláth, "Érzelmi Sérülés és Gyermekkori Kriminalitás"; Zoltán Varga, "Fiatalkorúak Büntetésvégrehajtásával Kapcsolatos Megfigyelések"; Péter Popper, "Fiatalkorú Bűnözők Személyiségvizsgálatának Néhány Tapasztalata"; and Rezső Hódosi, "Alkoholista Szülők Gyermekeinek Pszichológiai Problémái."

20. Just-Kéry and Lénárd, "A Gondolkodási Műveletek Előfordulása Kiscsoportos Óvodásoknál a Szervezett Foglalkozások Keretében."
21. Nóra Németh, "Megoldhatatlan Anya—Gyermek Kapcsolat."
22. Réti, "Az Iskolaérettség Pszichológiai Vizsgálata."
23. Gégesi, "Zárszó."
24. Majláth and Pick, "A Bűnöző Anya Szerepe egy Fiatalkorú Banda Bűncselekményeiben," p. 391.
25. Istvánné Kürti, "A Felnőttek Szerepének Tükröződése a Gyermek Cselekvéseiben," p. 51.
26. Gegesi, "Zárszó," p. 40.
27. See Annabella Horányi, "A Fővárosi Nevelési Tanácsadók Tevékenységéről"; Lieberman, "A Családi Csoportterápia Néhány Problémája"; and Kürti, "A Felnőttek Szerepének Tükröződése a Gyermek Cselekvéseiben."
28. Lucy Lieberman, "A Nevelési Tanácsadás Problémái Hazánkban."
29. Lajos Bartha, "Ifjúságunk Társadalmi Beilleszkedésének Pszichológiai Kérdései," p. 27.

MATERNALIZING NEED

1. For examples of these metaphors, see Berend and Ránki, *The Hungarian Economy in the Twentieth Century*, and Bruszt, "Without Us but for Us?"
2. For more on the economic changes brought about by the NEM, see Iván Berend and György Ránki, *Underdevelopment and Economic Growth: Studies in Hungarian Social and Economic History*; Kornai, *The Economics of Shortage*; Béla Balassa, "The New Growth Path in Hungary"; David Stark and Victor Nee, eds., *Remaking the Economic Institutions of Socialism: China and Eastern Europe*; and Róna-Tas, *The Great Surprise of the Small Transformation*.
3. Rév, "The Advantages of Being Atomized," and Goven, "The Gendered Foundations of Hungarian State Socialism."
4. Quoted in Bruszt, "Without Us but for Us?"
5. See Konrád, *Antipolitics*; Gal and Kligman, *The Politics of Gender after Socialism*; and Goven, "The Gendered Foundations of Hungarian State Socialism."
6. Szalai, "Some Aspects of the Changing Situation of Women in Hungary" and "From Informal Labor to Paid Occupations"; Enikő Bollobás, "Totalitarian Lib: The Legacy of Communism for Hungarian Women"; and Mária Neményi, "The Social Construction of Women's Roles in Hungary."
7. Szalai, "Some Aspects of the Changing Situation of Women in Hungary."
8. Mária Adamik, "Feminism and Hungary" and "How Can Hungarian Women Lose What They Never Had?"
9. Goven, "The Gendered Foundations of Hungarian State Socialism," and Verdery, "From Parent-State to Family Patriarchs."
10. This argument was first made in Joan Kelly-Gadol's classic 1979 article, "The Social Relations of the Sexes: Methodological Implications of Women's History." The article subsequently led to the blossoming of women's history.

11. Ferge, *A Society in the Making.*

12. By the mid-1970s, the Roma were also targeted, especially in the sphere of housing, where they were given slight preferences in the allocation of council flats—particularly in those regions with small Romany populations. Such treatment was part of the regime's "assimilation" program, an attempt to deal with ethnic differences through integration. For more on this program, see István Kemény, *A Magyarországi Cigányság Helyzete;* Gábor Havas, "A Tradícionális Teknővájó Cigánytelep Felbomlásánák Két Változata"; and Mihály Andor, ed., *Cigány Vizsgából.*

13. For examples of how women used the maternal in a variety of cases, see Koven and Michel, *Mothers of a New World.* For an exceptional historiography of U.S. women's use of the maternal, see Gordon, *Pitied but Not Entitled.*

14. For the French case, see Pedersen, *Family, Dependence, and the Origins of the Welfare State,* and Mary Stewart, *Women, Work, and the French State: Labor Protection and Social Patriarchy.* For more on race and the origins of the U.S. welfare state, see Mink, *The Wages of Motherhood.*

15. The only European country that came close was Sweden, which gave women two years of support after childbirth. For more on the Swedish case, see Sainsbury, *Gender, Equality, and Welfare States.*

16. See Goodwin, *Gender and the Politics of Welfare Reform.*

17. Koven and Michel, *Mothers of a New World,* and Sainsbury, *Gender, Equality, and Welfare States.*

18. Lisa Brush, "Love, Toil, and Trouble: Motherhood and Feminist Politics," and Gordon, *Pitied but Not Entitled.*

19. András Grád, "A Jogi Szabályozás Kapcsolata a Gyermekszületéssel és Gyermekvállalással."

20. Goven, "The Gendered Foundations of Hungarian State Socialism."

21. Grád, "A Jogi Szabályozás Kapcsolata a Gyermekszületéssel és Gyermekvállalással."

22. For a more complete list of these newly forbidden jobs, see Goven, "The Gendered Foundations of Hungarian State Socialism."

23. Balogh, *Nehéz Esztendők Krónikája.*

24. While other East European countries also introduced maternity-leave provisions in this period, they paled in comparison with Hungary's provisions. Most other countries provided mothers short amounts of paid leave. For instance, in 1966 the Romanian state granted women only two to three months of paid leave. Others coupled these short periods of paid leave with longer periods of unpaid leave. In 1973, the Soviet state introduced a new leave program: while it gave women only sixteen weeks of paid leave, it allowed them to take an additional eight months of unpaid leave. The Czechoslovak state took a similar approach; it gave women twenty-eight weeks of leave at 90 percent of their previous salaries and an additional two and a half years of unpaid leave. The Polish policy was almost identical to the Czech: Polish mothers were granted fully paid leave for twenty-four weeks, and they then had the option to take unpaid leave. For more on these regional policies, see Kligman, *The Politics of Duplicity;*

Madison, *Social Welfare in the Soviet Union;* and George and Manning, *Socialism, Social Welfare, and the Soviet Union.*

25. With time, these work requirements were relaxed. By the early 1970s, part-time workers and students became eligible for the grant. As a result, the percentage of eligible mothers increased in the grant's first decade. While only 57 percent of mothers were eligible in 1967, this percentage rose to 74 in 1970, 85 in 1974, and over 90 in 1978. For comprehensive data on GYES eligibility by region, age, education level, and family size, see KSH, *A Gyermekgondozási Segélyezés 10 Éve 1967–1976,* p. 5, and KSH, *A Gyermekgondozási Segély Igénybevétele és Hatásai,* p. 6.

26. Ferge, *A Society in the Making* , pp. 152, 104, 105.

27. There is a huge literature in Hungarian about the implications of GYES. For these analyses, see Erika Horváth, *A GYEStől a GYEDig;* Márkus, "A Nő Helyzete a Munka Világában"; and Gabriella Ernst, "A Munka, A Nő és a GYES Rendszere." For the few English discussions of the program, see Gal, "Gender in the Post-socialist Transition"; Adamik, "Feminism and Hungary"; Szalai, "Some Aspects of the Changing Situation of Women in Hungary; and Goven, "The Gendered Foundations of Hungarian State Socialism."

28. Author's interview #081123.

29. This is another way that the Hungarian policy differed from those of some of its neighbors. While the Soviet and Romanian states also granted mothers a fixed amount of money, the Poles distributed maternity-leave funds according to income tests. And the Czechs paid women a proportion of their previous salaries. In the 1980s, the Hungarian state began to follow this path by linking grant payments to women's salaries. But, in the period under consideration, all mothers received the same flat-rate payment.

30. KSH, *A Gyermekgondozási Segély Igénybevétele és Hatásai,* p. 21, and KSH, *A Gyermekgondozási Segélyezés 10 Éve 1967–1976,* p. 12.

31. KSH, *A Gyermekgondozási Segély Igénybevétele és Hatásai;* KSH, *A Gyermekgondozási Díj Igénybevétele és Hatásai;* and Ferge, *A Society in the Making,* p. 104.

32. Horváth, *A GYEStől a GYEDig,* and Márkus, "A Nő Helyzete a Munka Világában."

33. Ernst, "A Munka, A Nő és a GYES Rendszere," and Goven, "The Gendered Foundations of Hungarian State Socialism."

34. Andorka and Tóth, "A Jóléti Rendszer Jellemzői és Reformjának Lehetőségei," pp. 316–317, and KSH, *A Gyermekgondozási Díj Igénybevétele és Hatásai,* p. 56.

35. This kind of continuous use of GYES was a problem because these mothers did not meet the requirement of having twelve months of paid labor prior to the birth of their new children. Györgyné Forgó, "A Gyermekgondozási Segély Méltányossági Ügyek Elbírálása Során Szerzett Tapasztalatok."

36. Ibid., p. 110.

37. Ibid., pp. 110, 112.

38. For instance, a number of shorter leave provisions were reformed in this

period. In 1973, a special system of paid sick leave was established for mothers. The explicit justification for this provision was "to protect mothers" and "to permit them to fulfill the special responsibilities that accompany child rearing." As with GYES, Hungarian fathers were eligible for these benefits only if they were single parents. László Pongrácz, *Szociálpolitikai Ismeretek*, p. 151.

39. In this regard, Hungarian family allowances were also more extensive than those of other East European countries. For instance, in this period, the Soviet government provided allowances only to large families with four or more children. In other countries, such as Romania, family allowances were subjected to income tests. The Czechoslovak state was the only one in this period to offer similarly expansive allowances: in 1970, it extended allowances to all families with two or more children.

40. KSH, *A Gyermekgondozási Segélyezés 10 Éve 1967–1976*, p. 5.

41. That is, from my sample of 223 Gyámhatóság cases in the 1970s, roughly 10 percent involved appeals to switch the family allowance to the mother's name. Without national-level data I cannot assess whether this finding is representative of other districts.

42. Gyámhatóság case #013110: 219.

43. Gyámhatóság case #089110: 289.

44. In the earlier period, local-level caseworkers did have the option of applying for emergency aid that provided clients with one-time boosts to their incomes, yet they rarely used the option. And the amount of these funds paled in comparison with those distributed by enterprise unions.

45. Since almost no scholarly work has been done on the history of these local funds, there is little information on the politics underlying their creation. In my interviews with policymakers and government officials, I uncovered two explanations for their creation. Some policymakers claimed that the impetus came from the national government; it was part of the move to bolster women's reproductive roles. Of course, this shift was also consistent with the government's desire to scale back enterprise expenditures in order to increase production efficiency and productivity. Other policymakers claimed that these funds resulted from the work of local caseworkers themselves. Disappointed with their inability to support their clients directly, caseworkers demanded their own pool of resources. They were frustrated that they often had to remove children from their nuclear families and place them in their extended families or state institutions because of "simple financial problems." As one caseworker put it in an interview, "We needed a reward mechanism. We could not work without the means to applaud good behavior and punish the bad." Author's interviews #01311, 01314, 0802, 0809, 0803, 0810.

46. Author's interview #080211: 7.

47. In this regard, RNS differed from other discretionary programs in the region. In 1974, the Soviet state also introduced a cash-allowance program. But the Soviet policy was targeted at poor women; it was an income-tested program that provided small amounts of cash to poor mothers to purchase food for their children.

48. Ágota Horváth, "Egy Segély Anatómiája," p. 240.

49. Ibid., p. 242. Of those not employed, 22 percent were "housewives," 21 percent were on GYES, and 7 percent were on disability pensions.

50. KSH, *A Nők Helyzetének Alakulása a KSH Adatainak Tükrében 1970–1981*, p. 23.

51. Gyámhatóság institutional summaries. This number varied a great deal by district. The two districts of my research employed four workers in the late 1960s and between five and seven in the 1970s.

52. Gyámhatóság case #013661: 295.

53. Gyámhatóság case #0132213: 136.

54. Gyámhatóság case #013006: 301.

55. Gyámhatóság case #081124: 390.

56. Gyámhatóság case #0130006: 415.

57. Gyámhatóság case #083321: 631.

58. Gyámhatóság cases #081120: 193; 013006: 195, 199, 280; 370081124: 701.

59. Gyámhatóság case #0132215: 488.

60. Gyámhatóság case #0139121: 507.

61. For further examples of how these tests were used in the administration of RNS, see Horváth, "Egy Segély Anatómiája." Overall, Horváth's discussion of this program is relatively inattentive to its gendered agenda. While extremely insightful, Horváth examines RNS as a failed government attempt to alleviate poverty and not as a policy that articulated specific gender constructs. In part, this absence of a gender analysis is rooted in the lack of a feminist social-scientific tradition in Hungary: few sociologists in the period analyzed the social world through a gendered lens. Instead, they had other (equally important) political agendas. And Horváth's work exemplifies this type of analysis; she wrote in the 1980s, when sociologists were criticizing state-socialist welfare for not adequately meeting the needs of the materially deprived. For a longer discussion of this political agenda, see the introduction to Part Three.

62. Gyámhatóság cases #080211: 371, 391, 507, 611; 0132213: 136, 204, 233, 251.

63. Gyámhatóság case #080211: 377, 475.

64. Gyámhatóság cases #080211: 192, 222, 235; 0132214: 206, 391, 401.

65. Gyámhatóság case #080211: 222, 266, 509.

66. For more on the institutionalization process, see Mária Herczog, *A Gyermekvédelem Dilemmái*; Katalin Hanák, *Társadalom és Gyermekvédelem*; and András Dömszky, "A Gyermek és Ifjúságvédelem Magyarországon."

67. In the two districts of my research, I uncovered 117 cases of institutionalization, 98 of which involved such "mother blame."

68. As a caseworker said when I asked about a domestic-violence case: "This was not my job. It was for the woman to take care of. I protected the child. If the mother didn't do that, I gave the child to someone who did."

69. Gyámhatóság case #086678: 264.

70. Gyámhatóság case #080211: 266.

71. Gyámhatóság case #013006: 601.

72. Gyámhatóság case #013006: 415.

73. Gyámhatóság case #080211: 307.

74. Gyámhatóság case #0136615: 310. The irony is that this argument was used to institutionalize this woman's two children and to place them in large facilities with hundreds of other children, with shared beds.

75. Author's interview #013112: 4.

76. Ibid.

77. Ferenc Mérei, *Klinikai Pszichodiagnosztikai Módszerek,* and Alaine Polcz, *Világjáték.*

78. These observations were often quite surreal. Counselors would throw groups of children together and watch how they played. Depending on how well they interacted, there were labeled socially "mature" or "immature."

79. There were four possible outcomes here. First, counselors could keep a child in kindergarten for an extra year; particularly "slow" children were in this category. Second, they could advance a child to the first grade, but in a slow class. Third, they could put a child in a regular first-grade class. And fourth, they could accelerate a child into an advanced first-grade class.

80. To arrive at these data, I coded the 132 school exams in my sample and discovered that the mother's length of time on GYES was a key determinant of how a child fared in these exams. Because I did not control for other demographic factors, such as how many children the mother had or her education, occupation, or income, these findings remain suggestive. Yet other studies have uncovered similar GYES effects. One survey of young children found that those who remained at home with their mothers were evaluated as exhibiting more creativity, fantasy, and independent thinking; Szalai, "From Informal Labor to Paid Occupations."

81. Nevelési Tanácsadó case file #082116: 24.

82. Nevelési Tanácsadó case file #01322194: 75. Occasionally, counselors even recommended that these women remain on GYES for more time with future children. For instance, in 1974 one counselor advised a pregnant mother whose son was kept back a year to stay on GYES longer with her new child. The counselor warned that her son's poor performance was a sign of what was to come for her new baby without "adequate attention." Nevelési Tanácsadó case file #01322194: 61.

83. Nevelési Tanácsadó case file #082116: 36.

84. Nevelési Tanácsadó case file #082116: 127.

85. Nevelési Tanácsadó case file #082116: 201.

86. Nevelési Tanácsadó case file #01322194: 199.

87. Nevelési Tanácsadó institutional summary, document # 013221.

88. Nevelési Tanácsadó case file #01311992: 37.

89. Nevelési Tanácsadó case file #081182: 101.

90. Nevelési Tanácsadó case file #01322194: 51.

91. Nevelési Tanácsadó case file #01322194: 81.

92. In effect, the term "sexual abnormality" (*nemi rendellenesség*) was a

veiled reference to homosexuality. Counselors rarely made this reference explicit, but the meaning was clear in their analyses and treatment of these boys.

93. Since they saw these "abnormalities" as innate "tendencies," they often assured mothers that such "urges" could be suppressed with the right intervention. "It is like alcoholism," a counselor explained to an anxious mother. "Some have it, but, without access, it will never surface." Nevelési Tanácsadó case files #01322194: 169; 08182: 111, 181.

94. Nevelési Tanácsadó case file #081182: 181.

95. Mérei, *Klinikai Pszichodiagnosztikai Módszerek.*

96. László Tunkli, "Pszichológiai Munka a Fővárosi Nevelési Tanácsadókban."

97. Author's interview #03112: 3.

98. Nevelési Tanácsadó case file #081171: 275.

99. Nevelési Tanácsadó case files #081182: 39, 73, 99, 102, 298, 333; 132281: 13, 44, 60, 144, 179, 301.

100. Nevelési Tanácsadó case file #0132281: 57.

101. Nevelési Tanácsadó case file #0132281: 88.

102. Author's interview #0311–2.

103. Nevelési Tanácsadó case file #0132281: 261.

104. Nevelési Tanácsadó case file #0138819: 233.

105. It also surfaced in the different type of behavior that psychologists problematized in boys and girls. Boys' aloofness and hypermasculinity were rarely addressed, and neither were passivity and shyness in girls. Psychologists defined such behavior as consistent with gender norms. "His teacher complains that Tamás shows little interest in anything other than sports, music, and girls," wrote one psychologist in 1977. "I assured her this is normal adolescent behavior for boys." Nevelési Tanácsadó case file #081171: 151.

106. Nevelési Tanácsadó case file #0132281: 86.

107. Nevelési Tanácsadó case file #081171: 99.

108. Nevelési Tanácsadó case file #0132281: 202.

109. Nevelési Tanácsadó case file #081171: 20.

110. Nevelési Tanácsadó case file #081171: 89.

111. Nevelési Tanácsadó case file #0132281: 291.

112. Nevelési Tanácsadó institutional summary, document # 013221.

113. Author's interview #03112: 19.

114. Nevelési Tanácsadó case file #0132297: 299.

115. Nevelési Tanácsadó case file #081165: 87.

116. Nevelési Tanácsadó case file #013221: 169.

117. Author's interview #0311: 5.

118. Nevelési Tanácsadó case file #013299: 316.

119. Author's interview #03112: 2.

120. Nevelési Tanácsadó case files #013299: 11, 191, 211, 300.

121. Author's interview #013112: 4.

122. Nevelési Tanácsadó case file #081171: 310.

123. Nevelési Tanácsadó case file #0822116: 77.

124. Nevelési Tanácsadó case file #081165: 111.
125. Nevelési Tanácsadó case file #013112: 40.
126. Nevelési Tanácsadó case file #081171: 99.
127. Author's interviews #03112: 2, 01311: 17.

STRATEGIES OF EXPANSION

1. The issue of social rights is clearly quite complicated in this period. Given the lack of overall political rights, the population was restricted from participating formally in the social politics of the era. Yet, because most of the policies created in this period were allocated according to bureaucratically defined rules and accompanied by some sort of appeal mechanisms, it is possible to conceptualize them as social rights. For a more extensive discussion of the question of social rights in this era, see Deacon, *Social Policy and Socialism,* and Ferge, *A Society in the Making.*

2. See Lisa Brush, "Love, Toil, and Trouble," and Muncy, *Creating a Female Dominion in American Reform.*

3. See Koven and Michel, *Mothers of a New World;* Molly Ladd-Taylor, *Mother Work;* Pedersen, *Family, Dependence, and the Origins of the Welfare State;* and Goodwin, *Gender and the Politics of Welfare Reform.*

4. See Gordon, *Pitied but Not Entitled,* and Eileen Boris, "The Power of Motherhood: Black and White Women Redefine the Political."

5. As in my analysis of the welfare society, I take this regime on its own terms by examining its institutional modes of stratification. In other words, because the previous regime's collective focus tracked clients according to their institutional locations, I analyzed how client maneuverability in that regime varied by clients' institutional positions. By contrast, this regime's maternal focus stratified clients according to their mothering practices; thus, to understand client maneuverability in this regime, I compare the strategies employed by women who were labeled "good" and "bad" mothers.

6. Unfortunately, no reliable national data exist on the overall number of Hungarians connected to the welfare institutions of the period. Hence, it is difficult to determine whether the two districts of my research were representative. From interviews with caseworkers from other districts, it became clear that my two districts had slightly larger caseloads than the average: most Gyámhatóság caseworkers told me that their offices' caseloads hovered around 5,000 to 7,000, while other Child Guidance Centers seemed to average 350 to 400 new clients per year.

7. This drop was probably due to the introduction of RNS and the new surveillance techniques accompanying the program.

8. To arrive at these demographic overviews, I drew on the information welfare workers gathered in their case files. In other words, while state actors' classifications of their caseloads provided clues as to the overall number of "incompetent" and "competent" mothers, they offered few insights into who these

women were demographically. Thus, I reconstructed these portraits from my review of the 1968–1985 case files of four agencies. Interestingly, these demographic profiles resemble those of RNS recipients as described in Horváth, "Egy Segély Anatómiája."

9. Of course, some of these clients had only simple, bureaucratic needs that did not require extended contact with state caseworkers or counselors. In the Gyámhatóság, such clients included those who had to register newborns or to set legal guardianship; such cases constituted approximately 25 percent of the typical Gyámhatóság's caseload. In Child Guidance Centers, they included clients whose children just needed to take a school entrance exam. The goodmother label allowed these women to move in and out of these welfare offices relatively unscathed.

10. Júlia Szalai, "Some Thoughts on Poverty and the Concept of the Subsistence Minimum," pp. 302–303.

11. For similar arguments about the isolation that accompanied the GYES program, see Adamik, "How Can Hungarian Women Lose What They Never Had?"

12. Rudolf Andorka, Béla Falussy, and István Harcsa, "Időfelhasználás és Életmód," p. 136, and Andorka and Harcsa, "Long-Term Modernization of Hungarian Society," p. 42.

13. See Buda, "Ethnographic Perspectives on Alcohol Use and Abuse," Table 2.2.

14. Buda, "Ethnographic Perspectives on Alcohol Use and Abuse," p. 31, and KSH, *Az Alkoholizmus Kifejlődésének Tényezői*, p. 115.

15. The only issue that ranked higher than alcoholism was the population's financial troubles. For these survey data, see István György Tóth, "Opinions about Social Problems and Social Policies in Hungary."

16. Andorka and Harcsa, "Consumption," pp. 87, 89.

17. Andorka, Falussy, and Harcsa, "Időfelhasználás és Életmód," p. 129.

18. See Andorka and Harcsa, "Deviant Behavior," p. 147, and Zsolt Spéder, Borbála Paksi, and Zsuzsanna Elekes, "Anómia és Elégedettség a 90-es Évek Elején," pp. 92–93.

19. Gyámhatóság case #0132213: 157.

20. Gyámhatóság case #0130006: 415.

21. Gyámhatóság case #081124: 303.

22. Gyámhatóság case #0130006: 470.

23. Gyámhatóság case #080211: 161.

24. Gyámhatóság case #080211: 192.

25. Gyámhatóság case #080211: 222.

26. Gyámhatóság case #0132214: 191.

27. Nevelési Tanácsadó case file #013112: 62. The Esti Mese was a popular television program for children; it was broadcast throughout the country at the same time every night on one of the two state-run television stations.

28. Nevelési Tanácsadó case file #0132294: 218.

29. Nevelési Tanácsadó case file #032281: 171.

30. Nevelési Tanácsadó case file #082116: 201.
31. Nevelési Tanácsadó case file #0132281: 202.
32. Nevelési Tanácsadó case file #082116: 51.
33. Gyámhatóság case #081124: 176.
34. Gyámhatóság case #081124: 390.
35. Gyámhatóság case #0130006: 402.
36. Gyámhatóság case #0130006: 695.
37. Author's interviews #080211: 7, 12.
38. There are clear parallels between this use of RNS and Aid to Families with Dependent Children (AFDC) in the United States. As many have argued, AFDC enabled many unmarried women to obtain support without maintaining contact with their children's fathers. This situation changed as paternity investigations became a prerequisite for receiving Temporary Assistance to Needy Families and other such funds. For more on these debates in the United States, see Mink, *The Wages of Motherhood,* and Monson, "State-ing Sex and Gender."
39. Gyámhatóság case #080211: 235.
40. Gyámhatóság case #080211: 371.
41. Gyámhatóság case #0132213: 481.
42. Nevelési Tanácsadó case file #081171: 99.
43. Nevelési Tanácsadó case file #01322194: 206.
44. Gyámhatóság case #081129: 120.
45. Nevelési Tanácsadó case file #081124: 286.
46. Gyámhatóság case #0132213: 479.
47. Gyámhatóság case #080211: 141.
48. From the Szellő case file, it was impossible to tell whether Mrs. Szellő's beatings ended or she stopped reporting them. This is clearly one of the main limitations of my case-file data.
49. Gyámhatóság case #080211: 177.
50. Gyámhatóság case #080211: 402.
51. Gyámhatóság case #0132213: 310.
52. Author's interview #080211: 7.
53. Nevelési Tanácsadó case files #082211: 137, 151.
54. Nevelési Tanácsadó case file #0132294: 151.
55. Nevelési Tanácsadó case file #082211212: 123/89.
56. Nevelési Tanácsadó case file #0136611: 41.
57. Gyámhatóság case file #081169: 399.
58. Gyámhatóság cases #080211: 475, 01322214: 401, 080211: 539.
59. For instance, as one counselor told a mother in 1981, "Your son is ready for kindergarten. He will even go to an advanced class. You did something correct." Nevelési Tanácsadó case file #0136132: 198.
60. Author's interview #080211: 7.
61. Author's interview #013112: 4.
62. See Péter Somlai, "Kötelékek—Széltörésben," and Adamik, "How Can Hungarian Women Lose What They Never Had?"
63. Nevelési Tanácsadó case file #0132297: 299.

64. Nevelési Tanácsadó case file #081165: 195.
65. Nevelési Tanácsadó case file #081165: 669.
66. Nevelési Tanácsadó case files # 036615: 17, 41, 66, 91.
67. Nevelési Tanácsadó institutional summary, documents #08661, 08997.
68. Author's interview #03112: 4.
69. Nevelési Tanácsadó case file #013667: 49.
70. Nevelési Tanácsadó case files #0811565: 89, 081177: 99.
71. Author's interview #013112: 4.
72. Author's interview #03119: 2.
73. As with my breakdowns of "good" mothers, these data are only rough estimates. They were compiled from the institutional summaries of the offices I studied. Since these overviews were submitted to the Central Statistical Office on a yearly basis after 1968, they are also available in KSH, *Statisztikai Évkönyv*, 1968–1985.
74. Of the 20 percent not employed, 17 percent were on GYES, and 3 percent were housewives. Hence, these women's work positions were more similar to those of the general female population than were "good" mothers' positions.
75. Again, while I am certain that Romany women were overrepresented among "bad" mothers, it is impossible to give precise ethnic breakdowns since caseworkers could not state the race of their clients. Close to 15 percent of the "bad" mothers I studied were explicitly defined as Romany. But, without overall data on the ethnic composition of the entire caseload, this number is suggestive.
76. For this approximation of the number of Hungarians included in the second economy, see Szelényi and Manchin, "Social Policy under State Socialism," p. 113.
77. Szalai, "Some Thoughts on Poverty and the Concept of the Subsistence Minimum," p. 300.
78. Andrew Czeizel, "Alcohol Consumption by Females in Hungary."
79. Andrew Czeizel, "Female Alcohol Abuse and Pregnancy Outcomes in Hungary," Tables 6.3, 6.6, and 13.3. Because this study relied on self-reports, it is unclear whether working-class women really did abuse alcohol more often or whether they were simply more likely to report it.
80. Gyámhatóság case #081167: 111.
81. Gyámhatóság case #013669: 137.
82. In addition, many professional mothers claimed that they could not adhere to welfare workers' rigid child-rearing standards. In discussions with Gyámhatóság caseworkers, they admitted that their hectic work lives meant that their families rarely ate or relaxed together. These women often scoffed at state counselors' time formulas; they could hardly perform the basic household tasks, much less oversee their children's schoolwork or extracurricular activities. Thus, these women frequently missed meetings with counselors, sent their children to counseling sessions alone, and failed to carry out the child-rearing regimens dictated by psychologists—all of which led welfare workers to question their "commitment" to the family and ultimately their domestic competence.

83. *Pálinka* is a type of Hungarian liquor, known for its strong, inebriating effects. Gyámhatóság case #081172: 598.

84. Interestingly, I learned about this case from counselors themselves. Initially, this case was not part of my sample of files. After many counselors asked me whether I had come across the famous "pig case," I agreed to examine it. This was the only time that I purposefully inserted a case into my sample. Nevelési Tanácsadó case file #0136692: 173.

85. Gyámhatóság cases #081172: 196, 202, 312; 013017: 186, 229, 232. Nevelési Tanácsadó case files #0136692: 74, 130.

86. Gyámhatóság cases #081172: 370, 432.

87. Gyámhatóság cases #013665: 188. Nevelési Tanácsadó case files #013777: 406, 473.

88. Gyámhatóság case #0132221: 152.

89. Gyámhatóság case #0811672: 430.

90. Gyámhatóság case #0811672: 312.

91. Gyámhatóság case #0811672: 560.

92. Gyámhatóság case #0811661: 177.

93. Gyámhatóság case #0132221: 607.

94. Gyámhatóság case #0811672: 374.

95. Gyámhatóság case #0811672: 427. Counselors' use of the term *psychopathic* was not clinical. Rather, they seemed to use it to refer to severe depressive or self-destructive behavior (or both).

96. Gyámhatóság case #013002: 183.

97. Gyámhatóság case #080211: 399.

98. Gyámhatóság case #087750: 139.

99. Gyámhatóság case #013006: 555.

100. Nevelési Tanácsadó case file #08182: 189.

101. Gyámhatóság cases #081172: 401, 791; 013667: 512, 621.

102. Nevelési Tanácsadó case files #013699: 172, 310; 089957: 196, 222.

103. Nevelési Tanácsadó case file #089957: 401.

104. Gyámhatóság case #080211: 377.

105. Gyámhatóság case #080211: 302

106. Gyámhatóság case #081123: 394.

107. Gyámhatóság case #013667: 199.

108. Gyámhatóság case #081124: 394.

109. Author's interview #0811: 6.

110. Nevelési Tanácsadó case file #0132281: 161.

111. Author's interviews #01311: 5, 2, 7. Nevelési Tanácsadó case files #0132281: 71, 08182: 163.

112. Gyámhatóság case #081123: 431.

113. The institutionalization process was quite complex. In Budapest, it began with the forcible removal of children from their homes and their placement in GYIVI (Gyermek Védelmi Intézet), a temporary facility for endangered children. Minors remained in GYIVI until caseworkers found them places in more permanent children's homes (*gyermek otthonok*). This waiting period

could last for months. Once space was found, welfare workers contracted children out to homes all over the country. Parents had little say over where their children were placed; an overwhelming majority of them were taken to homes in remote towns and villages, so it was extremely difficult for parents to maintain ongoing contact. Most parents could visit only on weekends or holidays; a few were permitted to take their children back to Budapest for short home visits. In addition, parents were required to pay a portion of their children's living expenses, usually 20–40 percent of their wages. Those who could not pay these fees could take out loans from the Gyámhatóság, although failure to pay back these debts could lead to legal action. Usually, these institutional fees were taken directly out of parents' wages. Indirectly, this attachment of wages ended up marginalizing these parents at work by alerting enterprise accountants and supervisors that their children were institutionalized. This may be one reason why some parents refused to have their wages attached, even though caseworkers then considered these parents to be even more irresponsible. For more on this process, see György Konrád, *The Caseworker*; Hanák, *Társadalom és Gyermekvédelem*; and Herczog, *A Gyermekvédelem Dilemmái*.

114. Gyámhatóság case #081123: 195.
115. Gyámhatóság case #081123: 520.
116. Gyámhatóság case #013667: 475.
117. Gyámhatóság case #013667: 607.
118. Gyámhatóság case #081123: 152.
119. Gyámhatóság case #081123: 211.
120. Gyámhatóság case #081123: 699.
121. Gyámhatóság case #081123: 178 (special collection).

THE LIBERAL WELFARE STATE, 1985–1996

1. See Deacon, "Social Policy, Social Justice and Citizenship in Eastern Europe"; Ferge, "Social Citizenship in the New Democracies"; Júlia Szalai and Mária Neményi, *Hungary in the 1980s: A Historic Review of Social Policy and Urban Level Interventions*; and Júlia Szalai, "Social Participation in Hungary in the Context of Restructuring and Liberalization."

2. See Kornai, "Paying the Bill for Goulash Communism"; Peter Gedeon, "Hungary: Social Policy in Transition"; and Jan Adam, "Social Contract."

3. See István György Tóth, "A Jóléti Rendszer az Átmeneti Időszakban," and Andorka and Tóth, "A Jóléti Rendszer Jellemzői és Reformjának Lehetőségei."

4. For example, see Miklós Szántó, *Életmód Kutatás a Szocialista Országokban*; Emőke Bagdy, *Családi Szocializáció és Személyiség*; and László Cseh-Szombathy, *Családszociológia: Problémák és Módszerek* .

5. Zsuzsa Ferge, *A Society in the Making* and *Szociálpolitika Ma és Holnap*; Elemér Hankiss, "Kinek az Érdeke?"; and Haraszti, *A Worker in a Workers' State*.

6. Szelényi and Manchin, "Social Policy under State Socialism."

7. Szalai, "Some Aspects of the Changing Situation of Women in Hungary," pp. 300–303.

8. István Kemény, *A Magyarországi Cigányság Helyzete* and "A Magyarországi Cigány Lakosság"; István Hoóz, "A Cigány és a nem Cigány Népesség Társadalmi és Kulturális Helyzetében Lévő Fontosabb Különbségekről"; Havas, "A Tradicionális Teknővájó Cigánytelep Felbomlásánák Két Változata"; and Ottília Solt, *Méltóságot Mindenkinek: Első Kötet.*

9. Ottília Solt, "A SZETA, a Szegényeket Támogató Alap Szerveződése és Munkája."

10. Szelényi and Manchin, "Social Policy under State Socialism."

11. Rudolf Andorka, *Merre Tart a Magyar Társadalom?*

12. For example, see Ágnes Bokor, *Depriváció és Szegénység.*

13. The study culminated in an influential report that was widely distributed in the underground, emergent democratic opposition: Zsuzsa Ferge, Júlia Szalai, and György Petri, *Fordulat és Reform.* For descriptions of the study in English, see Szelényi and Manchin, "Social Policy under State Socialism," and Róna-Tas, *The Great Surprise of the Small Transformation.*

14. These sociologists also founded a new journal, *Szociálpolitikai Értesítő* (Social Policy Report), to disseminate their findings. For more on the goals of this journal, see Gyuláné Gayer, "Előszó."

15. Géza Gosztonyi, "Hatóság + Szolgálat," pp. 16–17.

16. Ibid., p. 17.

17. For reviews in English of the development of reformers' thinking, see Róna-Tas, *The Great Surprise of the Small Transformation;* Bockman, "Economists and Social Change"; and Jason McDonald, "Elite Economists and Political Change in Hungary since World War II."

18. László Antal, "Development—with Some Digression" and "Thoughts on the Further Development of the Hungarian Mechanism."

19. Tamás Bauer, "The Second Economy Reform and Ownership Relations: Some Considerations for the Further Development of the New Economic Mechanism."

20. Rezső Nyers, "Efficiency and Socialist Democracy."

21. For more on the official connections of reform economists, see Bockman, "Economists and Social Change," and Ervin Csizmadia, *A Magyar Demokratikus Ellenzék, 1968–1988.*

22. For a discussion of economists' influence in the opposition, see Erzsébet Szalai, "From the Belly of the Whale: The Crisis of the Hungarian Cultural Elite and the Dilemmas of the Intelligentsia"; Bockman, "Economists and Social Change"; McDonald, "Elite Economists and Political Change in Hungary since World War II"; and Csizmadia, *A Magyar Demokratikus Ellenzék.*

23. The study is cited in note 13 above. Although this report was never published formally, it is available in most Hungarian libraries, including the Szabó Ervin Könyvtár in Budapest. For discussions of the role of economists in this study, see Bockman, "Economists and Social Change," and Szelényi and Manchin, "Social Policy under State Socialism."

24. While my analysis of these consistencies is limited to the welfare arena, Eyal, Szelényi, and Townsley advance a similar, yet more general, argument about these groups' world-views: they flesh out the parallels between the ideology of monetarism adhered to by economists and the ideology of civil society propagated by dissidents (many of whom were social scientists). They show that there was an "elective affinity" between these ideologies—an affinity that, among other things, led to an antistatist stance and an obscuring of social inequality. Eyal, Szelényi, and Townsley, *Making Capitalism without Capitalists*, chap. 3.

25. Szelényi and Manchin, "Social Policy under State Socialism," and Pál Závada, *Gazdasági Reform, Szociális Reform.*

26. Andrea Szegő, "Gazdaság és Politika-Érdek és Struktúra," and Tamás Bauer, "A Második Gazdasági Reform és a Tulajdonviszonyok."

27. János Kornai, "Lasting Growth as the Top Priority."

28. Szelényi and Manchin, "Social Policy under State Socialism," and Hankiss, "Kinek az Érdeke?"

29. For more on the relationship between these global and local actors, see Lynne Haney, "Global Discourses of Need: Mythologizing and Pathologizing Welfare in Hungary."

30. See Harold James, *International Monetary Cooperation since Bretton Woods*, and Bockman, "Economists and Social Change."

31. L. W. Pauly, "Promoting a Global Economy: The Normative Role of the IMF," and Deacon, *Global Social Policy.*

32. World Bank, *Hungary Health Services: Issues and Options for Reform* and *Housing Policy Reform in Hungary.*

33. World Bank, *Hungary, The Transition to a Market Economy: Critical Human Resources Issues*, and International Monetary Fund, *Social Security Reform in Hungary.*

34. World Bank, *Hungary: Reform of Social Policy and Expenditures* and *Magyarország.*

35. Csizmadia, *A Magyar Demokratikus Ellenzék.*

36. István György Tóth et al., *Poverty, Inequalities, and the Incidence of Social Transfers in Hungary;* Szalai and Neményi, *Hungary in the 1980s;* and Júlia Szalai, *Poverty in Hungary during the Period of Economic Crisis* and *Urban Poverty and Social Policy in the Context of Adjustment: The Case of Hungary.*

37. Tóth, "A Jóléti Rendszer az Átmeneti Időszakban."

38. International Labor Organization, *Labor Market Developments in Hungary;* Organization for Economic Cooperation and Development, *Social and Labor Market Policies in Hungary;* and UNICEF, *Public Policy and Social Conditions* and *Central and Eastern Europe: Transition Public Policy and Social Conditions.*

39. Overall, these agencies played a relatively minor role in Hungary, particularly given the level of their involvement with other countries in the region. Because of the IMF and World Bank's stronghold in Hungary, there was less

space for other agencies. Thus, their roles were limited to funding special projects, policy studies, and programmatic evaluations. For more on the role of these agencies in the region, see Deacon, *Global Social Policy.*

40. For a classic formulation of the evolution of the intelligentsia and its relationship to the socialist state, see Szelényi and Konrád, *Intellectuals on the Road to Class Power.*

MATERIALIZING NEED

1. See Deacon, *Global Social Policy;* John Dixon and David Macarov, eds., *Social Welfare in Socialist Countries;* U. Götting, "Destruction, Adjustment, and Innovations: Social Policy Transformation in Eastern and Central Europe"; and Guy Standing and Daniel Vaughn-Whitehead, eds., *Minimum Wages in Central and Eastern Europe: From Protection to Destitution.*

2. See G. Cornia, *Income Distribution, Poverty, and Welfare in Transitional Economies: A Comparison between Eastern Europe and China;* M. Bruno, *Stabilization and Reform in Eastern Europe: A Preliminary Evaluation;* and Michael Förster and István Tóth, *Szegénység és Egyenlőtlenségek Magyarországon és a Többi Visegrádi Országban.*

3. See Guy Standing, "Social Protection in Central and Eastern Europe: A Tale of Slipping Anchors and Lost Safety Nets," and UNICEF, *Central and Eastern Europe: Transition Public Policy and Social Conditions.*

4. See Petr Mateju, "Winners and Losers in the Post-socialist Transition: The Czech Republic in Comparative Perspective," and Ornstein, "Transitional Social Policy in the Czech Republic and Poland."

5. See Einhorn, *Cinderella Goes to Market;* Corrin, *Superwomen and the Double Burden;* and Maxine Molyneux, "Women's Rights and the International Context in the Post-Communist States."

6. See Verdery, "From Parent-State to Family Patriarchs"; Éva Fodor, "The Political Woman? Women in Politics in Hungary"; Marilyn Rueschemeyer, ed., *Women in the Politics of Postcommunist Eastern Europe;* and Peggy Watson, "The Rise of Masculinism in Eastern Europe." For a different, and far more positive, evaluation of the effects of marketization on women's lives, see Szalai, "From Informal Labor to Paid Occupations."

7. For an overview of these arguments, see Nanette Funk and Magda Mueller, eds., *Gender and the Politics of Post-Communism,* and Gal and Kligman, *The Politics of Gender after Socialism.*

8. Esping-Andersen, *The Three Worlds of Welfare Capitalism.*

9. See Deacon, "Social Policy, Social Justice and Citizenship in Eastern Europe"; Klaus Nielsen, "Eastern European Welfare Systems in Comparative Perspective"; and Gedeon, "Hungary."

10. See Martin Potucek, "Current Social Policy Developments in the Czech and Slovak Republics"; Mácha, *Social Protection in the Czech Republic;* and Petr Mares and Ivo Mozný, *Poverty in the Czech Republic.*

11. See Ornstein, "Transitional Social Policy in the Czech Republic and

Poland," and Förster and Tóth, *Szegénység és Egyenlőtlenségek Magyaror-szágon és a Többi Visegrádi Országban.*

12. See Kornai, "Lasting Growth as the Top Priority" and "Paying the Bill for Goulash Communism"; Tóth, "A Jóléti Rendszer az Átmeneti Időszakban"; and Andorka and Tóth, "A Jóléti Rendszer Jellemzői és Reformjának Lehetőségei."

13. Coming from a quite different political perspective, others have pre-scribed a postsocialist "New Deal"—that is, a welfare state based on public-works programs and poor relief modeled after the Depression-era United States. See Iván Szelényi and János Ladányi, "Egy Posztkommunista New Deal Esélyei Kelet Közép Európában."

14. Tibor Nagy, "Hungarian Social Insurance Contributions as State Taxes," p. 305.

15. Zsuzsa Ferge, "A Magyar Segélyezési Rendszer Reformja II," p. 33.

16. See Júlia Szalai, "A Helyi Önkormányzatok Szociálpolitikájáról"; Ágota Horváth, "Törvény és Anarchia avagy Törvényes Anarchia"; and Ferenc Bárányi, *Szociálpolitikai Ismeretek.*

17. World Bank, *Magyarország: Szegénység és Szociális Támogatások.*

18. See Szalai and Neményi, *Hungary in the 1980s;* Horváth, "Törvény és Anarchia avagy Törvényes Anarchia"; and Bárányi, *Szociálpolitikai Ismeretek.*

19. István Harcsa, *Szociális Ellátás az Önkormányzatoknál (A Kísérleti Adatgyűjtés Tapasztalata).*

20. World Bank, *Magyarország,* p. 69.

21. See Ferge, *Szociálpolitika Ma és Holnap,* and Szalai, "Some Aspects of the Changing Situation of Women in Hungary."

22. Goven, "The Gendered Foundations of Hungarian State Socialism," p. 241.

23. Kata Beke, "A Kedv vagy a Lehetőség?" p. 15.

24. There was also a racialized undercurrent to this move from GYES to GYED. In addition to differing by class, GYES use patterns varied by race, with Romany women using the grant for longer periods of time. The shift to GYED was thus an attempt to convince more non-Romany Hungarians to have chil-dren and to stay on the grant longer.

25. KSH, *A Gyermekgondozási Díj Igénybevétele és Hatásai,* p. 8.

26. Little has been written on the history of these programs. The one exception is Horváth, "Egy Segély Anatómiája." Since she examines these funds through the late 1970s, her analysis stops just before they were fully means tested.

27. Author's interviews #08122: 12, 29.

28. Author's interview #08122: 17.

29. Author's interview #080211: 8.

30. Baxandall, "Reinventing Unemployment in Hungary."

31. Zsuzsa Ferge, "Unemployment in Hungary: The Need for a New Ideology," p. 162.

32. Ibid., p. 163.

33. Ibid., p. 164.

34. Moreover, those without high school degrees could receive these benefits only if they were enrolled in full-time retraining programs—a requirement not imposed on better-educated workers.

35. They then received 60 percent of their previous wages for an additional six months. For more on these changes, see Bárányi, *Szociálpolitikai Ismeretek;* World Bank, *Magyarország;* and Csaba Bánfalvy, *A Munkanélküliség.*

36. The program (Hosszú Távú Munkanélküliek Szociális Támogatása) provided recipients a stipend that amounted to the minimum wage.

37. This reliance becomes even clearer when we consider that these recipients tend to pool funds from more than one source. For instance, roughly 40 percent of recipients of social assistance rely on funds from more than one program. For these data, see Harcsa, *Szociális Ellátás az Önkormányzatoknál,* p. 30.

38. Put another way, local-level social assistance constituted 15 percent of the household income of those below the poverty line; the corresponding percentage for those above the poverty line was 6 percent. World Bank, *Magyarország,* p. 48.

39. For example, of the more than five hundred parliamentary acts and decisions passed from 1990 to 1994, only four impinged on the operation of these programs; they did so by making slight adjustments to benefit levels. Hungarian Parliamentary Record, 1990–1994. These records are available in the Hungarian Parliamentary Archives. They can also be reviewed on the Internet at http://www.kerszov.hv/kzlcim/kzl.

40. This was a campaign slogan of the Hungarian Small Holders Party, which was in the governing coalition with the Hungarian Democratic Forum (MDF).

41. In addition to these ideological impediments to reform, the MDF government did not consider reform to be fiscally necessary; it seemed to believe that an economic upsurge was forthcoming, which would allow for the maintenance of these programs. See Gedeon, "Hungary."

42. The Bokros Plan included other measures: it devalued the forint, cut medical subsidies, created new rules for paid sick leave, and levied new import taxes on "luxury goods."

43. More specifically, the plan stipulated that only families with monthly incomes below 15,000 forints per person would remain eligible for these programs—a cut-off that was below even the official subsistence level.

44. Importantly, not all the politicians from these parties supported the plan. The day it was announced, three ministers from the Socialist party resigned—including the minister of welfare. In interviews, these politicians expressed anger that they had not been consulted about the plan before its introduction. They were also concerned that the plan was unnecessarily harsh and even premature; they faulted the government for not even experimenting with less severe measures. For more on this opposition, see Péter Kertész, "Vélemények a Szociális Ellátórendszer Átalakításáról."

45. The Bokros Plan was debated several times in the Hungarian Parliament.

The initial debate occurred in 1995, immediately after the plan was announced. The plan was then subjected to Constitutional Court review, which led to a second round of debates in the spring of 1996. The Parliament has subsequently held additional debates on reform, including an extensive discussion in the fall of 1999. My analysis relies on records from all these debates. For an in-depth description of the second round of debates, see Joanna Goven, "New Parliament, Old Discourse? The Parental Leave Debate in Hungary."

46. See Hungarian Parliamentary Record, November 1999, speech by Katalin Aszondi.

47. In a provocative analysis of this political discourse, Eyal, Szelényi, and Townsley view such budgetary formulations as examples of the postcommunist "ritual of sacrifice." They argue that budgetary restrictions are framed as exercises in civic education—as a way not only to mend the "wrongdoings" of state socialism but also to teach virtue, responsibility, and delayed gratification. Eyal, Szelényi, and Townsley, *Making Capitalism without Capitalists.*

48. Hungarian Parliamentary Record, November 1999, speech by Béla Kádár.

49. Quoted in Kertész, "Vélemények a Szociális Ellátórendszer Átalakításáról," p. 6.

50. "Hiányozni Fog a Családi Pótlék," *Magyar Hírlap,* March 20, 1995.

51. For examples of these appeals, see Hungarian Parliamentary Record, February 1996, speeches by Terézia Szilágyi, Zoltán Pokorni, and Mrs. József Torgyán; and Hungarian Parliamentary Record, November 1999, speeches by József Torgyán, Iván Szabó, and József Szájer.

52. The one exception here was a remark made by an MP from the Small Holders Party, which explicitly framed the child-care grant as a way to compensate labor not recognized by the market. See Goven, "New Parliament, Old Discourse?" for a discussion of this and a different argument about how the politics of motherhood played into these debates.

53. The one substantive change the court made to the plan regarded its timing: the court took issue with the speed with which the reforms were introduced, and it then ordered the government to give families ample time to prepare for such profound policy changes.

54. It would be inaccurate to present these social scientists as a homogenous group. After attending many of their post-Bokros workshops and meetings, I realized that political differences divided them. On one side were those who opposed the plan on principle; they remained devoted to welfare universalism. On the other side were those who opposed the plan for more professional reasons; they faulted the government for not consulting with them before formulating the reforms. By late 1995, these groups seemed to have found common ground around the issue of the social minimum and thus were able to launch a fairly consistent intervention into reform politics.

55. This six-year cut-off was another important change; prior to the Bokros Plan, family allowances were given until a child turned eighteen.

56. According to Goven, the abolishment of GYED was a key component of

the World Bank's reform agenda; the Bank assumed that returning to a flat-rate grant would draw better-skilled, more productive, and higher-paid women back into the labor force. Goven, "New Parliament, Old Discourse?" p. 291.

57. Of course, this argument mistakenly equates discretionary welfare programs with a smaller state sector. As Hungarians have begun to discover, discretionary welfare states are extremely expensive to operate. What the state gains from income and means testing usually goes back to support the enormous bureaucracy required to sustain a targeted welfare state. Thus, according to most analyses, welfare expenditures have increased in Hungary with the advent of targeting. See István György Tóth, "Welfare Programs and the Alleviation of Poverty," and Andorka and Tóth, "A Jóléti Rendszer Jellemzői és Reformjának Lehetőségei."

58. One of the main holdouts here was Zsuzsa Ferge, Hungary's most prominent and respected welfare-state scholar. As she explained to me in an interview (February 28, 1995), "Everyone thinks universalism is dead. Not for me. I will continue interjecting [it] into the debate. I will annoy them with my universalism."

59. More specifically, in 1995 the family-allowance system supported 1.5 million families and 2.56 million children. By 1997, these numbers had fallen to 1.23 million families and 2.11 million children—a decrease of roughly 20 percent. Bárányi, *Szociálpolitikai Ismeretek*, p. 77; World Bank, *Magyarország*, pp. 42, 52; and KSH, *Magyarország*, p. 18.

60. Interview with Gábor Barna, April 5, 1994.

61. For an example of such political fluctuations, one need look only two years down the road: after their victory in the 1998 parliamentary elections, the FIDESZ-MPP (Fiatal Demokraták Szövetsége–Magyar Polgári Párt) government revised these programs yet again. Although it is beyond the historical scope of this study, in 1999 the governing coalition replaced the Bokros Plan's income tests with what amounted to life-style tests. Echoing the ideas they expressed in the Bokros debates, these government officials set for these programs new eligibility requirements that stressed recipients' behavior and morals. For instance, instead of linking eligibility to income, they linked it to criteria like children's school attendance and evidence of appropriate parenting. They also gave local Gyámhatóság offices the right to revoke assistance to anyone deemed "unfit." Thus, rather than turning these programs into social entitlements, the government tied them to life-style.

62. Initially, the ministry wanted them to work within the framework of Child Guidance Centers. Worried that their "distinctive" approach would be diluted, these social scientists pushed for their own institutional network. For more on these struggles, see Gosztonyi, "Hatóság + Szolgálat"; Gábor Hegyesi, "A Szociális Munka"; and Magda Révész, "Hungarian Family Helping Centers: Theory and Practice."

63. That is, the term *family* signified their move away from children; the term *support* marked their attempt not to be punitive; the term *service* indicated

their desire to provide voluntary assistance; and the term *center* marked their intention to be noncoercive and charity-like.

64. Author's interview #0311: 7.

65. Author's interviews #013112: 2, 5; 080211: 18, 20.

66. Author's interviews #013112: 5; 080211: 6.

67. Author's interview #013112: 4.

68. Author's interview #0311: 7.

69. Author's interview #080211: 8. Although derogatory, this comment had a kernel of truth to it: social workers from Family Support Service Centers were better educated than their Gyámhatóság counterparts. A 1997 study of social workers found that 87 percent of them had college degrees. By contrast, only 24 percent of Gyámhatóság workers had such degrees. Ágota Horváth, "Szociális Munkások," pp. 31, 33, 35.

70. Author's interview #080211: 21.

71. Művelődési Minisztérium, *Statisztikai Tájékoztató: Gyermekvédelem*, p. 68.

72. Author's interview #080211: 28.

73. For an example of these instruments, see Mihály Andor, Ágota Horváth, and Emília Horváth, "Egy Budapesti Kerület Szociálpolitikájáról," p. 320.

74. Author's interview #080211: 9.

75. Gyámhatóság case #0811776: 815.

76. Throughout this chapter and the next, most of my empirical data and quotations are ethnographic observations and thus do not have citations.

77. For another account of caseworkers' narrow definition of child protection, see Herczog, *A Gyermekvédelem Dilemmái*.

78. Author's interview #013112: 24.

79. Gyámhatóság case #0137794: 712.

80. Gyámhatóság case #0811776: 909.

81. Author's interview #080211: 8.

82. László Katona and Judit Szabó, "Temetés, Tüzelő, Napközi: Diszkrecionális Segélyezés A Családsegítő Központokban."

83. This is an approximation, based on coding my field notes for different cases I observed.

84. These numbers were compiled by a disgruntled social worker. He calculated them because he was angry that some social workers gave away a disproportionate amount of the center's resources to a few clients. He broke the numbers down by client and social worker. These revelations created quite a stir in the office. His memo was immediately deemed a "secret" by the office head, and the social worker found another job a few weeks later.

85. Author's interview #080211: 21.

86. Család Segítő case file #0822110: 15.

87. Author's interview #013112: 26.

88. KSH, *Népjóléti Statisztikai Évkönyv*, p. 243.

89. Gyámhatóság case #0137794: 792.

90. Gyámhatóság case #08009: 1002.

91. Because turnover rates are so high, Gyámhatóság offices are reluctant to keep (or share) data on their employees. In the two districts of my research, few caseworkers lasted for more than two years. And when I returned to the field in April 2000, roughly five years after I completed my research, only one of the more than twenty caseworkers I had worked with was still employed in the Gyámhatóság.

92. Author's interview #080211: 11.

93. Put another way, 70 percent of them worked in blue-collar jobs or administrative jobs in unrelated fields before moving into social work. Horváth, "Szociális Munkások," p. 42.

94. Author's interview #080211: 21.

95. In particular, in 1996, 33 percent of them earned less than 16,000 forints per month, 37 percent earned 17,000–23,000 forints per month, and 29 percent earned over 24,000 forints per month. When these wages are compared with data on the social minimum included in Table 16, it is clear that the majority of them lived just above the subsistence level. For these wages data, see Horváth, "Szociális Munkások," p. 37.

96. Author's interview #080211: 8.

97. Gyámhatóság case #081998: 992. In her account, this caseworker made a metaphorical connection between Rákóczi Square, a notorious gathering place for prostitutes, and the Rákóczi war of independence, which occurred in the early eighteenth century.

STRATEGIES OF EXCAVATION

1. See Deacon, "Social Policy, Social Justice and Citizenship in Eastern Europe," and Götting, "Destruction, Adjustment, and Innovations."

2. See Ferge, "Social Citizenship in the New Democracies"; Claire Wallace, "Gender, Citizenship, and Transition"; Claus Offe, "The Politics of Social Policy in East European Transition: Antecedents, Agents, and Agenda of Reform"; and Deacon, *Global Social Policy*.

3. Szalai, "Social Participation in Hungary in the Context of Restructuring and Liberalization" and "From Informal Labor to Paid Occupations"; Gábor Hegyesi, "Social Work in Hungary: New Opportunities in a Changing Society"; and Isadora Hare, *New Developments in Hungarian Social Work*.

4. For public-opinion data on these welfare reforms, see "Hiányozni Fog a Családi Pótlék," *Magyar Hírlap*, March 20, 1995.

5. By even the most generous estimates, new nonstate agencies devoted to the homeless, battered women, and the Roma reach only a few thousand Hungarians—a number that pales in comparison with the hundreds of thousands of clients connected to state institutions.

6. For the most influential of these arguments, see Kornai, "Lasting Growth as the Top Priority" and "Paying the Bill for Goulash Communism."

7. See Tóth, "A Jóléti Rendszer az Átmeneti Időszakban" and "Welfare Programs and the Alleviation of Poverty."

8. In constructing a view of this welfare regime from "below," I found my case-file data to be somewhat limiting. For the previous welfare regimes, I illuminated client strategizing by studying the dynamics of inclusion: I took a random sample of case files as representative of the client population and analyzed it for institutional patterns. Yet such an approach did not work for this period; it would have obscured the dynamics of exclusion and missed those who were shuffled out of welfare offices. Here is where my ethnographic work proved critical: it enabled me to supplement the case-file analysis and to gain a sense of who fell outside and inside the new welfare boundaries.

9. World Bank, *Magyarország*, p. 11. Moreover, the decline in the number of employed Hungarians was even more dramatic: from 1990 to 1995, the overall employment rate dropped by 25 percent, and the women's employment rate by 20 percent; Förster and Tóth, *Szegénység és Egyenlőtlenségek Magyarországon és a Többi Visegrádi Országban*, p. 4. According to one Hungarian researcher, from 1989 to 1993 more jobs were lost than were created during the entire state-socialist period; János Tímár, "A Foglalkoztatás és Munkanélküliség Sajátosságai a Posztszocialista Országokban." For more on these trends, see Katalin Kovács and Mónika Váradi, "Women's Life Trajectories and Class Formation in Hungary"; Andorka and Harcsa, "Long-Term Modernization of Hungarian Society"; Mária Frey, "Nők a Munkaerőpiacon"; and Ferge, "A Magyar Segélyezési Rendszer Reformja II."

10. Ferge, "A Magyar Segélyezési Rendszer Reformja II," p. 32.

11. Frey, "Nők a Munkaerőpiacon," Table 8.

12. For these data, see ibid. and Beáta Nagy, "Karrier Női Módra," Table 1. For an argument about how these trends led to the "upward mobility of women," see Szalai, "From Informal Labor to Paid Occupations."

13. Szalai, "From Informal Labor to Paid Occupations," p. 205.

14. Tamás Kolosi and Endre Sík, "The Scope of the State and Private Sectors," p. 82.

15. Thus, by most accounts real wages dropped between 25 and 32 percent from 1989 to 1995. See Andorka and Harcsa, "Long-Term Modernization of Hungarian Society," p. 35, and Förster and Tóth, *Szegénység és Egyenlőtlenségek Magyarországon és a Többi Visegrádi Országban*, p. 3, for these data.

16. This percentage was higher for women in management positions (80 percent), but lower for women in semiskilled and unskilled positions (62 percent); Nagy, "Karrier Női Módra," p. 43.

17. Andorka, Falussy, and Harcsa, "Időfelhasználás és Életmód," p. 136.

18. See Kovács and Váradi, "Women's Life Trajectories and Class Formation in Hungary," and Fodor, "The Political Woman?"

19. Andorka and Harcsa, "Long-Term Modernization of Hungarian Society," p. 42, and Andorka, Falussy, and Harcsa, "Időfelhasználás és Életmód," pp. 129, 136.

20. Buda, "Ethnographic Perspectives on Alcohol Use and Abuse," Table 5.2.

21. For these data, see Czeizel, "Alcohol Consumption by Females in Hungary," Tables 6.3 and 6.8. Another indication of the severity of this problem

was Hungary's high rate of alcohol-related deaths: in 1992, Hungary had the highest rate of cirrhosis and hepatitis deaths in the developed world. For example, among men, Hungary's alcohol-related death rate was 104 per 100,000, compared with Romania's rate of 49.7, Austria's rate of 40.2, and Italy's rate of 38.4. Buda, "Ethnographic Perspectives on Alcohol Use and Abuse," Table 5.1.

22. Zsuzsanna Elekes, "Devianciák, Mentális Betegségek," Table 5, and Rudolf Andorka, "Dissatisfaction and Alienation," p. 150.

23. Personal communication with volunteers from Nők a Nőkért Együtt az Erőszak Ellen Egyesület and Nők Háza.

24. For a few examples, see "Családi Háborúk," *Nők Lapja* 40 (1994): 20; "Mit Tegyünk Ha Bántalmaznak?" *Nők Lapja* 40 (1994): 21; "Erőszak a Házasságban," *Nők Lapja* 42 (1994): 50.

25. Krisztina Morvai, *Terror a Családban: A Feleségbántalmazás és a Jog.*

26. Ibid. See also Olga Tóth, *Violence in the Family.*

27. For instance, Hungarian social scientists Katalin Kovács and Mónika Váradi found that the withdrawal of state support in the workplace left many lower- and working-class women with fewer resources to resolve their everyday problems. Once central to these women's communal and familial networks, the workplace lost its social significance, and the result perhaps was to push some women to state institutions to meet needs previously addressed through work networks. Kovács and Váradi, "Women's Life Trajectories and Class Formation in Hungary."

28. Something about Mrs. Kaltner piqued my interest when I met her, prompting me to mine the Gyámhatóság archives for her paper trail. These case materials, combined with our ongoing office discussions, enabled me to piece together a picture of her institutional trajectory. Gyámhatóság case #01311221: 398.

29. Home visits were extremely rare for these kinds of women: welfare workers visited the newly excluded only when ordered to do so by the court. Usually, court-ordered visits were limited to child-custody and visitation cases, which continued to constitute up to 10 percent of the Gyámhatóság's caseload.

30. These Hungarian rates are much higher than those of other East European countries. For instance, in this same period, 15 percent of the Polish population and 11 percent of Czechs sought welfare assistance. For these comparative data, see Förster and Tóth, *Szegénység és Egyenlőtlenségek Magyarországon és a Többi Visegrádi Országban,* and Ferge, "A Magyar Segélyezési Rendszer Reformja II," p. 31.

31. This percentage was slightly higher than the rates compiled by these institutions, which were 52 percent and 56 percent. While this difference could be related to my case sample, it may also have to do with the fact that these institutions collected unemployment data on clients themselves and omitted unemployed family members. When I coded my data, I included both forms of unemployment, which probably explains why I arrived at a higher percentage.

32. Frey, "Nők a Munkaerőpiacon," Table 11.

33. István Harcsa, *Szociális Ellátás az Önkormányzatoknál 1994–1996*, p. 31.

34. Ferge, "A Magyar Segélyezési Rendszer Reformja II," and KSH, *Magyarország.*

35. Moreover, because clients could not subsist on public assistance, many participated in the unofficial economy to make ends meet. During the 1990s, the nature of the unofficial economy shifted. Under state socialism, second-economy work was performed outside the bounds of the formal state sector or was conducted alongside state work in intrafirm markets (or both). In contemporary Hungary, it is performed outside formal markets themselves—that is, such work provides goods and services for those shut out of the market. For many clients, this category includes unreported work as traders of affordable consumer goods or as child/elderly-care providers. Of course, unofficial work also means engaging in the illegal economy, which burgeoned during the 1990s. Female clients are now subjected to a new traffic in women and children: the international trade in women's bodies and adoptable children. For more on these hazards, see Lenke Fehér, "Bűnözés és Prostitúció," and Kligman, *The Politics of Duplicity.*

36. Rudolf Andorka and Zsolt Spéder, "A Szegénység Magyarországon 1992–1995," p. 44.

37. Ibid., pp. 44–45, and Förster and Tóth, *Szegénység és Egyenlőtlenségek Magyarországon és a Többi Visegrádi Országban*, pp. 12–13.

38. The main difference here is healthcare; as of 1997, Hungary still had a national healthcare system that guaranteed assistance to all citizens. Of course, the quality of care varied greatly and was linked to one's ability to "pay" for special (or even decent) treatment.

39. This dual sense of deprivation may explain why surveys showed that only 17 percent of Hungarians claimed to be satisfied with their income level, and only 25 percent were satisfied with their standard of living. It also may explain why studies showed that Hungarians rated their general well-being as being higher in the Kádár era. In one survey, Hungarians ranked the 1970s as the most prosperous period in recent history for both their families and in general. György Hunyady, *Stereotypes during the Decline and Fall of Communism*, pp. 261, 267, 270, 274.

40. In addition, during this same period, state housing construction declined by 50 percent. József Hegedűs and Iván Tosics, "Hungary," pp. 251, 261.

41. Ibid., pp. 256–257.

42. Ibid., p. 257.

43. For example, while 11 percent of Hungarian flats lacked running water and 13 percent lacked private bathrooms, the rental stock was dominated by flats that lacked such basic amenities; Andorka and Spéder, "A Szegénység Magyarországon 1992–1995," p. 43.

44. Gábor Iványi, *A Hajléktalanok*, p. 41.

45. KSH, *A Kommunális Ellátás Fontosabb Adatai*, p. 17, and Hegedűs and Tosics, "Hungary," p. 265.

46. Andorka and Spéder, "A Szegénység Magyarországon 1992–1995," p. 40.

47. Andorka and Harcsa, "Long-Term Modernization of Hungarian Society," p. 45.

48. Ibid., p. 28.

49. Andorka and Spéder, "A Szegénység Magyarországon 1992–1995," p. 45.

50. Fradi is a Hungarian soccer team.

51. Although female clients shared these experiences of abuse with other groups of women, they also faced physical threats from other sources because they lived in neighborhoods plagued by crime and violence. The overall crime rate rose by 131 percent from 1989 to 1995, while the number of arrests increased by 300 percent in the same period. For these data, see István Várvó, "A Bűnözés és Mérésének Módszerei," p. 60, and Fehér, "Bűnözés és Prostitúció," Tables 1–3. In some areas of Budapest, these rates were much higher. Moreover, the police came down hard on certain "target" populations. For some groups, especially the Roma, the police proved to be part of the problem. The overall number of reported police brutality cases increased almost as much as the crime rate. Hence, as members of communities plagued by crime and police surveillance, many clients had new needs for physical protection and security. Human Rights Watch, *Rights Denied: The Roma of Hungary*, pp. 25–26.

52. KSH, *Népjóléti Statisztikai Évkönyv* , pp. 138–139. In addition, women complained of serious disorders far more often than men: in 1983, 15 percent of Hungarian women were diagnosed with a "serious" disorder, while by 1995 the percentage had increased to 23; Elekes, "Devianciák, Mentális Betegségek," Table 17, and KSH, *Népjóléti Statisztikai Évkönyv*, p. 139.

53. KSH, *Népjóléti Statisztikai Évkönyv*, p. 139.

54. Andorka and Spéder, "A Szegénység Magyarországon 1992–1995," p. 52; Andorka, "Dissatisfaction and Alienation," p. 154; and Spéder, Paksi, and Elekes, "Anómia és Elégedettség a 90-es Évek Elején," p. 496.

55. Szelényi, Szelényi, and Poster, "Post-Communist Political Culture in Hungary," pp. 470–471, and Péter Róbert, "Consciousness of Inequality," p. 124.

56. Gyámhatóság case #031213: 853.

57. Gyámhatóság case #062667: 901.

58. Gyámhatóság institutional summary.

59. My account of Mrs. Zsigó's case relies almost exclusively on data I collected in my fieldwork—that is, observations of her interactions with welfare workers and conversations I had with her. I also reviewed her assistance applications and home-visit reports through 1994. Gyámhatóság case #08122134: 989.

CONCLUSION

1. Esping-Andersen, *The Three Worlds of Welfare Capitalism*.

2. See Orloff, "Gender and the Social Rights of Citizenship"; O'Connor,

Orloff, and Shaver, *States, Markets, and Families;* and Sainsbury, *Gender, Equality, and Welfare States.*

3. Fraser, *Unruly Practices.*

4. See Brown, "Mothers, Father, and Children"; Mimi Abramovitz, *Regulating the Lives of Women: Social Welfare Policy from Colonial Times to the Present;* and Catharine MacKinnon, *Toward a Feminist Theory of the State.*

5. See Orloff, "Gender and the Social Rights of Citizenship" and "Gender in the Welfare State"; Hobson, "Solo Mothers, Social Policy Regimes, and the Logics of Gender"; and Sainsbury, *Gendering Welfare States.*

6. Nancy Fraser and Linda Gordon, "A Genealogy of Dependency: Tracing a Keyword in the US Welfare State."

7. Sainsbury, *Gender, Equality, and Welfare States.*

8. See Haney, "Homeboys, Babies, Men in Suits."

References

Abramovitz, Mimi. *Regulating the Lives of Women: Social Welfare Policy from Colonial Times to the Present.* Boston: South End Press, 1988.

Adam, Jan. "Social Contract." In *Economic Reforms and Welfare Systems in the USSR, Poland, and Hungary,* edited by Jan Adam. New York: St. Martin's Press, 1991.

Adamik, Mária. "Feminism and Hungary." In *Gender and the Politics of Post-Communism,* edited by Nanette Funk and Magda Mueller. New York: Routledge, 1993.

———."How Can Hungarian Women Lose What They Never Had?" Paper presented at the conference "Gender in Transition," Collegium Budapest, January 23, 1995.

Adams, Julia. "Feminist Theory as Fifth Columnist or Discursive Vanguard: Some Contested Uses of Gender Analysis in Historical Sociology." *Social Politics* 5 (1998): 1–16.

Andor, Mihály, ed. *Cigány Vizsgából.* Budapest: Művelődési Kutató Intézet, 1982.

Andor, Mihály, Ágota Horváth, and Emília Horváth. "Egy Budapesti Kerület Szociálpolitikájáról." *Aktív Társadalom Alapítvány* 3 (1995): 299–323.

Andorka, Rudolf. *Merre Tart a Magyar Társadalom?* Budapest: Antológia Kiadó, 1996.

———."Dissatisfaction and Alienation." In *A Society Transformed: Hungary in Time-Space Perspective,* edited by Rudolf Andorka, Tamás Kolosi, Richard Rose, and György Vukovich. Budapest: Central European University Press, 1999.

Andorka, Rudolf, Béla Falussy, and István Harcsa. "Időfelhasználás és Életmód." In *Társadalmi Riport,* edited by Rudolf Andorka, Tamás Kolosi, and György Vukovich. Budapest: TÁRKI, 1990.

Andorka, Rudolf, and István Harcsa. "Consumption." In *Social Report,* edited by Rudolf Andorka, Tamás Kolosi, and György Vukovich. Budapest: TÁRKI, 1990.

————."Deviant Behavior." In *Social Report,* edited by Rudolf Andorka, Tamás Kolosi, and György Vukovich. Budapest: TÁRKI, 1990.

————. "Long-Term Modernization of Hungarian Society." In *A Society Transformed: Hungary in Time-Space Perspective,* edited by Rudolf Andorka, Tamás Kolosi, Richard Rose, and György Vukovich. Budapest: Central European University Press, 1999.

Andorka, Rudolf, and Zsolt Spéder. "A Szegénység Magyarországon 1992–1995." *Esély* 4 (1996): 25–53.

Andorka, Rudolf, and István Tóth. "A Jóléti Rendszer Jellemzői és Reformjának Lehetőségei." *Közgazdasági Szemle* 1 (1994): 1–29.

Antal, László. "Development—with Some Digression." *ACTA Oeconomia* 23 (1979): 257–273.

————. "Thoughts on the Further Development of the Hungarian Mechanism." *ACTA Oeconomia* 29 (1982): 199–224.

Bagdy, Emőke. *Családi Szocializáció és Személyiség.* Budapest: Tankönyvkiadó, 1977.

Baksay, Zoltán. *A Munkaerőhelyzet Alakulása és a Munkanélküliség Felszámolása Magyarországon, 1945–1949.* Budapest: Akadémiai Kiadó, 1983.

Balassa, Béla. "The New Growth Path in Hungary." In *The Hungarian Economy in the 1980s: Reforming the System and Adjusting to External Shocks,* edited by Josef Brada and István Dobozi. Greenwich, Conn.: JAI Press, 1988.

Bálint, István. "Baleseti Veszély és Egyéni Veszélyeztettség." *Pszichológiai Tanulmányok* 5 (1963): 327–343.

Bálint, István, and Tibor Hódos. "Futószalagon Dolgozó Ruhaipari Munkások Neurózisának Vizsgálata." *Pszichológiai Tanulmányok* 4 (1962): 237–254.

Bálint, István, and Mihály Murányi. "Pszichológiai Tényezők Hatása a Könnyűipari Balesetek Megoszlására." *Pszichológiai Tanulmányok* 3 (1961): 323–341.

Balogh, Sándor. *Parlamenti és Pártharcok Magyarországon, 1945–1947.* Budapest: Kossuth Könyvkiadó, 1975.

————. *A Magyar Népi Demokrácia Története, 1944–1962.* Budapest: Kossuth Könyvkiadó, 1978.

————. *Nehéz Esztendők Krónikája, 1949–1953: Dokumentumok.* Budapest: Gondolat, 1986.

Balogh, Sándor, and Ferenc Pölöskei, eds. *Agrárpolitika és Agrárátalakulás Magyarországon, 1944–1962.* Budapest: Akadémiai Kiadó, 1979.

Bánfalvy, Csaba. *A Munkanélküliség.* Budapest: Magvető Kiadó, 1997.

Bárányi, Ferenc. *Szociálpolitikai Ismeretek.* Szeged: JGYF Kiadó, 1999.

Bartha, Lajos. "Ifjúságunk Társadalmi Beilleszkedésének Pszichológiai Kérdései." *Pszichológiai Tanulmányok* 8 (1965): 11–28.

Bauer, Tamás. "A Második Gazdasági Reform és a Tulajdonviszonyok." *Mozgó Világ* 11 (1983).

————. "The Second Economic Reform and Ownership Relations: Some Considerations for the Further Development of the New Economic Mechanism." *Eastern European Economics* 22 (1984): 33–87.

Baxandall, Phineas. "Reinventing Unemployment in Hungary: Politics, Pensions, and Patterns of Work." Paper presented at the American Political Science Association annual meeting, San Francisco, August 30, 1996.

Beke, Kata. "A Kedv vagy a Lehetőség?" *Élet és Irodalom*, January 15, 1982.

Berend, Iván. *A Szocialista Gazdaság Fejlődése Magyarországon, 1945–1968.* Budapest: Kossuth Könyvkiadó, 1976.

Berend, Iván, and György Ránki. *Hungary: A Century of Economic Development.* New York: Harper & Row, 1974.

———. *Underdevelopment and Economic Growth: Studies in Hungarian Social and Economic History.* Budapest: Akadémiai Kiadó, 1979.

———. *The Hungarian Economy in the Twentieth Century.* London: Croom Helm, 1988.

Bock, Gisella, and Pat Thane, eds. *Maternity and Gender Policies: Women and the Rise of the European Welfare State, 1880–1950.* New York: Routledge, 1991.

Bockman, Joanna. "Economists and Social Change: Science, Professional Power, and Politics in Hungary, 1945–1995." Ph.D. diss., University of California, San Diego, 2000.

Bokor, Ágnes. *Depriváció és Szegénység.* Budapest: Társadalomtudományi Intézet, 1985.

Bollobás, Enikő. "Totalitarian Lib: The Legacy of Communism for Hungarian Women." In *Gender and the Politics of Post-Communism*, edited by Nanette Funk and Magda Mueller. New York: Routledge, 1993.

Bonnell, Victoria. *Iconographies of Power.* Berkeley: University of California Press, 1998.

Boris, Eileen. "The Power of Motherhood: Black and White Women Redefine the Political." In *Mothers of a New World: Maternalist Policies and the Origins of Welfare States*, edited by Seth Koven and Sonya Michel. New York: Routledge, 1993.

Boris, Eileen, and Peter Bardaglio. "The Transformation of Patriarchy: The Historic Role of the State." In *Families, Politics and Public Policy*, edited by I. Diamond. New York: Longman, 1983.

Böröcz, József, and Ákos Róna-Tas. "Small Leap Forward: Emergence of New Economic Elites in Hungary, Poland, and Russia." *Theory and Society* 24 (1995): 751–781.

Brown, Carol. "Mothers, Fathers, and Children: From Private to Public Patriarchy." In *Women and Revolution*, edited by L. Sargent. Boston: South End Press, 1981.

Bruno, M. *Stabilization and Reform in Eastern Europe: A Preliminary Evaluation.* IMF Staff Papers, vol. 39, no. 4. Washington, D.C.: International Monetary Fund, 1992.

Brush, Lisa. "Love, Toil, and Trouble: Motherhood and Feminist Politics." *Signs* 21 (1996).

Bruszt, László. "Without Us but for Us? Political Orientation in Hungary in the Period of Late Paternalism." *Social Research* 55 (1988).

Buda, Béla. "Ethnographic Perspectives on Alcohol Use and Abuse." In *Alcohol Consumption and Alcoholism in Hungary*, edited by D. P. Agarwal, B. Buda, A. E. Czeizel, and H. W. Goede. Budapest: Akadémiai Kiadó, 1997.

Burawoy, Michael. "Neoclassical Sociology: From the End of Communism to the End of Classes." *American Journal of Sociology* 106 (2001).

Burawoy, Michael, and János Lukács. *The Radiant Past: Ideology and Reality in Hungary's Road to Capitalism*. Chicago: University of Chicago Press, 1992.

Burawoy, Michael, and Katherine Verdery, eds. *Uncertain Transition: Ethnographies of Change in the Postsocialist World*. Lanham, Md.: Rowman & Littlefield, 1999.

Connell, Robert W. *Gender and Power*. Stanford, Calif.: Stanford University Press, 1987.

Cook, Linda. *The Soviet Social Contract*. Cambridge, Mass.: Harvard University Press, 1993.

Cornia, G. *Income Distribution, Poverty, and Welfare in Transitional Economies: A Comparison between Eastern Europe and China*. UNICEF Occasional Papers, Economic Policy Series 44. New York: UNICEF, 1994.

Corrin, Chris. *Superwomen and the Double Burden: Women's Experience of Change in Central and Eastern Europe and the Former Soviet Union*. Toronto: Second Story Press, 1992.

Családjogi Törvények (CsJT). Budapest: Közgazdasági és Jogi Könyvkiadó, 1993.

Cseh-Szombathy, László. *Családszociológia: Problémák és Módszerek*. Budapest: Gondolat, 1979.

Csizmadia, Ervin. *A Magyar Demokratikus Ellenzék, 1968–1988*. Budapest: T-Twins Kiadó, 1995.

Czechoslovak Ministry of Social Affairs. "Czechoslovakia." In *Social Welfare in the Socialist Countries*, edited by John Dixon and David Macarov. New York: Routledge, 1992.

Czeizel, Andrew. "Alcohol Consumption by Females in Hungary." In *Alcohol Consumption and Alcoholism in Hungary*, edited by D. P. Agarwal, B. Buda, A. E. Czeizel, and H. W. Goede. Budapest: Akadémiai Kiadó, 1997.

———."Female Alcohol Abuse and Pregnancy Outcomes in Hungary." In *Alcohol Consumption and Alcoholism in Hungary*, edited by D. P. Agarwal, B. Buda, A. E. Czeizel, and H. W. Goede. Budapest: Akadémiai Kiadó, 1997.

David, Henry. *Family Planning and Abortion in the Socialist Countries of Central Europe*. New York: Population Council, 1978.

Deacon, Robert. *Social Policy and Socialism*. London: Pluto Press, 1986.

———. "Social Policy, Social Justice and Citizenship in Eastern Europe." In *Social Policy, Social Justice and Citizenship in Eastern Europe*, edited by Robert Deacon. Aldershot, England: Avebury, 1992.

———. *Global Social Policy: International Organizations and the Future of Welfare*. London: Sage, 1997.

Dessewffy, Tibor, and András Szántó. *"Kitörő Éberséggel" A Budapesti Kitelepítések Hiteles Története*. Budapest: Háttér Könykiadó, 1989.

Dixon, John, and David Macarov, eds. *Social Welfare in the Socialist Countries.* New York: Routledge, 1992.

Dömszky, András. "A Gyermek és Ifjúságvédelem Magyarországon." In *A Gyermekvédelem Nemzetközi Gyakorlata,* edited by L. Csókay, A. Dömszky, V. Hazsai, and M. Herczog. Budapest: Pont Kiadó, 1994.

Einhorn, Barbara. *Cinderella Goes to Market: Citizenship, Gender, and Women's Movements in East Central Europe.* London: Verso, 1993.

Elekes, Zsuzsanna. "Devianciák, Mentális Betegségek." In *Szerepváltozások: Jelentés a Nők Helyzetéről,* edited by G. Tóth and K. Lévai. Budapest: TÁRKI, 1997.

Ernst, Gabriella. "A Munka, A Nő és a GYES Rendszere." *Munkaügyi Szemle* 3 (1986): 182–198.

Esping-Andersen, Gøsta. *The Three Worlds of Welfare Capitalism.* Cambridge: Polity Press, 1990.

Eyal, Gil, Iván Szelényi, and Eleanor Townsley. *Making Capitalism without Capitalists: The New Ruling Elites in Eastern Europe.* New York: Verso, 1998.

Fehér, Ferenc, Ágnes Heller, and George Márkus. *Dictatorship over Needs.* Oxford: Blackwell, 1983.

Fehér, Lenke. "Bűnözés és Prostitúció." In *Szerepváltozások: Jelentés a Nők Helyzetéről,* edited by G. Tóth and K. Lévai. Budapest: TÁRKI, 1997.

Fehérváry, István. *Börtönvilág Magyarországon 1945–1956.* Budapest: Magyar Politikai Foglyok Szövetsége, 1990.

Ferge, Zsuzsa. *A Society in the Making: Hungarian Social and Societal Policy 1945–1975.* New York: Sharpe, 1979.

———. *Fejezetek a Magyar Szegénypolitika Történetéből.* Budapest: Magvető Kiadó, 1986.

———. *Szociálpolitika Ma és Holnap.* Budapest: MTA, 1987.

———. "Recent Trends in Social Policy in Hungary." In *Economic Reforms and Welfare Systems in the USSR, Poland, and Hungary,* edited by Jan Adam. New York: St. Martin's Press, 1991.

———. "Unemployment in Hungary: The Need for a New Ideology." In *Social Policy, Social Justice and Citizenship in Eastern Europe,* edited by Robert Deacon. Aldershot, England: Avebury, 1992.

———. "Social Citizenship in the New Democracies: The Difficulties of Reviving Citizens' Rights in Hungary." *International Journal of Urban and Regional Research* 20 (1993): 99–114.

———. "A Célzott Szociálpolitika Lehetőségei." Paper presented at the conference "A Jóléti Rendszer Reformja," ELTE Szociálpolitika Tanszék, Budapest, March 24, 1995.

———. "A Magyar Segélyezési Rendszer Reformja II." *Esély* 1 (1996): 25–42.

Ferge, Zsuzsa, Júlia Szalai, and György Petri. *Fordulat és Reform.* Budapest: MTA, 1985.

Fodor, Éva. "The Political Woman? Women in Politics in Hungary." In *Women in the Politics of Postcommunist Eastern Europe,* edited by Marilyn Rueschemeyer. New York: Sharpe, 1994.

———. "Gender in Transition: Unemployment in Hungary, Poland, and Slovakia." *East European Politics and Societies* 11 (1997): 470–500.

———. "Power, Patriarchy, and Paternalism: An Examination of the Gendered Nature of State Socialist Authority." Ph.D. diss., University of California, Los Angeles, 1997.

Forgó, Györgyné "A Gyermekgondozási Segély Méltányossági Ügyek Elbírálása Során Szerzett Tapasztalatok." *Szociálpolitikai Értesítő* 6 (1987): 108–127.

Förster, Michael, and István Tóth. *Szegénység és Egyenlőtlenségek Magyarországon és a Többi Visegrádi Országban.* Budapest: TÁRKI, 1998.

Fraser, Nancy. *Unruly Practices.* Minneapolis: University of Minnesota Press, 1989.

Fraser, Nancy, and Linda Gordon. "A Genealogy of Dependency: Tracing a Keyword in the US Welfare State." *Signs* 29 (1993): 4–31.

Frey, Mária. "Nők a Munkaerőpiacon." In *Szerepváltozások: Jelentés a Nők Helyzetéről,* edited by G. Tóth and K. Lévai. Budapest: TÁRKI, 1997.

Funk, Nanette, and Magda Mueller, eds., *Gender and the Politics of Post-Communism.* New York: Routledge, 1993.

Gál, László. *Szociálpolitikánk Két Évtizede.* Budapest: Kossuth Könyvkiadó, 1969.

Gal, Susan. "Gender in the Post-socialist Transition: The Abortion Debate in Hungary." *East European Politics and Societies* 8 (1994): 256–286.

Gal, Susan, and Gail Kligman. *The Politics of Gender after Socialism.* Princeton, N.J.: Princeton University Press, 2000.

———, eds. *Reproducing Gender: Politics, Publics, and Everyday Life after Socialism.* Princeton, N.J.: Princeton University Press, 2000.

Gayer, Gyuláné. "Előszó." *Szociálpolitikai Értesítő* 1, no. 1 (1983): 1–6.

Gedeon, Peter. "Hungary: Social Policy in Transition." *East European Politics and Societies* 9 (1995): 433–458.

Gégesi, Pál. "Zárszó." *Pszichológiai Tanulmányok* 8 (1965): 347–349.

George, Vic, and Nick Manning. *Socialism, Social Welfare, and the Soviet Union.* New York: Routledge, 1980.

Gille, Zsuzsa. "Cognitive Cartography in a European Wasteland: Multinational Capital and Greens Vie for Village Allegiance." In *Global Ethnography: Forces, Connections, and Imaginations in a Postmodern World,* edited by Michael Burawoy, Joseph A. Blum, Sheba George, Zsuzsa Gille, Teresa Gowan, Lynne Haney, Maren Klawiter, Steven H. Lopez, Seán Ó Riain, and Millie Thayer. Berkeley: University of California Press, 2000.

Gönczöl, Katalin, László Korinek, and Miklós Lévai, eds. *Kriminológiai Ismeretek Bűnözés Bűnözéskontroll.* Budapest: Corvina Press, 1999.

Goodwin, Joanne. *Gender and the Politics of Welfare Reform.* Chicago: University of Chicago Press, 1997.

Gordon, Linda. *Heroes of Their Own Lives: The History and Politics of Family Violence.* New York: Viking Penguin, 1988.

———. *Pitied but Not Entitled: Single Mothers and the History of Welfare.* Cambridge, Mass.: Harvard University Press, 1994.

Gosztonyi, Géza. "Hatóság + Szolgálat." *Esély* 4 (1993): 14–35.

Götting, U. "Destruction, Adjustment, and Innovations: Social Policy Transformation in Eastern and Central Europe." *Journal of European Social Policy* 4 (1994).

Goven, Joanna. "The Gendered Foundations of Hungarian State Socialism: State, Society and the Anti-politics of Anti-feminism." Ph.D. diss., University of California, Berkeley, 1993.

———. "New Parliament, Old Discourse? The Parental Leave Debate in Hungary." In *Reproducing Gender*, edited by Susan Gal and Gail Kligman. Princeton, N.J.: Princeton University Press, 2000.

Grád, András. "A Jogi Szabályozás Kapcsolata a Gyermekszületéssel és Gyermekvállalással." In *Terhesség—Szülés—Születés*, edited by Á. Losonczi. Budapest: MTA, 1979.

Gustafsson, Siv. "Childcare and Types of Welfare States." In *Gendering Welfare States*, edited by Diane Sainsbury. London: Sage, 1994.

Gyáni, Gábor. *A Szociálpolitika Múltja Magyarországon.* Budapest: MTA, 1994.

Hagan, John. "The Everyday and the Not So Exceptional in the Social Organization of Criminal Justice Practices." In *Everyday Practices and Trouble Cases*, edited by A. Sarat, M. Constable, D. Engel, V. Hans, S. Lawrence. Evanston, Ill.: Northwestern University Press, 1998.

Hanák, Katalin. *Társadalom és Gyermekvédelem.* Budapest: Kiadó, 1983.

Haney, Lynne. "From Proud Worker to Good Mother: Gender, the State, and Regime Change in Hungary." *Frontiers* 14 (1994): 113–150.

———. "Homeboys, Babies, Men in Suits: The State and the Reproduction of Male Dominance." *American Sociological Review* 61 (1996): 759–778.

———. "But We Are Still Mothers: Gender and the Construction of Need in Post-socialist Hungary." *Social Politics* 4 (1997): 208–244.

———. "Engendering the Welfare State." *Comparative Studies in Society and History* 40 (1998): 748–767.

———. "Feminist State Theory: Applications to Jurisprudence, Criminology, and the Welfare State." *Annual Review of Sociology* 26 (2000).

———. "Global Discourses of Need: Mythologizing and Pathologizing Welfare in Hungary." In *Global Ethnography: Forces, Connections, and Imaginations in a Postmodern World*, edited by Michael Burawoy, Joseph A. Blum, Sheba George, Zsuzsa Gille, Teresa Gowan, Lynne Haney, Maren Klawiter, Steven H. Lopez, Seán Ó Riain, and Millie Thayer. Berkeley: University of California Press, 2000.

Hankiss, Elemér. "Kinek az Érdeke?" *Heti Világgazdaság*, November 27, 1982.

Haraszti, Miklós. *A Worker in a Workers' State.* Harmondsworth, England: Penguin Books, 1977.

Harcsa, István. *Szociális Ellátás az Önkormányzatoknál (A Kísérleti Adatgyűjtés Tapasztalata).* Budapest: Központi Statisztikai Hivatal, 1995.

———. *Szociális Ellátás az Önkormányzatoknál 1994–1996.* Budapest: Központi Statisztikai Hivatal, 1998.

Hare, Isadora. *New Developments in Hungarian Social Work.* Washington, D.C.: National Association of Social Workers Press, 1993.

Havas, Gábor. "A Tradicionális Teknővájó Cigánytelep Felbomlásánák Két Változata."*Kultúra és Közösség* 9 (1976): 38–52.

Hegedűs, József, and Iván Tosics. "Hungary." In *Housing Policy in Europe*, edited by Paul Balchin. New York: Routledge, 1997.

Hegyesi, Gábor. "A Szociális Munka." In *Szociális Segítő*, edited by Zsuzsa Ferge. Budapest: MTA, 1991.

———. "Social Work in Hungary: New Opportunities in a Changing Society." In *Profiles in International Social Work*, edited by M. C. Hokenstad. Washington, D.C.: National Association of Social Workers Press, 1992.

Herczog, Mária. *A Gyermekvédelem Dilemmái*. Budapest: Pont Kiadó, 1997.

"Hiányozni Fog a Családi Pótlék." *Magyar Hírlap*, March 20, 1995.

Hobson, Barbara. "Solo Mothers, Social Policy Regimes, and the Logics of Gender." In *Gendering Welfare States*, edited by Diane Sainsbury. London: Sage, 1994.

Hodos, George. *Show Trials: Stalinist Purges in Eastern Europe, 1948–1954*. New York: Praeger, 1987.

Hódosi, Rezső. "Alkoholista Szülők Gyermekeinek Pszichológiai Problémái." *Pszichológiai Tanulmányok* 6 (1964): 615–626.

Hoóz, István. "A Cigány és a nem Cigány Népesség Társadalmi és Kulturális Helyzetében Lévő Fontosabb Különbségekröl." *Állam és Jogtudomány* 4 (1975): 49–66.

Horányi, Annabella. "A Fővárosi Nevelési Tanácsadók Tevékenységéről." In *Nevelési Tanácsadás Elmélete és Gyakorlata*, edited by Annabella Horányi. Budapest: Tankönyvkiadó, 1985.

Horowitz, Ruth. *Teen Mothers: Citizens or Dependents*. Chicago: University of Chicago Press, 1995.

Horváth, Ágota. "Egy Segély Anatómiája." In *Oktatásról és Társadalom-politikáról*, edited by Zsuzsa Ferge. Budapest: Szociológiai Kutató Intézet, 1982.

———. "Törvény és Anarchia avagy Törvényes Anarchia." In *Aktív Társadalom Alapítvány* 3 (1995): 261–298.

———. "Szociális Munkások." *Nemzet és Statégia* 13 (1997): 1–54.

Horváth, Erika. *A GYEStől a GYEDig*. Budapest: Kiadó, 1986.

Human Rights Watch. *Rights Denied: The Roma of Hungary*. New York: Human Rights Watch, 1996.

Hunyady, György. *Stereotypes during the Decline and Fall of Communism*. New York: Routledge, 1998.

Illyés, Gyula. *The People of the Puszta*. Budapest: Corvina Press, 1967.

International Labor Organization. *Labor Market Developments in Hungary*. Budapest: ILO-CEET, 1994.

International Monetary Fund. *Social Security Reform in Hungary*. Washington, D.C.: IMF Fiscal Affairs Department, 1990.

Iványi, Gábor. *A Hajléktalanok*. Budapest: Sík Könyvkiadó, 1998.

James, Harold. *International Monetary Cooperation since Bretton Woods*. New York: Oxford University Press, 1996.

Jowitt, Kenneth. "Soviet Neo-traditionalism: The Political Corruption of a Leninist Regime." *Soviet Studies* 35 (1983): 275–297.

Just-Kéry, Hedvig, and Ferenc Lénárd. "A Gondolkodási Műveletek Előfordulása Kiscsoportos Óvodásoknál a Szervezett Foglalkozások Keretében." *Pszichológiai Tanulmányok* 5 (1963): 241–258.

Katona, László, and Judit Szabó. "Temetés, Tüzelő, Napközi: Diszkrecionális Segélyezés A Családsegítő Központokban." *Esély* 5 (1992): 52–57.

Kelly-Gadol, Joan. "The Social Relations of the Sexes: Methodological Implications of Women's History." In *The Signs Reader*, edited by E. Abel and E. Abel. Chicago: University of Chicago Press, 1983; originally published in 1979.

Kemény, István. *A Magyarországi Cigányság Helyzete.* Budapest: Fővárosi Szabó Ervin Könyvtár, 1972.

———. "A Magyarországi Cigány Lakosság." *Valóság* 1 (1974): 63–72.

Kertesi, Gábor, and Gábor Kézdi. *A Cigány Népesség Magyarországon.* Budapest: Socio-type Kiadó, 1999.

Kertész, Péter. "Vélemények a Szociális Ellátórendszer Átalakításáról." *Magyar Hírlap*, March 21, 1995.

Klaus, Alyssa. *Every Child a Lion: The Origins of Maternal and Infant Policy in the U.S. and France, 1890–1920.* Ithaca, N.Y.: Cornell University Press, 1993.

Kligman, Gail. *The Politics of Duplicity: Controlling Fertility in Ceausescu's Romania.* Berkeley: University of California Press, 1998.

Klinger, András. "A Társadalmi Rétegenként Differenciált Termékenység Alakulása Magyarországon." *Demográfia* 4 (1961): 91–102.

Klinger, András, B. Barta, and G. Vukovich. *Fertility and Female Employment in Hungary.* Geneva: International Labor Organization, 1982.

Kollár, István. *The Development of Social Insurance in Hungary over Three Decades.* Budapest: Táncsics Publishing, 1976.

Kolosi, Tamás, and György Majláth. "Érzelmi Sérülés és Gyermekkori Kriminalitás." *Pszichológiai Tanulmányok* 6 (1964): 537–548.

Kolosi, Tamás, and Endre Sík. "The Scope of the State and Private Sectors." In *A Society Transformed: Hungary in Time-Space Perspective*, edited by Rudolf Andorka, Tamás Kolosi, Richard Rose, and György Vukovich. Budapest: Central European University Press, 1999.

Konrád, György. *The Caseworker.* New York: Harcourt, Brace, 1974.

———. *Antipolitics.* New York: Henry Holt, 1984.

Kornai, János. *The Economics of Shortage.* Amsterdam: North Holland Publishing, 1980.

———. "Bürokratikus és Piaci Koordináció." *Közgazdasági Szemle* 9 (1983): 1025–1037.

———. "Lasting Growth as the Top Priority." Discussion Paper 7. Collegium Budapest, 1992.

———. "Paying the Bill for Goulash Communism." *Social Research* 63 (1995): 943–1040.

Kovács, Katalin, and Mónika Váradi. "Women's Life Trajectories and Class

Formation in Hungary." In *Reproducing Gender*, edited by Susan Gal and Gail Kligman. Princeton, N.J.: Princeton University Press, 2000.

Koven, Seth, and Sonya Michel, eds. *Mothers of a New World: Maternalist Politics and the Origins of Welfare States*. New York: Routledge, 1993.

Kovrig, Bennett. *Communism in Hungary: From Kun to Kádár*. Stanford, Calif.: Hoover Institution Press, 1979.

Központi Népi Ellenőrzési Bizottság (KNEB). *Lakáshelyzet*.National Archives, Budapest, 1967.

Központi Statisztikai Hivatal (KSH). *Az Élelmiszer Fogyasztás Alakulása Magyarországon*. Budapest: Társadalmi Statisztikai Főosztály, 1957.

———. *Statisztikai Évkönyv*. Budapest: Társadalmi Statisztikai Főosztály, 1960–1996.

———. *Háztartásstatisztika*. Budapest: Társadalmi Statisztikai Főosztály, 1961.

———. *A Nők Helyzete a Munkahelyen és a Családban*. Budapest: Társadalmi Statisztikai Főosztály, 1962.

———. *The Standard of Living*. Budapest: Társadalmi Statisztikai Főosztály, 1962.

———. *Budapest a Szocializmus Útján 1950–1960*. Budapest: Társadalmi Statisztikai Főosztály, 1963.

———. *Az Alkoholizmus Kifejlődésének Tényezői*. Budapest: Társadalmi Statisztikai Főosztály, 1972.

———. *Társadalmi Szolgáltatások, 1960–1971*. Budapest: Társadalmi Statisztikai Főosztály, 1972.

———. *A Gyermekgondozási Segélyezés 10 Éve 1967–1976*. Budapest: SZOT Társadalombiztosítási Főigazgatóság, 1976.

———. *A Gyermekgondozási Segély Igénybevétele és Hatásai*. Budapest: Társadalmi Statisztikai Főosztály, 1981.

———. *A Nők Helyzetének Alakulása a KSH Adatainak Tükrében 1970–1981*. Budapest: Társadalmi Statisztikai Főosztály, 1982.

———. *Háztartásstatisztika*. Budapest: Társadalmi Statisztikai Főosztály, 1985.

———. *A Nők Helyzete a Munkahelyen és Otthon*. Budapest: Társadalmi Statisztikai Főosztály, 1988.

———. *A Gyermekgondozási Díj Igénybevétele és Hatásai*. Budapest: Társadalmi Statisztikai Főosztály, 1989.

———. *Time Series of Historical Statistics, 1867–1992*. Budapest: Társadalmi Statisztikai Főosztály, 1992.

———. *A Kommunális Ellátás Fontosabb Adatai*. Budapest: Társadalmi Statisztikai Főosztály, 1995.

———. *Népjóléti Statisztikai Évkönyv*. Budapest: Társadalmi Statisztikai Főosztály, 1995.

———. *Magyarország*. Budapest: Társadalmi Statisztikai Főosztály, 1998.

Kunzel, Regina. *Fallen Women, Problem Girls: Unmarried Mothers and the Professionalization of Social Work, 1890–1945*. New Haven, Conn.: Yale University Press, 1993.

Kürti, Istvánné. "A Felnőttek Szerepének Tükröződése a Gyermek Cselekvéseiben." *Pszichológiai Tanulmányok* 7 (1965): 245–258.

Ladd-Taylor, Molly. *Mother Work.* Cambridge, Mass.: Harvard University Press, 1991.

Lampland, Martha. "Biographies of Liberation: Testimonials to Labor in Socialist Hungary." In *Promissory Notes: Women in the Transition to Socialism,* edited by Sonya Kruks, Rayna Rapp, and Marilyn Young. New York: Monthly Review Press, 1989.

———. *The Object of Labor: Commodification in Socialist Hungary.* Chicago: University of Chicago Press, 1997.

———. "Standards for Stalinists: The Science of Socialist Production in Hungary, 1948–1953." Paper presented at the annual meeting of the American Sociological Association, Chicago, August 1999.

Lénárd, Ferenc, and Erzsébet Bánlaki. "Az Érzelmek Felismerése Arckép Alapján 7–17 Éves Korban." *Pszichológiai Tanulmányok* 3 (1961): 267–280.

Lieberman, Lucy. "A Nevelési Tanácsadás Problémái Hazánkban." *Magyar Pszichológiai Szemle* 18 (1964): 17–24.

———. "A Családi Csoportterápia Néhány Problémája." *Pszichológiai Tanulmányok* 8 (1965): 73–79.

Litván, György. *The Hungarian Revolution of 1956: Reform, Revolt, and Repression 1953–1963.* New York: Longman, 1996.

Lomax, William, ed. *The Hungarian Workers' Councils of 1956.* Boulder, Colo: Social Science Monographs, 1990.

Mácha, Martin. *Social Protection in the Czech Republic.* Prague: Center for Research on Social Transformation, 1998.

MacKinnon, Catharine. *Toward a Feminist Theory of the State.* Cambridge, Mass.: Harvard University Press, 1989.

Madison, Bernice. *Social Welfare in the Soviet Union.* Stanford, Calif.: Stanford University Press, 1968.

Majláth, György, and Imre Pick. "A Bűnöző Anya Szerepe egy Fiatalkorú Banda Bűncselekményeiben." *Pszichológiai Tanulmányok* 4 (1962): 517–532.

Makkai, Toni. "Social Policy and Gender in Eastern Europe." In *Gendering Welfare States,* edited by Diane Sainsbury. London: Sage, 1994.

Mares, Petr, and Ivo Mozný. *Poverty in the Czech Republic.* Prague: Center for Research on Social Transformation, 1996.

Márkus, Mária. "A Nő Helyzete a Munka Világában." *Kortárs* 14 (1970): 222–251.

Mateju, Petr. "Winners and Losers in the Post-socialist Transition: The Czech Republic in Comparative Perspective." *Innovation* 9 (1996): 371–390.

McDonald, Jason. "Elite Economists and Political Change in Hungary since World War II." Ph.D. diss., University of California, Berkeley, 1992.

McIntosh, Mary. "The State and the Oppression of Women." In *Feminism and Materialism,* edited by A. Kuhn and A. Wolpe. London: Routledge, 1978.

Mérei, Ferenc. *Klinikai Pszichodiagnosztikai Módszerek.* Budapest: Medicina Könyvkiadó, 1974.

Mink, Gwendolyn. *The Wages of Motherhood.* Ithaca, N.Y.: Cornell University Press, 1995.

Mód, Aladárné. "Születésszám és Életszínvonal." *Demográfia* 4 (1961): 21–36.

Molyneux, Maxine. "Women's Rights and the International Context in the Post-Communist States." *Millennium: Journal of International Studies* 23 (1993): 1–27.

Monostori, Judit. "Kinek Kiszámítható a Segélyezés?" *Esély* 6 (1994): 63–89.

Monson, Renee. "State-ing Sex and Gender." *Gender and Society* 11 (1997): 279–295.

Morvai, Krisztina. *Terror a Családban: A Feleségbántalmazás és a Jog.* Budapest: Kossuth Könyvkiadó, 1998.

Muncy, Robin. *Creating a Female Dominion in American Reform, 1890–1935.* New York: Oxford University Press, 1991.

Művelődési Minisztérium. *Statisztikai Tájékoztató: Gyermekvédelem.* Budapest: Tudományszervezési és Informatikai Intézet, 1988.

Nagy, Beáta. "Karrier Női Módra." In *Szerepváltozások: Jelentés a Nők Helyzetéről,* edited by G. Tóth and K. Lévai. Budapest: TÁRKI, 1997.

Nagy, Tibor. "Hungarian Social Insurance Contributions as State Taxes." *Legal Development and Comparative Law* 8 (1986): 299–329.

Neményi, Mária. "The Social Construction of Women's Roles in Hungary." *Replika* 7 (1996): 83–91.

Németh, Nóra. "Megoldhatatlan Anya—Gyermek Kapcsolat." *Pszichológiai Tanulmányok* 3 (1961): 751–766.

Népesség Tudományi Kutató Intézet (NTKI). *Közlemény: Alkoholizmus.* Budapest: Népesség Intézet, 1968.

Nielsen, Klaus. "Eastern European Welfare Systems in Comparative Perspective." In *Comparative Welfare Systems,* edited by Brent Greve. New York: St. Martin's Press, 1996.

Nyers, Rezső. "Efficiency and Socialist Democracy." *ACTA Oeconomica* 37 (1986): 1–13.

O'Connor, Julia, Ann Orloff, and Sheila Shaver. *States, Markets, and Families: Gender, Liberalism, and Social Policy in Australia, Canada, Great Britain, and the United States.* New York: Cambridge University Press, 1999.

Offe, Claus. "The Politics of Social Policy in East European Transition: Antecedents, Agents, and Agenda of Reform." *Social Research* 60 (1993): 649–674.

Organization for Economic Cooperation and Development. *Social and Labor Market Policies in Hungary.* Paris: Organization for Economic Cooperation and Development, 1995.

Orloff, Ann. "Gender and the Social Rights of Citizenship." *American Sociological Review* 58 (1993): 303–328.

———. "Gender in the Welfare State." *Annual Review of Sociology* 22 (1996): 51–78.

Ornstein, Mitchell. "Transitional Social Policy in the Czech Republic and Poland." *Czech Sociological Review* 2 (1995): 179–196.

Országos Gyermek és Ifjúságvédelmi Tanács. *A Gyermek és Ifjúságvédelem Mai Helyzete.* Budapest: Országos Gyermek és Ifjúságvédelmi Tanács, 1962.

Pauly, L. W. "Promoting a Global Economy: The Normative Role of the IMF." In

Political Economy and the Changing Global Order, edited by R. Stubbs and G.R.G. Underhill. London: Macmillan, 1994.

Pedersen, Susan. *Family, Dependence, and the Origins of the Welfare State: Britain and France, 1914–1945.* New York: Cambridge University Press, 1993.

Pető, Andrea. *A Munkások Életkörülményei Magyarországon az 1950-es Években.* Budapest: MTA, 1992.

———. "As He Saw Her": Gender Politics in Secret Party Reports in Hungary during the 1950s." In *Women in History—Women's History: Central and East European Perspectives,* edited by A. Pető and M. Pittaway, Working Paper Series 1. Budapest: CEU History Department, 1997.

Pető, Iván, and Sándor Szakács. *A Hazai Gazdaság Négy Évtizedének Története, 1945–1985.* Budapest: Közgazdasági és Jogi Könyvkiadó, 1985.

Pittaway, Mark. "Industrial Workers, Socialist Industrialization, and the State in Hungary, 1948–1958." Ph.D. diss., University of Liverpool, 1998.

Polcz, Alaine. *Világjáték.* Budapest: Pont Kiadó, 1999.

Pongrácz, László. *Szociálpolitikai Ismeretek.* Budapest: Munkügyi Kutató Intézet, 1986.

Pongrácz, Tiborné, and Edit Molnár, eds. *Élettársi Kapcsolatok Magyarországon.* Budapest: Népességi Intézet, 1992.

Popper, Péter. "Fiatalkorú Bűnözők Személyiségvizsgálatának Néhány Tapasztalata." *Pszichológiai Tanulmányok* 4 (1962): 533–550.

Potucek, Martin. "Current Social Policy Developments in the Czech and Slovak Republics." *Journal of European Social Policy* 3 (1993).

Réti, László. "Az Iskolaérettség Pszichológiai Vizsgálata." *Pszichológiai Tanulmányok* 5 (1963): 289–304.

Rév, István. "The Advantages of Being Atomized." *Dissent* 34 (1988): 335–349.

Révész, Magda. "Hungarian Family Helping Centers: Theory and Practice." Paper presented at the National Association of Social Workers Annual Conference, Orlando, Florida, 1993.

Róbert, Péter. "Consciousness of Inequality." In *A Society Transformed: Hungary in Time-Space Perspective,* edited by Rudolf Andorka, Tamás Kolosi, Richard Rose, and György Vukovich. Budapest: Central European University Press, 1999.

Róna-Tas, Ákos. *The Great Surprise of the Small Transformation.* Ann Arbor: University of Michigan Press, 1997.

Rueschemeyer, Marilyn, ed. *Women in the Politics of Postcommunist Eastern Europe.* New York: Sharpe, 1994.

Sainsbury, Diane, ed. *Gendering Welfare States.* London: Sage, 1994.

———. *Gender, Equality, and Welfare States.* New York: Cambridge University Press, 1997.

Skocpol, Theda. *Protecting Soldiers and Mothers.* Cambridge, Mass.: Harvard University Press, 1992.

Solt, Ottília. "A SZETA, a Szegényeket Támogató Alap Szerveződése és Munkája." In *Szociális Segítő,* edited by Zsuzsa Ferge. Budapest: MTA, 1991.

———. *Méltóságot Mindenkinek: Első Kötet.* Budapest: Beszélő, 1998.

Somlai, Péter. "Kötelékek—Széltörésben." *Család, Gyermek, Ifjúság* 8 (1994): 3–4.

Spéder, Zsolt. "Szegény Nők és Férfiak." In *Szerepváltozások: Jelentés a Nők Helyzetéről,* edited by G. Tóth and K. Lévai. Budapest: TÁRKI, 1997.

Spéder, Zsolt, Borbála Paksi, and Zsuzsanna Elekes. "Anómia és Elégedettség a 90-es Évek Elején." In *Társadalmi Riport,* edited by Tamás Kolosi, György Tóth, and György Vukovich. Budapest: TÁRKI, 1998.

Standing, Guy. "Social Protection in Central and Eastern Europe: A Tale of Slipping Anchors and Torn Safety Nets." In *Welfare States in Transition: National Adaptations to the Global Economy,* edited by Gosta Esping-Andersen. London: Sage, 1996.

Standing, Guy, and Daniel Vaughn-Whitehead, eds. *Minimum Wages in Central and Eastern Europe: From Protection to Destitution.* Budapest: Central European University Press, 1995.

Stark, David. "Path Dependence and Privatization Strategies in East Central Europe." *East European Politics and Societies* 6 (1992): 17–54.

———. "Recombinant Property in East European Capitalism." *American Journal of Sociology* 101 (1996): 993–1027.

Stark, David, and László Bruszt. *Postsocialist Pathways: Transforming Politics and Property in East Central Europe.* Cambridge: Cambridge University Press, 1998.

Stark, David, and Victor Nee, eds. *Remaking the Economic Institutions of Socialism: China and Eastern Europe.* Stanford, Calif.: Stanford University Press, 1989.

Stewart, Mary. *Women, Work, and the French State: Labor Protection and Social Patriarchy.* Kingston, Ontario: McGill University Press, 1989.

Swain, Nigel. *Hungary: The Rise and Fall of Feasible Socialism.* New York: Verso, 1992.

Szakszervezetek Országos Tanácsa (SZOT). *Szociálpolitikai Tájékoztató.* Budapest, 1953.

Szalai, Erzsébet. "From the Belly of the Whale: The Crisis of the Hungarian Cultural Elite and the Dilemmas of the Intelligentsia." Working Paper Series 12. Collegium Budapest, 1996.

Szalai, Júlia. *Poverty in Hungary during the Period of Economic Crisis.* IBRD World Development Report. Washington, D.C.: International Bank for Reconstruction and Development, 1990.

———. "Some Thoughts on Poverty and the Concept of the Subsistence Minimum." In *Social Report,* edited by Rudolf Andorka, Tamás Kolosi, and György Vukovich. Budapest: TÁRKI, 1990.

———. "Some Aspects of the Changing Situation of Women in Hungary." *Signs* 17 (1991): 152–170.

———. "Social Participation in Hungary in the Context of Restructuring and Liberalization." In *Social Policy, Social Justice and Citizenship in Eastern Europe,* edited by Robert Deacon. Aldershot, England: Avebury, 1992.

————. *Urban Poverty and Social Policy in the Context of Adjustment: The Case of Hungary.* Washington, D.C: World Bank, 1992.

————. "A Helyi Önkormányzatok Szociálpolitikájáról." *Aktív Társadalom Alapítvány* 3 (1995): 240–260.

————. "From Informal Labor to Paid Occupations: Marketization from Below in Hungarian Women's Work." In *Reproducing Gender,* edited by Susan Gal and Gail Kligman. Princeton, N.J.: Princeton University Press, 2000.

Szalai, Júlia, and Mária Neményi. *Hungary in the 1980s: A Historic Review of Social Policy and Urban Level Interventions.* Washington, D.C: World Bank, 1993.

Szántó, Miklós. *Életmód Kutatás a Szocialista Országokban.* Budapest: Kossuth Könyvkiadó, 1978.

Szegő, Andrea. "Gazdaság és Politika-Érdek és Struktúra." *Medvetánc* 2/3 (1982): 49–92.

Szelényi, Iván. "Urban Inequalities under State Socialist Redistributive Economies." *International Journal of Comparative Sociology* 1 (1978): 61–87.

————. *Urban Inequalities under State Socialism.* Oxford: Oxford University Press, 1983.

Szelényi, Iván, and György Konrád. *Intellectuals on the Road to Class Power.* New York: Harcourt, Brace, 1979.

Szelényi, Iván, and János Ladányi. "Egy Posztkommunista New Deal Esélyei Kelet Közép Európában." *Kritika,* January 1996.

Szelényi, Iván, and Róbert Manchin. "Social Policy under State Socialism: Market Redistribution and Social Inequalities in East European Socialist Societies." In *Stagnation and Renewal in Social Policy,* edited by Gøsta Esping-Andersen. New York: Sharpe, 1987.

Szelényi, Szonja. *Equality by Design: The Grand Experiment in Destratification in Socialist Hungary.* Stanford, Calif.: Stanford University Press, 1998.

Szelényi, Szonja, Iván Szelényi, and Winifred Poster. "Post-Communist Political Culture in Hungary." *American Sociological Review* 61 (1996): 466–477.

Tímár, János. "Economic Reform and New Employment Problems in Hungary." In *Economic Reforms and Welfare Systems in the USSR, Poland, and Hungary,* edited by Jan Adam. New York: St. Martin's Press, 1991.

————. "A Foglalkoztatás és Munkanélküliség Sajátosságai a Posztszocialista Országokban." *Közgazdasági Szemle* 7–8 (1994): 633–647.

Tóth, István. *A Nemzeti Parasztpárt Története, 1944–1948.* Budapest: Kossuth Könyvkiadó, 1972.

Tóth, István György. "Opinions about Social Problems and Social Policies in Hungary." In *Social Report,* edited by Rudolf Andorka, Tamás Kolosi, and György Vukovich. Budapest: TÁRKI, 1990.

————. "A Jóléti Rendszer az Átmeneti Időszakban." *Közgazdasági Szemle* 4 (1994): 313–340.

————. "Welfare Programs and the Alleviation of Poverty." In *A Society Transformed: Hungary in Time-Space Perspective,* edited by Rudolf

Andorka, Tamás Kolosi, Richard Rose, and György Vukovich. Budapest: Central European University Press, 1999.

Tóth, István György, Rudolf Andorka, Michael Förester, and Zsolt Spéder. *Poverty, Inequalities, and the Incidence of Social Transfers in Hungary*. Budapest: TÁRKI, 2000.

Tóth, Olga. "Családformák és Együttélési Minták a Mai Magyar Társadalomban." In *Szerepváltozások: Jelentés a Nők Helyzetéről*, edited by G. Tóth and K. Lévai. Budapest: TÁRKI, 1997.

———. *Violence in the Family*. TÁRKI Social Policy Working Paper 12. Budapest: TÁRKI, 1999.

Tunkli, László. "Pszichológiai Munka a Fővárosi Nevelési Tanácsadókban." *Pszichológiai Tanulmányok* 29 (1975): 269–275.

UNICEF. *Public Policy and Social Conditions*. Economies in Transition Regional Monitoring Report 1. New York: UNICEF, 1993.

———. *Central and Eastern Europe: Transition Public Policy and Social Conditions*. Florence, Italy: UNICEF Child Development Centre, 1997.

Varga, Zoltán. "Fiatalkorúak Büntetésvégrehajtásával Kapcsolatos Megfigyelések." *Pszichológiai Tanulmányok* 6 (1964): 549–564.

Várvó, István. "A Bűnözés és Mérésének Módszerei." In *Kriminológiai Ismeretek: Bűnözés-Bűnözéskontroll*, edited by Katalin Gönczöl, László Korinek, and Miklós Lévai. Budapest: Corvina Press, 1999.

Verdery, Katherine. "From Parent-State to Family Patriarchs: Gender and Nation in Contemporary Eastern Europe." *East European Politics and Societies* 8 (1994): 225–255.

Walder, Andrew. *Communist Neo-traditionalism*. Berkeley: University of California Press, 1986.

Wallace, Claire. "Gender, Citizenship, and Transition." *Social Politics* 4 (1996): 237–242.

Watson, Peggy, "The Rise of Masculinism in Eastern Europe." *New Left Review* 98 (1993): 71–82.

Wolchik, Sharon. *Women, the State, and Party in Eastern Europe*. Durham, N.C.: Duke University Press, 1985.

———. "Reproductive Policies in the Czech and Slovak Republics." In *Reproducing Gender*, edited by Susan Gal and Gail Kligman. Princeton, N.J.: Princeton University Press, 2000.

World Bank. *Housing Policy Reform in Hungary*. Report 9031-HU. Washington, D.C.: World Bank, 1990.

———. *Hungary, the Transition to a Market Economy: Critical Human Resources Issues*. Report 8665-HU. Washington, D.C.: World Bank, 1990.

———. *Hungary Health Services: Issues and Options for Reform*. Report 8772-HU. Washington, D.C.: World Bank, 1990.

———. *Hungary: Reform of Social Policy and Expenditures*. Washington D.C.: World Bank, 1992.

———. *Magyarország: Szegénység és Szociális Támogatások*. Budapest: World Bank, 1996.

Závada, Pál. *Gazdasági Reform, Szociális Reform*. Budapest: MTA, 1983.

Index

abortion: ban on, 6, 32, 92, 275n59; liberalization after Stalin's death, 262n8; relegalization in Hungary in 1956, 92; restrictive law of 1973, 92; in Romania, 92

adoption, 47

after-school programs, 146

agency, client maneuverability contrasted with, 17

Aid to Families with Dependent Children (AFDC) (U.S.), 229, 287n38

alcohol abuse: alcohol negatively subsidized, 37; in "bad" mothers, 148, 149, 150–51, 156, 158, 159, 288n79; in Dávid case, 75; and domestic violence, 74, 221; by female welfare clients, 225; increase in liberal welfare state, 210–11, 300n21; increase in maternalist welfare state, 135–36; men with alcohol problems as public disturbances, 155; and poverty, 195–96; in welfare society, 67, 74; in Zsigó case, 228

Alliance of Free Democrats, 184

Antall-Boross government, 184

Ápolási Segély (nursing grants), 183–84, 185

appliances, household, 68, 136

architectures of need: as differently encoded by different regimes, 9; gender in constructing, 13; in liberal welfare state, 10, 11, 173–205; in

maternalist welfare state, 10, 11, 99–130; qualitative change in, 17; quantitative change in, 16; the state constructing, 7; in welfare society, 10, 11, 25–61

árvaszék, 45

Átmeneti Segély (transitional aid), 183, 184, 185

austerity, 186

autonomy, client maneuverability contrasted with, 17

"bad" mothers, 147–59; alcoholism in, 148, 149, 150–51, 156, 158, 159, 288n79; blame put on the father, 133, 152–55, 160; demographic characteristics of, 147; domesticity tests failed by, 149–51; employed outside the home, 147–48; ethnicity of, 147, 288n75; institutionalization of children of, 116–17, 147, 154, 157–59, 289n113; in liberal welfare state, 219; as married, 148; medical and psychiatric exams for, 157; needs of, 147–48; the "pig case," 151; punitive welfare practices for, 133, 152, 155–59, 160; and second economy, 148

battered-women shelters, 211

"beef-stew case," 49

behavioral disorders, 121–23

benefits-in-cash, enterprises providing in welfare society, 26, 39, 42–44

benefits-in-kind: enterprises providing in welfare society, 26, 39, 41–42. *See also* services
birth control (contraceptives), 6, 32, 92, 275n59
birthrate: decline after relegalization of abortion, 92, 276n1; decline after World War II, 32, 267n41; 1984–1990, *180*; as stable during mid-1950s, 91–92
block grants, 177
Bokros, Lajos, 185
Bokros Plan, 183–90; Constitutional Court review of, 187, 296n53; debate over, 186, 295n45; eligibility cut-offs for, 187–88; opposition to, 186–88, 295n44; other elements of, 295n42; political defense of, 186; United States' welfare reform compared with, 229; welfare workers' benefits cut by, 201
boys: mothers blamed for behavioral disorders of, 121–22; mothers blamed for sexual behavior of, 122–23; oedipal problems attributed to, 124; stereotypical gender attributes promoted for, 125, 284n105
Boza case, 158–59
Bruszt, László, 5
Budapest: crime rates in, 303n51; data for this study drawn from, 18–19; demography of RNS recipients in, 111; institutionalization procedure in, 289n113; localization of welfare in, 177; mothers feeling isolated in, 145; Rákóczi Square, 195, 203, 228, 299n97; women employed outside the home in, 33, 65. *See also* Csepel enterprises; ipartelep; szegénytelep
Burawoy, Michael, 7
bureaucratic state coordination, 5, 6, 30, 206

canteens, 41
castration anxiety, 123, 124, 128
Central Committee of Hungarian Trade Unions, 40

Central Committee on Social Insurance, 40
centralized planning. *See* economic planning
charity initiatives, 206
childcare: after-school programs, 146; council, 37–38; enterprise, 38, 41, 59; extended family for solving problems with, 56–57, 82; for "good mothers," 146; for single mothers, 76, 82, 83; in welfare society, 37–38. *See also* Gyermekgondozási Díj; Gyermekgondozási Segély; maternity leave
child custody: "bad" mothers given unfavorable decrees, 152, 157; "good mother" criteria in, 116; professional women given unfavorable decrees, 117–18
Child Guidance Centers (Nevelési Tanácsadók): behavioral interventions of, 121–23; bureaucratic needs of clients of, 286n9; caseloads increasing, 1968–1985, 134, 285n6; class bias in, 126–27; clients connecting paternal and maternal in counseling, 140–41; clients' sense of isolation, 145; on competent mothers, 134; data for this study collected from, 19, 250; domesticity tests by, 136, 138–39; educational interventions of, 120–21; establishment of, 11, 99, 113; ethnic bias in, 126, 127–28; ethnographic fieldwork in, 252; family experts employed in, 11, 113; and Family Support Services Centers, 190–91; Gyámhatóság as viewed by, 119, 120; hierarchy in, 120, 128; on incompetent mothers, 147; interviews with counselors from, 257; mothers targeted by, 119; the "pig case," 151; psychological counseling at, 123–26; scientific maternalism and familial expertise in, 119–28; support groups held by, 146; welfare apparatus bifurcating with, 99

legal advisors (*jogászok*), 113
liberal welfare state, 163–236;
architecture of need in, 10, 11, 173–
205; assembly-line nature of welfare
work in, 222–23; Bokros Plan, 183–
90; case categories in this study, 20;
case-file data as limiting for, 300n8;
casework as piecework in, 191–99,
204–5; client maneuverability in,
18, 206–36, 245; destigmatization
strategies for, 228–33; discretionary
welfare practice in, 190–204;
eligibility tests as exclusionary
mechanisms, 208–9; gender identities allowed in, 17, 244, 245, 246;
gender in conception of neediness of,
13; in Hungarian welfare system
periodization, 9, 11–12; the included
in, 218–33, 234–35; international
agencies in creation of, 169–71, 204;
limitations of, 222–28; narrow
interpretation of need in, 16, 176,
233–35, 241; the newly excluded,
208–18, 234–35; overview of, 10;
pathologizing welfare clients, 199–
204, 205, 235, 247; policies of, 175–
90; processes of exclusion in, 211–
16; professionals designing, 9, 165–
69, 204; reductionist approach to
clients' problems in, 194–95; sex
segregation in, 16; social divisions
fueled by, 233; state layers as
compatible in, 239; strategies of
reinclusion, 216–18; welfare rolls
increasing in, 218, 301n30; women
forced to turn to private networks
in, 16, 243
linear programming, 94, 119–20
local cultural centers (*müvelödési
házak*), 145
local government: assistance for long-
term unemployed, 183; council
childcare, 37–38; council flats, 38–
39, 83, 221, 269n76, 279n12; in
decentralization of welfare funding,
12, 176–77; discretionary welfare
funds given to, 109; maternalist poli-

cies of, 109–12; officials interviewed
for this study, 257; supplementary
assistance plans of, 183–84, 185,
295n38; trade unions and, 40
Local Government Act of 1990, 176
local-level analyses, 14–15, 17

male alcoholics, 135, 211
male unemployment, 209
Manchin, Róbert, 266n23
manual workers: average monthly
income, 1950–1965, 35; GYED
program use by, 179; percentage of
labor force using GYES, 1970–1978,
106
marital allowances, 44
markets: democratization linked to,
169; difficulties in paying "market
price," 220; economists' commitment to marketization, 167, 168; liberal welfare state forcing women to
turn to, 243; as mechanism to economists, 94; New Economic Mechanisms on, 94, 99; in post-1989 era, 5;
for redressing social inequalities,
266n31; in reform socialism, 5; in
restructuring of Hungarian welfare
system, 165; single mothers affected
by marketization, 220; and unofficial
economy of 1990s, 302n35. See also
privatization
marriage: in constitution of 1949, 28;
enterprise housing for couples, 42,
271n104; in Family Law of 1952, 29;
marital allowances for newly
married workers, 44; women given
property rights in, 29. See also
divorce; married women
married women: "bad" mothers as,
148; complaints about men and family life, 66–67, 71–75; family
allowance paid to, 108, 281n41;
Gyámhatóság caseworkers used by,
70–75; improving their material and
work lives, 67–71; individualized
strategies used by, 87; "living separately" from their husbands, 75;

Temporary Assistance to Needy Families (U.S.), 287n38
theaters, state subsidies for, 269n84
therapy (psychological), 124–25
time-management training for mothers, 126
tobacco, 37, 269n67
Townsley, Eleanor, 292n24, 296n47
trade unions: as data source for this study, 259; emergency aid distributed by, 44, 79–80, 109; in enterprise re/distribution, 40, 60; and maternity-leave administration, 106; new labor regulations reducing role of, 104; workers' needs interpreted by, 27
transitional aid (Átmeneti Segély), 183, 184, 185
transitologists, 5, 7, 8
Turnabout and Reform (*Fordulat és Reform*) (Ferge, Szalai, and Petri), 168–69, 291n13

unemployment (*munkánelküliség*): female unemployment lagging behind male, 209; Gyámhatóság and, 47–48; increasing in 1990s, 209, 219, 300n9; increasing with end of full employment, 173; local government assistance for long-term unemployed, 183; as officially abolished, 31; official rate of, 1990–1996, 181, 182; work sought by the unemployed, 223–24. *See also* unemployment compensation
unemployment compensation: full employment replaced by, 181–83, 184; funding of, 176; in 1950s, 31, 266n35; number of recipients, 1990–1995, 185
unions. *See* trade unions
United States, 229, 287n38
utilities, price increases for, 220

vacations: enterprises subsidizing, 41, 59; married women with children having differential access to, 69, 274n27

Váradi, Mónika, 301n27
verbal abuse, 141
violence, domestic. *See* domestic violence
visitation in divorce cases, 53–54, 83, 117

wages: children institutionalized due to low, 198; fall in real wages in 1990s, 210, 300n15; family affected by welfare society policy on, 59; family wage abolished, 34; gender-based wage differential, 66, 136, 210; for Gyámhatóság caseworkers, 271n118; increasing after 1956 revolution, 39; as increasing from 1955 to 1965, 36; minimum wage levels, 35; welfare society policies, 34–36, 39; for welfare workers, 299n95
welfare: as defined in this study, 12–13. *See also* welfare reform; welfare regimes; welfare state
welfare capitalism: bringing Eastern Europe into line with Western, 174–75; bringing Hungary into line with Western, 171; in Eastern European periodization, 5; Esping-Andersen's model of, 174
"welfare cheats," 199, 201–2, 226, 230
welfare liberalism, 204, 246–48
"welfare queen" myth, 202
welfare reform: Bokros Plan compared with United States', 229; Eötvös Lóránd University conference on, 237; interpretive shifts accompanying, 242
welfare regimes: defined, 8; East European welfare trajectories, 174; gender in evaluation of, 13, 242–46; interpretive and redistributive apparatuses in, 8, 240–41; layered view of state in analysis of, 238–42; policies and practices interacting in, 239. *See also* Hungarian welfare system
welfare society, 23–88; architecture of need in, 10, 11, 25–61; broad interpretive and narrow re/distributive dimensions of, 16, 60–61, 87, 101,

this study, 259; as enterprise benefit-in-kind, 41–42, 269n77; facilities for women's well-being, 145; female workers organizing, 69; single mothers using, 79, 83

working-class women: and Child Guidance Centers practices, 127; as excluded from liberal welfare system, 209; GYES program use by, 177; in liberal welfare state system, 219. *See also* manual workers

World Bank, 169–70, 184, 185, 204, 233, 292n39, 296n56

world games, 120, 123, 151

Zsigó case, 226–28

www.ingramcontent.com/pod-product-compliance
Lightning Source LLC
Chambersburg PA
CBHW020334270326
41926CB00007B/175